R00427 47931

D0204917

Y

25.00

RB
17
.F57
W55
1984

Williams, Trevor I.

Howard Florey,
    penicillin and
    after

DATE			

CHICAGO PUBLIC LIBRARY
CONRAD SULZER REGIONAL LIBRARY
4455 LINCOLN AVE.
CHICAGO, ILLINOIS 60625

MAY   1985
© THE BAKER & TAYLOR CO

HOWARD FLOREY

Penicillin and after

HOWARD FLOREY

(Photo: Dr W. H. Feldman, Mayo Clinic)

Howard Florey

PENICILLIN AND AFTER

BY

TREVOR I. WILLIAMS

OXFORD UNIVERSITY PRESS

1984

Oxford University Press, Walton Street, Oxford OX2 6DP

London New York Toronto
Delhi Bombay Calcutta Madras Karachi
Kuala Lumpur Singapore Hong Kong Tokyo
Nairobi Dar es Salaam Cape Town
Melbourne Auckland

and associated companies in
Beirut Berlin Ibadan Mexico City Nicosia

Oxford is a trade mark of Oxford University Press

Published in the United States
by Oxford University Press, New York

© Trevor I. Williams, 1984

All rights reserved. No part of this publication may be reproduced,
stored in a retrieval system, or transmitted, in any form or by any means,
electronic, mechanical, photocopying, recording, or otherwise, without
the prior permission of Oxford University Press

British Library Cataloguing in Publication Data
Williams, Trevor I.
Howard Florey.
1. Florey, Howard, Baron Florey
2. Pathologists—Great Britain—Biography
I. Title
616.07′092′4   RB17.F57
ISBN 0-19-858173-4

Library of Congress Cataloging in Publication Data
Williams, Trevor I.
Howard Florey, penicillin and after
Bibliography: p.
Includes index.
1. Florey, Howard, Baron Florey, 1898-1968.
2. Pathologists—Great Britain—Biography.
3. Pathologists—Australia—Biography. 4. Penicillin—
History. 5. Microbiological synthesis—history
I. Title. [DNLM: 1. Physicians—biography.
2. Penicillins—history. 3. Florey, Howard W. (Howard
Walter), Sir., 1898-   . WZ 100 F636W]
RB17.F57W55   1984   616.07′092′4 [B]   84-7845
ISBN 0-19-858173-4 (U.S.)

R00427 47931

Typeset by DMB (Typesetting), Oxford
Printed in Great Britain by
St Edmundsbury Press,
Bury St Edmunds, Suffolk.

PREFACE

At first sight, the life of Florey is already adequately documented. After his death the Royal Society published, in its *Biographical Memoirs*, a fifty-page *éloge* prepared with meticulous attention to detail by his close colleague in the Sir William Dunn School of Pathology, Professor Sir Edward Abraham. In 1979 the Oxford University Press published an admirable biography—*Howard Florey: the Making of a Great Scientist*—by Professor Gwyn Macfarlane, who knew him well in Oxford for more than twenty years. Both these biographies are authoritative, in that the authors had access to Florey's personal papers. Additionally, Lennard Bickel, an Australian writer, published in 1972, under the title *Rise up to Life*, a comprehensive biography designed for a wide readership.

The justification for the appearance of the present work is that the space available to Abraham in his memoir was not sufficient to do justice to every facet of Florey's life and Macfarlane's study reviews his life in depth only up to about 1942: the remaining twenty-six years are dealt with very briefly in a sixteen-page Epilogue. My own book is designed to complement Macfarlane's and is in effect a mirror-image of it: I have begun with a short Prologue which deals with Florey's life up to his appointment to the Chair of Pathology in Oxford in 1935, thus making it possible to devote the greater part of the book to the remaining years of his life, about which relatively little has been written. There is thus an overlap of several years between Macfarlane's book and mine, but this is necessary in order to present the development of penicillin as a continuous story. It is to be understood, however, that there is no question of a two-part biography: the two books are designed for independent reading.

Although penicillin was the central episode in Florey's life, it was by no means his sole claim to fame. Over a long working life he made important contributions to research in other fields, and it was, indeed, these and not penicillin which earned him his FRS in 1941; he was closely identified from its inception with the Australian National University, of which he eventually became

Chancellor; he served for five years as President of the Royal Society; and he ended his life as Provost of The Queen's College, Oxford. These diverse interests present considerable biographical problems. While these facets of his life are logically dealt with as separate entities, each was inevitably influenced by other concurrent activities: if one thread is followed too long, the reader is left in ignorance of relevant action elsewhere. Chronology thus inevitably conflicts with thematic continuity and it has, therefore, been necessary to find compromises, except in the case of the Australian National University. This was a matter of great and continuing concern to him throughout virtually the whole of the period of his life with which this book is concerned, but for geographical and other reasons it was an interest in parallel, rather than in series, with his other activities. For this reason it has been dealt with almost entirely within the space of a single chapter. Partly because it concerned him so actively and for so long, and partly because it is a story that has not hitherto been recorded in any detail, it is the longest chapter in the book.

Purely by chance, Macfarlane's decision effectively to end his biography around 1942 dovetailed exactly with my own interest, for in that year Florey, on the recommendation of Sir Robert Robinson, invited me to work in the Sir William Dunn School of Pathology on the chemistry of some new antibiotics. To be associated in this way with such a powerful group of original research workers engaged in a project of national importance was an extraordinary stroke of good fortune, and I should like to acknowledge the patience and kindness shown to me as a young and inexperienced graduate, not least by Dr. Ernst Chain, my immediate supervisor. Apart from being of lasting benefit to my subsequent career, the experience is significant in the present context in that it gave me an opportunity, over a period of three years, of seeing Florey in action at the climax of the penicillin project. Subsequently, our paths crossed from time to time— sometimes at scientific meetings and not infrequently on trains between Oxford and Paddington—and in the fullness of time he became Provost of my own college in Oxford. To some extent, therefore, this biography draws on my own personal knowledge and experience. It would not have been conceived, however—let alone completed—without a great deal of help and encouragement from many sources, and the list of those whose active assistance

I must acknowledge is so long that the reader may be led to suppose that my own contribution has been quite modest.

First and foremost, this book reflects Lady Florey's determination that there should be an authoritative public record of the whole of her late husband's life and work. Shortly after his death she initiated a move of great importance to the attainment of this objective: this was to ensure that all his personal papers and other archival material were preserved for the benefit of posterity. The greater part of them she entrusted to the Royal Society where they occupy some 450 box-files. A generous grant from the Wellcome Trust made it possible for them to be professionally classified and indexed, a service of immeasurable value to any serious biographer. She concluded, however, that the considerable archival materials relating to the Australian National University were most suitably entrusted to that institution and in 1969 they were dispatched to Canberra, where they are lodged in the Menzies Library.

Lady Florey has naturally taken a keen and active interest in the preparation of this biography and I have benefited greatly from her personal knowledge and constructive comments. She has read the final text as now published and I am happy to know that it has earned her approval. It has been read and approved, too, by his children, Mrs. J. McMichael and Professor Charles Florey; I am grateful to them for some comments on points of detail, which have been incorporated.

I am particularly indebted to Professor Macfarlane. He has allowed me to draw very freely on his own biography—especially in writing my Prologue, which covers Florey's early life—and has read the whole of my typescript and made many constructive comments on it. Additionally, I have profited greatly from a number of informal talks with him.

Oxford was the centre of Florey's professional life and I have to acknowledge the help of many other people associated with the University who have given me much help and advice. In particular, I have to thank Dr. Norman Heatley—for many years a close colleague of Florey at the Sir William Dunn School—for reading the whole of the typescript with meticulous care and making many useful suggestions for its amendment and improvement. It was read, too, by Professor Sir Edward Abraham, also a close collaborator with Florey at Oxford, who corrected me on several points of detail. At an early stage in the project Professor Henry Harris, Florey's successor at the Sir William Dunn School of Pathology, and previously associated with him in research, gave me some helpful background information. I also greatly enjoyed, and profited from, discussion with Mr. J. H. D. Kent, whose technical assistance over more than forty years—at Cambridge, Sheffield, and Oxford—so admirably complemented Florey's own experimental genius.

As a corporate body The Queen's College has not identified itself with this work, but I have been greatly helped by several individual Fellows, past and present. Professor George Temple was a mine of entertaining and useful information about the College and its inmates over the years in question. Mr. J. O. Prestwich, Senior Fellow at the time of Florey's death, also gave me much helpful information. To Dr. P. L. Miller I am indebted for information on the Florey European Studentships. Professor David Jenkins of the University of Leeds, Chaplain and Domestic Bursar of Queen's in Florey's time, very kindly sent me a copy of the Address he gave on the occasion of the unveiling of a memorial plaque in St. Nicholas Church, Marston, in 1980, from which I quote. Finally, Professor J. L Harley was kind enough to read the whole of the chapter dealing with Florey's Provostship, and corrected me on many points of detail.

Florey had a long association with Lincoln College and I am indebted to two former Rectors—Lord Murray of Newhaven and Sir Walter Oakeshott—for giving me the benefit of some personal recollections. Late in his life he was associated also with Wolfson College, as the first Chairman of the Trustees. In this connection I have to acknowledge the help of Sir Isaiah Berlin, first President of the College. Through his successor, Sir Henry Fisher, I was granted permission to consult the Trustee's Minutes. Still in the context of Oxford, I have to thank Dame Janet Vaughan, formerly Principal of Somerville College, for giving me some of her recollections of Florey, particularly during his time as Provost of Queen's when they found they had many problems in common.

When the book was well advanced I was able, through the ready kindness of Lady Chain, to consult the papers of Sir Ernst Chain relating to his years in Oxford. These were then being classified by the Contemporary Scientific Archives in Oxford, where Mrs. J. Alton and Miss Julia Nathan-Jameson were most helpful. The availability of this important material made possible some constructive revision of the text.

It is not generally realized—and indeed he himself had surprisingly little knowledge of it—that although Florey was a native-born Australian his father and forebears came from the area around Standlake and Bampton, villages only a dozen miles from Oxford. This led Mrs. A. J. Goadby, then living in Standlake, to construct a genealogical tree tracing his family back as far as 1588. I am most grateful to her for allowing me to reproduce this.

In consulting the Florey archives at the Royal Society in London I have been much helped by the Librarian, Mr. N. H. Robinson, and his staff. There is also much relevant and interesting material in the files of the Medical Research Council in London. I am grateful to Sir James Gowans—now the Secretary of the Council and a former research worker in the Sir William Dunn School of Pathology—for not only allowing me access to these but arranging for the relevant material to be flagged for easy consultation. Again in London, I have to thank Dr. C. J. Hackett, who co-ordinated the arrangements for the commemorative plaque unveiled in Westminster Abbey in 1982, for information on the moves which led up to this.

Florey's long, and sometimes tempestuous, relationship with the Australian National University was of such importance in his later life that it had to be dealt with in some detail, but a major difficulty arose from the fact that all the relevant archival material that needed to be consulted had been lodged in Canberra. This difficulty was generously and happily resolved by the University— through the then Vice-Chancellor, Professor D. A. Low—who awarded me a Visiting Fellowship to go to Canberra in 1981 and consult all the archival material there. In doing so, I had much friendly help from Mr. Alan Burnett of the Chancellery staff, and Mr. Andrew Bennett of the John Menzies Library. The visit also provided a valuable opportunity to meet and talk with a number of people associated with Florey in the early days of the University. These included Sir Mark Oliphant and Sir Keith Hancock, both original members, with Florey, of the Academic Advisory Committee; Sir Leslie Melville and Sir Leonard Huxley, former Vice-Chancellors; Dr. H. C. Coombs, who succeeded Florey as Chancellor; and Mr. R. A. Hohnen, who was Registrar from 1949 to 1968. Professor Adrien Albert, the first Professor of Chemistry in the John Curtin School of Medical Research, was away from Canberra at the time, but very kindly came to see me later in Oxford. Additionally, I was able to have discussions with Professor F. J. Fenner, formerly Professor of Microbiology and Director of the John Curtin School; Professor R. Porter, now Director and Howard Florey Professor of Medical Research in the John Curtin School; and his colleagues Professor F. W. E. Gibson, Professor Bede Morris, and Professor D. J. Brown. I met also Professor J. A. La Nauze, who had arranged for the relevant part of the Florey archive to be moved from Oxford to Canberra. Subsequently, I received through the Vice-Chancellor much helpful comment on the draft of the chapter dealing with Florey's relationship with the University. A visit to Melbourne provided an opportunity for a long and informative talk at the Howard Florey Institute with Professor R. D. Wright, now Sir R. Douglas Wright, who was very closely associated with Florey in the initial conception of the Australian National University, and to meet Florey's niece, Dr. Joan Gardner. This was my first visit to Australia and I should like to put on record my appreciation of the friendly and helpful way in which I was received by all concerned.

In designing the John Curtin School, Florey received much assistance from Dr. A. G. Sanders of the Sir William Dunn School of Pathology—his companion on his wartime visit to Moscow—who made several visits to Canberra in this connection. After Sanders' death in 1980 all his correspondence, draft plans, and other papers relating to the design and building of the School were made available to me. This proved an important source of new information, much of which has been incorporated in the relevant chapter.

Florey was a dedicated academic with a passion for research, and it is appropriate that my acknowledgement should be first to those who have helped me to depict this side of his life. That it has been so freely forthcoming—and in many instances proffered—is a measure of the esteem in which Florey was held. It cannot be too strongly stressed, however, that penicillin would have remained a laboratory curiosity had not the pharmaceutical industry overcome the many problems associated with its large-scale production. That the United States embarked upon a massive wartime programme for the industrial production of penicillin

owes much to Florey's powers of persuasion displayed during his
visit there with N. G. Heatley in 1941. From this stemmed the
availability of penicillin for the treatment of Allied battle casualties from D-Day onward, and the subsequent development of
a completely new industry that made penicillin generally and
cheaply available throughout the world. For this reason alone the
early history of the penicillin industry demands our attention
here, but there are other important and relevant considerations.
At a very early stage the question of patenting penicillin arose but
—deferring to the advice of Sir Edward Mellanby and Sir Henry
Dale—Florey decided that this would be quite unethical even if
it were practicable. After the War, however, the correctness of
this decision was questioned and accusations were made—in
Parliament and elsewhere—that America had not only 'stolen'
penicillin from Britain but made her pay royalties on American
patents. Although Florey concealed his emotions better than
most people, this public criticism undermined his self-confidence
and distressed him greatly. I therefore make no apology for
devoting a fair amount of space to examining these issues, the
more so as they have not hitherto been discussed in any generally
available publication. For the opportunity to do so—and, indeed,
to embark upon this biography at all—I am indebted to the
generosity of the Squibb Corporation, through the good offices
of Dr. Robert H. Ebert, formerly Chairman of their Committee
on Social Responsibility. They provided a subvention sufficient
for me not only to devote a great part of my time, over a period of
six years, to the writing of this biography, but to visit the United
States in order to study at first hand the various issues alluded to
above. They made available a great deal of documentary material
and enabled me to meet some members of their staff who were
concerned, but left me free to draw my own conclusions. Within
the Squibb organization I must thank for their encouragement
and support Mr. Ross Reid, Senior Vice President and General
Counsel; Mr. William R. Luney, Vice President and Secretary;
and Mr. Grant Wolfkill, Vice President Public Affairs. Dr.
George B. Mackaness, President of the Squibb Foundation for
Medical Research, was kind enough to read the three chapters
concerned with industrial production of penicillin and I am
grateful for his friendly and helpful comments. I also profited
greatly from discussions with Mr. Robert Alpher, formerly with

their Patents Department, Mr. Harry L. Yale, who has written a short history of the development of penicillin at Squibb, and Dr. Julian Aurelius.

The same visit to the United States made it possible for me to meet Mr. William H. Helfand, Senior Vice President of Merck Sharpe and Dohme International, an authority on the history of the wartime industrial development of penicillin in the United States. By him I was introduced to Professor David L. Cowen, of Rutgers University, also an authority on the history of penicillin. Both have read the relevant chapters and I am most grateful to them for their constructive comments.

Wartime problems—in particular the havoc wrought by German air-raids—made it very difficult for the British chemical industry to make more than a very modest contribution to penicillin production until after the War. Nevertheless, the contribution of British industry—together with material laboriously prepared in Oxford—was crucial to Florey for his own clinical trials. His most important source was the firm of Kemball Bishop, at Bromley-by-Bow, now a part of Pfizer Limited at Sandwich, Kent. I am most grateful to Pfizer's for making the relevant files freely available to me and to Dr. L. M. Miall, now retired, who during the War was closely concerned with the liaison with the Sir William Dunn School at Oxford. A second important British source of penicillin was ICI, and I am grateful to them for making available to me archival material from both their headquarters in London and at Trafford Park, Manchester, where their penicillin production unit was situated.

Public concern over the patenting situation with regard to penicillin was a major factor in the setting up of the National Research Development Corporation (now British Technology Group) to control the exploitation of publicly supported research. I am indebted to Mr. B. S. W. Mann for directing my attention to two helpful publications on cephalosporin, the second major antibiotic success of the Sir William Dunn School, which—in contrast to penicillin—was fully and very advantageously protected by patents from the outset.

When penicillin was a proven success Florey had no difficulty in finding funds to support his research, but in the early days the position was very different. For this reason he always had a particular regard for the Albert and Mary Lasker Foundation in

New York: it was, he used to say, the only body that gave him money without his even asking for it. I am grateful to Mrs. Mary Lasker for providing me with details of this and also some helpful background information.

In acknowledging the help I have received from so many quarters, I must stress that the views expressed, and any errors of commission and omission, are my responsibility alone. Omissions there certainly are, if only because the susceptibilities of those concerned and still alive demand consideration. As George Arnold put it: 'The living need charity more than the dead'.

Finally, I have once again to thank Mrs. Yvonne Rue for converting a confused and heavily corrected manuscript into a crisp and elegant typescript.

Oxford   T. I. W.
May 1983

ACKNOWLEDGEMENTS

Frontispiece: Dr. W. H. Feldman, Mayo Clinic; Fig. 2: Reprinted by permission form *Nature, Lond.* 201, 444 (1964). Copyright 1964 Macmillan Journals Limited; Plate 1: Oxford Museum Services, Woodstock; Plate 9: The Nobel Foundation, Stockholm; Plate 11: Australian National University; Plate 14: Australian National University; Plate 15: Charles Florey; Plate 16: W. E. van Heyningen; Plate 17: Mrs. L. Rees, Murmur-y-Nant, Corris Uchaf; Plate 18: Dr. C. J. Hackett; Plate 19: Australian High Commission.

CONTENTS

PLATES
(Plates fall between pp. 176 and 177 of the text.)

1. Shoemaker's tools found in the roof of the home of Florey's grandfather.
2. A souvenir of Florey's Spitzbergen expedition of 1924.
3. An example from Florey's paper with N. E. Goldsworthy on antibiosis.
4. Heatley cylinder-plate assay method.
5. Florey with J. H. D. Kent injecting a solution into the tail of a mouse.
6. Heatley's original counter-current apparatus used for extracting penicillin from crude culture fluid.
7. Later penicillin extraction apparatus.
8. Pure crystalline penicillin.
9. Presentation of Nobel Prizes in Stockholm, 1945.
10. Mrs. Mary Lasker.
11. The John Curtin School of Medical Research, Canberra, 1955.
12. Margaret Jennings.
13. Dr. N. G. Heatley.
14. Florey opening the John Curtin School of Medical Research, Canberra, 1958.
15. Ethel Florey.
16. Florey's sister Anne.
17. Florey in 1962.
18. The memorial to Florey in Westminster Abbey.
19. The Australian fifty-dollar bank note commemorating Florey's contribution to the development of penicillin.

1
PROLOGUE: THE THRESHOLD OF FAME

In many ways 1935 may be regarded as a turning-point in the life of Howard Florey, for it saw the beginning of a chain of events which was to translate him from a distinguished scientist acknowledged by his academic peers to a public figure of international repute. Behind him lay the early distinction of the Rhodes Scholarship which brought him to England as a young man and a series of appointments, and experience abroad, that had allowed him to develop both his individual genius for experiment and the ability to organize research teams and manage university departments. In that year he was appointed, at the early age of thirty-six, to a Chair at Oxford, which had long been his goal. Ahead lay the fruits and consequences of success: the triumph of penicillin; Fellowship, and eventually the Presidency, of the Royal Society; a Nobel Prize; a Life Peerage and the Order of Merit; the Provostship of Queen's College, Oxford; and the Chancellorship of the Australian National University. Inevitably, however, these later years were powerfully influenced by earlier ones and before chronicling his later life we must pause to take stock of them.

Florey was born in Adelaide, the capital of South Australia. He was thus a native Australian and always had a strong affection for that country: in later life, indeed, his loyalty was to be the cause of anguish, and some misunderstanding with his compatriots, when he had to decide whether to remain in Britain or return to hold high office in Australia. He was, however, a first-generation Australian, for his father came from Oxfordshire: it was by a strange quirk of fate that, after a family journey half-way round the world, Florey's greatest achievements were made within a few miles of the home of his forebears. There are still many Floreys around Oxford who are distant connections.

Early years in Adelaide
Joseph Florey, Howard's father, was born in 1857 in Bampton,

where his father Walter was a bootmaker (Plate 1). As a boy Joseph moved with his father to Islington and also entered the bootmaking trade. In 1878 he married Charlotte Ames, daughter of a workmate, by whom he had two daughters, Charlotte (1880) and Anne (1882). Unhappily, his wife contracted tuberculosis—for which there was then no effective medical treatment—and in 1882 he resolved to emigrate to Australia, settling in the then comparatively new township of Adelaide, in the hope that the better climate would improve her health. There they settled in a small house, Argylle Cottage, in the suburb of Parkside. But his hopes proved vain and she died in 1886.

During her last years Charlotte was nursed by a Mrs. Wadham, a widow with a daughter, Bertha, in her early twenties. After Charlotte's death in 1886 Mrs. Wadham apparently remained as housekeeper, an arrangement which Joseph could by then well afford. His trade had progressed far beyond that of a village boot-maker and he was well established as a manufacturer, with a factory in Pultney Street. In 1889 Joseph married Bertha and a year later the family moved to a new and larger house in Fisher Street, Malvern. There two more daughters were born, Hilda (1891) and Valetta (1892). There, too, on 24 September 1898, was born the only son of the family, Howard Walter: his second name, we may suppose, was given after his grandfather from Bampton. As a matter of passing interest, his birth certificate recorded him as Walter Howard Florey. This discrepancy came to light half a century later, when he applied for a visa for a visit to South America. A zealous official insisted that he registered with the South Australian authorities a formal declaration that he had always been known as Howard Walter.

Meanwhile, encouraged by Bertha—an energetic and practical woman—Joseph's business flourished and extended far beyond Adelaide, with branches in other states. He was more than comfortable; he had become rich and in the process had, not unnaturally, acquired social ambitions. His house at Malvern, and a country cottage ten miles away at Belair, no longer satisfied him and in 1906 he purchased a large house, 'Coreega', in the fashionable Mitcham area. The move was ill-judged. In the course of no more than a century Australia had evolved its own system of society, with boundaries as sharp and generally observed as those of Britain. Rich they might be, but the Floreys were

FLOREY

Robert m. Elizabeth **Tomson**
bur. 18 Apr. 1625
= 24 Aug. 1588

Thomas m. Mary
bap. 1 May 1589   bur. 7 Oct 1658
bur. 6 Sep 1677

Thomas m. Katherine **Potter**
bap. 7 Feb. 1629
= 4 Dec 1656 b.o.t.p.

Robert m. Sarah
bap. 8 Apr. 1672   bur. 30 Dec. 1707

Robert m. (2) Ann
bap. 21 Dec. 1707   bur. 28 May 1783 widow

Richard m. (2) Mary **Hill**
bap: 18 Jul. 1756   bur. 18 Jul. 1814 (60)
bur. 9 Nov. 1837 (83)
= 18 Dec. 1784 b.o.t.p.

Joseph m. Hannah **Walton**
bap. 30 Nov 1788   bur. 6 Mar 1867 (76)
bur. 27 Jul 1834 (45)
= 26 Dec. 1812 at St Peters in the East,
Oxford

Walter m. Mary Ann **Hendy** (23) dau.
bap. 19 Sep. 1830   Thomas Hendy bootmaker
(father cordwainer)
aged 23 at marriage
bootmaker
= 25 Sep. 1853 at
St Leonard's Shoreditch

Joseph m. (2) Bertha Mary **Wadham**
born 5 Jan. 1857
at Bampton

Howard Walter
born 24 Sep. 1898
at Adelaide

All events taken from Parish Registers
of Standlake, Oxon, except where stated.
b.o.t.p. = both of this parish.
bap   = baptised
bur.   = buried
Figures in brackets represent ages.

ranked as trade and as such did not fit into the aristocratic society of Mitcham. Writing from England to his mother in 1925, Florey remarked: ' . . . if I recollect, there were very few people that had truck with us before I left'. This seems not to have worried Joseph unduly, as his business occupied most of his time and took him away a great deal. For Bertha, tied to Mitcham by the demands of a growing family, things were very different. Naturally, she wished to take part in the local social life, but she was out of her element and her efforts to gain acceptance tended, if anything, to make her even less welcome. Among the few exceptions, but important ones, were their next-door neighbours, an Irish family by the name of Clampett. The father was a Canon of Adelaide Cathedral and his daughter, Mollie, became a lifelong friend of Howard. Howard was the younger of the two, but by only 18 months, and they went together by horse-drawn tram to a local school, Unley Park.

Howard soon outgrew his dame-school and in 1908 he moved on to Kyre College, a private school for about a hundred boys. Three years later, at thirteen, it was time for him to move on again, this time to St. Peter's Collegiate School. This was modelled on an English public school—the Headmaster was Canon A. G. Girdlestone, a graduate of Magdalen College, Oxford—but took both boarders and day-boys; it was as one of the latter that Howard was entered, though it involved a long daily journey by tram. Here he proved himself a good all-rounder; he was soon top of his class, won four scholarships, and did well at athletics. In this respect the boy set the pattern for the man; many factors contributed to his later success but versatility at a high level, and capacity for sustained hard work, were among the essentials. We get a glimpse, too, of another important aspect of his character. Despite his vigorous involvement in school life he seems to have had difficulty in forming a close friendship with any of his schoolfellows. As a day-boy he was not bound to the school and he found his main pleasure and relaxation in wandering in the wild country around 'Coreega', often in the company of Mollie Clampett.

Adolescence is difficult for anybody, but all the evidence is that these were on balance happy years. He fitted well enough into school life and at home, as the youngest member of his family and the only boy, he clearly came in for his fair share of spoiling.

In his twenties he recalled this as having disadvantages: 'It is a terrible thing to be the only son, and the youngest at that. Everyone puts you under the obligation to do well.' A minor cloud was his health. He was prone to what would then be called 'chesty' conditions and these developed into attacks of pneumonia in 1912 and 1914. Possibly these early experiences contributed to his introverted attitude to his health in adult life, an attitude which, incidentally, later inspired some aspects of his research work.

In any circumstances, school is only a short stage on the road to adult life and must inevitably be the prelude to major changes. For Florey there was no exception, but for his whole generation there was the added complication of the outbreak of the First World War in August 1914. Before this, however, there were important changes within the family. Bertha was a woman of strong character and for many years dominated her two step-daughters, Charlotte and Anne, both of whom remained at home to carry out mundane household duties. Hilda, however, showed more determination and in 1906 entered Adelaide University to study medicine. This had been founded in 1874; a medical school was soon established and from the beginning had admitted women as well as men. This liberal attitude contrasted with that then prevailing in Britain, where Sophia Jex-Blake began in the 1870s her campaign for allowing women to graduate in medicine. Even so, women medical students were rare in Adelaide and Hilda was the only one of her year. She graduated in 1912 and then specialized as a pathologist. Eventually she found a clinical appointment in Melbourne and married a medical man, John Gardner: sadly, he died of tetanus in 1929. Also in 1912 Anne, then 30 years of age, finally exercised her independence and enrolled as a student nurse in Launceston, Tasmania. It is said that this important decision was influenced by the nurse engaged to look after Howard in his first attack of pneumonia. After qualifying she joined the Queen Alexandra Nursing Service, in which she was awarded a decoration, and served during the First World War in the Middle East; eventually she found work in Britain where, in the fullness of time, she was to meet her brother Howard on his arrival in 1922. Valetta, despite having aspirations as a pianist, remained at home.

The extent to which this flurry of medical activity influenced Florey's own choice of career must be a matter for speculation, but it can hardly have failed to have had an effect. At St. Peter's he had acquired a keen interest in chemistry from one of his teachers, J. S. Thompson, and he seems in his early teens to have determined on a career in scientific research. Later, physics began to compete with chemistry, but he soon realized that his mathematical ability was scarcely sufficient. His headmaster, Canon Girdlestone, himself a science graduate, was dubious about career prospects in Australia in chemical research. In such circumstances, it was inevitable that he would in any event have considered medicine as an alternative, offering an assured living as well as the possibility of research. The first-hand experience of his sister must have played some part in the making of his final decision.

The fulfilment of this intention was not easy at that particular time, however. His father's business, once so prosperous, was running into serious, and ultimately fatal, difficulties, the result of a combination of poor health and an unfortunate choice of business associates. In 1916 he raised mortgages on 'Coreega', on the country cottage, and on some 1000 acres of land bought as an investment. This staved off disaster until his death in 1918. Fortunately, Howard, showing his usual form, had won both the Young Exhibition at Adelaide University and a state bursary, so that his training would cost nothing. Thus he could pursue his medical studies with an easy conscience so far as dependence on his father was concerned. But, as with many Australians of his age, his conscience was troubled in another way. The War in Europe dragged on and the end was not in sight; most young men of his age went off to fight. Most of his contemporaries leaving St. Peter's were enlisting as volunteers—there was no conscription—and he had a strong feeling that he should join them. His family sought to dissuade him, advancing such arguments as his position as the only son; his father's failing health and business difficulties; and his own medical history of bronchial ailments. It was pointed out, too, that doctors as well as soldiers were urgently needed, and the government issued special badges to be worn by those in reserved occupations. Eventually, these arguments prevailed and he enrolled at the University in March 1916, just ten years after his sister Hilda. But it was a decision about which he was never really happy. As he expressed it laconically in a letter to his father in July 1915: 'I don't want to go, but

I ought to, and that's the whole position . . . '.

Medical training

In later life, Florey was inclined to be somewhat disparaging about the Medical School at Adelaide. In 1926 he wrote: 'I only know it as it was, of course, and I can't say too much bad about most of it'. In the light of circumstances, this seems a little harsh. Adelaide in those days was very different from what it is now. Although half as big again as France, South Australia in 1912 had a population of less than half a million, more than half living in Adelaide. The first settlement there had been made only 80 years previously, and the university itself had been established no more than 40 years. It was a small university in a country still struggling to establish its place in the world: as such, its standards were necessarily different from those of the established universities of Europe and North America with which, at the time of writing, Florey had just become familiar. Its resources were limited and its reputation was not such as to make it easy to attract, still less to retain, really able staff. In 1924, Florey himself toyed with the idea of putting in for a vacant lectureship there—which it seems he would almost certainly have got, and then the course of history would have been different—but eventually gave the idea up because of the limited research facilities. William Bragg, destined like Florey to be a Nobel Laureate, was another Adelaide graduate who had left in search of a more challenging environment. In short, the Medical School seems to have been no worse than one would expect, and its problems were aggravated at that particular time by the absence of many younger men on war service. Even so, there were some colourful and stimulating characters among the staff. One such was Archibald Watson, officially Lecturer in Anatomy. He was a graduate of Göttingen and had studied under Pasteur in Paris. He taught also physiology and pathology, indicative of a breadth of interest that must have struck a responsive chord in Florey. Watson in his time was reputed to have been involved in piracy and body-snatching. Given to amorous intrigues, he was, nevertheless, one of the few who was actively unkind to woman students. He was also a keen motor cyclist and several of the students acquired machines; Florey already had one, a Triumph, bought originally for the journeys between school and 'Coreega'. Uncomfortable though they might be on rough, dusty roads, motor cycles conferred a welcome degree of mobility on their owners and made possible journeys to the sea or to neighbouring beaches. In later life, however, he felt these machines to be far too dangerous to let his son have one.

With the end of the War in 1918, many of the medical staff returned to Adelaide from active service. Among them was C. T. C. de Crespigny, reportedly a good teacher with experience of pathology, who returned as an Honorary Physician. Unlike Watson he made himself agreeable to the women students, Florey's future wife among them, and in this context we shall encounter him again. These changes affected Florey relatively little, however, because by the time of this postwar reorganization he had completed his preclinical work and embarked on clinical work in the hospital. It seems to have been at this stage that disillusionment with Adelaide set in: the teachers seemed to him more interested in what the textbooks said than in the symptoms displayed in the wards and instead of admitting their ignorance sought to conceal it under a mask of pomposity. Years after, when he was in England, he recalled that de Crespigny advised a student that 'it is far better for you to learn what is in your books. It is not for you to question.' For a young man gifted with a perpetually questioning mind such an attitude was anathema, and it perhaps contributed to the antipathy Florey felt towards him later for more personal reasons.

On 15 September 1918 Joseph Florey died in Melbourne, where he had gone on business. Hilda's husband, Dr. John Gardner, attended him in a severe heart attack, but nothing could be done and he died before Bertha could arrive. The practical consequences were serious for the family: his shoe company went into liquidation and the ordinary shareholders got nothing. The principal assets remaining were 10 000 preference shares, valued at some £7000, which Bertha had shrewdly acquired in her own name. 'Coreega', heavily mortgaged, was sold in 1920 and Bertha and her two daughters moved to a bungalow in Glenunga Avenue, Glen Osmond. Later again they moved to a smaller house on the Fullerton Estate in South Adelaide.

Of Florey's reaction to his father's death we know nothing; though there is ample evidence that he could feel strong emotion he always had difficulty in expressing it. Yet by his own account, expressed in letters of the 1920s, he reproached himself for his attitude to his family. Of his mother he wrote: 'It's truly horrible that I don't give her anything. I've tried and the failure will probably haunt me all my life. I really think its because I've never been able to tell her anything that mattered. . . . She was strong-willed and I was obstinate.' Again, when he had thoughts of bringing his mother and two sisters to England he wrote: 'My conscience is Banquo's ghost. I feel I am making a beastly mess of the whole show, and my mistakes rebound on so many people.'

This was a difficult period in Florey's life. On the one hand, he had a clearcut ambition to make his career in research, but saw all too clearly that the opportunity for this in Adelaide was lacking. On the other, he had a sense of duty—not as strong as his ambition—urging him to stay and support his mother and sisters. In the end, of course, he opted for his career and it is hard to see how anyone could blame him; the family, it is true, had fallen on hard times, but they were still far from destitute and at that time his mother, still in her fifties, was in good health. Nevertheless, he blamed himself, and when the time came to leave Adelaide he wrote: 'I'm sad at heart, and I'm dreading the family goodbye tomorrow. I shan't see my mother again probably, and I've been a beast—that's the rub. If a chap could dispense with a conscience, or be like Elija and push off in a chariot.'

In spite of these misgivings, having made his decision he stuck firmly to it. Characteristically, he aimed high: in August 1920 he applied for a Rhodes Scholarship to Oxford. These were highly prestigious awards, founded by Cecil Rhodes for the benefit of colonial and American students. The Trustees demanded evidence not only of high academic achievement but of prowess at sport and high moral character. His failure to enlist was evidently still on his mind, for in his application he explained his reasons at some length. In December of that year Florey received news that his application had been successful. Apart from the honour, the value of the awards (£300 p.a.) was high by the academic standards of the day. For most young men of his age and background this would have been sufficient in itself, but Florey at once began to make stipulations. The problem was that the award should be taken up at Oxford in October 1921, but he wished to stay in Adelaide until December of that year in order to take his final qualifying examinations. The normal solution would have been either to have deferred taking up the award for a year or to take his finals after finishing at Oxford. Florey, however, wanted to start at Oxford a term late, in Hilary term 1922. Possibly the thought was in his mind that if he left Adelaide without qualifying he would have to return, if only to take the examination. In the end he got his way, as he usually did in similar situations in later years.

This problem resolved, Florey settled down to work steadily for his final examinations, scheduled for the end of November. Whatever his views on the clinical teaching at Adelaide, he seems to have made up his mind to comply with the strictly orthodox requirements of his examiners. Nevertheless, his results for once fell short of his normal high standard; he did not gain the honours he expected and thus did not achieve the Everard Scholarship he had hoped for.

As everybody knows, examinations are chancy affairs; most candidates do pretty much as predicted but some do not run true to form. Where the results fall short of expectations, the reason is sometimes apparent: lack of application, sheer bad luck with the papers, illness, emotional upsets, and so on. In Florey's case we can only speculate within these general limits. Health may have been a contributory factor: we know that in May he had had an attack of enteritis; he remarked that 'with my hypochondriacal nature [I] was certain it was typhoid'. Boredom, too, may have played its part: as we have noted, he found the teaching inflexible and unimaginative. But we have good reason to suppose that, as with so many students at that stage of their career, preoccupation with romance was partly to blame.

Although Florey always found it difficult to establish close personal relationships with anybody, it seems that his attitude towards girls was typical of young men of his age and generation. This qualification is necessary, for we must remember that in these matters society of sixty years ago, and Australian society certainly no less so than that of Britain, was a great deal more straitlaced than it is now; only the United States was more liberal. Clearly, Florey had had a pleasant boy-and-girl relationship with Mollie Clampett while at school, but she lost her heart to his friend Tom Bowen, and they married when he came back from the War. More serious, apparently, was an attachment to Nancy Lamphee, sister of Alan Lamphee, a fellow medical student.

In his last year in Adelaide, however, his affection was transferred to Mary Ethel Hayter Reed, also a medical student but three years younger than he. Their first meeting seems to have been a matter of chance. At that time, Florey was editor of the *Review*, published by the Adelaide Medical Students Society. Looking round for material, he suggested in January 1920 that, as one of the few women medical students, she might care to write on the not very original theme of 'women in medicine'. She accepted his invitation to discuss this over tea at 'Coreega' and from that point their friendship ripened rapidly until Howard, at least, felt himself to be in love; Ethel was strongly attracted but less sure of herself.

Like most love affairs this one did not run smoothly. Some of the reasons were inherent in the social conventions of the day; others stemmed from the nature of the two personalities concerned. Under the first heading, there was the difference in family background. As we have remarked, trade came low in the social pecking order and the inmates of 'Coreega' made little headway with their neighbours; no doubt the barriers were even less surmountable when Joseph Florey ran into financial difficulties. Ethel's father was a banker, manager of the Adelaide branch of the Bank of Australasia, and he and his wife were conscious of their higher social status, evidenced by their large house in the most fashionable part of the city. A little surprisingly, Florey allowed himself to be intimidated and it was a long time before he visited Ethel's home, The Red House. With the typical frankness that did not always endear him to those he addressed, he told Ethel bluntly: 'Your parents appal me'. This was after Mrs. Reed had rebuffed him when he had telephoned, in May 1921, to enquire anxiously about Ethel's health during an attack of pleurisy. Again at a practical level, they had rather limited opportunity to get to know each other. As students, both were working hard—Howard in particular, with his finals in sight. Moreover, in 1921 he was absent from Adelaide for some time—first on a working holiday at Mildura, up the Murray River, and later as an unqualified medical assistant at Broken Hill Hospital. Even at that stage in their acquaintance, money may also have been an inhibition. Howard, with his expectations dashed by his father's ruin, was very conscious that he had only himself to depend on— and possibly some obligation to his family—in embarking on a career not lavish in its financial rewards. Ethel, as a banker's daughter, would surely have had urged on her the advantages of security, especially in a household where, despite its pretensions, money was not plentiful. On both sides financial prudence would be natural.

On the personal level, there were evident disparities. Although women were admitted to the Medical School, only those with a sense of dedication and purpose would avail themselves of the opportunity. From the outset Ethel was determined to make a career in medicine in her own right and, with reason, was confident of her ability to do so. Her ambition was no doubt pitched lower than Howard's, and might have been satisfied within the confines of Adelaide—of which she was openly proud—but it was real enough. Howard, in this respect, was nearer to Watson than to de Crespigny. He was sceptical of the role of women in medicine; in a letter from Oxford to Ethel he conceded no more than that they might make 'good average general practitioners'. Tact was not his strong suit as a young man, though he learnt to exercise it later. In an earlier letter to Ethel, written just before he left Australia, he said ' . . . you may not be brilliant at your work, but what is that?' Such comments must have tried the patience of an intelligent and popular young woman not lacking in friends of both sexes.

Nevertheless, it would be wrong to take too seriously these expressions of male superiority, quoted somewhat at random. The most devoted of couples are liable to fall into disputes in which both overstate their cases and then regret it. Nevertheless, they were indicative of a conflict of outlook existing from the start of their relationship. There was more to unite than divide them and during his remaining time in Adelaide they clearly enjoyed each other's company at social events such as tennis parties and on more intimate occasions when they could explore each other's beliefs in a diversity of subjects from music to philosophy, from literature to religion. In short, they seem to have behaved very much like any other young couple strongly attracted to each other but not yet ready to link their fortunes irrevocably.

On 11 December 1921 Florey left Port Adelaide bound for Hull as surgeon on board the freight liner *SS Otira*, a post he had taken to gain a free passage to England. Medically, the voyage was undemanding but his hasty temper, which was to remain a well-known characteristic until the later years of his life, led him into a major row with the captain, whom he had at the outset written off as 'an absolute dud'. They parted acrimoniously when the ship docked at Hull on 24 January 1922.

It needs little imagination to sense his feelings on that day, for it was very literally a turning-point in his life. Until that time he had not travelled beyond South Australia and New South Wales. The climate of Adelaide is similar to that of the Mediterranean: by contrast, he arrived in Hull—not the most attractive of cities at the best of times—on the coldest winter day recorded for five years. As he went south by train to London snow was falling, the first he had ever seen. Behind he had left his family and his friends; in particular he had left Ethel, with whom there was no formal engagement but certainly an understanding. Ahead lay a world of which he knew little save that its way of life and social conventions were very different from those to which he was accustomed. The prestige of his Rhodes Scholarship ensured him a flying start, but it was of limited duration and he was uneasily conscious that he might in the future be called upon to support his mother. The financial uncertainties of a career in research favoured neither marriage nor family commitments.

Nevertheless, it is not to be supposed that any such misgivings lay too heavily upon him. Ahead lay three years at Oxford with all its high tradition of scholarship and promise of future advancement. A cold and cheerless journey to London brought him back into touch with his old life; his sister Anne, who had made her way to England and become matron in a boys' school at Abingdon, near Oxford, met him at King's Cross. After two days in London, during which he visited his uncle James Florey at Stoke Newington, he finally completed his long journey to Oxford.

Oxford 1922-24

As he had a choice of colleges, Florey had elected to enter Magdalen, very probably because it was that of his old headmaster in Adelaide, who meanwhile had retired to Bath. On other grounds, the choice is perhaps a little surprising. Oxford as a whole was still very much an upper-class institution, drawing its students mainly from the Public Schools, and Magdalen was just about top of the social scale; prewar it had been the choice of the royal family for the future Edward VIII. This was scarcely the most appropriate environment for a brash young 'colonial' of middle-class origins. Some other colleges—such as Queen's, of which he was later to become Provost—had a more mixed intake. In the event, however, things worked out well enough: in the first flush of enthusiasm he wrote to Ethel telling her that Magdalen was the most beautiful of all the colleges and The High, in which it is situated, the finest street in Europe. The climate depressed him, however, and he found it hard to adjust to after the sunshine of Australia.

Today, Rhodes Scholarships are regarded as an enlightened conception but in 1922 they were still viewed with suspicion by many Oxford dons: no good would come, they thought, from this invasion by barbarians unversed in the classical tradition. Florey was fortunate in that the President of his college was an advocate of the scheme and showed some interest in him. For his part, he had a proper reverence for Oxford and its traditions but had no intention of subscribing to them unreservedly. His letters home are full of tart comments on aesthetic students, vapid girls, and the dowagers of north Oxford. His lack of social grace, to which at that stage of his life he gave little thought, often landed him in difficulties. Nevertheless, his circle of acquaintance was generally indulgent and seems to have taken any awkwardness in his manner in good part; indeed, he probably enlivened a rather stuffy atmosphere. At any rate, towards the end of his first year he could send word home that: 'Sometimes I think I am more or less liked here'.

Florey's determination to complete his medical studies at Adelaide before coming to Oxford landed him in an immediate difficulty. He had elected to join the honour school of physiology but as he arrived a term after the course began he had to wait two terms before another started. An advantage was that he had a delightful, leisured first two terms in Oxford, with plenty of time for the river in summer. For the moment he had to content himself with more elementary work, which he found irksome because he had already covered much of the ground. As at Adelaide, he viewed his teachers with a questioning eye, and found some of them wanting: they were given to 'saying absurd things with a convincing air'. At the same time he was more than willing to recognize talent where it existed. At the end of his first term he wrote to Ethel: 'Its a wonderful place . . . one is humbled by one's own insignificance. I got very little, intellectually, from the chaps at Adelaide Varsity. Quite the reverse here. I feel I have all to gain and little to give.' In particular, he came under the spell of Sir Charles Sherrington, who had been appointed Waynflete Professor of Physiology in 1913; he had already made his mark at Liverpool with the publication in 1906 of his *Integrative action of the nervous system*. He had reorganized his department and transformed it into what was probably the best centre for neurophysiology in the world. In 1922 he was 65 years of age and at the height of his powers. He was President of the Royal Society (1920-5) and also President of the British Association for the Advancement of Science, then a far more influential body than it is now. A man of great sensitivity, he was also a talented poet. He was to go on to be awarded the OM (1924) and a Nobel Prize (1932). In many respects Florey's career was to parallel his.

Sherrington was not only a great research worker but also a dedicated teacher determined to inspire his students with his own enthusiasm and bring out the best in them. When Sherrington spoke to him personally only a few weeks after his arrival in Oxford, the event was momentous enough to be recorded in Florey's next letter to Ethel. It was in fact, the beginning of an association which was powerfully to influence Florey's whole career. Before the end of term he had been to tea with the Sherringtons—where he was somewhat taken aback to find women smoking and by the rapid changes in Lady Sherrington's complexion—but for the moment this seemed of no particular significance.

Throughout his life, Florey was fond of travelling and he spent his first vacation away from Oxford. For a time he stayed with his Uncle James in London, enjoying art galleries and concerts, two other lasting pleasures. While there he visited another Australian who had come from Adelaide as a Rhodes Scholar. This was Hugh Cairns; he was two years older than Florey, coming to Oxford in 1919, but they seemed not to have known each other in Australia. From London he went on to join his sister Anne, who was staying with friends near Salisbury: family ties were not forgotten.

At Oxford he had formed another friendship that was to prove very significant. This was with an American Rhodes Scholar,

John Farquhar Fulton, also at Magdalen. Through him, Florey was introduced to Harvey Cushing, who was spending some time working with Sherrington. Cushing was then Moseley Professor of Surgery at Harvard and had an international reputation as a pioneer of neurosurgery, specializing in long and painstaking operations on the brain. In 1946 John Fulton was to write what is regarded as the definitive biography of Cushing, who died in 1939.

By this time Florey had been in England for no more than six months but already he was building up that wide circle of influential acquaintance which was to stand him in such good stead in later years. Fulton went on to become Professor of Physiology at Yale and Cairns, after working for a year with Cushing at Harvard in 1926, came back to head a new neurosurgical unit at the London Hospital and then at Oxford in the Chair of Surgery, one of several clinical professorships established by the Nuffield Benefaction. Florey was also making contacts in English society, supposedly, as he said, because they thought him 'quaint'. In London he had met Lady Frances Ryder; she was the daughter of the Earl of Harrowby, a partner in the banking firm of Coutts. He met also a Miss Kerr, apparently a connection of the Marquess of Lothian, who had been a Lady-in-Waiting to Queen Victoria. From his sister's friends in Salisbury he went on to stay with a rich old lady in Sherborne, who entertained him with tours by motor-car: Florey was entranced by the Dorset countryside, so different from Australia. Such company, which in those days commanded more general respect than it does in our more egalitarian times, in no way overawed him: in his letters to Ethel they all tended to be referred to as 'old ducks'.

The first Long Vacation gave Florey ample opportunity to indulge his taste for foreign travel, then very cheap; one could live comfortably on £2 per week on the Continent, more cheaply than at home. He learnt on arriving at a new place to make for some small hotel near the station, which he generally found to be cheap, clean, and friendly. From his experiences then he retained a gift for picking out the pleasant small hotel at sight. He visited Brussels, Cologne, Bonn, Nuremberg, and Vienna, where he spent three months at the American Medical School. He enjoyed travel, not only for its own sake, but also for the new opportunities if gave him to enjoy music and art. But such trips were not wholly in pursuit of pleasure. Conscious of his lack of knowledge of languages—on his journey from Brussels he had been dependent on 'an old duck from Cambridge who knows French and German like a native'—he worked hard to learn German, then, much more than now, a useful attribute for a research worker. Making use of Linguaphone courses, he also learnt some basic French, Italian, and Spanish.

Returning to Oxford for the Michaelmas term, he was able to start in earnest on the final honours course in physiology and showed himself back in form by gaining a first-class degree. This was one out of only five awarded in a class of 64: to his pleasure, his friend John Fulton was one of the others. Enlivened by this success he set off to spend the following Long Vacation on a more ambitious tour of Europe. He had decided on this, rather than on hospital work which he had done at the Radcliffe Infirmary in April, on the basis that it would broaden his mind and that he might not have such opportunities in later life. There is reason to suppose, however, that one factor in his decision was an invitation from two Czech girls, whom he had met the previous year in Vienna, to join them in the Carpathians. Clearly he spent an enjoyable holiday with them but found time to visit also Germany, Austria, Hungary, and Italy.

At this stage, Florey still had a year and a term left of his Rhodes Scholarship, and his intention was to spend this in pharmacological research, but fate decreed otherwise. His first-class degree in physiology and his fine earlier record had marked him out—even in Oxford, where good scholarship abounded—as a person of promise. Clearly it had impressed Sherrington, who in July invited him to come to his Department in Oxford as a Demonstrator. Naturally, Florey accepted without hesitation. To work under a man of such distinction was doubly advantageous; it offered both first-rate experience in research and useful prestige for the future. An additional cause for satisfaction was that Fulton, too, was a demonstrator in Sherrington's department. The only news which marred his satisfaction was that, after being short-listed, he had narrowly missed a fellowship at Merton. Later, this was offset by the award of the Gotch Memorial Prize—£5 and a medal.

The initial research with Sherrington proved a disappointment; neurophysiology involved a good deal of delicate work with electrodes, which had little appeal for Florey. Before Christmas he had switched to other work on the contraction of blood capillaries.

This was the basis of his Oxford BSc thesis and of his first published paper. This change of plan seems not to have upset Sherrington—who may well have encouraged him, in the belief that neurophysiology was not his line—at whose home he was still a frequent visitor. Indeed, Sherrington was clearly mindful of his interests, for he encouraged Florey to put in for the John Lucas Walker studentship at Cambridge; in May, he learned that he had been successful, in open competition. This was a boost to his ego—especially as it was for research in pathology rather than physiology—and encouraged his hopes that he might in time climb the higher rungs of the academic ladder. Financially he would be no better off, however; the stipend was £300 p.a., the same as the Rhodes Scholarship, though he could have £200 to buy apparatus.

Throughout his life he had a deep affection for Sherrington and used always to remember his birthdays. Near the end of Sherrington's long life, when he was physically but not mentally incapacitated, Florey went to Eastborne to visit him in the nursing home in which he lived.

Cambridge was not entirely strange to him, for he had already visited the University and made contacts there. They included Joseph Barcroft, for whom a special Readership in Physiology had been created in 1919, and H. R. Dean, who had been appointed Professor of Pathology in 1922.

The Arctic expedition

Between winding up his affairs in Oxford and taking up his new appointment in Cambridge, Florey embarked on further travels, but of a kind very different from those he had previously enjoyed. In June 1924 he was invited to join as medical officer the Oxford University Arctic Expedition, then on the point of leaving for a programme of scientific exploration in Spitsbergen. It was, in fact, a mixed expedition, eight members coming from Oxford, three from Cambridge, nine from the Services, and one from the National Physical Laboratory. Four Norwegians were in charge of the dogs and sledges.

In strictly scientific terms the expedition achieved little of note. An aeroplane, allegedly the first used in Arctic exploration, proved nothing but a nuisance. The wireless operator developed pleurisy and Florey felt it essential to get him to hospital, necessitating a difficult voyage through pack ice. On the return journey, the ship ran aground and all ballast had to be thrown overboard. Eventually Florey reached Tromsö safely, and returned home in mid-September via Sweden and Denmark.

In other senses, however, the expedition was very fruitful: on Florey, and no doubt many of his companions, the adventure made a lifelong impression, and he always made a point of attending the Club's annual reunion dinner if he possibly could. On the one hand, it was for him a unique experience to be committed to a small group of mixed interests and nationalities who had of necessity to rely wholly on themselves. On the other, the majesty of the Arctic made a powerful impression on him. He records that it induced in him a particularly strong sense of that 'loneliness of spirit' which seems always to have been part of his life. While he always had a great circle of acquaintance, he was essentially a loner and had real difficulty in getting close to anybody. During the previous Christmas vacation he had written to Ethel lamenting that 'the fact is I really haven't got a friend as I conceive the term, and am quite incapable of having one . . . It must be something wrong with me.' Nevertheless, this feeling was not always reciprocated. Charles Elton, an ecologist who later became Director of the Bureau of Animal Population at Oxford, has recorded that the time he spent alone with Florey at the base camp in Spitsbergen was the beginning of what he, at least, regarded as a lifelong friendship. Fulton, too, almost the only man whom Florey addressed by his first name, was surely in the same category.

Cambridge

Sherrington's concern for Florey extended to recommending him as a member of the Senior Common Room at his old college, Caius. The Master at that time was Sir Hugh Anderson, who shared Sherrington's interest in the physiology of the nervous system. As always, Florey devoted a good deal of time and energy to various ball games. In the summer he played tennis but with an aggressive determination to win that made him an unpopular opponent in an age and environment when tennis was a social pastime as much as a competitive game. He played for the County a couple of times and today he would have the makings of a good professional player. In the winter he played some hockey, apparently with more enthusiasm than skill. He also played golf on the Gog Magog golf course, reserved for graduate members of the University. There he would have encountered the famous 'Trinity Circus', a group of Trinity men, mostly physicists and mathematicians, headed by Rutherford. They played bad golf and talked noisy shop on Sunday mornings, and the Club was not best pleased with them. Nevertheless, they were all eminent men who were, or became, Fellows of the Royal Society; Rutherford and F. W. Aston were Nobel Laureates. In 1924 this group included F. G. Mann and Geoffrey Taylor. Florey never joined this select golfing clique, but was very gratified to receive an invitation from the Master of Caius to join the Rayleigh Club as one of six associate members. It, too, was very select, the membership being limited to twelve, including Rutherford and J. J. Thomson.

The way in which Florey was taken up by older people of standing—whether they were rich old ladies or eminent academics—calls for some comment, for the ability to call on strategically placed acquaintances was an important factor in his success in later life. There is no reason to suppose that there was any deliberate social or professional climbing about it beyond what is reasonable in an ambitious young man with his career to make; on the contrary, the trivia of social life made no appeal to him and he found the common room talk of Oxbridge boring. Clearly, therefore, people liked him for what he was. Wherein the attraction lay is another matter. Academics, of course, attach great importance to intellectual ability and his record was eloquent testimony to his possession of this. Proficiency in experimental research is held in particular esteem among scientists and Florey's dedication to his laboratory work was self-evident. Yet these were qualities taken almost as a matter of course in postgraduate life in Cambridge at that time; if you lacked them, you would scarcely be there at all. Why should giants such as J. J. Thomson, then 68, and Rutherford, aged 53, admit Florey to the very select circle of the Rayleigh Club? He was not of their discipline, nor even of a discipline for which physicists had any particular regard, nor was he a member of Trinity. In the non-academic world, knowledge of the fate of blood cells, and of cerebral control of the blood supply to the dog's colon, were scarcely social attributes. If we are seeking a common factor, it is perhaps to be found in his forthright views and astringent way of expressing them. Not a man to suffer fools gladly, he was never backward in expressing his own opinion bluntly and tersely, and usually very much to the point. At the same time he usually, though not always, contrived to avoid giving offence by his readiness to listen to reasonable arguments to the contrary. Perhaps a fair comment is that people in many walks of life found Florey what for lack of a better generalization might be called 'good value', a phrase he often used himself.

While research was always very much the centre of his life—and to the end he was eager to embark on new techniques, such as electron microscopy—he could not pursue it free from distraction. For one thing he had his career to think of, and on Sherrington's advice applied for—and in due course won—a Rockefeller Fellowship to enable him to gain experience of new techniques in America. He had hopes of returning to take up an official Fellowship at Caius and with this in mind was busy writing the thesis that would support his candidature. He had, too, to do some teaching in bacteriology, of which his knowledge was by then only rudimentary. More seriously, he had digestive problems which pulled him down considerably. By his own experiments, he diagnosed this as achlorhydria, a condition in which the stomach fails to produce sufficient hydrochloric acid. This, coupled with a profusion of mucus—a secretion in which he acquired a lasting scientific interest—led him to suspect dire trouble, such as pernicious anaemia or even cancer. He 'worked himself into a sweat' and went off to London to seek privately the professional advice of his friend Cairns: he was relieved to find that the condition was likely to prove chronically troublesome but not serious, provided he took some care with his diet. Charles Bolton, an eminent consulting physician at University College Hospital, London advised on treatment and told him never to allow a surgeon to open him up for exploratory purposes. Accordingly, he adopted a system of self-medication, taking dilute hydrochloric acid to restore the gastric balance. This discoloured his teeth and probably led to the tightlipped smile characteristic of later years.

This somewhat secretive approach to ill-health may well have stemmed not only from natural stoicism but from anxiety that, if it were known, it might prejudice future appointments on which so much depended. Much later in life, when he was a victim of angina, he certainly concealed it for this reason; as a professor his job was secure, but a suspicion of physical disability might well have debarred him from consideration for some of the high offices which eventually came his way.

As the only son he was concerned about his mother and sisters in Adelaide. Although their circumstances could not properly be called straitened, they were certainly reduced compared with the old days at Coreega. This, too, was inevitably a distraction. But far overshadowing all this, so far as his private life was concerned, was his relationship with Ethel, and to this we must now return.

A postal courtship

While they were together in Adelaide, Howard and Ethel were clearly mutually attracted but there was no formal engagement: so far as affection can be quantified, it is perhaps true to say that he was rather fonder of her than she of him. Neither was committed and after they parted there could have been no cause for recrimination if one or the other had formed an attachment for another partner. More often than not this would have been the natural outcome in the circumstances. In the 1920s communication with Australia was very different from what it is now. Today, a subscriber in Oxford or Cambridge can telephone Adelaide by direct dialling at a moderate rate and be connected in a moment. Then, there was no such service; the telegraph was available for brief and urgent messages, but for all practical purposes, personal communication was possible only by post. Moreover, post then meant surface mail, taking some six weeks for delivery, the same as the passenger service. The sender could not expect a reply in less than three months. Such delay is not conducive to maintaining the links of ordinary friendship, let alone allowing friendship to develop into romance and romance into a formal engagement and marriage. Yet this is in fact what happened over five long years, during which no meeting between them took place. Looked at in retrospect it was not a promising recipe for a successful marriage nor, unhappily, did it prove to be so.

Since this long courtship was conducted wholly by correspondence, the letters themselves must be the main source of information about its course. Fortunately, from the historical point of view, almost all Howard's letters, around one hundred and fifty in all, were kept by Ethel and survive. Her letters to him, on the other hand, were almost all destroyed by Howard himself. When he learnt in 1925 that his application for a Rockefeller Fellowship for research in America had been successful he decided to burn those he had not destroyed already rather than leave them at Oxford exposed to 'the possibility of prying eyes'. There is a suggestion, however, that he had some misgivings afterwards, for he excused himself to Ethel, saying:

You won't think I don't value your letters? I think I could answer all questions thereon by heart—I've read them all so many times.

Although only one side of the correspondence still exists, much of the other can reasonably be inferred.

Looked at objectively the letters have many points of interest. Not least is the lack of passion; that this may have been felt is very possible, but the intimate endearments one expects to find in love letters are rare. Perhaps this is not altogether surprising, for in Adelaide only the beginnings of courtship had been possible. Had they remained together their individual interests and attitudes, their likes and dislikes, and—above all—their views on marriage would have emerged in conversation, and never been committed to paper at all. As it was, both parties had to seek to understand each other's inner nature almost by question and answer. From the biographer's point of view, this has its advantages. We have on record Florey's explicit views on a wide variety of subjects: his ambitions; the idiosyncrasies of his contemporaries; his taste in literature, music, and art; his religious belief; his attitude towards women; and much else beside. A particular point of interest is that as both were medically qualified Florey includes a great deal of technical information about the progress of his research, both successes and failure. We must remember, however, that people change with age and experience, and views expressed by a young and enthusiastic Florey in the 1920s are not necessarily ones to which he would have subscribed in his maturity. He himself makes this very point in one of his letters: 'I only hope you won't pick up each phrase and award it marks of approval or disapproval. . . . ' The same may be said of Ethel. During these years she was still isolated in Adelaide, initially completing her studies and later practising medicine in what was still very much a man's world. Of the broader vistas opened to Howard by his Rhodes Scholarship she had no direct experience nor, indeed, was she very much in touch with those who had. In forming a judgement of her nature, we must not rely unduly on the evidence of what she wrote and did in these early years.

Of interest, too, are the uncertainties that emerge, especially on Ethel's part. Characteristically, Florey does not hesitate to punctuate his wooing with some pretty astringent personal comments; at times, however, he is conscious of having overstepped the mark and writes conciliatory letters to repair the damage. Ethel can be equally spirited, but in a rather different way; she is less concerned with finding fault with Howard personally than with considering how differences between them would create difficulties if they were married. Events were to show that Ethel's view of their matrimonial prospects was the more realistic.

For the moment, however, we have got ahead of events. The earliest letters make it clear that marriage was in their thoughts, but Florey—apart from other considerations—was preoccupied with his career and financial problems. During his first spring in Oxford, he wrote:

give me the chance to write to you and know you better . . . Magdalen will be simply a paradise in summer. If we were married, we ought to live here.

But a few months later, his tone was a little different:

I told you how I stand financially. In three years I'll be in precisely the same position, and I couldn't ask you to marry me then, even.

Florey's concern over money has sometimes been misconstrued. As a young man with no private means or capital, trying to establish himself—and later a wife and family—in a profession notoriously ill-paid, it was natural that long-term financial security should loom large. In everyday matters he could be as generous as the next man.

Understandably, Ethel found this desultory and sometimes disparaging correspondence frustrating and in the summer of 1922 she wrote saying she thought their relationship should be ended. Florey, then staying in Vienna as part of his long vacation tour, certainly did not reject this out of hand for after so long he, too, was conscious of frustration and uncertainty. On the other hand, he had been brought up in the tradition that having pledged yourself you stuck by your proposal. In the end, he wrote begging her to reconsider the matter, saying that, for his part, he would wait for years if necessary. For the moment, however, Ethel was adamant and there was a break in the correspondence for several months. When it was renewed, there was some change of attitude. Ethel's feelings towards him had not changed for better or for worse, but Adelaide was beginning to pall. She, too, wanted to taste the fuller life that England could offer; Howard welcomed this, but not the prospect that she might bring her mother.

So the affair ebbed and flowed during his first two years in Oxford, and his acceptance of the invitation to join the Spitsbergen expedition did not help matters. Ethel, cast down by ill-health and problems of her own, appears to have persuaded herself that even if Howard would not consider returning to Adelaide to take up the vacant lectureship in physiology of which he was virtually assured, he might at least have come on a brief visit so that they could talk together and resolve their differences one way or another. Howard, however, seems never to have contemplated this possibility; on the face of it this is curious, for it was quite feasible and he could at the same time have seen his mother and sisters. The Spitsbergen expedition was an exciting and attractive adventure, and one that left a lasting impression on him, but it was not something that could be represented as furthering his career in research. Months later he expressed repentance:

You were disappointed that I went to Spitsbergen instead of coming home, and that I didn't take the Adelaide job. I feel a perfect beast in the way in which I am treating you.

Meanwhile, however, marriage was again in prospect, and soon after arriving in Cambridge he wrote suggesting that they might become formally engaged. Ethel went to see Mrs. Florey in Adelaide and seems to have been kindly received, though Howard later accused his mother of having been lukewarm in her attitude to Ethel. Perhaps he was not best pleased at his mother's comment that Ethel did not seem the sort of girl who would tolerate sloppy dress; he might no longer be able to take off his collar and tie in the evening, as was his wont.

By the following April Florey had received sufficient encouragement to say that he would write formally to Ethel's father to request her hand in marriage—the only immediate obstacle to this major step was that he did not know his initials! In fact, however, he seems not to have got round to writing this letter until six months later, by which time he was in America. But still there were bigger obstacles than this. Ethel's health was not good and she feared tuberculosis, with which she was all too familiar from her medical experience; de Crespigny had advised her against leaving Australia to brave the rigours of English winters. Worse, she had incautiously mentioned the possibility of her hearing being impaired. Florey reacted immediately, and tactlessly, by saying that if he had to shout at her marriage was out of the question. Later, he maintained that he had not taken her seriously, but lasting damage had been done. In fact Ethel did become very deaf, and this was to be a cause for dissension.

For the moment, however, romance was in the ascendant. Lady Sherrington had allayed his financial fears by saying that her married son managed very well on £400 p.a. and in July he got word that his application for a Rockefeller Fellowship had been successful. Elated, he wrote to Ethel: 'I'll have £400 clear of . . . expenses. . . . If you think it can be done, I'll marry you as soon as you like in America.'

Once again postal delays caused complications. On second thoughts, he wrote proposing that he should come to Adelaide at the end of his Rockefeller award and they should be married there. Ethel, meanwhile, had written agreeing to join him in America in six months. A variety of other alternatives were explored and were confused by letters crossing in the post, one suggestion being dispatched before the previous one had been commented on, but nevertheless marriage within the year seemed assured. For the moment, however, we must consider the professional use to which Florey put the Rockefeller Fellowship in America, since this was to prove of considerable importance to his career.

America 1925

The present pre-eminence of the United States in most fields of scientific and medical research is too well known to need stressing, but half a century ago—when Florey gained his Rockefeller award—the situation was very different. If we take Nobel Prizes as a yardstick, not inappropriate in the present context, the position was that since they were first awarded in 1901 only three out of 75 (none in physiology or medicine) had gone to America up to 1925; virtually all the others had gone to Europe. In 1976, America astonished the world by winning every prize, and had by then gained 100 out of just over 300 awarded: almost exactly half of them had been in physiology or medicine. Nevertheless, in the 1920s excellent research was being done in the best American laboratories and there was plenty for a young man to learn in the way of new techniques. No doubt one factor which influenced Florey's choice was his encounter with Harvey Cushing, the pioneer American neurosurgeon, in his early days in Oxford.

In the event, however, the direct benefits of this visit to America were, for reasons outside Florey's control, not very great. He sailed for New York in the Cunarder *Coronia* on 19 September 1925, with the intention of working with Robert Chambers at Cornell Medical School. Chambers had made a name for himself with the development of a micromanipulator with which most delicate operations could be carried out at a cellular level: this could have been very valuable in connection with Florey's work on the blood vessels of the brain. As it turned out no micro-manipulator was immediately available, so Florey, with characteristic impatience, arranged at short notice to go and work in the laboratory of A. N. Richards at Philadelphia; Richards was Professor of Pharmacology in the University of Pennsylvania (1910-46), well known for his work on kidney fuction, involving some delicate cannulation of fine blood vessels in Bowman's capsule.

This change of plan apparently suited him, for he had found New York dirty and expensive; moreover, Philadelphia offered the pleasure of its splendid Symphony Orchestra. Nevertheless, he found it 'dull and monotonous' and he sought introductions to other former Rhodes Scholars. Positively to seek companion-ship was rather out of keeping; possibly the reason was that things were going badly again with Ethel, mainly as a result of postal delays. Before she had received either his letter proposing marriage in Adelaide or a later one suggesting that it should take place in New York in August, Ethel wrote to say that she would join him in America in April. Instead of being pleased, as she might have expected from his earlier eagerness, Howard prevari-cated, pleading the high cost of living in America. And so it went on, plans being changed almost as soon as they were formulated.

Events came to a crisis in November. Ethel, we must suppose because she had by then received Howard's suggestion of coming to Adelaide in the following August, announced that she would not come to America after all. Furious, and perhaps jealous because he saw the hand of de Crespigny in this, he sent back a reply so intemperate that he was driven to sending a cable to mitigate its impact before she received it, and following it by a further letter, full of apology and remorse. When she did eventually receive his 'appalling' letter Ethel took it very well indeed, and conceded that:

It's all—or nearly all—quite true . . . but at least I've the satisfaction of knowing that I told you, time and time again, that I was not by any means the perfect person you imagined . . . it would be better for me to wait and go to England where I would have some means of supporting myself . . . if you were too disgusted with me altogether.

A rather sad but revealing letter came a week later when, presumably, she had received Howard's letter of apology:

at least I stuck to a resolution that I made when we first talked about getting married. That was that no matter what I had to give up, I should never voluntarily stand in the way of your career in the smallest possible thing. Cannot you see how torn in two I am, between you on the one hand and my profession which, after eight years of it has filled my life and thoughts and interest pretty fully?. . . . But you know I am quite prepared to give the whole thing up when I marry you. But, in return, I must feel absolutely certain of your unreserved and entire love for the rest of my life.

Ethel's dilemma is clear enough, and the problem of combining a career with the role of wife and mother was much less easily resolved then than it is now. This letter touches also on another point of difference: Ethel liked doctoring and Howard liked research. Worse, Florey had a contempt for clinicians and made no secret of it. Shortly before they were married he wrote: 'Like all clinicians you are not in a position to prove your ideas'.

The correspondence continued during the remainder of Florey's stay in America, but on a calmer note. It was tacitly accepted that Ethel would come to England in August and they would marry there. Meanwhile Florey had had important news to tell her. In November he received an invitation from Dr. Philip Panton to take up a research appointment at the London Hospital; the letter made it clear that the suggestion had received the approval of Sherrington and Dean. It seemed to be a splendid opportunity for research, with good facilities, and the salary was £850 p.a. with a five-year tenure. The invitation was, in fact, to be the first holder of a newly endowed Freedom Fellowship. The only snag was that the London Hospital wanted him to take up the appointment as soon as possible, and this would mean cutting short his American visit. Typically, Florey tried to temporize, on the ground that the techniques he was learning in America would be useful in his new work. In the end, a compromise was reached and he returned to England in May.

As a further boost to morale, he very shortly received a second invitation, in the form of a cable, this time of a job in the Physiological Laboratory at Cambridge, under Joseph Barcroft—famous for his work on the respiratory function of the blood—who had just succeeded J. N. Langley as professor. Sizing up the situation, Florey decided that the Cambridge facilities were no better than London's and that the salary would almost certainly be less. For the moment, therefore, Cambridge was refused. In the event, he had miscalculated. A letter to him from Barcroft miscarried; had he received it he would have known that the Cambridge job was also worth £850 p.a., plus a college fellowship. The post went to a Russian, Gleb von Anrep, who soon moved on to take up a professorship of physiology in Cairo.

Christmas was spent at Boston with his old friend John Fulton, who had become Professor of Physiology at Yale. Apart from the general pleasure of agreeable society, the occasion provided an opportunity for several meetings and talks with Harvey Cushing, then Professor of Surgery at Harvard. He met also the Swedish physiologist A. J. Carlson, who invited him to spend a few weeks with him in Chicago. There he met also another rising young physiologist, A. C. Ivy. This visit—again the result of chance— was very significant; Carlson and Ivy were both interested in gastroenterology and Florey was fired with enthusiasm to embark on research on the role of mucus in the intestinal tract, a subject to which his own gastric problems had already directed his attention. No time was wasted: he learned operative techniques from Ivy and wrote to Ethel pressing her to analyse the gastric juices of some of her child patients suffering from gastroenteritis and collect data from the post-mortem room. All must be kept secret, however, for fear that his 'great idea' might be plagiarized by others. Ethel took this sudden demand on her limited time in good part but was sceptical of the results; first she doubted whether gastroenteritis really existed and, later, pointed out that Howard was quite mistaken in supposing that 'kids swallowed stomach tubes easily'. Howard replied lamely that 'this was only what he had been told', Possibly, however, he had been influenced by the readiness with which he himself could swallow a stomach tube—'almost like breakfast'—in investigating his own gastritis. At that time the work on mucus was necessarily limited, but it was to be one of Florey's main research interests.

On leaving Chicago—where the Symphony Orchestra had provided 'welcome relaxation'—his ultimate destination was New York, but first he wanted to see something of Canada, visiting Toronto, Ottawa, Montreal, and Quebec. Finally he ended his tour where he had intended to begin—in Chambers' laboratory at New York. Again he was unlucky, for the whole department was moving into new quarters. With little more than a month to go not much could in any case be achieved, but he nevertheless did some interesting—and, he believed, original—research on the contraction of lacteals. Ruefully, however, he wrote to Ethel a few days later that much of his observation had been made half a century earlier by A. Heller, a German pathologist. Nevertheless, there was sufficient originality in his research to make a paper for the *Journal of Physiology*; this appeared in 1927.

On 4 May the tour was ended; Florey sailed for England to fulfil his promise to start work at the London Hospital under Panton. Writing to Ethel during the voyage he said: 'I've really had a most enjoyable and instructive time in America. I would like to go back some time.' In later life, he used to say that he felt more at home in the tougher American scene than he did in England. He was probably well into his fifties before he entirely lost the feeling that in England he was something of an outsider. In 1929 he attended the International Physiological Congress in Boston, but his crucial return visit was in 1941 when he came to seek aid for the large-sclae production of penicillin. Then, his experience of the country—and above all his friendship with Richards and Fulton—was to prove invaluable.

London 1926

Florey landed at Plymouth on 13 May, the day after the end of the General Strike, and was able to get up to London without delay to meet Panton and his new colleagues. His accommodation was not quite ready, so he accepted an invitation from Barcroft to spend a week in Cambridge; it was only then that he learnt the true nature of the appointment he had refused. However, he was made much of, and he was invited—no doubt as a sequel to the Spitsbergen expedition—to a dinner given by the Vice-Chancellor to mark the inauguration of the Scott Polar Institute. It was made clear that they were still anxious to attract him back to Cambridge. Indeed, the Master of Caius suggested that he should apply for a College Fellowship, and gave a strong hint that Florey would be a strong candidate for a new Chair of Experimental Medicine which it was hoped to establish. He was invited to spend the weekend at Royston with Lord Knutsford—an eminent banker and in his younger days a prominent sportsman—Chairman of the London Hospital.

London was to prove rather a disappointment. Within a month he was writing to Ethel from Cambridge:

I'm feeling very restless so I have migrated here for a few days to work in Barcroft's lab. I'm rather fed up with the London Hospital.

The causes were manifold but seem mainly to have arisen from conflicts of personality. Within the hospital there were conflicts between clinicians and research workers. The former had not adjusted themselves to the advent of pathology as a scientific discipline; the latter resented carrying out analyses for fee-charging consultants. There were wearisome disputes at a lower level; Florey describes a trying weekend, punctuated with domestic squabbles, spent with the Pantons. It is clear, however, that his own hasty temper did not contribute to harmony in the laboratory. Nevertheless, his research progressed. He continued his work on mucus and the lymphatics and embarked on a programme of tetanus research with Paul Fildes, the start of a lifelong association. At the same time he was busy writing the thesis that he was to submit in support of his application for a fellowship at Caius, and another for a Cambridge PhD.

On top of all this, there was a last-minute flurry of uncertainty about Ethel's journey to England. She had booked to leave Australia on 24 September in the *Moreton Bay* and Howard had hoped to join her at Marseilles. In the event, however, it proved that her last port of call was Port Said and they had to arrange to meet at Plymouth. Then, on her side of the world, Ethel was subjected to a final dilemma. For several years she had suffered from enlarged cervical glands and these suddenly increased in size. It was felt best that they should be removed before she left, and as expected they proved tuberculous. Doctors and parents then combined to urge her to reconsider, even at that eleventh hour, her plan to go to England with its notoriously cold damp climate. She herself was assailed with doubts lest she exposed Howard to 'the risk of possible heavy expenses added to an invalid wife'.

Nevertheless, the doubts were resolved and Ethel sailed as planned. There is no contemporary record of their meeting but from a note penned by Howard some years later it is clear that the lighthearted romance of young lovers was not apparent. Howard had visions of Ethel waving excitedly from the deck as he approached; in the event, he had to search the ship to find her. On the journey to London she yawned in his face. At the lodgings they took for a couple of weeks before they were married, she twice abandoned him to join acquaintances she had met on the boat. But these were comments made years later in a spirit of acrimony and they may well not fairly represent the real situation. Moreover, we lack Ethel's version; what the reality was we can only conjecture.

The marriage took place on 19 October 1925 at Holy Trinity, Paddington. Ironically, for he was among those who had sought to dissuade her from coming to England at all, the bride was given away by de Crespigny. Ominously, Ethel succumbed almost at once to a throat infection but they were soon able to get away for a short honeymoon in Rome. On their return, Howard was called on to honour an undertaking he had given earlier—that in consideration of Ethel's health they would live outside London. Accordingly, they rented a furnished house, Heather Lodge, at Chobham some thirty miles from London. For many young married people this would have seemed an idyllic arrangement, and commuting into London was quite common practice. For Florey, however, the journey to the London Hospital proved irksome and it was difficult to reconcile railway time tables with research programmes and the routine of family life. Whenever he could he visited Oxford or Cambridge, and was always a welcome visitor in the research laboratories there.

The travel situation was relieved in the summer of 1926 by a move to a flat in Belsize Square on the high, and supposedly healthy, ground of Hampstead. Nevertheless, it was still not a situation that a man of Florey's ambition and temperament would accept for longer than he need. In the event, the opportunity he wanted came quickly. His application to Caius was successful and he was elected to an Unofficial Fellowship; at the time this status was important as it enable him to hold the post while living and working in London. Much more important, however, was the unexpected vacancy of the Huddersfield Lectureship in Special Pathology early in 1927: Florey was offered the post and accepted with alacrity. In the autumn of the same year he was installed in Dean's department in Cambridge.

Cambridge 1927-32

Apart from professional advancement, the move to Cambridge had important practical advantages. In the first place, he now had an income of about £900 p.a., not inconsiderable in 1927. It was possible to buy, jointly, a house, albeit on mortgage; the Floreys settled in a semidetached house at 75 Cavendish Avenue, within easy cycling distance of the laboratory. His Unofficial Fellowship at Caius was made official, giving him rooms in college. Morale was boosted in 1928, by two major awards in physiology, both from Oxford.

From the moment of his arrival, there was no lack of things to be done. On the research front he began three major lines of research: with Alan Drury on cerebral blood pressure; with L. J. Witts on blood transfusion by injection into the peritoneum; and with Barcroft on the blood supply to the spleen. On his very first day he had, unknowingly at the time, an extraordinary stroke of good fortune in securing as his personal technician a young boy named Jim Kent. With his impatience, his intensity of application, and his long hours Florey was no easy taskmaster but on that day began a fruitful association which was to last for forty years: J. H. D. Kent was undoubtedly among the more important of Florey's discoveries. As part of his new responsibilities Florey was involved in teaching, and he took part in a radical revision of the teaching course in pathology.

In their long correspondence both Ethel and Howard had had dreams of combining their medical skill and experience in joint research. London had provided no opportunity for this but a trial was made at Cambridge. Unhappily, it was not a great success. Ethel's deafness was at least partially to blame, for she sometimes failed to hear, or misunderstood, Howard's peremptory instructions. However, they did publish two joint papers in 1929; in one they had A. N. Drury as a third collaborator, in the other A. Szent-Györgyi, a brilliant young Hungarian biochemist who was to win a Nobel Prize for Medicine in 1937 for his work on the physiological role of vitamin C.

Friction at the laboratory was matched by friction at home. Ethel was a keen gardener and capable dressmaker, but was less successful as a housewife—a weakness which became apparent on the rather rare occasions when they were entertaining. On such occasions there were uninhibited comments on both sides—the very fault that Howard had so much deplored when staying with the Pantons. Thus early in the marriage there was evidence of discord, though Professor Macfarlane has argued plausibly that allowance must be made for a natural lack of reticence between Australians who had no inhibitions about being outspoken; both being Australian was also in itself a bond between them. Nevertheless, friction there clearly was, and Cambridge society was divided in its sympathies—some seeing a nagging wife and others an overbearing husband. The situation was not improved by a visit in the summer of 1928 from Ethel's parents, for whom Howard had never had any great liking. All the same, they seem to have been generous enough, buying a car and taking them off on a tour of Britain and the Continent; better still, they left the car with the Floreys when they returned to Australia.

Late that year Ethel became pregnant. With her usual bad luck, she had a difficult time, suffering much from sickness. In the middle of it Howard, at Sherrington's instigation, was invited to go and work in Madrid for six weeks with Ramon y Cajal, a neurohistologist who had won a Nobel Prize as long ago as 1906. It was a great opportunity to learn useful new techniques and Florey was pleased to go. He was insistent, however, that Ethel should go with him and many thought that the long overland journey, in the heat of the summer, was an unreasonable imposition. Ethel herself seems, however, to have been quite game to go and this would have been in keeping with what we know of her character. Certainly she enjoyed it, and no harm was done. That it was not an experience either wished to forget seems clear from the fact that when the child was born—on 26 September—they called her Paquita Mary Joanna.

The year 1929 was memorable in another way, for in that year the department moved into the new pathology building, and Florey now had excellent facilities in a suite of rooms on the top floor. His overseas trip to Madrid was only one of several. In 1929 he went to the International Physiology Conference in Boston; he worked for three weeks with Paul Bouin in Strasbourg in 1931, taking Ethel and Paquita with him, and with August Krogh—yet another Nobel Laureate—in Copenhagen. He had received the important Thruston Award for research. To many, it must have seemed that he was an exceedingly fortunate young man who could now afford to relax and enjoy the undoubted pleasures of academic life in prewar Cambridge. Florey already had other ideas, however; his objective was a professorship. What his motives may have been—apart from a natural desire to get to the top of his professional tree—we can only conjecture. On his own statement, the financial aspect—about which both the Floreys were somewhat obsessional—was a powerful incentive; a professorship was better paid and the longer it was held the greater the pension. Much later, when he surprised many people by giving up his professorship at Oxford to become Provost of Queen's College, he advanced a similar reason. There were, however, undoubtedly other considerations, one of which was that professors had considerable control over the research of their departmental colleagues and could raise funds; they could, if they so wished, tackle a particular problem on a team basis instead of individually. Again, the social status of a professor was undeniably higher than that of a lecturer, a consideration to which Florey was certainly not indifferent.

In the 1930s the British academic world was fairly static. Unlike the 1960s, when there was a rash of new universities and great expansion of the old ones, there were relatively few established professorships and the creation of new ones was rare. It was, therefore, a fairly predictable world; short of the death of an existing incumbent it was fairly easy to see when and where opportunities would occur. Surveying the scene, it was clear that Cambridge had little to offer for some time to come: Barcroft was 56 and Dean only 49. True, there had been talk of a new Chair of Experimental Medicine, but nothing had come of it; in fact it was not established until 1945, so Florey did well not to count on it. At Oxford, Sherrington was 71 (though he did not in the event retire until 1936), but Georges Dreyer, the pathologist, was only 55. The provincial universities were more promising and Florey evidently made up his mind to try his luck there. Two opportunities quickly came up, Liverpool in 1928 and Bristol a year later. Florey thought seriously about applying for each of them and sought the advice of Sherrington, who seems at least to have thought Bristol suitable, but in the event he applied for neither. Then, unexpectedly, the Chair of Pathology at Sheffield fell vacant, in 1931, following the sudden death of J. S. C. Douglas. When the appointment was advertised Florey was in Strasbourg working with Bouin, and on his return he was sufficiently interested to go to Sheffield to see something of the department at first hand. What he saw impressed him and he decided to apply for the job, and in December he learnt that he had been elected.

With benefit of hindsight, his success is not surprising; in later years virtually any university in the world would have been proud to have claimed him as a professor. In 1931, however, things were very different. It is true that he had a good record for research, with already some 30 papers to his credit, and powerful backers such as Sherrington. Nevertheless, there were points to be counted against him. First and foremost, many pathologists of the day—grounded in the clinical tradition—declined to acknow-ledge him as one of their number; he was, they maintained, no more than a physiologist. Sir Robert Muir, Professor of Pathology at Glasgow, said flatly 'There is no pathologist named Florey'. Florey said nothing at the time but years later, when the fact that he had never done a post mortem no longer mattered, he com-mented publicly—'and, of course, he was right.' Secondly, his notoriously hasty temper had not endeared him to everybody; he himself acknowledged that he was aggressive at the interview, and it is said that he refused to accept the post if membership of the British Medical Association—'that pack of bloody trade unionists'—was made a condition. Thirdly, there was a strong field, more than a dozen applications being received. One of those shortlisted with Florey was J. B. Duguid, then Lecturer in Pathology at the Welsh National School of Medicine; his disappointment at missing Sheffield was assuaged in the following year when the University of Wales acknowledged his merit by appointing him to the vacant Chair of Pathology and Bacteriology, in which he made important contributions to the study of atherosclerosis to which Florey later turned. Finally, at 34, Florey was—by the standards of the day—young to gain a professorial appointment.

Equally, one may wonder why Florey chose Sheffield. Opportunities had, of course, to be taken where they occurred but Sheffield is as different from Oxford or Cambridge—or Adelaide for that matter—as it could well be. Moreover, the climate is not good and, especially in those days, the smoky atmosphere was not favourable to respiratory problems. Bristol, by contrast, is milder and the university and the best residential area are on high ground; not long previously it had been a fashionable spa. Moreover, Oxford—on which there is evidence his sights were really set, perhaps with Sherrington's chair in mind—was easily accessible by road or rail.

In the absence of evidence to the contrary, we must suppose that the attraction of Sheffield lay in either the facilities or the staff. The former cannot have been the main attraction, for the accommodation was considerably less spacious than he had at Cambridge. So far as the latter were concerned two men in particular must have appealed to him as colleagues. One was Edward Mellanby, a dedicated experimentalist, who had been appointed Professor of Pharmacology in 1920 and elected Fellow of the Royal Society five years later. He was a Cambridge man and had been much influenced by Gowland Hopkins and his work on vitamins; he himself did important work on vitamin D. In 1933 he was to become Secretary of the Medical Research Council, of which he was already a member. This was an important source of funds for academic research—and in this capacity was later to prove important for the support of Florey's own work. The other senior man of immediate interest was J. B. Leathes, appointed Professor of Physiology in 1915. He, too, was a Fellow of the Royal Society, to which he had been elected in 1911. He appears to have shared Florey's views on the way in which physiology and pathology should be integrated with clinical medicine. A further reason, no doubt, was that Sheffield was recognized as a stepping-stone to higher things; Dean himself had once occupied the chair for which Florey applied. It is conceivable, too, that the reputation of Yorkshire men for robust and outspoken expressions of opinion appealed to him as an Australian. In later years he always expressed himself as having been happy there: 'There are very nice people in Sheffield'.

Sheffield 1932-35

The Floreys arrived in Sheffield in March 1932 and were immediately faced by the realities of provincial life. In those days professors were of greater importance in local society than they are today and were expected to live in some style. The Cambridge house proved impossible to sell and they eventually let it; in Sheffield they rented a large Victorian house—now Florey Lodge, a hall of residence—standing in an acre of garden. The upkeep was considerable and staffing on a scale scarcely credible today was deemed essential: a cook, housemaid, gardener, and nannie were engaged. Wages, it is true, were low—a housemaid would then earn around £26 p.a., plus her keep—but any financial advantage in the move must have been swallowed up. It was worth £1000 p.a., only £100 more than he was getting at Cambridge.

The responsibilities of the job made serious inroads into time available for research. The medical school was small—admitting no more than fourteen students a year—but there was quite a heavy teaching load to which was added some teaching for dental students. Dental pathology was unknown territory to Florey, but with characteristic determination he made good the deficiency. The professor of pathology was, at least nominally, in charge of pathological services for four hospitals serving a population of a million people; it is clear that Florey did much to improve these services. Last, but by no means least, a service had to be provided for clinical consultants, from whom he had glowing testimonials when he left. In spite of this, research was quickly resumed, mainly on the role of the cell in inflammation and the effect of infection on tissue. The invaluable Kent came with him, despite a miniscule and precarious wage; it was some months before the Medical Research Council made reasonable, but not lavish, provision.

While Florey was at Cambridge research on mucus had taken a new direction. In 1922 Alexander Fleming, Lecturer in Bacteriology at St. Mary's Hospital London had discovered an enzyme, lysozyme, which had a powerful solvent (lytic) effect on certain bacteria. It proved to be widely present in bodily secretions, including mucus. Fleming at once published his results in three papers in the *Proceedings of the Royal Society* and the *British Journal of Experimental Pathology*. The significance of this discovery for his own research at Cambridge was apparent to Florey and with N. E. Goldsworthy he turned his attention to the lysozyme content of mucus. This led, in 1930, to the publication—also in the *British Journal of Experimental Pathology*—of an account of 'Some properties of mucus, with special reference to its antibacterial functions' (Plate 3). This publication is doubly important. On the one hand it marked the beginning of Florey's interest in the phenomenon of antibiosis, namely the inhibition of the growth of one organism by another. It also marked the first crossing of the paths of Florey and Fleming, for—until he mastered the techniques for himself—Florey sought Fleming's help in making the necessary assays of lysozyme. However, since this research on lysozyme is so intimately related to the later work on penicillin, it is appropriate to defer consideration of it in detail until later.

For most of his life Florey had the reputation of being a stormy petrel and it is scarcely surprising to see him involved in a flurry of excitement less than a year after arriving at Sheffield. In 1932 the chair of pathology at Guy's Hospital, London, fell vacant and none of the applicants were felt to be of the calibre to fill it. In February 1933 an approach was made to Florey to see if he would consider it. He was certainly prepared to be tempted; it was a prestigious appointment, at the heart of affairs, and worth £1200 p.a. There were protracted but inconclusive negotiations and then, suddenly, on 15 July he received a formal offer. In the circumstances he had no alternative but to inform the Vice-Chancellor at Sheffield. Hurried discussion took place, as a result of which Florey was offered £1200 p.a. if he would stay. Apart from Florey's obvious merit, a factor in the decision must have been that Leathes and Mellanby had just been lost, the former by retirement and the latter, as we have noted, to be Secretary of the Medical Research Council. This offer Florey decided to accept but to the embarrassment of all concerned Guy's prejudged the issue and published a notice of his acceptance in *The Times* of 26 July. The whole episode was unfortunate, but he was able to use Sheffield's evident anxiety to keep him as a lever to obtain staff there at the same level as similar departments elsewhere, a matter on which he went to some trouble to inform himself. Among the most valuable of his new recruits was a South African pathologist, Beatrice Pullinger, who had exceptional experience of both research and clinical work; before coming to Sheffield she had been Clinical Pathologist at the Mount Vernon Hospital. They worked closely together at Sheffield in work on the lymphatics, and later she went with Florey to Oxford for a short time, during which they worked closely together to organize a new course in general pathology.

Among Florey's skills was the ability to keep several distinct lines of research going at the same time and in different places. His interest in tetanus, on which he had collaborated with Paul Fildes in London, was no doubt heightened by the death of his brother-in-law—Hilda's husband—from this infection in 1929. The immediate cause of death is exhaustion from severe muscular spasms. Florey conceived the idea that if those spasms could be prevented the body might eliminate the toxin and the patient would recover. It was well known that curare—a drug obtainable from an arrow poison used by Indians in South America—would stop such spasms; unfortunately in so doing it caused general paralysis, including paralysis of the respiratory muscles. In 1929, however, the American hygienist Philip Drinker announced his invention of the iron lung, primarily for victims of poliomyelitis. With Fildes, in London, and his colleague at Sheffield H. E. Harding, Florey tried—though with not much success—to develop a form of treatment combining paralysis with curare and the mechanical maintenance of respiration. This involved visits to Oxford to learn from Sherrington the techniques of using curare. Also at Oxford, he continued collaboration with one of his earliest friends there, Harry Carleton, on the physiology of fertilization and the development of spermicides of practical use as contraceptives.

While professional life prospered, the domestic situation deteriorated sadly. The Floreys' taste for Spain led them to spend a family holiday there in 1933, with the unfortunate result that Ethel—whose health was still by no means good—contracted infective hepatitis. At the very end of the year she became pregnant for the second time and again suffered miseries from sickness. When their son, Charles, was born on 11 September 1934 his health gave cause for concern as he suffered from pyloric stenosis—a condition that causes frequent vomiting. Such a combination of circumstances would test even a happy marriage but when they were set against a background of already constant bickering the result was disastrous. The couple became estranged to the extent that they communicated virtually only in writing, and Ethel was thinking in terms of a legal separation. In the climate of the day, so very much more censorious than it is now, divorce could scarcely have been in question: the grounds were very restricted and the social and professional penalties severe. In a recent biography the historian A. J. P. Taylor recalls how in the 1950s he was the first Fellow in Oxfod to be divorced and not resign his Fellowship. Howard replied to her own written complaints and set out his own grievances in a long memorandum which is still preserved; the dispute is a sad reminder of the trivialities which can obsess highly intelligent, and basically well-meaning people when they are overstressed. It is not an episode by which either should be judged, or would have wished to have been judged.

At the end of his own bitter effusion Howard is conciliatory: much has been lost but much can still be retrieved:

Let us both resolve to do our utmost to heal the breach which has grown up and I am sure we will be successful. Now that we know some at least of the reasons for one another's discontent, it may be easier to be forgiving and charitable.

It was in this spirit that they faced yet another domestic upheaval; their Sheffield house had been their fourth home in five years.

The return to Oxford

There is no doubt that a chair at Oxford had long been Florey's objective, and in 1934 an unexpected chance of attaining it arose. In the summer of that year Georges Dreyer, Professor of Pathology, died suddenly in his 62nd year. Dreyer, Danish by birth, had been appointed to the chair of pathology when it was created in 1907. After graduating in Denmark he had spent some time at the State Serum Institute in Copenhagen and this experience was reflected in the immunological research he carried out at Oxford; he also did research in bacteriology, and devised the so-called sigma test for syphilis, a modified Wassermann reaction. He initially presided over a vigorous research school, but at the time of his death he was, for reasons which will become apparent, head of a department housed in a splendid new building with rather little going on in it. Nevertheless, the potential for his successor was enormous and Florey lost no time in applying for the post; Sherrington was his principal supporter and adviser.

In making appointments of this kind an electoral board is set up to assess the candidates, to shortlist the best of them, and make the final choice. Gwyn Macfarlane has given a vivid account of the way in which the electoral board was set up in this instance; the background moves that influenced its composition; and the dramatic end to its deliberations. In the event, the choice of candidates ultimately narrowed to two: one was Florey and the other was M. J. Stewart. The latter was Florey's senior by 13 years; he had been Professor of Pathology at Leeds since 1918 and was a morbid anatomist in the traditional mould. His supporters on the board would certainly have included the redoubtable Sir Robert Muir of Glasgow, who had passed such scathing comment on Florey's candidature at Sheffield. It was to be expected, too, that Sir Farquahar Buzzard, Regius Professor of Medicine at Oxford, would favour Stewart as the orthodox candidate. Indeed, we know that when Florey learnt the composition of the board his hopes were dashed; all but one, he thought, would be against him, and the rest ready to follow whatever lead was given them.

The one exception was all important, however. This was Edward Mellanby, briefly his colleague at Sheffield, who had become Secretary of the Medical Research Council; he was a powerful man in a powerful position. But when the board convened on 22 January 1935 Mellanby was not there; no word had come from him and of necessity they had to proceed without him. The argument apparently ended in favour of Stewart but before an irrevocable decision had been reached Mellanby arrived; his train from Paddington had been two hours late. It says much for his force of personality and powers of persuasion that not only was the discussion reopened but the final vote went in favour of Florey; he was asked to take up his new appointment on 1 May 1935.

This day was undoubtedly the turning-point in Florey's career. With his appointment to a chair at Oxford his goal had been achieved so far as advancement in the university world was concerned, though we may reasonably surmise that the thought of other distinctions—notably Fellowship of the Royal Society—must have been in his mind. Had he missed this opportunity he would clearly still have had a distinguished career, but it is doubtful whether elsewhere he could have gathered together the various threads which led to the start of the penicillin project three years later. It is interesting to reflect that the course of the history of medicine—and, indeed, of the history of mankind—hung briefly on the timekeeping of the Great Western Railway.

2

EARLY YEARS AT THE SIR WILLIAM DUNN SCHOOL OF PATHOLOGY

A first consequence of the return to Oxford was the need to find a family house, and the Floreys were fortunate in being able to rent a University property at 16 Parks Road. By chance, its name was The Red House, the same as Ethel's old home in North Adelaide; practical though she was, she might have taken this as a good omen. It was a substantial late Victorian house, typical of north Oxford. Though not so large as the one they had had at Sheffield, and with a smaller garden, it was adequate for them and their two children. On what was then a substantial salary of £1700 p.a. they could well afford a nannie, Doris Wheeler—who later became Mrs. Kent—a domestic staff of two, and a part-time gardener, especially as the Cambridge house was at last sold for nearly £1000. The Red House had an open view over the University parks and was situated on the fringe of the area, lying in the angle between Parks Road and South Parks Road, which houses the principal science departments. Florey's own laboratory was only a few minutes' walk away and the well-stocked Radcliffe Science Library—as essential as laboratory facilities for the pursuit of serious research—was literally across the road. The Chair carried with it a Fellowship at Lincoln College in the centre of the city; this, too, was only a few minutes' walk from the house and the laboratory. It is one of the smaller and older Oxford colleges, dating from 1427, and it had rather more of a scientific flavour than most. Florey found it a welcome refuge and made much use of its amenities; it played an important role in his life and he remained a Fellow, latterly an honorary one, until his death. Ethel, partly because of her ill-health and deafness, was never a very successful hostess and the college was an excellent place at which to entertain guests. Domestically, therefore, they were as comfortably situated as they well could be.

Professionally, the new appointment fulfilled a long-cherished ambition. As Ethel wrote to Valetta when she heard the news,

'The Oxford Chair has been his Mecca for many years'. But although the potential was great his immediate inheritance was meagre. His greatest asset was a truly magnificent laboratory. In 1922 Dreyer was in full flight in research, with nearly 100 papers to his credit.[1] He approached the Trustees of Sir William Dunn— a former Lord Mayor of London—about the possibility of a grant to provide a new building for the Department of Pathology, then occupying accommodation which was later to house the Department of Pharmacology. Surprisingly quickly this move bore fruit and a grant of £100 000 was forthcoming. The foundation stone of the new building was laid in 1923 and it was formally opened in March 1927. When Florey arrived in 1935 it was thus only eight years old.

In those days the grant was a munificent one and Dreyer made the most of his opportunity. He planned the building with the most careful regard to the needs it would have to fulfil in both teaching and research; two important features were an exceptionally well-equipped workshop in the basement and a separate animal house at the rear to provide the necessary experimental materials. The design and the quality of the furnishing and fittings were at a level far higher than could even be contemplated today; they included a marble hall and a fine oak staircase. The professorial suite was spacious: a large laboratory for experimental work, and a panelled study with sleeping facilities and a bathroom, valuable aids to comfort when protracted experiments were to be conducted.

With such splendid facilities—at that time unsurpassed anywhere—and with a professor in charge whose enthusiasm and skill in research was widely recognized, great things could be expected. In the event, however, Dreyer suddenly flagged. After 1923 he published only six research papers until his sudden death in 1934. He lost his enthusiasm for the struggle to raise pathology in Oxford to the status of a Final Honour School. Indeed, he paid only cursory visits to the laboratory. Inevitably, efficiency and morale slumped generally; standards of teaching, research, and technical services declined. Students scarcely troubled to attend lectures and classes if they could avoid them.

This surprising sea-change in Dreyer is generally attributed to an unlucky piece of research he carried out in 1923, when he published an article on a new vaccine which seemed effective in preventing tuberculosis in animals.[2] There were hopes that it might be successful in preventing human tuberculosis—then much less tractable than it is now—but unfortunately the press became aware of this before adequate tests could be carried out. Under pressure, the Medical Research Council carried out a clinical trial, which showed the vaccine to be ineffective. Quite unfairly, this discredited Dreyer and from that moment he virtually withdrew from research: a contributory cause seems to have been a general deterioration in his health. Years later, Florey was to be criticized because of his reluctance to give information on penicillin—and on occasion other matters—to the press; in so doing, it may well be that he had in mind the unhappy experience of his immediate predecessor.

Although the Sir William Dunn School of Pathology was certainly a victim of lost heart in leadership, there was another reason for its decline. Although the Trustees had made an exceptionally generous grant towards the building and its equipment, there was quite inadequate provision for running it, which was a University responsibility. This, it may be remarked, was no unusual situation and one which afflicts some University laboratories even at the present day. When Florey took up office only about one-third of the available accommodation was being utilized. Students attending classes numbered only about a dozen, whereas there were facilities for around fifty.

In addition, Florey inherited lodgers in the form of the Standards Laboratory of the Medical Research Council, responsible for maintaining standard cultures and sera for diagnosis of enteric pathogens. This was entirely autonomous, under the control of an experienced bacteriologist, A. D. Gardner. He was some 14 years older than Florey, very different in temperament, and had himself been a candidate for the professorship. The general expectation, and no doubt that of Gardner himself, was that the two would be incompatible and the Standards Laboratory would have to move. In the event this did not happen. Gardner stayed on, and in 1936 was appointed Reader in Bacteriology, with the title of Professor. In retrospect, this is not so surprising a decision as it may then have seemed. For the time being, at least, the space occupied was not needed and the unit paid a very welcome rent of £600 p.a. Florey, with his convinced belief in a multidisciplinary approach to medical research, had need of the advice of a good bacteriologist, and Gardner's competence was not in question. Additionally, he had held an Oxford appointment for some twenty years and was knowledgeable on University politics, about which Florey still had much to learn, as he was soon to discover. Last, but certainly not least, the unit was, in the last analysis, under Mellanby's control and Florey must have been well aware of the strong support the latter had given him when his election was under consideration. Events showed the wisdom of the decision. Gardner proved a valuable colleague within the department until 1948, when he was appointed Regius Professor of Medicine.

From his predecessor Florey inherited two young men of undoubted talent for both, like him, had come to Oxford as Rhodes Scholars. One was a Canadian, R. L. Vollum, who was Demonstrator in Bacteriology. The other was a fellow Australian, B. G. Maegraith, Demonstrator in Pathology, who was to go on to a distinguished career as Professor of Tropical Medicine at Liverpool (1944-72). Dr. A. G. Gibson, a member of the selection committee which had appointed Florey, was attached to the department as a pathologist, but was primarily concerned with clinical work at the Radcliffe Infirmary. Additionally Miss M. Campbell-Renton and Miss Jean Orr-Ewing continued as part-time research workers. Dr. E. W. Ainley Walker, who after Dreyer's death had served as acting head of the department for the third time, decided to retire. Florey acquired a major asset, however, in the shape of the excellent workshop under the direction of a most able mechanic, S. W. Bush. It was underutilized and spent much time in doing paid work for other departments; Florey himself had had apparatus made there while he was at Sheffield.

Such, in brief, was the situation inherited by Florey. From Sheffield he brought the competent and every-loyal Jim Kent as his personal technician. In the summer he was followed by Dr. Beatrice Pullinger, who was appointed Demonstrator in Pathology. Last, but by no means least, Miss P. J. Smart (later Mrs. Turner) was appointed secretary to the department, a task which she discharged with great efficiency for some thirty years; the University awarded her an honorary degree on her retirement in 1976. When Florey left in 1962 to become Provost of Queen's (see Chapter 11) he paid her a typically laconic, but none the less sincere, compliment. He informed his successor, Henry Harris, that he need have no anxiety over administration because Mrs. Turner saw to it all—for the Professor it was 'a piece of cake'.

With this diverse team he had two immediate tasks to perform. Firstly, he had to revise and modernize the teaching course in pathology and bacteriology and he set about this with characteristic vigour. Although to the end of his life his first love was research, he was always punctilious in fulfilling his obligations towards students; no doubt he had very much in his mind what he regarded as the poor teaching of medicine at Adelaide. In this respect his ideas were bigger than his purse, and lack of cash thwarted his ambition; initially, his entire departmental budget, excluding his own salary, was not much more than £3000 p.a. Nevertheless, much was achieved, and within a surprisingly short time the course was revitalized: the technicians, on whom devolved much of the additional work, responded well when given a lead. No doubt Kent's vigorous example gave them a new standard at which to aim.

The new teaching course, with which Beatrice Pullinger was closely concerned, was of a pioneer character. Traditionally, medical students were taught in the hospitals in terms of 'special pathology': that is to say, the pathology of the lungs, stomach, and so on. Florey's two-term course was based on general changes and on experimental work—for example processes of inflammation, degeneration, neoplasia, and the like. At that time there was no clinical school at Oxford and students went to the London hospitals; there they joined others who had been taught along different lines and initially this naturally created practical problems. Over the years, however, the London hospitals moved towards the Oxford method, especially after the publication of the lectures in book form in 1954 (p. 299).

His second task was to get a new programme of research under way and here too financial stringency was to prove, not only then but for some years ahead, a considerable handicap. Very largely, he had to depend on recruiting people who in one way or another were self-propelled, usually with the aid of some kind of scholarship. The University had been slow to recognize science as a proper subject for academic inquiry, and there was still a strong traditionalist element which regarded money spent on scientific research as money diverted from better purposes. For a time, soon after Florey's appointment, it looked as though some really substantial funds might become available, for the preclinical sciences at least, from an unexpected source. Lord Nuffield, already a substantial University benefactor, became interested in an ambitious scheme to promote medicine and medical research in Oxford. The protagonist on the University side was Hugh Cairns. Like Florey, who was his junior by only two years, he was a graduate of Adelaide and had come to Oxford as a Rhodes scholar, but, as mentioned, the two seem to have met for the first time at the London Hospital.

Cairns had worked with Harvey Cushing in America, on a Rockefeller Fellowship; the latter had been so impressed by Cairns' research that he had persuaded the Rockefeller Foundation to establish a neurosurgical unit for Cairns in London. This, however, by no means satisfied his ambition and he turned his thoughts to reviving a scheme in which the Rockefeller Foundation had been interested some years previously. In 1927 it had offered to support in Oxford an institute for clinical research but the scheme foundered owing to the inability of the local medical factions at Oxford to agree. In the summer of 1935 Cairns revived it in a more ambitious form, including the establishment of a medical school at Oxford; at that time medical graduates had to go elsewhere, usually to London, to complete their training. Cairns had the 1927 failure very much in mind and realized that success in a new bid would depend upon a great deal of patient lobbying of interested parties. In particular, the conflicting interests of the clinical and preclinical departments would have to be reconciled. For the former, he sought the support of Sir Farquahar Buzzard—like himself a neurologist and at that time in a very influential position as Regius Professor of Medicine. Buzzard in turn enlisted the support of, among others, William Goodenough, Treasurer of the Radcliffe Infirmary, and A. D. Lindsay, Master of Balliol and then Vice-Chancellor. Lindsay had strong views on education which, as Lord Lindsay of Birker, he pursued after the War as Principal of the University College of North Staffordshire (now Keele University). This powerful combination could scarcely fail to impress the clinical camp, but to carry the day, the support of the preclinical professors was no less essential. For this, it was natural that Cairns should turn to Florey, who had so providentially appeared on the scene and had a reputation for strong advocacy of projects in which he was interested; if his support could be enlisted, his preclinical colleagues might well follow his lead.

So considerable a scheme could not, of course, have been canvassed without reasonable expectation that very substantial finance would be forthcoming to support it. In this respect hopes rested on Lord Nuffield, already a considerable benefactor of the Radcliffe Infirmary: he had lately founded there the Nuffield Institute for Medical Research. The Director was J. A. Gunn, who concurrently occupied the Chair of Pharmacology: from 1937 he devoted himself full-time to the Institute as Professor of Therapeutics. The hopes of the University were not disappointed. In the autumn of 1936 Nuffield announced that he would contribute £1¼ million—shortly afterwards increased to £2 million—towards the proposed scheme of medical expansion. He also made it known that he would give a further £1 million towards the foundation of a new graduate college 'to encourage research especially but not exclusively in the field of social studies'. This eventually emerged as Nuffield College, incorporated in 1958; Nuffield is said to have privately referred to it as the Kremlin, because its studies seemed to him more socialist than social.

By the standards of the day the Nuffield Benefaction was princely and the expectation was that it would be used to advance medicine at Oxford on all fronts. In the event, however, the preclinical departments, whose support had been so assiduously wooed, were disappointed; not only did the lion's share go to the clinical departments at the Radcliffe Infirmary, but new laboratories were established there virtually in competition with existing ones in the Parks Road science area. The latter received only the benefit of reflected glory. The episode therefore did little to relieve Florey's financial problems though no doubt he found it a useful lesson in University politics and confirmation of his inborn misgivings about clinicians. It did not, however, do any permanent damage to his relationship with Cairns, with whom he was to have close connection in the future. It must be noted, however, that at a later date he did receive important research grants from the Nuffield Benefaction.

Clemenceau's sentiment that war is much too serious a thing to be left to the military found a parallel in Florey, who believed that medical research should not be left to medical men. He was convinced that progress could be made only by combining the knowledge and skills of a wide range of scientific disciplines. Today this is so widely recognized that it is no longer a matter for argument, but Florey deserves much credit for being in the forefront of those who transformed the climate of opinion within a few decades. He himself was well versed in basic medical sciences such as physiology, bacteriology, and histology and the associated experimental techniques and he was well able to guide others doing research with him in these fields. But the no less important fields of chemistry and biochemistry were, comparatively speaking, a closed book to him. The latter was, indeed, a subject which had established itself virtually within his own lifetime. One of its great proponents was Frederick Gowland Hopkins, who had made a great impression on Florey during his time at Cambridge. He had been appointed Professor of Biochemistry there in 1914 and in 1924 had moved into the splendid new Sir William Dunn Institute of Biochemistry, endowed by the same Trustees as the School of Pathology in Oxford. Like Florey, Hopkins was convinced that many biological problems could be solved only in chemical terms, and his own classic researches on the vitamins had forcibly demonstrated the truth of this thesis.

One of Florey's first tasks after settling in at Oxford was to seek the services of a biochemist to complement the skills of his biologically oriented research team. This proved difficult, partly because biochemistry was still a comparatively young science, and so the number of practitioners was small, and partly because pathology, still closely identified with clinicians, was not at first sight an attractive field for biochemists with their careers to make. Florey was fortunate in having as his neighbour in South Parks Road Sir Robert Robinson,[3] Waynflete Professor of Chemistry in the Dyson Perrins Laboratory, who was perhaps the greatest organic chemist of his day and another future President of the Royal Society. Robinson was some fourteen years Florey's senior and generally regarded with considerable awe, but they got on well together. One thing at least they had in common: neither was given to suffering fools gladly. It was perhaps helpful, too, that Robinson had spent three years in Sydney (1912-15) as professor of Chemistry and was thus familiar with the Australian temperament. Jointly they applied in 1935 for a two-year grant from the Medical Research Council for one of Robinson's students, E. A. H. Roberts, to work with Maegraith on lysozyme.

Another close neighbour was Professor Rudolph Peters, head of the Department of Biochemistry since 1923. He was a former student of Gowland Hopkins and had been elected to Fellowship of the Royal Society in the year in which Florey returned to Oxford. It was natural that Florey should turn his attention to him in his search for a biochemical recruit. For a time it looked as though he might have attracted H. M. Sinclair, but this approach came to nothing. He considered, too, N. W. Pirie, then Demonstrator in Hopkins's department at Cambridge, who would have liked to have come. In the event neither possibility materialized, but they are evidence of Florey's judgement. Sinclair went on to a distinguished career in nutrition, being particularly identified with the role of polyunsaturated fatty acids; Pirie later became head of the biochemistry department at Rothamsted Experimental Station and gained his Fellowship of the Royal Society in 1949.

Though it came to nothing, Florey's interest in Pirie had what proved to be an immensely important consequence. Hopkins found himself unable to release Pirie immediately, as Florey wished, but shortly wrote recommending as an alternative a young biochemist who had just completed a PhD thesis. This was Ernst Boris Chain, who was to be Florey's close collaborator in the penicillin work and ultimately to share with him a Nobel Prize for it.

Chain and his research will necessarily feature very prominently later in this book and it is, therefore, necessary to say something of his background. He was born of Jewish parents in Berlin on 19 June 1906; his father was of Russian origin, his mother German. His father, who died when he was only fourteen years of age, was a chemical industrialist with a factory at Adlershof, where he made various salts of copper, manganese, nickel, and other metals.[4] As a boy, his son determined to study chemistry and did so at the Friedrich-Wilhelm University in Berlin, graduating in 1930; his interest in the biological aspects of chemistry led him to study physiology as a subsidiary subject. From the University he went as a research worker to the Institute of Pathology in the large Charité Hospital in Berlin. There he worked for his Dr.Phil degree, making an investigation of the important class of natural products known as phospholipids, such as lecithin, and the enzymes that decompose them. He was also a talented musician, so much so that in 1930 he had to make a deliberate choice whether to follow music or science as a profession. Fortunately, as it was to turn out, he chose science but throughout his life music gave him intense pleasure.

As for so many others of Jewish descent, the advent of Hitler to power in 1933 was a personal tragedy. Chain, who had become a naturalized German citizen in 1928, left the country and came to England; his mother and sister remained behind and were killed by the Nazis during the War. Through the good offices of J. B. S. Haldane, to whom he had written and sent reprints of some research papers, he continued his research on phospholipids at University College London under Sir Charles Harington. Haldane later recommended him to Gowland Hopkins at Cambridge and he went there as a PhD student, still working on phospholipids. At that time he had no money, but was fortunate enough to receive a grant from a Jewish organization. This was arranged by Dr. Redcliffe Salaman, a trustee of Jews' College. Salaman was a medical man and had been Director of the Pathological Institute in the London Hospital, but made his name as perhaps the world's leading authority on the potato; he was then Director of the Potato Virus Research Station in Cambridge University.

For the moment Chain, who had arrived in England with only £10 in his pocket, was self-sufficient, but his future was uncertain. He had no hopes of a university appointment in England and his thoughts were turning to the possibility of moving on to Canada or Australia. It was, therefore, a very pleasant surprise when, one day in 1935, Hopkins came to his laboratory and enquired if he would be interested in going to work with Florey in Oxford as a Departmental Demonstrator. The proposal that Florey made was attractive. Chain was to organize a biochemical section in the Sir William Dunn School and have virtually a free hand in developing it. In Chain's own words:

The only problem that he himself suggested was that I should become interested in elucidating the mode of action of the bacteriolytic substance lysozyme. He himself had been interested in this substance for some years. He had found that it was secreted by various sections of the gut and he believed that it had something to do with the natural defence mechanisms against bacterial invasion and also possibly something to do with protection against gastric ulcers.[5].

In view of Florey's sustained interest in lysozyme we may surmise that his proposal that Chain should investigate it was more in the nature of a stipulation than a suggestion. The grant available—£200 p.a.—was not princely but for those days adequate. By the end of 1935 he was settled in lodgings in Walton Street. Characteristically, one of his first actions was to rent a piano; this was his favourite instrument and in later years he went to some trouble to dispel the belief that he was a violinist, an instrument he did not even play.

For the moment, however, his luck failed him: very soon after arriving he fell ill with what proved to be a grumbling appendicitis: eventually the offending appendix was removed while he was on a visit to Paris early in 1936. Florey was understanding and helpful and visited him while he was in hospital in Oxford:

Florey was very nice to me at that time and he did everything he could to help me and I started to work in the middle of 1936 on the problem he suggested to me [lysozyme] as well as on my own problems—the biochemical mode of action of snake venoms and related toxic substances.[6].

With convalescence his situation improved. With his cousin, Mme Anna Sacharina, he moved into a flat at 21 Bardwell Road, similarly near to the laboratory. Ths snake venom work was a logical extension of what he had been doing at Cambridge, where he had discovered that certain venoms act on lecithin to form lysolecithin. The toxic action was due to inhibition of glycolysis by interference with the action of coenzyme A (CoA) which plays an essential role in the so-called Krebs' metabolic cycle.

Thus was established a scientific collaboration which was to prove immensely fruitful, but for the moment we must resume our survey of the way in which Florey strengthened his research team. One of his colleagues in Cambridge had been A. Q. Wells, a bacteriologist with a particular interest in tubercular infection in voles, through which he hoped to develop a vaccine for use in medicine. This was, of course, a field with which the laboratory had been closely identified under Dreyer. He and Florey had already published a joint paper in 1931 on a photographic technique for measuring small volume changes in living organs, especially the trachea, in which they were interested as a centre of mucus secretion. Another valuable recruit, who supported himself with a postgraduate scholarship from Magdalen, was a zoologist, P. B. (later Sir Peter) Medawar, also destined for a brilliant career; after various senior academic appointments he became director of the National Institute for Medical Research at Mill Hill in 1962. Another member initially self-supporting was A. G. Sanders,[7] a graduate of St. Thomas's, who came in 1936 to work for a Dr.Phil; he remained for the rest of his working life and, as we shall see, was associated with Florey in several major ventures. Florey never forgot the flying start in life he had received from holding a Rhodes Scholarship at Oxford and it must have given him particular pleasure to welcome an American Rhodes Scholar who wished to work in his department. This was Robert H. Ebert, who later became Dean of Harvard Medical School. He held his Scholarship from 1936 to 1939 and they published two papers together. It was, indeed, his personal and professional magnetism which enabled Florey to build up a run-down department; able, ambitious young research workers now sought the privilege of working under him, just at he had been privileged to work under such a giant as Sherrington 15 years earlier. Nearly 50 years later, when complaints were being made in the United States that professors did not adequately supervise their research students, Ebert recalled:

Things were very different then, it was more important to do the work thoroughly and to be sure of it. . . . Florey was totally familiar with everything that went on in the lab.[8].

Up to this time Florey had published some 50 research papers, many of them jointly with collaborators, and they had covered a variety of subjects. While mucus secretion was a continuing interest he had made contributions to such diverse topics as the contraction of lacteals; the treatment of tetanus; and the functions of Brunner's glands in the duodenum. While they showed much originality both in concept and in experimental technique it is fair to say that they fell within generally recognized fields of research. He had now reached a stage in his career—40 years of age and with a prestigious Chair which he would in all probability occupy for the rest of his working life—at which it would be normal for any dedicated research worker with a command of his own to consider strategy rather than tactics. He had the tenure and resources to concentrate his efforts on some particular target, though this would, of course, have to be compatible with the teaching requirements of the department and the diversity of research projects already being pursued by his colleagues. In the event it was, of course, penicillin which he pursued as his main objective and which proved such a brilliant success. This success, and the public acclaim it brought, so profoundly affected his life that we must digress considerably in an attempt to elucidate the complex circumstances leading up to it.

The route to penicillin was as oblique as G. K. Chesterton's road to Birmingham by way of Beachy Head, but at least it seems clear that the starting-point was Florey's lifelong interest in mucus originating, at least in part, in his study of his own anomalous gastric secretion. As a matter of course every serious research worker makes himself as familiar as possible with work already done in his chosen field and those closely related to it. He would, therefore, have quickly become aware of work carried out by Alexander Fleming at St. Mary's Hospital Medical School in London and described over the period 1922-7 in five papers in the *Proceedings of the Royal Society* and the *British Journal of Experimental Pathology*. The latter had then been only recently launched (1920), partly on the initiative of Fildes, and was to be the journal of choice for many of Florey's own research papers; his first in it appeared in 1927.

At that time Fleming[9] was some 40 years of age. He was the son of a Scottish farmer, born in Ayrshire in 1881, and his early education was at the village school and later Kilmarnock Academy. A few years after his father's death he had come to London, at the age of 13, in order to live with an older brother, a medical practitioner. He continued his education at the Regent Street Polytechnic and then, having to support himself as best he could, spent four years in a shipping office in the city. Then a small legacy made it possible for him to resume his studies and he entered St. Mary's Hospital as a medical student: he did well, graduating MB, BS as a gold medallist. His work had attracted the attention of Sir Almroth Wright—Principal of the Institute of Pathology and Research at St. Mary's and Professor of Experimental Pathology in London University—who engaged him in 1906 as his assistant in the Inoculation Department. He was to remain at St. Mary's for the rest of his life, first as Lecturer in Bacteriology, later as Professor (1928), and finally as Principal of the Wright-Fleming Institute of Microbiology, successor to the old Inoculation Department. Of Almroth Wright[10] we shall hear more later. For the moment suffice to say that he was an influential figure in the medical world, having gained both a Knighthood and Fellowship of the Royal Society in 1906. In research, his interest was in the natural defences of the body against bacterial infection. His name is particularly identified with antityphoid vaccination—introduced in the British Army, with highly successful results shortly before the Boer War—with the agglutination test for undulant fever, and—with that of S. R. Douglas—with the supposed role of opsonin in stimulating phagocytes (leucocytes) in the blood to ingest invading bacteria. He was a man of wide interests and possessed a powerful intellect which he directed to the problems of philosophy as well as of science; Fleming found him a stimulating chief.

In 1922 Fleming made, apparently without premeditation, a remarkable observation. As a professional hospital bacteriologist his daily occupation was the culture of bacteria on a variety of artificial media, partly for his own research purposes and partly to identify them for his clinical colleagues. Suffering from a head cold he decided to make a culture of a drop of his own nasal secretion. Not surprisingly, a mixed bag of organisms developed; what was surprising was that one of the colonies was being dissolved (or lysed, to use the technical term). This colony he subcultured and again tested it with nasal secretion, with the same result: the cloudy bacterial culture cleared rapidly. The bacteria he named *Micrococcus lysodeikticus* and the dissolving agent—apparently belonging to the class of organic catalysts known as enzymes—was called lysozyme. It was quickly shown that lysozyme was present in a variety of bodily secretions—including tears and saliva—as well as in egg-white and certain plant tissues. It was also shown that many other species of bacteria were sensitive, to some degree at least, to lysozyme. This discovery was doubly interesting. On the one hand, it was a phenomenon not previously observed. On the other, it held out the promise of practical applications in medicine. Clearly, a substance normally present in bodily secretions such as tears and saliva could not be toxic to human tissues; it might therefore serve as an antibacterial agent to control infection. These hopes were not fulfilled: pathogenic bacteria—that is to say those associated with disease—generally proved not susceptible to lysozyme. On this score, however, it could be plausibly argued that pathogenic bacteria were pathogenic simply because, through some process of natural selection, they had acquired immunity to lysozyme. Nevertheless, for those who could read it there was an important lesson to be learnt. In the early years of this century it was commonly supposed that substances toxic to bacteria were necessarily toxic also to human cells. If this was so, it was futile to look for chemical agents which would destroy bacteria that had invaded the body, for they would also destroy the patient. In 1909 Paul Ehrlich, in Germany, discovered an exception to his apparent rule: his arsenical Compound 606 (Salvarsan) proved effective in the treatment of human syphilis. But it was a far from ideal drug, with unpleasant side-reactions, and even its successor, Neosalvarsan, introduced in 1911, left much to be desired. Moreover, it was without effect on most other pathogenic organisms. Although Ehrlich coined the word chemotherapy, now one of the most important fields of medical science, his 'magic bullet', as he called it, was not regarded as of major importance by the clinicians.

Florey's interest in lysozyme was aroused by his existing interest in mucus. Although this was a widely encountered animal secretion, its role was not clear. In some circumstances, no doubt, it was essentially a lubricant but it might well have several roles. Could one of these be to protect the body against infection by virtue of lysozyme contained in it? Some colour had been given to this by an observation that vitamin A deficiency causes susceptibility to infection of the colon and that this is associated with cessation of mucus secretion. To test this hypothesis it was necessary to make an extensive survey of gastric secretions from various sources and measure their lysozyme content. This he did at Cambridge in collaboration with a fellow Australian, N. E. Goldsworthy, with the aid of a grant of £50 p.a. for three years from the Medical Research Council. Initially, Florey sent samples to Fleming for their lysozyme content to be assayed, but he quickly learned the technique for himself. Their results[11] were interesting, but inconclusive. Although lysozyme was widely found in the mucus of healthy animals it was present in widely varying amounts and sometimes absent altogether. Yet there was no apparent difference in the animals' resistance to bacterial infection. They concluded that any antibacterial property of mucus must be mechanical rather than chemical; its high viscosity made it an effective barrier between the lumen of the gut and the intestinal wall. Incidentally, however, they noticed and described another phenomenon which was to be of great significance later; certain normal intestinal bacteria, notably *Bacillus coli*, inhibited the growth of the test organisms used for the assay of lysozyme. This was, however, no more than a particular example of the well-known phenomenon of microbial antagonism for which the term *antibiosis* had been used as early as 1899 by H. Marshall Ward,[12] Professor of Botany at Cambridge.

Although these experiments were inconclusive they by no means quenched Florey's interest, for the whole question of immunity to infection, both natural and acquired, was of fundamental importance. Lysozyme, it seemed clear, was not the answer, but might it not be just one example from a group of antibacterial enzymes which included some active against pathogenic bacteria such as staphylococci and streptococci? This suggested two lines of enquiry. Firstly, to pursue the investigation of lysozyme—as the bird in hand—with a view to isolating it and identifying its chemical nature. Secondly, to seek other enzymes with anti-bacterial properties and, if found, investigate them similarly.

Florey's efforts to pursue this work at Cambridge met with little success. Putting mucus on one side, he carried out a survey of the lysozyme content of various mammalian tissues.[13] He persuaded a bacteriological colleague, Ashley Miles—later Director of the Lister Institute—to test the antibacterial potency of various tissue extracts. But progress, as he realized, depended on the collaboration of a properly qualified biochemist. Briefly, but on a basis too limited to be productive, this was forthcoming from Marjory Stephenson, then Reader in Chemical Microbiology in Gowland Hopkins's department.

Concurrently, he was pursuing another line of enquiry which was perhaps more relevant than it then seemed to what came later. This was on the physiological basis of contraception, pursued with H. M. Carleton, a histologist.[14] This involved study not only of the mechanism of fertilization but of various spermicidal agents designed to prevent it. Here, again, the need was for a 'magic bullet', a chemical agent—such as certain organo-mercury compounds—that would act selectively against spermatozoa but not affect the surrounding tissue. The existence of such selective agents for spermatozoa at least did nothing to diminish the hope that they might exist also for pathogenic bacteria.

At Sheffield, Florey had almost immediately tried to further his lysozyme work. He arrived in March 1932 and in May he wrote to Sir Walter Fletcher, Mellanby's predecessor as Secretary of the Medical Research Council, seeking a grant towards the support of a biochemist to investigate the possible role of anti-bacterial substances in natural immunity. Boldly (for those days) he hoped that £400 or £500 p.a. might be forthcoming, but the best Fletcher could do was suggest that he might organize some sort of collaboration with some biochemist already in Sheffield. For a couple of years, Florey did in fact collaborate with Sylvia Harrison, the biochemist wife of D. C. Harrison of the Department of Pharmacology. However, this was no more productive than the similarly contrived collaboration with Marjory Stephenson in Cambridge and in any event ended after a couple of years when Harrison was appointed Professor of Biochemistry at Belfast.

Despite this lack of progress, Florey retained his keen interest in lysozyme and we have noted that very soon after his appointment in Oxford he approached Sir Robert Robinson and arranged for E. A. H. Roberts, a student in his department, to collaborate in chemical work on lysozyme. It is thus apparent that his interest in the mode of action of antibacterial substances in general, and of lysozyme in particular, had been continuously sustained since 1929, when he made his first approach to the Medical Research Council. It is against this background that we must view Florey's invitation to Chain to join him at Oxford. Hitherto we have spoken of biochemists as though they were a single species; in reality, they were by then so firmly established as a profession that a considerable degree of specialization had begun to emerge among them—in the same sort of way as it does among, say, artists, musicians, or writers. The snake venom on which Chain was working was, in a purely chemical sense, not dissimilar to lysozyme—both being enzymes—and thus many of the techniques developed for investigating one were applicable to the other. He had, too, been studying the enzymes that decompose phospholipids.

For the time being, however, Chain continued to work with snake venom rather than lysozyme and quickly brought his research to a successful conclusion. He succeeded in isolating the active constituent of the venom; identified it chemically; and showed that its toxic action was due to interference with an essential biochemical stage in the respiratory process.

Meanwhile the research on lysozyme by Roberts and Maegraith—for which he had succeeded in getting a further grant of $1280 from the Rockefeller Foundation in 1936—had proved fruitful. They had succeeded in effecting a considerable degree of purification and in 1937 E. P. Abraham—who was working with Robinson as a DPhil student—succeeded in crystallizing it: he was later to join Florey in the Sir William Dunn School of Pathology. This provided an appropriate starting-point for Chain, who had completed his snake venom work; he was joined in 1937 by an American Rhodes Scholar, L. A. Epstein (later Falk), in an investigation of the nature and mode of action of lysozyme. They confirmed that it was indeed an enzyme and that its action was directed specifically against a polysaccharide in the cell wall of *Micrococcus lysodeikticus* and other lysozyme-sensitive organisms. To identify the polysaccharide it was necessary to grow substantial quantities of the bacteria in Winchester bottles—a technique in which the advice of Professor Gardner was helpful—and separate and fractionate the bacterial cells. With this material it was possible to show that the cell-wall component destroyed by lysozyme was a simple derivative of glucose-N-acetylglucosamine. The destruction of this by lysozyme accounted for the disintegration and lysis of the cells orginally observed by Fleming. Today, when research techniques are so much more sensitive and versatile, this would not rank as a remarkable achievement but with the techniques available immediately before the last War it was unquestionably a brilliant success.

As things stood, however, it was something of a self-contained success; it did not immediately suggest a further line of fruitful investigation. Indirectly, none the less, it initiated new research which was to culminate in the development of penicillin as a chemotherapeutic agent in a class on its own. The distinctive feature of lysozyme was its unusual combination of two properties. On the one hand it was innocuous to human tissue; on the other, it was lethal to certain bacteria. Its disappointing feature was that the bacteria it destroyed were not those of practical significance in medicine. Although little serious effort had been put into it, nothing had come of Florey's proposal to search for other lysozyme-like enzymes which might be useful in chemotherapy. Nevertheless, the investigation—apart from its intrinsic scientific interest—was instructive in establishing beyond doubt that there were natural substances capable of destroying bacteria and harmless to human cells. From this grew a decision by Florey and Chain to conduct a survey of all the antibacterial substances known to exist in nature, with a view to investigating some which seemed particularly interesting. However, to understand just how and why this decision was reached we must return once again to Fleming's laboratory at St. Mary's Hospital. Here, in 1928, he made the crucial discovery of the antibacterial activity of penicillin, a discovery which a dozen years later Florey and Chain were quite independently to turn into one of the most powerful weapons in the medical armoury.

There are historians of science who believe in an objective rather than a subjective approach to the subject, subordinating priority of discovery to the discovery itself. In the eighteenth century the distinguished chemist James Keir had argued that 'Knowledge is important, but whether the discovery is made by one man or another is not deserving of consideration'. This is a defensible view, and for many people a history of penicillin shorn of the personalities involved might suffice. In later life, when the hurly-burly was over and he had, as he put it, 'joined that undistinguished company which crawls along the frontiers of science with a hand lens examining phenomena which many would consider of small importance'—Florey gave his own considered view on this point:

What probably matters as much as anything in the battle of priorities is the accuracy and compendiousness of the description and the comprehensiveness of the explanation of the phenomena. In other words, perhaps we should not be deflected too much from our work by attempts to be first in the field but should strive as artists to get the maximum pleasure from our experiments and thereby savour that great joie de vivre so often experienced by the experimentalist—for it is the struggle for perfection that gives so much satisfaction.[15]

Such a view cannot suffice, however, for a biography such as this, for the clash of personalities between the three principals—Fleming, Florey, and Chain—materially affected all their lives. We must remember, too, that for the professional research worker priority of discovery is—rightly or wrongly—of great career importance. To climb Everest or reach the South Pole is a great thing in itself: to be the first to do so is a different matter again. Despite the plethora of accounts already published (the most important of which are to be found among the references for this chapter) we must recall the sequence of events and try to resolve some continuing discrepancies.

About the circumstances of the discovery itself there is no dispute of consequence. It is common practice to grow bacteria on sterilized nutrient jelly based on agar-agar, a seaweed product. This jelly is sterilized in flat glass dishes (Petri dishes), some three inches (7.5 cm) in diameter, with loose-fitting glass lids. The jelly is inoculated with the organism to be cultured, the lid is replaced, and the covered dish is placed in an incubator at a suitable temperature, about blood-heat or thereabouts in the case of human pathogens. Under these favourable conditions single or small groups of bacteria will grow into small colonies, from which they can be subcultured.

In the ordinary course of events Fleming, like any other similarly employed bacteriologist, would have large numbers of Petri dishes stacked around his laboratory: when they were no longer required they would be sterilized—because many of the bacteria might be pathogenic and dangerous—and washed ready for reuse. In 1928 Fleming was making a study of staphylococci—bacteria common in human infections but by no means as dangerous as the streptococci—as a background to a contribution he was writing for inclusion in the *System of Bacteriology in Relation to Medicine* being compiled under the auspices of the Medical Research Council. When he went off on holiday in the summer he left behind a stack of dishes on which he had been working. Going through these on his return to St. Mary's in September, he noted one that struck him as unusual. A plate on which numerous staphylococcal colonies had grown had accidentally become contaminated with a spore from which a circular mould colony had developed. This was not in itself a matter for any concern, for the dish had already outlived its usefulness, but Fleming noticed that in the vicinity of the mould colony the staphylococcal colonies had virtually disappeared, leaving only a faint ghost behind to show where they had been. That this should have caught his attention, when it might well have been ignored by others is scarcely surprising; his earlier work on lysozyme had given him a keen interest in any instance of bacterial lysis. It appeared, and Fleming certainly supposed, that the mould colony produced some antibacterial substance which had diffused outwards from it through the jelly and destroyed the staphylococcal colonies in its path. On this supposition he made a subculture of the mould on a nutrient broth and he showed that after a few days this broth was highly active against a wide range of pathogenic bacteria—including staphylococci, *Streptococcus pyogenes*, and *Pneumococcus*—even when diluted up to 800 times. Fleming himself had no special knowledge of moulds but persuaded a mycologist colleague at St. Mary's, C. J. La Touche, to identify it for him. La Touche considered it to be *Penicillium rubrum*, though later the American mycologist C. Thom showed that it was in fact the very similar *Penicillium notatum*. On the strength of this, Fleming called his antibacterial broth penicillin; only later was this name give to the active principal of the broth, a white crystalline solid.

On the face of it, then, the discovery was straightforward enough. A mould spore blew in from the street and settled on Fleming's staphylococcal culture. As it grew it produced a potent antibacterial substance which diffused outwards and destroyed the bacterial colonies in its path. It was seemingly a commonplace occurrence but Fleming's trained eye noticed its significance. In fact what happened was a great deal more complicated, as has been shown by Ronald Hare,[16] himself a distinguished bacteriologist who qualified in 1924 and also went on to work under Almroth Wright in the Inoculation Department.[17] His experimental attempts to reproduce Fleming's discovery showed that an exceptional combination of circumstances—which need not concern us here—led to the phenomenon observed in Fleming's historic Petri dish. The essence of the matter is that only actively growing staphylococci are lysed by penicillin; mature colonies are unaffected. This is incompatible with the traditional story that the relatively slow-growing mould infected an incubated plate. Hare believes that either deliberately or by chance Fleming left some unincubated plates aside when he went on holiday. On these the bacteria would grow, though relatively slowly, in the normal ambient temperature of the laboratory in midsummer. A cold spell, such as occurred between 28 August and 6 September

1928, would have slowed down the growth of the staphylococci and, as it were, enabled the mould to get ahead of them. It is an interesting and plausible theory which indicates that the odds against Fleming's plate behaving as it did were far longer than is generally supposed. It is significant that Fleming himself was never able to reproduce his original result. It was not to be the only instance of chance playing an important part in the history of penicillin.

It seems likely, too, that the popular belief that the mould spore blew in through the open window of Fleming's laboratory facing Praed Street is incorrect, even though he himself subscribed to it, and his official biographer, André Maurois, refers to 'The mysterious mould from Praed Street'.[18] Bacteriologists prefer not to work near open windows—for very fear of contaminants blowing in—and according to Hare, Fleming's were particularly inaccessible even if he had wanted to open them. His theory is that the source was internal, most probably the laboratory of La Touche who was growing a variety of moulds as part of a study of their role in causing asthma. Hare[19] has plausibly suggested that Fleming was reluctant to admit that conditions in the laboratories at St. Mary's were such that mould spores escaped and drifted about in the air. Fleming himself demonstrated that the strain of *Penicillium* which contaminated his plate was indistinguishable from one later supplied to him by La Touche.

The 'ifs' of history always provide a good basis for speculation, and those connected with Fleming's original discovery are very interesting. Nevertheless, they do not affect the subsequent development of penicillin, which would have been the same whether Fleming's plate grew in accordance with popular belief or with Hare's sophisticated explanation. The end result was that he had isolated a specific mould, *Penicillium notatum*, which when grown on a suitable nutrient broth conferred strong antibacterial activity on it. We must now consider what he proceeded to do with his 'mould juice', for this is highly relevant to the claims and counterclaims made by him and others later.

First, as is normal, he published an account of his discovery and first experiments in a journal with which we are already familiar, the *British Journal of Experimental Pathology*.[20] This had then been established for ten years and his paper would be widely read by professional colleagues with similar interests. The full title of the paper is significant: 'On the antibacterial action of cultures of a *Penicillium*, with special reference to their use in the isolation of *B. influenzae*'. One of the main tasks of a bacteriologist is to prepare pure cultures of organisms of interest to him; the availability in the laboratory of agents which differentially eliminate contaminants would therefore be of great value. From the title he chose, Fleming clearly saw a major use for penicillin in preparing pure cultures of the influenza bacillus. But it is clear that he also had in mind possible therapeutic uses, for he drew attention to certain relevant properties of the broth. That it had been shown to be active against a number of pathogenic bacteria was not in itself significant. Plenty of well-known substances—carbolic acid, for example, Lister's original antiseptic—had this property; the trouble was that they were general toxins, as poisonous to the cells of living animals as to bacteria that had invaded them. The interest of penicillin was that while it destroyed certain infective bacteria the active broth—as indicated by simple experiments with mice—was no more toxic to animals than the original broth. But this was a long way from establishing that pure penicillin, which eventually proved to be a million times more concentrated than Fleming's crude material, would prove to be non-toxic. When he investigated the action of the broth on leucocytes—the disease-countering blood cells in which St. Mary's had a very particular interest—he found that they were apparently unaffected. Finally, the active principle of the broth was very diffusible: an important property if it were to be used, for example, in contact with pus or blood clots. The broth was also very unstable: it lost its activity quite quickly.

Fleming made only limited clinical trial of his mould broth, using it against a number of local infections such as conjunctivitis, infected wounds, and sinusitis. He did not attempt to use it against deep-seated infections. Some success was achieved but the results were not spectacular and excited little interest—even Fleming himself gave it only limited attention. Indeed, two of his young colleagues—F. Ridley and S. R. Craddock—apparently displayed more enthusiasm than he did himself. Ridley, who later had a distinguished career as an ophthalmologist at Moorfield's Hospital, had had some biochemical training and had worked with Fleming on lysozyme. Together, under difficult conditions and with very simple apparatus, Ridley and Craddock set about concentrating penicillin by a process based on vacuum distillation. In this, water can be boiled away at a much lower temperature than normal: at the normal boiling-point penicillin is rapidly deactivated. They succeeded in preparing for Fleming solutions which although still very impure, were about ten times more potent than the original broth and free of protein. This work was never published and Fleming made only perfunctory and incomplete reference to it in his 1929 paper; for such details as we have we are indebted to Hare.[21] It was soon discontinued when the two workers concerned left St. Mary's, Ridley to go to Moorfields, and Craddock to the Wellcome Research Laboratories at Beckenham; again according to Hare, Fleming made no attempt to retain them so that their work on penicillin could be continued. Hare also states[22] that Craddock discovered that staphylococci became resistant to penicillin after quite brief exposure to it. This very important fact was never published; it was rediscovered in Oxford ten years later.

In later life Fleming was to imply that from the outset he recognized the potential therapeutic value of penicillin and that it was only lack of biochemical resources that stood in the way of his developing it himself in 1930. In fact, he can have paid only cursory attention to the biochemical work of Ridley and Craddock. The latter's laboratory notebook, summaries of which were placed daily on Fleming's desk, show that by the spring of 1929 they had demonstrated that penicillin was soluble not only in water but in at least three organic solvents—ether, acetone, and alcohol. Yet in his original paper, Fleming dismisses the solubility of penicillin, crucial to its isolation, in two sentences—and even then gets it wrong. He does not mention acetone; he states that it is insoluble in ether; and ends by saying that it is insoluble in chloroform, which Ridley does not seem to have investigated at all.[23].

That Fleming was keenly interested in his original discovery is not to be questioned, but it is equally clear that his enthusiasm for developing it was minimal. As lawyers say, *res ipsos loquitur*: if Fleming had had an inkling of penicillin's unique properties in 1930 it is inconceivable that he would not immediately have put aside all other work, as far as possible, and concentrated on it. With so great a prize in prospect, the problem of enlisting the necessary biochemical assistance could surely have been solved.

Nor, as Hare has pointed out, would he have so readily allowed himself to be rebuffed by the clinicians when he sought to treat septic wounds.

In point of fact, Fleming at that time had no means of evaluating penicillin. The antagonism between the mould *Penicillium notatum* and certain bacteria was not demonstrably different from many other examples of antibiosis that had been described in the scientific literature over the previous thirty years and more. Some of them might perhaps yield clinically useful products but—Salvarsan notwithstanding—medical opinion was not optimistic about chemotherapy. Almroth Wright's department, with its deep belief in immunological methods, was not conducive to the blossoming of such optimism, though the force of this argument has perhaps been overstated. The sulphonamides, which demanded a radical revision of medical opinion on chemotherapy, still lay in the future. Not until much more preliminary research had been done did a glimpse of the true nature of penicillin begin to emerge. Nevertheless, this is the start of what Gwyn Macfarlane[24] has rightly called the 'Fleming Myth'. To the way in which this was later unscrupulously exploited by St. Mary's Hospital we will return later, but for the moment we must record that after 1931 Fleming's own interest in penicillin lapsed almost entirely; he did nothing, he promoted nothing, he published nothing, and he made no public mention of it.

But if Fleming himself was half-hearted, interest in penicillin did not lapse altogether. At the London School of Hygiene and Tropical Medicine in Gower Street, also part of London University, Professor Harold Raistrick was engaged in general research on the biochemistry of micro-organisms, including a mould known as *Penicillium chrysogenum*. As a matter of course he saw the paper on *Penicillium notatum* and asked Fleming for a culture of it, which he received. Raistrick and his colleagues were generally interested in substances produced by micro-organisms and not specially in those having antibacterial activity. As Professor of Biochemistry, Raistrick had staff and facilities appropriate for an attempt to isolate penicillin, and he entrusted the task mainly to two of his colleagues, P. W. Clutterbuck and Reginald Lovell (the latter was a trained bacteriologist who later went on to be Professor of Veterinary Bacteriology in London University). Although they failed to isolate penicillin—a task much more difficult than they could have discerned—they did establish some important facts. Firstly, they showed that the mould would grow, though more slowly than on broth, on a wholly synthetic substrate known as Czapek-Dox medium; this resulted in a more manageable starting material. Secondly, they confirmed Ridley and Craddock's observation that penicillin was more stable under slightly acid conditions than in the slightly alkaline condition of the fermentation liquid. Thirdly, they confirmed that considerable concentration could be effected by vacuum distillation, even though a good deal of penicillin disappeared in the process. Finally, they managed to extract penicillin by means of ether from the residue left after distillation and from a weakly acid solution, but when the ether was allowed to evaporate the penicillin was deactivated. One thing at least was clear; penicillin was a very labile (easily decomposed) substance which would survive only the mildest treatment.

At this point the attempt was abandoned. The results were published as only part of a paper[25] dealing also with other topics. This abandonment is interesting in itself: it does not suggest that Fleming gave any of the workers concerned the idea that the isolation of penicillin would be a major medical achievement. On the contrary, Lovell has implied[26] that Fleming's interest in the progress of his work was perfunctory. Yet years later, as Hare[27] has also pointed out, Fleming complained that the attempt at isolation was not pursued as vigorously as he wished and failed through lack of bacteriological co-operation. All the evidence suggests that the attempt was abandoned simply because penicillin proved intractable and there was no indication that it was more interesting than many other mould products which could be isolated much more readily.

Fleming apparently made only one more attempt to isolate penicillin. In 1934 he asked Lewis Holt, a chemist in the Inoculation Department, to have a shot at it. Holt apparently realized that penicillin was soluble in certain organic solvents—such as ether—which were insoluble in water: he himself chose amyl acetate, a common laboratory solvent, possibly because it is much less highly flammable than ether and thus safer to work with, and no doubt conscious of the fact that Almroth Wright was terrified of explosions. He found that if the filtered mould juice medium was made slightly acid and shaken with a little amyl acetate, the penicillin went into the solvent. If the penicillin-containing solvent was then shaken with a little water made mildly alkaline with bicarbonate, the penicillin went back into the aqueous phase but unhappily it rapidly became deactivated. Again, Fleming seems to have given Holt little encouragement or sense of urgency, and he lost heart; the results were never even published and as his notebooks have not survived it is difficult after this lapse of time to be quite clear about what Holt really did. Holt may have been unlucky, for the process he devised seems similar in principle to that successfully developed some years later at Oxford.

Hare, who worked closely with Fleming at St. Mary's from 1926 to 1930 has the following comment to make on Fleming's own attempts to make practical use of penicillin:

Fleming evidently did think that penicillin might be of value when used locally, even though his attempts to employ it can only be described as feeble.[28]

He goes on to quote similar assertions by various contemporaries of Fleming. In particular he quotes Craddock, who knew him well, in a letter written soon after Fleming's death:

He thought it had possibilities in 1928 or early 1929, and he mentioned this in his original paper. But the instability, the cost of production and the very impure product convinced Flem that there was very little future in the stuff. His opinion of penicillin became very hardened after our failures to refine and preserve it. And so he classified it with lysozyme and regarded it as hopeless.[29].

Craddock might perhaps have added that Fleming had been discouraged, too, by his own unpublished observation that staphylococci quickly became resistant to penicillin.

Hare succinctly states that it was not the biochemical barrier that daunted Fleming but his failure to see that it was worth surmounting:

Its similarity to other agents known to be useless, its ability to induce resistance on the part of previously sensitive organisms, its paucity in the fluid, in which it was produced, and above all its instability made it (penicillin) the real villain of the piece.[30]

In this first phase, only one other person seems to have made any serious attempt to isolate penicillin. This was an American worker, R. D. Reid,[31] who also reached the conclusion that the instability of penicillin seriously militated against its possible medical use. There is no evidence that his research was in any way inspired by Fleming personally.

There, for the moment, the matter rested. Notwithstanding claims made years later with the benefit of hindsight, including those of Fleming, it seems clear that by 1935 there was not one person in the world who believed in penicillin as a practical aid to medicine. The practical difficulties of preparing penicillin in a form suitable for clinical trial are in themselves sufficient explanation, but quite apart from this a major discovery made in 1932 had directed attention to a different and apparently far more promising alternative.

In 1927 Gerhard Domagk,[32] director of research in experimental pathology and bacteriology for I. G. Farbenindustrie, had embarked on a systematic search for a chemical agent that would combat the most serious infections to which man was prone, such as streptococcal septicaemia, meningitis, tuberculosis, osteomyelitis, and pneumonia, the latter rightly feared as 'the captain of the men of death'. The grounds for hope were slender but none the less real. To Ehrlich's Salvarsan had been added in 1926 the synthetic antimalarial Plasmoquine. J. Morgenroth had shown that a derivative of an alkaloid related to quinine (ethyl hydrocuprein hydrochlorate) could cure experimental pneumonia infections in mice, but had the fatal defect of causing severe damage to the optic nerve.

With the great resources of the I.G., then the world's leading chemical company, it was possible to conduct a long-term investigation without pressure for quick results. This involved three separate phases. Firstly, a systematic investigation of the effects of very many different compounds on a range of pathogenic bacteria. Secondly, to determine the toxicity of active compounds towards experimental animals. Thirdly, to test the most promising substances that emerged against experimental or natural infections in animals and—ultimately—man. It is interesting that now, 50 years later, we still have to use essentially the same laborious screening process to identify biologically useful chemical agents whether they be drugs, insecticides, fungicides, and the like; we are only just within sight of being able to make useful deductions about a substance's biological activity simply on the basis of its known chemical structure.

It was five years before a significant result was obtained but then it proved a major success. In 1932 two I.G. dyestuffs chemists synthesized a new dye, Prontosil Rubrum, which they hoped would prove a useful red dye for leather. In preliminary animal protection tests it proved spectacularly successful in controlling haemolytic streptococcal infection in mice: 14 control animals died within four days, 12 treated animals survived. It appears, however, that for one reason or another difficulties arose and Domagk did not publish the experimental results until 1935.[33] Various explanations of this long delay have been advanced. One supposes that it proved difficult to produce consistently successful results, possibly due to variations in the virulence of the streptococcal strains used. Another, for which Hare[34] has advanced reasons, is that the I.G. discovered at an early date that the antibacterial activity did not reside in the whole Prontosil molecule but in a moiety of it identified as sulphanilamide. Sulphanilamide, however, had been prepared as early as 1908 by an Austrian chemist, Paul Gelmo, and it could not, therefore, be patented. Hare suggests that the real reason for the delay, and the German reluctance to make Prontosil available for research purposes, was that they were desperately, but unsuccessfully, trying to prepare patentable variants of sulphanilamide suitable for chemotherapy. The point is not irrelevant here, for the question of patents was to prove of major importance in more ways than one in the development of penicillin. Even if this supposition is correct, it reflects no discredit on the I.G., which was a strictly commercial enterprise and entitled to regard Domagk's project as a speculative investment. Without knowing the total effort deployed it is hard to estimate cost, but in present-day terms we could be talking of an outlay of around £½ million over the period 1927-35.

The importance of this work was immediately perceived and stimulated clinical trials and research at many other centres. Success in the treatment of the many manifestations of haemolytic streptococcal infection—including puerperal fever, infected wounds, and acute rheumatic fever—was recorded all over the world. Research quickly produced two important results. Firstly, success was recorded in the treatment of a number of other serious infections including cerebrospinal meningitis, pneumonia, and gonorrhoea. Secondly, and perhaps more important, J. Trefouel, at the Pasteur Institute in Paris, quickly showed and published the fact that sulphanilamide—the parent compound of Prontosil—was just as active as the dye itself. The speed with which this was done lends colour to the suspicion that the I.G. themselves were aware of it at an early stage. Apart from invalidating the German patents, the importance of this lay in the fact that sulphanilamide was a much simpler and cheaper chemical than Prontosil. There ensued a worldwide flurry of activity to synthesize sulphonamide derivatives that might be useful chermotherapeutic agents; a year after they had put Prontosil on the market the I.G. announced that more than 1000 derivatives of sulphonamide had been made; by 1942 this had risen to 3600. Very few of these proved to be of interest—which might account for the fact that the I.G. chemists came up with nothing useful between the discovery of Prontosil and the publication of their results. But, looking ahead a little, it may be noted that sulphapyridine (1938) and sulphathiazole (1940) were introduced with dramatic results on pneumonia mortality. Sulphadiazine (1941) was particularly valuable for epidemic cerebrospinal meningitis and sulphaguanidine (1940) for intestinal infections. The new drugs were not used only for treating established infections; surgeons quickly realized their prophylactic value, with dramatic results on postoperative mortality.

Interest in the new discovery was as high in Britain as elsewhere. Sulphapyridine, for example, is better known as M & B 693, and emanated from the laboratories of May and Baker. At Queen Charlotte's Hospital, Leonard Colebrook and Maeve Kenny, in 1935, demonstrated that mortality from puerperal fever could be reduced from 20 to 4.7 per cent.[35] At the time, these results were so impressive that an accompanying editorial in the *Lancet* urged readers to interpret them cautiously. At this point Ronald Hare dramatically enters the story again; he accidentally pricked himself in his laboratory at Queen Charlotte's, where he was then working, and picked up a streptococcal infection as a result. He became gravely ill and he believes that probably his life was saved by the Prontosil that Colebrook administered.

At the Middlesex Hospital, in the late 1930s, Florey's old friend Paul Fildes—together with D. D. Wood who later became Reader (in 1946) and then Professor of Microbiology at Oxford—was investigating the nutritional requirements of streptococci and identified p-aminobenzoic acid as an essential factor. They also discovered that this substance neutralized the antistreptococcal effect of sulphanilamide. This led to the interesting Fildes-Wood theory of the action of sulphonamides.[36] Chemically, the two substances are very similar and they supposed that in their ignorance, as it were, of their need for p-aminobenzoic acid the bacteria consumed the equally attractive sulphonamide, with fatal results.

In these post-penicillin days, with popular interest centred on antibiotics, it is difficult to recapture the intense interest generated by the sudden arrival of the sulphonamides nearly half a century ago. The outstanding importance of Domagk's work was recognized by the award to him of a Nobel Prize for Medicine in 1939, but the Nazis would not allow him to receive it; he was even arrested by the Gestapo in consequence. In 1936 Hitler had been furious when Carl von Ossietsky had been awarded the Nobel Peace Prize in 1936, and decreed that in future no German was to accept a Prize. After the war Domagk did receive his medal but unluckily under the rules of the Nobel Foundation the prize money by then had been reabsorbed into the fund.

Apart from its direct impact on medical practice this new development had two important consequences. Firstly, it changed the climate of opinion: no longer could it be argued that Ehrlich's dream of a magic bullet was impossible to attain. Secondly, however, the almost limitless possibilities of ringing the changes on sulphanilamide by chemical synthesis directed attention away from natural products and the problems of handling them; it seemed that synthetic drugs had quite as much to offer, and quite probably more, with much less trouble and expense.

Florey, with his longstanding interest in the antibacterial properties of lysozyme, must have followed these developments with particular interest. The shift of emphasis towards synthetic drugs was immaterial from the point of view of his research; his interest in lysozyme was primarily to elucidate what part it played in the natural defences of the body against infection. Nevertheless, he had a personal interest in sulphanilamide. In 1932 his young nephew, son of Hilda Gardner, died of meningitis following a mastoid operation; he must have reflected that had the sulphonamides been available the boy might have been saved. Four years later he had even greater cause to think along these lines. Early in 1936 Hilda wrote from Melbourne to say that their mother was dying of cancer and that if Howard wished to see her again he must come soon. Hasty arrangements were made for a visit by all the family in the Long Vacation but not long before their departure date Paquita had to have an emergency operation for an acute mastoid infection. She was treated postoperatively with sulphanilamide and made a good recovery, but as a precaution Florey took with him a supply of the drug; this was apparently the first to reach Melbourne.

Despite the sadness of the occasion, the family made the best of the unexpected journey in their various ways. Although mortally ill—she died on 27 November, after the Floreys had returned to Oxford—Bertha contrived to put a brave face on things. Ethel and the children went off to visit her parents and friends in Adelaide, and Howard—predictably—spent some time in local laboratories. In particular, he visited the Physiology Department of Melbourne University and there met a young research worker named R. D. Wright, who so impressed him that he arranged for him to spend a year in Oxford. Wright was a man robust in physique and in speech, and universally known as 'Pansy' Wright. He was also a successful research worker and was co-author with Florey of two papers on intestinal secretion. Later, as we shall see, Florey's friendship with Wright was to prove an essential link in the chain of events which led to his close involvement in the foundation of the Australian National University, which commanded much of his attention for the last twenty-five years of his life. Indeed, it was so powerful a magnet that there were times when it seemed strong enough to draw him back permanently to Australia.

Sadly, Florey had to part from his mother in Melbourne with the certainty that he would never see her again. He joined Ethel and the children in Adelaide and they were back in Oxford in October, in time for the start of the Michaelmas term. There he found installed a new recruit to his research team: this was Dr. Margaret Jennings, who had been a demonstrator in the Pathology Department of the Royal Free Hospital, London. She was to become a close collaborator in much of his research; between 1938 and 1967 she was co-author with him of some thirty papers and, with other members of the department, a joint author of the massive two-volume work on *Antibiotics* published by the Oxford

University Press in 1949. Their collaboration in research led to a long and devoted personal relationship which culminated, after Ethel's death in 1966, in their marriage only a few months before the end of his own life. This, however, is the concern of later chapters and for the moment we need only say something about her early career.

The University of Oxford is nothing if not conservative, not least in its attitude to women. In 1879 two colleges for women were opened—Lady Margaret Hall, conducted on the principles of the Church of England, and Somerville—but not until the end of the century were women admitted to all honours schools. Even then, however, they were not permitted to take degrees; for this they had to wait until 1920. In Australia, as we have seen, a more liberal attitude had long prevailed. Thus when Margaret Augusta Fremantle entered Lady Margaret Hall in 1924 women had been accorded full privileges only four years earlier; in fact, her college was admitted as a full College of the University only in 1960. Initially, she was admitted to read English, but then changed to PPE (Philosophy, Politics and Economics). Only at the end of her first year did she turn to medicine, having found that some women were actually reading it. She was born in 1904 and came of an aristocratic family. Her father—whose practical turn of mind found expression in a fine workshop and a keen interest in rifle shooting—was the third Baron Cottesloe and her grandmother was a daughter of the second Earl of Eldon; the first Earl had been High Steward of Oxford University at the beginning of the nineteenth century. Fremantle was the family name and there was a strong naval tradition; no less than four Fremantles became Admirals.[37] Thomas Francis Fremantle was one of Nelson's captains at Copenhagen and Trafalgar; the family possessed a treasured scrap of paper supposed to carry Nelson's first writing with his left hand. The city of Fremantle in Australia was named after Charles Howe Fremantle by Sir James Stirling, Governor of Western Australia. Although not naturally assertive by nature, Margaret showed a firm determination in seeking a place at Oxford; two younger sisters went to Girton College, Cambridge. With such a background it is perhaps surprising that she should eventually have made a career for herself in medical research. After graduating in the Honours School of Physiology in 1928, just three years after Florey, she went on to do her clinical training at the Royal Free Hospital in London, completing it in 1933, and was then appointed successively house physician and assistant pathologist there. Those who knew her well at that time describe her as very capable at her job and exceptionally diligent. It was while qualifying that she had met and married Denys Jennings. With the quiet determination she showed throughout her life, she continued her medical career. After a brief spell as house surgeon at the Princess Elizabeth Hospital for children, she went back to the Royal Free Hospital in 1935 as A. M. Bird Scholar in Pathology. There she had a good training in bacteriology and for a time was responsible for all the bacteriological work. The following year both she and her husband joined Florey's research staff in Oxford: Florey accepted her on the recommendation of R. A. Webb, then Professor of Pathology at the Royal Free and a former colleague at Cambridge: he said 'she would work her fingers to the bone'. Her husband, Dr. Denys Jennings—who had trained at New College, Oxford, and then at St. Thomas's—had found a position at the Radcliffe Infirmary. In Germany he had mastered the then new technique of gastroscopy and did some incidental experimental work at the Sir William Dunn School of Pathology in connection with the gastric secretion of young pigs. A year later she was appointed to the Schorstein Research Fellowship in Medical Science. This was a prestigious University award, tenable for two years, made only every third year. On its expiration she was appointed Demonstrator in the Department of Pathology. There she was to have a long career in research and teaching being University Lecturer in Pathology from 1945 until she retired in 1972. Her marriage was less successful than her research; it ended in separation early in the war, when Jennings went off to join the Navy, and finally in divorce in 1946.

In 1936, however, all this still lay in the future and for the moment we must return to Florey and his development of a research strategy for his new department. In the interest of clarity it is perhaps easiest first to describe the strategy that emerged and then move on to the much more difficult and controversial question of the relative contribution to its choice and fulfilment of those involved.

As we have recorded, in the course of their original investigation of lysozyme Florey and Goldsworthy had noted that growth of one of the organisms they were testing for lysozyme sensitivity was inhibited in the region of growth of *B. coli* (now known as *Escherichia coli*) on an agar plate. This so particularly attracted their attention that they added an appendix to their paper, in which they discussed the inhibition of one bacterium by another. Primarily on the basis of an extensive review of the literature by G. Papacostas and J. Gaté,[38] they drew attention to the fact that microbial antagonism was then a well-known phenomenon and the possibility of exploiting it medically for controlling infection had already been explored by earlier workers over a period of half a century. To this earlier work we will return later; for the moment we will merely note the fact that there was no intrinsic novelty in Fleming's observation of *P. notatum*. It has often been remarked that they did not quote Fleming's paper which had appeared the previous year, but it can be convincingly argued that it would have been surprising rather than otherwise if they had done so. If they wanted to draw attention to antibiosis as a general phenomenon it would be natural to quote a very recent general review, itself citing several hundred references, such as that of Papacostas and Gaté, rather than a single recent example such as Fleming's.

The isolation of lysozyme and Chain's brilliant demonstration of its mode of action did not in itself point the way to further progress along this particular line. It is not surprising, therefore, that Florey's thoughts turned again to the broader aspects of microbial antagonism to which he and Goldsworthy had directed attention in their lysozyme paper. Chain, too, must have been familiar with this work because as a matter of course he would have read every paper published on lysozyme.

In the circumstances it was inevitable that Florey and Chain should have discussed antibiosis together and this led to a joint agreement to explore its possibilities as a topic for a joint research programme. As a preliminary, it was agreed that Chain should make a detailed survey of the more recent literature to make himself familiar with what had already been published by other workers. In the course of this he collected a couple of hundred references, including many drawn from Papacostas and Gaté's review and Fleming's paper of 1929. The latter it would have been virtually impossible for him to have missed, for it had appeared in a journal which he would for professional reasons have seen issue by issue and to which the library of the Sir William Dunn School of Pathology subscribed. What is surprising is that it attracted his particular attention among so many other comparable examples of antibiosis. The reason seems to have been that—thanks to a remote chance that we have already discussed—penicillin appeared to destroy bacteria by lysis, and this seemed to put it into the same category as lysozyme. In the event three micro-organisms were initially selected for investigation— *P. notatum, Bacillus subtilis*, and *Bacillus pyocyaneus* (now *Pseudomonas pyocyanea*). Significantly, all three had been reported as having a bacteriolytic action, like lysozyme. *B. pyocaneus* had been investigated by numerous workers since 1899; pyocyanase, the dried raw material, had not only been used in clinical trials but had been made available commercially.

Interestingly, in view of the way in which things developed, both Florey and Chain were later insistent that at that time they were not concerned with therapeutic possibilities. Anything that advanced medical knowledge was, of course, of potential use but both of them claimed that the original motivation was scientific investigation of an interesting natural phenomenon. Thus Chain states:

I should like to point out that the possibility that penicillin could have practical use in clinical medicine did not enter our minds when we started our work. . . .[39]

At first sight this is difficult to reconcile with the terms of an application for research funds made to the Rockefeller Foundation in November 1939. This was drafted by Chain and sent off, after minimal alteration, by Florey. The section entitled 'A Chemical Study of the Phenomenon of Bacterial Antagonism' stated explicitly:

They [the antagonistic substances] act on a large variety of pathogenic micro-organisms. They seem therefore to possess great potentialities for therapeutic application. . . . In view of the possibly great practical significance of antagonistic substances produced by bacteria against bacteria it is proposed to study systematically the chemical fundamentals of the phenomenon with the aim of obtaining in purified state and suitable for intravenous injection bacteriolytic and bactericidal substances against various kinds of pathogenic microorganisms.[40]

Possibly the explanation of the discrepancy lies in the context;

it could be argued that the application's chance of success would be greater if the proposed research was presented as not only interesting and original but useful. Against this, however, the Rockefeller Foundation had insisted on the application being made for a biochemical rather than a medical project.

This is a point to which we will return later. For the moment we will simply accept the fact that some time in 1938 Florey and Chain mutually agreed on a joint scientific investigation of the phenomenon of microbial antagonism. This marked the beginning of a new phase of penicillin research that was, in a few short years, to lead to its industrial production as a chemotherapeutic agent of unrivalled efficacy and its worldwide use. How this was brought about forms the subject of the following chapter.

3

LAUNCH OF THE
PENICILLIN PROJECT

In the last chapter it was argued that by 1935 not one person in the world believed in penicillin as a practical aid to medicine. This is not to say, however, that there was no interest in the practical possibilities of the phenomenon of antibiosis, of which penicillin was a single example. On the contrary, there had not only been a sustained interest in antibiosis (p. 59) for half a century but a number of workers had quite specifically suggested that it might be used clinically to combat bacterial infections. As early as 1887 C. Garre[1] had demonstrated that the growth of *Staphylococcus pyogenes* was prevented by *Bac. fluorescens putidus* and had attributed this to the production by this latter organism of a specific, easily diffusible substance which did not at all affect its own growth but inhibited that of *Staph. pyogenes*. On the strength of such experiments he predicted that bacteriotherapy might be used for fighting already established infections. About the same time another French bacteriologist, V. Babès, remarked that a further and wider study of this reciprocal action of bacteria may lead to new ideas in therapeutics. Florey himself had an early encounter with antibiosis in his work on lysozyme, and in his 1930 paper with Goldsworthy had drawn particular attention to a recent French review which cited some 200 examples. Much later, when penicillin was firmly established, he and his colleagues at Oxford found time to make a much more exhaustive historical study of the literature and found that interest had been far wider than they had supposed.[2] As early as 1903, for example, A. Lode[3] had published pictures of circular zones of inhibition on Petri dish cultures of *Staph. aureus* deliberately contaminated with colonies of *Pseudomonas pyocyanea*; to the untutored eye, these are very difficult to distinguish from Fleming's famous plate.

Research on *Ps. pyocanea* is of more than passing interest as exemplifying the kind of work that was being done around the world long before the discovery of penicillin. In 1894, for example, N. Pane had claimed that rabbits experimentally infected with anthrax (*B.anthracis*) were protected if simultaneously inoculated with *Ps. pyocyanea*. Around the same time C. R. Charrin and L. Guignard experimented with the filtered medium on which the organism had grown—the exact equivalent of Fleming's mould juice; they reached the very significant conclusion that the active chemicals concerned were more toxic to bacterial cells than to some types of animal cells. This principle of differential toxicity is, of course, fundamental to the whole concept of chemotherapy. In the early years of this century R. Emmerich and O. Löw, in Germany, introduced a derived soluble product which they called 'pyocyanase'. This was extensively used clinically on the Continent up to the First World War and there are many published references to it,[4] especially in the treatment of diphtheria using an oral spray. The distinguished Austrian bacteriologist T. Escherich endorsed its claims in 1906:

The resumption of these endeavours [the chemical treatment of infection] first became possible when the march of science made known to us a substance which possessed a highly bactericidal capacity and at the same time did not harm the tissues as did previously known antiseptics.[5]

Suddenly, after what has been called the 'pyocyanase disturbance', medical interest lapsed almost as quickly as it had arisen; there are few references to its use after 1914, though it appears to have been on sale in Germany as late as 1936. Various reasons for this decline have been adduced, one of which is simply that the quality of the commercial product was allowed to deteriorate and many samples were quite inactive. Apart from this, it is now clear that pyocyanase is not a very good antibiotic and exaggerated claims were made for it on the basis of insufficiently controlled clinical trials. Nevertheless, it did have a considerable vogue, and both Almroth Wright and Fleming— both active in the field at the time—must have been well aware of its existence and the claims made for it.

But though clinical interest in pyocyanase lapsed, scientific research continued. In 1924-25 F. Wrede and E. Strack, in Germany, isolated a specific antibacterial substance, pyocyanine, from the culture medium. They identified its chemical structure and later prepared it synthetically. It forms beautiful deep blue crystals and it is from these that the name *pyocyanea* ('blue pus') derives. In the 1930s a number of workers investigated the anti-bacterial properties of the substance and confirmed its selective action. Generally speaking, however, its relatively high toxicity and low activity, compared with other available antiseptics, did not encourage its medical use. Nevertheless, it is interesting that *Ps. pyocyanea* was one of the three organisms specifically named by Florey and Chain in their application for research funds to the Rockefeller Foundation in 1939 (p. 79). Pyocyanine was, in fact, later investigated in Oxford by their colleague, Miss R. Schoental, who published her results in 1941.

So far, we have quoted European examples, but meanwhile the phenomenon of antibiosis had not passed unnoticed on the other side of the Atlantic. There in 1923, Selman Waksman—a soil microbiologist at Rutgers University—had noted zones of growth inhibition around colonies of Actinomyces, but not until 1936 did he turn his attention, with J. W. Foster, to a systematic study of antibiosis—'The associative and antagonistic phenomena among micro-organisms'. In 1939, René Dubos,[6] his former student, isolated a crystalline antibiotic, tyrothricin, from the culture medium of *B. brevis*; subsequently this was in fact shown to be a mixture of two antibiotics, gramicidin and tyrocidine. Tyrothricin was very active against a range of pathogenic bacteria at dilutions up to about one part per million, and early animal protection tests showed that a single intraperitoneal injection of 2 mg into mice gave a significant degree of protection against massive infections with pneumococci. It was clear, however, that, like pyocyanine, various toxic manifestations precluded its parenteral administration—that is, intravenously, intramuscularly, or subcutaneously. Nevertheless, it is interesting that tyrothricin is still sometimes encountered as an ingredient in certain pro-prietary throat pastilles and was listed in the British National Formulary for 1982.

To Waksman and his research we shall return later, but it is worth noting at this point that he went on to discover four antibiotics which found practical application, of which the best known is streptomycin. His work in this field earned him a Nobel Prize in 1952. From 1938 Waksman was consultant to Merck and Company of Rahway, New Jersey, one of the big American chemical companies. Initially, his advice was sought primarily in the field of citric acid manufacture, but from 1939 Merck extended the scope of the arrangement to cover antimicrobial substances of microbial origin. It was to be a cooperative venture; Merck was to patent promising discoveries and pay Rutgers a royalty on any sales that eventuated. This arrangement seemed fair and straightforward at the time, but it was destined to land the University and Waksman in very deep trouble. That is a story we shall come to later (p. 296-7); for the moment we should note two important points. The first is that by 1938-39 a leading American pharmaceutical manufacturer was sufficiently interested in the therapeutic possibilities of antibiosis to put money into research on it, if only as a speculative venture. From the beginning of 1940 three Merck staff members were deputed to study the isolation of therapeutic substances from micro-organisms. This invites comparison with the I.G.'s support for Domagk (p. 71). The second, more immediately relevant, is that penicillin was included in their original list of substances to be investigated. A culture of *P. notatum* was obtained from Dr. Fritz Schiff of the Beth Israel Hospital, New York, and by the autumn of 1940 purification work was in hand with a first batch of 9 litres of culture medium.[7] By that time several other American pharmaceutical companies were showing an interest. E. R. Squibb, for example, had made a survey of the penicillin literature as early as October 1936; other companies that had shown interest were Eli Lilly, Lederle, Winthrop, Parke Davis, and Upjohn. We must be clear, however, that it is customary for chemical companies to maintain a watching brief on interesting new fields without necessarily having any immediate intention of active involvement or seeing any special significance in them.

This digression into the early history of antibiosis and its possible therapeutic possibilities, affording no more than a glimpse of what was going on worldwide, has, of course, been made with a purpose—that of demonstrating that in 1938 Florey and Chain were not venturing into some *terra incognita* where no one, except Fleming, had previously ventured; there was already a long history of somewhat desultory and inconclusive exploration and some current activity. Both have put themselves firmly on record in this particular point. Thus Florey, in 1949, wrote:

When the reader has further considered the chemical, bacteriological and animal experiments which have been carried out with *Ps. pyocyanea*

... he will appreciate that the work done with this organism was comparable in scope and in imagination with the outburst of energy in the antibiotic field which began in 1940 ... it is difficult to believe from the records that pyocyanase was worthless when prepared in an active state, as it appears to have been around 1908. These older workers had nearly all the ideas which are too readily supposed to be of quite recent origin—their misfortune was that they happened to be working with a rather toxic antibiotic preparation.[8]

Much later (1971) when the historical perspective was sharper, though memories about detail perhaps less clear, Chain expressed himself similarly:

I believe that the field of microbial antagonism had become ripe for study when we started our investigations in 1938. The existence of antibacterial substances produced by micro-organisms had been well documented with many examples and it was of obvious interest to study their biological and biochemical properties. We would have started our research programme in these substances even if Fleming's paper had not been published and if we had not done so someone else in some other laboratory in the world would have taken the initiative. As a result some interesting antibacterial substances would have been discovered, as they later were, and following this a general screening programme for organisms capable of producing antibiotics would have started. This would undoubtedly have revealed the existence of the penicillin-producing penicillia. The development of the antibiotics field might have been delayed by a few years but it would, inevitably, have taken place with the same final results which we have now.[9]

History provides countless examples of similar situations; a sequence of events creates a situation where a major discovery is in the air, ready to be plucked from it. Wireless communication—with its later ramifications into radio, television, and radar—is an obvious example. Equally, history rightly reserves a special accolade for those who take the decisive step. In the case of penicillin there is no doubt that it was Florey and Chain who jointly set in train the research programme that made penicillin available to the world as a chemotherapeutic agent of unrivalled excellence. In a perfect world, we might regard the venture as simply an agreed collaboration between two experienced research workers each contributing their own particular expertise—one medical, the other biochemical. It did, indeed, start in this way but differences of such magnitude later arose between them that the allocation of credit became an important issue. As these differences substantially affected the lives of both Florey and Chain we must perforce give some consideration to them.

The starting point, beyond question, was lysozyme. As we have seen, there is ample evidence that Florey had had a continuing interest in this ever since his Cambridge days. He had realized that progress depended on the possibility of isolating lysozyme and elucidating its chemical nature. One of his first tasks on arriving in Oxford had been to secure the collaboration of Sir Robert Robinson in this work. His invitation to Chain to join him in Oxford was clearly to have a qualified biochemist as a general collaborator, but he made it clear (p. 53) that one field of collaboration was to be lysozyme. Chain, as we have seen, applied himself very successfully to this and published his results, with Epstein, in 1940. Simultaneously he was carrying out research on snake venom and collaborating with other members of the department—with Isaac Berenblum on the determination of phosphate, as part of a study of the metabolism of cancer tissue, and with N. G. Heatley and Berenblum on a new type of micro-respirometer. Heatley, another biochemist who figures prominently in the penicillin story, had also come from Cambridge, in 1936; there he had been working under Joseph Needham, an able biochemist who later made an international reputation for himself as an orientalist with his *Science and Civilisation in China*, a monumental work of immense erudition. Heatley's skills included a remarkable flair for devising micro methods in the laboratory: the micro-respirometer mentioned above was entirely his own conception and design. Chain had been instrumental in getting Heatley to Oxford: he arrived while Florey was away in Australia and was Chain's research assistant until 1939.

As a matter of course, every experimental scientist scans the existing literature to discover what work has already been published on his particular project. This is done partly to obtain useful background information and partly to avoid the embarrassment of repeating and describing work already done by others and thus seeming to seek credit for it. We can recall Florey's chagrin, for example, in finding that his observation of the contraction of the lacteals in 1926 had been very accurately recorded by A. Heller as long ago as 1869. As a normal part of his research on lysozyme, Chain studied the existing literature on bacterial antagonism, with a special interest in those where the destruction was by lysis. In the circumstances it was not merely likely, but virtually inevitable, that he would come across Fleming's original paper on penicillin: it will be remembered that because of a very exceptional combination of circumstances (p. 64) the staphylo-coccal colonies on the mould-contaminated culture plate were lysed. Chain states explicitly that it was the evidence of lysis that particularly caught his attention:

When I saw Fleming's paper for the first time I thought that Fleming had discovered a sort of mould lysozyme which, in contrast to egg white lysozyme, acted on a wide range of . . . pathogenic bacteria.[10]

So far, there is every reason to suppose that Chain had arrived at this point entirely on his own initiative. He had followed routine procedure and there was no occasion for him to have mentioned it to Florey or anybody else. But it is clear that he was turning over in his mind the possibility of investigating other examples of bacterial antagonism, especially those involving lysis.

At this stage the two men were on easy terms, so far as the great disparity in their temperaments and backgrounds allowed. Apart from meetings in the laboratory, at the end of the working day they sometimes walked part of the way home together through the University parks—Florey to his house in Parks Road, Chain to his flat in Bardwell Road. In the nature of things, such talk would be desultory, but it would be surprising indeed if it had not involved a certain amount of professional shop—their indi-vidual researches, the work of the laboratory, and so on. On the evidence of a surviving manuscript note,[11] Chain chose such an opportunity to mention to Florey his growing general interest in bacterial antagonism, and the latter at once recalled his own earlier interest, which he had expressed in the appendix—'inhibition of one bacterium by another'—to his 1930 paper on lysozyme with Goldsworthy (p. 78). In Chain's own words:

During the course of this work E. C. became interested in the phenom-enon of bacterial antagonism and began a survey of the literature in this field. In discussions between H. W. F. and E. C., H. W. F. mentioned that he had been interested in the phenomenon of bacterial antagonism since 1929 and informed E. C. about the existence of French mono-graph in this field. After numerous discussions between H. W. F. and E. C. it was decided between them to make a systematic study of the field of bacterial antagonism, with a view to study the biological and chemical properties of substances produced by certain micro-organisms which were responsible for their antagonistic action towards other micro-organisms.[12]

So far, all seems unexceptional. Through their mutual interest in lysozyme they had developed a common interest in the phenomenon of antibiosis, a field just becoming ripe for closer investigation. The basis for collaboration was entirely logical. Florey was exceptionally well qualified to do the biological work, but had no illusions that his biochemical knowledge was more than elementary. Chain was a first-rate biochemist but in no way qualified to carry out biological experiments. In particular, he had no licence to carry out experiments with live animals. For Florey, responsible for the running of a department pursuing a number of research programmes, there was an additional attraction, which also did not escape Chain, whose long-term future was by no means secure, since his three-year grant from the British Empire Cancer Campaign was nearing its end. He was anxious to stay in Britain and had applied for naturalization, which was granted in April 1939. There was then a severe financial crisis: the department had an overdraft of £500. Again to quote Chain:

At that time my work, in fact, the development of the whole biochemical section in the Institute of Pathology at Oxford, was greatly handicapped by lack of funds, so much so that one day I was told by Florey in very categorical terms that we had no funds at all, and that we had to stop ordering anything whatever it was, even if it were a piece of glass rod; I remember this very well, this particular event.[13]

Such an investigation as they now proposed would be of a long-term nature and if a grant could be raised at all it might be given for several years. This would give welcome relief, for the financial prospects were indeed grave. In June 1939 an application to the Nuffield Fund Research Committee for a grant of £200 p.a. to enable Dr. Jennings to continue her research on gut function had not only been turned down, but turned down in a way that Florey thought offensive; he sought, and got, an apology. He confided his difficulties to Mellanby, complaining that 'It would seem that the University almost wish to make it as difficult as possible to carry on. You may gather that I am fed up.'

Mellanby offered cold comfort, saying that such frustration was 'the natural condition of the normal man'. This was followed by an angry exchange about an application Gardner had made to the Medical Research Council for a small grant to cover the cost of laboratory material. Florey had not even seen this application and was justifiably annoyed when Mellanby said it indicated a 'frankly deplorable' state of affairs in Florey's department:

I gather from your second paragraph that the Council think I am seriously at fault. . . . Perhaps this is so, but I hardly think they know all the relevant facts. However, I am needing no urging to reduce here. It is a great deal easier to stop than to start research: five people have gone this year and by the end of next I expect to have reduced the numbers by twelve, including Maegraith. It will then be possible to run the rump with what the University provides.[14]

The implication was that Florey had put his research interests above his department's teaching obligations. Whatever the justification, these sharp exchanges did nothing to improve his relations with the MRC. Nevertheless, some help was secured. It was agreed that the grant to N. G. Heatley, who was due to go to Copenhagen in September to work at the Carlsberg Laboratory on a Rockefeller Fellowship, should be transferred to Dr. Jennings.

It was against this somewhat unfavourable background that Florey made, three days after the outbreak of war, his first plea for direct support by the MRC for the proposed programme of research on microbial antagonism. It is too long to quote *in extenso* but the following significant points were made in it:

1. The investigation would include Fleming's penicillin.
2. Dubos' very recent work on tyrothricin was cited as evidence of the general promise of the field of antibiosis.
3. The 'possible great practical importance' of the bactericidal agents involved was specifically mentioned.
4. It was claimed that 'penicillin can easily be prepared in large quantities and is non-toxic to animals, even in large doses'.
5. It was stated that 'in our opinion the purification of penicillin can be carried out easily and rapidly'.

So far as the first of these points is concerned, there is no evidence that the fateful decision to include penicillin was made at the insistence of Chain. Indeed, Florey once told Heatley that Chain was initially very much attracted by gramicidin and that it was he who insisted that penicillin should have priority.[15] Chain has acknowledged that Florey's knowledge of penicillin was at least good as his own:

I told Florey about my finding in the literature of penicillin. Though he never mentioned the word penicillin to me during our frequent conversations, he appeared to be familiar with the substance and asked me whether I was aware that, in 1933, a group of well-known and successful natural-product chemists, the late Professor Raistrick and two of his colleagues, had worked on it, but could not make any progress because of its instability. I had not heard of this paper, but read it immediately after my talk with Florey.[16]

The insistence on the great therapeutic potentialities of the research programme—which both were later to deny vehemently—has already been discussed (p. 79). The presumption is that this was introduced to strengthen the claim for a grant, rather than with any serious expectation that it would prove true. There is no doubt, however, that the evidence of activity against staphylococci must have been a factor.

The claim that penicillin (meaning presumably the active culture medium) could easily be prepared in large quantities is defensible, for it is essentially a matter of scaling up a laboratory experiment. But the claim that it 'is non-toxic to animals, even in large doses' reads strangely. The whole basis of the well-founded argument against the claims later made by Fleming was that neither he nor anybody else could determine the toxicity of penicillin until it had been at least partially purified. Again, the expectation that penicillin could be easily and rapidly purified was at variance with the evidence then available and was no doubt an expression of Chain's normal optimism. The reality, as he acknowledged years later (1951) in an (unpublished) letter to the Editor of the *Evening Standard*, to whose accounts of the history of penicillin he took great exception—doubtless aggravated by the Beaverbrook connection with St.Mary's—was very different:

Though the first extraction of penicillin was a relatively easy matter, its further purification up to the final state of purity proved to be a very difficult chemical problem which kept whole groups of chemists in England and in the United States busy for quite a long time.[17]

This application to the MRC had one important result. It was agreed that a grant currently made to another research worker who was leaving the department, could be transferred to Chain; this assured him of a grant of £300 p.a. for three years, with £100 for expenses. But otherwise Mellanby's response was disheartening in the extreme. He agreed that the project was interesting and possibly of practical importance, but Florey's request for £100 to get it started could only be 'remembered'. For the moment all that could be made available was £25! So was born perhaps the most important medical research programme ever launched.

This pitifully small offer was received on 8 September 1939. By a lucky coincidence Dr. H. M. Miller, of the Rockefeller Foundation, with whom Florey had maintained friendly relations, was visiting Britain and called on Florey on 1 November. He intimated that an immediate application to the Foundation for research funds might be successful but stressed that if he was to promote it, it would have to be of a biochemical nature, since he himself was a member of the Natural Sciences (and not the Medical) Division of the Foundation. This suited Florey, for any application for support of a medical research programme by the Foundation would have to be routed through Mellanby at the MRC and might be thwarted. As it was, he was sailing very near the wind and there was a very considerable row later when Mellanby discovered what had happened. By then, however, penicillin was on the high-road to success and his displeasure no longer mattered.

The application to the Rockefeller Foundation was quickly prepared and dispatched to Dr. Warren Weaver in New York only three weeks after Miller's visit. It seems to have been drafted by Chain with some advice from another colleague, E. S. Duthie—which would be natural as it was basically biochemical— and received minimal amendment by Florey. In the event it sought support for two research programmes: one for 'a chemical study of the phenomenon of bacterial antagonism and the other for a study of the mucinases (enzymes that destroy mucin)'. By prevailing standards, Florey pitched his request pretty high: £1,670 p.a. ($7700) for salaries and current expenses, plus up to £1000 ($4600) for equipment. He made it clear, moreover, that he had in mind a protracted programme:

In the present unsettled state [war with Germany] it would no doubt be advantageous to review the position annually but I should not like the responsibility of organising the proposed work on less than a presumption of three years duration at least.

The answer was swift and fulfilled their expectations. The Rockefeller Foundation made a recurrent grant of $5000 (£1100) p.a. but for five years not three. Naturally they were jubilant, and Chain recalls:

This was very welcome news indeed. I remember very well celebrating it in our room at Bardwell Road with him [Florey], my cousin Mrs. A. Sacharina, and a friend Doctor R. Klibansky, who was just present at that time in our flat.[18]

At long last the programme they had been talking about for more than a year could go ahead.

Even then, however, all was far from plain sailing, for in the meantime the war had started and various contingency plans were being put into effect that, apart from the general national upheaval, affected the department. It became the headquarters of the Emergency Public Health Laboratory Service, shortly placed under the direction of G. S. (later Sir Graham) Wilson. Florey's first intimation of this had come in a letter from Mellanby dated 14 March 1938, saying that the Medical Research Council had been asked to help create an auxiliary bacteriological scheme to help the regular Public Health authorities in the event of war. For obvious reasons it had to be decentralized and Oxford was to serve the south and west. Florey replied by return, saying that he would be glad to have something useful to do. For the moment the scheme was purely a paper organization, but on 26 August 1939 a fateful telegram was received: 'Emergency Laboratory Scheme being made effective. Transport and personnel will begin arriving Monday, possibly sooner.' The MRC files throw an amusing sidelight on the varied kinds of problems that had to be solved. Early in September the Council was informed:

We have engaged temporarily an office boy and messenger as follows. He is Peter J. Bliss, 176 The Moors, Kidlington, Oxford. He is fifteen years of age and will be paid at the rate of 14 shillings per week under the running account [surely appropriate!] pending any instructions to the contrary.

Gordon Sanders was put in charge of the Oxford Area blood transfusion service, for which accommodation was found close by in the New Bodleian Library. Ethel was glad to find a new opportunity for professional employment in organizing the medical staff concerned with blood donors. Preparations had to be made to receive additional medical students evacuated from London. Apart from these organizational distractions, the investigations of microbial antagonism was only part of the departmental research effort, though it was to assume increasing importance. In particular, the work on mucus was being continued and from October 1939 Florey directed, at the request of the Medical Research Council, a research programme on shock. This involved attendance at meetings of the MRC Shock Committee (later Committee on Traumatic Shock). Shock was a serious, and often fatal consequence of severe physical injury, and had suddenly acquired increased importance in face of the prospect of heavy battle and air-raid casualties. It was, unfortunately, a condition whose aetiology was still obscure, as Florey reminded Mellanby.

The real difficulty is that no one can give a firm answer to simple questions. One lot maintains that shocked people start off with a high BP, others deny it and so on over a number of simple points.

There was, therefore, no lack of research to be done by Florey and his colleagues at Oxford and collaborators at other centres. It was a time-consuming task, of which the first product was a succinct review of current ideas.[19]

The outbreak of war also had immediate domestic consequences. In the expectation, unfulfilled as it happened, of immediate air-raids some of the civilian population, especially children, were evacuated from potential danger areas. Paradoxically, the Florey children went to St. Austell in Cornwall, for safety and six children and two teachers, from London, sought the safety of the Red House.

But the declaration of war had its advantages. Heatley gave up his intention to work with Linderstrøm Lang in Copenhagen and at the very last moment it was arranged that he could hold at Oxford the Rockefeller Fellowship he had been awarded. His position in the department was different, however; he no longer worked under the direction of Chain but as personal assistant to Florey. This was an early indication of intra-departmental strains which were to become more serious later. Although Heatley had, and never lost, a great respect for Chain's intellectual capacity he did not find him an easy colleague. It was, therefore, very much more congenial for him to work with Chain than under him. Florey was sensitive to such undercurrents and skilled at unobtrusively relieving awkward situations. Abraham, holding a Rockefeller Fellowship in Stockholm in the Institute of Hans von Euler, also made his way back to Oxford in November 1939 and joined the Sir William Dunn School of Pathology on 1 January 1940, with an MRC grant to work on the wound shock programme.

In later years, much prominence was given to the so-called penicillin team, as though this were some sort of task force assembled to deal specifically with the investigation of this particular aspect of microbial antagonism. It is true that as the research developed additional staff were recruited to deal with problems that arose, and to enlarge the scope of the work and the speed with which it could be pressed forward, but initially no special arrangements were made. This was, of course, no more than a measure of the success of Florey's deliberate policy of building up a multidisciplinary group that could be deployed as required on a variety of medical research programmes. When the first paper on penicillin was published in 1940, the co-authors with Florey were Chain, Gardner, Heatley, Margaret Jennings, Jean Orr-Ewing, and Sanders; all had been in the department long before the decision to investigate microbial antagonism had been taken. By contrast, in the same year Florey's name appeared on no less than six other published research papers, on such diverse topics as the lymph system and capillary contraction (with Ebert and Sanders) and the control of gastric mucus secretion by the vagus nerve (with Margaret Jennings).

The 1939 application to the Rockefeller Foundation proposed a general investigation on microbial antagonism but named three specific organisms by way of example—*B. pyocyaneus, B. subtilis* and *P. notatum*; the common link was that, like lysozyme, they all produced substances that destroyed bacteria by dissolving (lysing) them rather than by producing toxic substances that killed them outright and, as it were, left the bodies on the field of battle. The application did not limit them to these three, or indeed to any particular organisms, but Chain stated that 'a beginning has already been made here with the purification of the bactericidal substances produced by *Penicillium notatum* and *B. pyocyaneus*. . . . This work will be carried out with Professor

A. D. Gardner and Professor H. W. Florey on the bacteriological and animal experimental side.'

In view of conflicting claims made later, Chain's statement that 'a beginning has already [i.e. in November 1939] been made here' needs comment. According to Chain:

> I was asked by Florey to formulate an application [to the Rockefeller Foundation] for our research project. . . . A few months later, towards the beginning of 1939, we received the reply that our application had been agreed. . . . In 1939 N. G.Heatley was due to go to Dr. Linderstrom-Lang's Laboratories at the Carlsberg Institute in Copenhagen, Denmark, but after the war had broken out he returned to our department, and Florey asked me whether I had any objection to Heatley joining the penicillin work. I agreed, of course.[20]

In fact, Chain's memory was at fault; the Rockefeller application was actually not dispatched until November 1939 and the resulting grant was actually approved by the University of Oxford on 12 March 1940. As his notebooks prove, Heatley had been working full-time on penicillin from the beginning of October 1939, and the implication that he did so only after the Rockefeller grant had been notified must therefore be incorrect. Chain's error over the date of the application indicates that a start had been made in 1938, but all the evidence indicates that no experimental work on penicillin was done in Oxford before the late summer of 1939. Interestingly, Heatley, too, had some prior knowledge of penicillin; in the early 1930s it was mentioned in a lecture he attended at Cambridge and this sufficiently aroused his interest to make him seek out and make an abstract of Fleming's original paper.

As we have noted, the investigation of *B. pyocyaneus* was carried out by Regine Schoental. The investigation of *B. subtilis*—which M. Nicolle, as early as 1907 had shown to be active against several species of pathogenic bacteria, including pneumococci—was not pursued at Oxford. In 1947 an active substance named subtilin was isolated from it elsewhere, but it found no clinical use because of its toxicity.[21] Thus, so far as Florey and Chain were directly concerned, the field was narrowed to penicillin. The die was cast.

For the moment the ball was necessarily firmly in the chemical court. The first need was to produce mould juice and to extract from it enough sufficiently pure penicillin* for its biological properties to be evaluated; it was only at that stage that Florey could make his contribution. The production of the crude liquid was no great problem, for the growth of *P. notatum* on a liquid medium is in essence no different from the fermentation of fruit juices by yeast, an age-old process practised by innumerable amateur as well as professional winemakers. Not quite so straightforward, perhaps, for the medium must be protected with particular care from infection by other organisms: the temperature must be fairly closely controlled; the fermentation must be stopped at the right moment, before the accumulated penicillin begins to disappear; and the ordinary laboratory is not designed to deal with the considerable volumes that were quickly found necessary. The biggest single problem was to avoid contamination during fermentations lasting several days. It was found as early as 1940 that a number of airborne contaminants produce an enzyme (penicillinase) that rapidly destroyed penicillin.

For convenience, a wholly synthetic (Czapek-Dox) medium† was used (p. 69), except for the addition of a little yeast extract which was found to speed up growth though it did not appear to increase the yield. This had to be inoculated with Fleming's strain of *P. notatum*. By a strange coincidence this was already available in the laboratory. Dreyer, Florey's predecessor, had been interested in a class of bacteriolytic agents, known as bacteriophages, discovered by Frederick Twort in 1915. He thought that Fleming's penicillin might be some kind of bacteriophage and in 1929 had obtained a culture of the mould; this had been maintained at Oxford ever since by Miss Campbell-Renton. According to Heatley, Vollum said that he had 'played about' with *P. notatum* and his culture may have been independently obtained.[19] There was thus no occasion for any direct request to be made to Fleming, who consequently was not aware of renewed interest in his mould.

---

*Fleming used the term penicillin to describe his crude mould juice: the Oxford workers used it to describe the active substance that conferred antibacterial activity. Florey used to say that if Oxford had coined a different name for the purified material, a great deal of trouble with Fleming might have been avoided.

†Czapek-Dox medium is essentially a 4 per cent solution of glucose in water, with addition of salts of sodium, potassium, magnesium, and iron.

The early stages of most investigations of new physiologically active substances present a fundamental problem, in that it is only through their biological effects that their presence can be detected and their concentration measured. Direct methods of estimation are generally inapplicable until some considerable knowledge has been gained of the physicochemical nature of the substance under investigation. Such problems arise, for example, in the investigation of new vitamins and hormones. Often the observed biological effect becomes apparent only slowly. Consequently, it may take days or weeks to discover what success has been achieved in a particular attempt at purification, and this will determine the speed at which the research programme as a whole can be pushed forward. It follows, therefore, that the development of a rapid assay method is of the utmost importance in any investigation of biologically active material of unknown nature; penicillin was no exception to the general rule.

In an investigation of microbial antagonism the biological property to be used to monitor the active substance is, of course, its antibacterial activity against a specified test organism. Two main alternative procedures are available. Firstly, a dilution method can be used: a measured amount of the solution to be assayed is serially diluted until the antibacterial effect is no longer observable when it is added to a measured suspension of the test organism. The more concentrated the original solution, the more it can be diluted until its antibacterial effect disappears. While reliable, such methods are time-consuming and demand the observance of sterile conditions at all stages. Secondly, diffusion methods can be employed; in effect, this normally involves deliberately producing something rather resembling Fleming's now familiar contaminated plate. Briefly, a Petri dish is seeded with an appropriate test organism, such as *Staph. aureus*, and a drop of the solution whose antibacterial potency is to be assayed is placed on it; the plate is then incubated overnight. In the morning the culture plate will be covered with a uniform dull film of bacterial growth except for sharply defined circles of clear agar surrounding each drop of applied test solution.

In 1939 there was nothing novel in principle in such tests—which had been described in the very early literature—nor in the fact that to the trained eye they gave a quantitative measure of antibacterial activity: the larger the disc of inhibition the higher the antibacterial activity of the solution that had been applied. However, in the hands of Heatley, with his flair for delicate experimental techniques, this method was considerably refined (Plate 4). Small glass (later porcelain) cylinders were obtained, some 7 mm in diameter and 9 mm in height. In carrying out an assay the cylinder was placed on the agar and filled with the test liquid, using a pipette; from the size of the cylinders, it is clear that only a very small volume of liquid was required for each test. The test was standardized in other ways: the subculturing of the test organism to keep its sensitivity constant; the composition of the nutrient agar; the duration and temperature of incubation; and so on. Heatley's use of cylinders derived from Goldsworthy and Florey's 1929 paper.

Normally, five or six cylinders would be put on each plate. When the test was finished, the diameter of the clear circle of growth-free agar round each cylinder was measured to give a semi-quantitative measure of the activity of the solution; this was quickly and easily done by placing the plate over a glass scale illuminated from underneath. Under standardized conditions (an arbitrary penicillin standard was set up in March 1941) the diameter of the ring gives a measure of the activity of the solution against the test organism.

This plate-and-cylinder assay method was of fundamental importance not only to the progress of the Oxford research programme but to the huge international penicillin venture that followed it. The basic unit of penicillin activity became known as the Oxford unit and over the years literally hundreds of millions of such assays were carried out. One commercial firm alone is said to have set up as many as 3000 plates daily—each carrying five to six cylinders—and various devices were introduced to mechanize the process.

At Oxford the preparation of the test plates and the sterilization of the cylinders became another routine task for the technicians. Normally, solutions were allowed to accumulate during the day and the assay plates were set up at night, ready to be examined in the morning. Early in 1942 Florey discovered that if the cylinders were briefly warmed in a flame they would melt a little agar and adhere firmly to the plate; among other advantages this prevented the risk of leakage round the base. It was necessary to judge the heat of the cylinders rather carefully before applying them to the agar: 'the noise accompanying the operation should be a short "psst!" rather than a prolonged sizzle', he advised those learning the technique. As the research advanced, the psst! of cylinders became a familiar sound at the end of each day's work.

It must be stressed that, initially, the Oxford unit was not an absolute one. Its importance lay in the fact that it enabled different solutions to be precisely compared and thus the process of concentration on the one hand, or loss of activity on the other, could be monitored. It was quite an arbitrary unit, as was made clear in an early Oxford publication (1941):

The Oxford unit is 'that amount of penicillin which when dissolved in 1 c.cm of water gives the same inhibition as . . . [a certain partly purified] standard [solution].

This is a very important point, for it emphasizes that even at this stage nobody had any notion of the intrinsic antibacterial activity of pure penicillin. Not until much later, when pure crystalline penicillin had been isolated, was this possible; it was then established that pure crystalline penicillin has an activity of approximately 2000 Oxford units per milligram.* In mid-1943, Florey and Chain[22] believed that 'pure penicillin contains about 1000 units per milligram'. It is interesting to note that the original Oxford standard had an activity of only four to five units per mg: that is, it was only around 0.25 per cent pure!

The development of a simple, quick, and reliable assay method for penicillin was of crucial importance. It provided a ready means of testing the potency of the crude broth, so that it could be harvested at the point of maximum activity, and of evaluating the success or otherwise of attempts to extract purified penicillin from it. Later, at the time of clinical trials and subsequent general introduction into medical practice, it still remained essential. Heatley's contribution to the penicillin research programme has been generally underestimated, but his development of this assay method alone gives him a substantial claim to recognition.

Initially, penicillin was prepared in vessels of all sorts and sizes, maintained in an ambient temperature of 24°C (75°F). To pre-

---

*The word 'approximately' is used because by then it had been shown that penicillin was not a single substance but a mixture of closely related ones. Oxford penicillin was penicillin F, characterized by a 2-pentenyl group; American penicillin (penicillin G) contained a benzyl group derived from a constituent of the corn-steep liquor on which the mould was grown (see p. 172).

vent contamination after inoculation with *P. notatum* the opening of each vessel was plugged with cottonwool; as we have remarked, the prevention of contamination was the major problem at this stage. Later, sterilization of both vessels and culture medium became routine. The development of penicillin activity was regularly monitored and normally reached a maximum after 8-12 days. The liquid was then poured off and worked up to extract the penicillin; the vessels were then cleaned and sterilized for re-use. One advantage of this use of a multiplicity of small vessels was that if contamination did occur the whole batch was not lost. For a time the experiment was tried of drawing off the active liquid—golden yellow in colour—from underneath the thick felt of mould growth on the surface, and then replacing it with a succession of fresh culture solutions. However, the incidence of contamination was such that this eventually proved not worth while and the practice was discontinued after some eighteen months.

To demonstrate the magnitude of the further task of extracting penicillin from the crude culture fluid it is convenient to invoke knowledge which in fact was acquired only much later. In those early days, two thousand vessels would be required to produce a total of about 60 mg of pure penicillin. In effect, the crude medium contained only one part of penicillin in 10 million.

Why the mould produces penicillin at all is still obscure: the common pathogenic organisms—so deadly to man—are scarcely a threat to its existence in nature. The supposition is that it is no more than the casual end product of some metabolic process important for other reasons, much as some plants produce highly toxic substances, like strychnine and nicotine, which are not demonstrably useful to them. Unfortunately, as it grows the mould produces many other complex chemical species, such as pigments, alcohols, proteins, etc.; the penicillin molecules are in a minority, jostling round in an ocean of water with multiplicity of others, like rare pieces of coral on a pebble beach. Moreover, as earlier investigators had discovered, penicillin is unstable under certain conditions and this closed the door on many conventional separation processes. It is destroyed by heat; by acid and alkali; by certain metal ions, such as those of copper; and by a variety of organic chemical reagents. The net result was that only the mildest of separation processes were applicable, and two proved of paramount importance. The first was solvent transfer or back extraction (distribution between two immiscible solvents); the second was chromatography.

Back extraction depends on the simple fact that certain liquids are immiscible and when shaken together quickly separate into two distinct layers; oil and water are familiar examples. In the laboratory, a wide range of solvents immiscible with water are available, such as chloroform, ether, carbon disulphide, and amyl acetate. If a mixture of substances is shaken with two such solvents some constituents will go into one solvent and others into the other, and thus some degree of separation can be achieved. The two liquid phases are conveniently separated by means of a funnel fitted with a tap in its stem; the tap is opened to draw off the denser lower layer of liquid and closed just as the upper one is about to run through. This is a very old method of chemical separation, and separating funnels were in use at least as early as the seventeenth century. By extracting from a large volume into a smaller one a corresponding degree of concentration may be effected.

Chromatography, too, is a separation technique of respectable antiquity, dating at least from the middle of the last century.[23] Basically, it depends on the fact that certain powders, such as fullers' earth, have the power of absorbing dissolved substances on their surfaces; the degree of absorption depends on the nature of the powder, the nature of the solvent, and the nature of the dissolved substance. Some solvents can reverse the process and wash off from the powder substances absorbed by it from other solvents. Chromatography makes use of this kind of differential absorption in a dynamic way. If a tube is filled with a suitable powder and a solution of the mixture is allowed to percolate through it, the individual constituents of the mixture will gradually collect in bands across the tube. If the bands are then separated mechanically the absorbed substances in them can be washed off with another solvent. Needless to say, the technique is in practice not quite as easy as it may sound, and needs considerable skill and judgement on the part of the research worker. Nevertheless, by the 1930s it was well established and, significantly, had found particular favour with chemists investigating natural products. In this field it had the double advantage of requiring little advance knowledge of the chemical nature of the substance to be isolated, and of exposing it to only the mildest conditions.

A specific example of the use of chromatography in natural

product chemistry was the isolation by the Russian botanist M. S. Tswett, of the principal plant pigments, cholorphyll and carotene, in 1906.[24] In the early 1930s the Swiss Nobel Laureate Paul Karrer, among others, made extensive use of chromatography to isolate carotenoid pigments from various natural sources—higher plants, algae, fungi, and bacteria. In 1939, the year which we have now reached, E. A. Doisy—who shared a Nobel Prize for Medicine with Henrik Dam—had a conspicuous success when he and his colleagues isolated vitamin K_1 (the antihaemorrhagic factor) by chromatographic methods alone. From 6000 lb (2700 kg) of kiln-dried alfalfa they extracted 1.3 g of pure vitamin K_1;[25] thus the original substance contained less than 0.001 per cent by weight of active material. In view of the emphasis already laid on the importance of Heatley's assay method for penicillin, it is worth recording that vitamin K_1 assays each required at least ten chicks and took four days to complete. Finally, because it brings us right into the Sir William Dunn School of Pathology, we may mention the classic researches by Hieger in 1930-33 on the isolation and identification of 3:4-benzpyrene as a potent carcinogen in coal-tar. At Oxford, Berenblum and Schoental[26] were investigating the carcinogenic properties of shale oil and isolated 3:4-benzpyrene from it chromatographically to the extent of 0.01 per cent. Even simpler, but less effective than chromatography, was merely to shake a crude solution of penicillin with a strong absorbent such as charcoal (of the type then used for gas-masks); filter off the charcoal with the penicillin attached to it; and then wash the absorbed penicillin off with a different solvent.

Thus there were available two well-tried processes of chemical separation eminently suitable for the particular process in prospect and, as we shall see, they sufficed for the task. Unfortunately, the initiation of the use of back extraction at Oxford was to prove so serious a source of controversy between Chain and his colleagues that we must examine the circumstances in some detail.

The generally accepted version is that in the course of an informal discussion between Florey, Chain, and Heatley, the latter suggested that the back extraction method should be attempted with the crude culture medium; if it were made slightly acid the penicillin could be extracted into ether, as Raistrick had shown, and then quickly extracted back into water at neutrality. Chain pooh-poohed this suggestion, partly because he still thought that penicillin might be an enzyme—and thus likely to be 'denatured' by ether—and partly because penicillin was known to be sensitive to acid. Florey intervened—on his precept that 'if you don't ask you don't get to find out' (p. 254)—to suggest that Heatley might as well try; there was nothing much to lose because it was a simple experiment involving very little trouble or material. Chain allegedly grumbled that this would be a good way for Heatley to discover that it would not work. In fact, Heatley's first trials, made on 9 March 1940, proved the feasibility of the method. In due course the back extraction process (using amyl acetate) was to prove the basis of commercial production of penicillin.

Chain's version is different.[27] According to him, he did not discount the possibility of success but reminded Florey that their agreeement was that all chemical work should be his responsibility: Heatley, it will be recollected, by that time was not working under Chain but was Florey's personal assistant. What Florey and Heatley both interpreted as an indication that Chain thought the idea farfetched was no more than a gesture of annoyance on his part at what he regarded as their joint trespass on his preserve. If chemical work was to be done, then he should be the one to do it. That he did not protest further, at the risk of provoking a quarrel, he attributed to the weakness of his personal position as a German-Jewish refugee. At that time he had only recently been naturalized and was very anxious not to become involved in any controversy that might seem to have antisemitic undertones. He also believed that in any dispute he would inevitably come off second best because Mellanby would support any action that Florey might take.

To those not involved, and after a long lapse of time, the episode may seem trivial. When the first paper on penicillin came to be published no individual credit for particular work was assigned to any of those concerned. But we cannot dismiss it lightly here; the matter was far from trivial to Chain, for it was one of several episodes that poisoned his relationship with both Florey and Heatley. Rightly or wrongly, it not only upset him very much at the time but there is abundant evidence that it rankled with him for the rest of his life. In 1979, only six months before he died, he was still anxious to vindicate himself[28] on this particular point. Florey was always equally firm about the truth of his own version; on more than one occasion he lamented to Heatley that the crucial conversation had not been recorded on tape, thus putting an end to the argument once and for all.

Whatever agreement there was between Florey and Chain was, of course, quite informal, as is normal in such circumstances; demarcation issues do not normally assume such importance among research workers as they do among, say, trade unionists. It is difficult, therefore, to see that any great impropriety was committed, whatever the circumstances. The undisputed facts are that it was Heatley who proposed exploring the possibility of purifying penicillin by back extraction; that it was he who, with Florey's approval, carried out the crucial experiment; and that it was this method that was used by Florey's team and later adopted as an essential part of commerical processes. Perhaps a fair conclusion is not that less credit should be given to Chain but more to Heatley.

The importance of the back-extraction method was twofold: it gave a more concentrated solution of penicillin, and it eliminated some associated impurities. The next important step was to attempt to prepare a stable solid preparation. This would be easier to store and handle, and, because it could be dispensed by weight, experimental work could be put on a firmer quantitative basis. But once again the instability of pencillin limited the experimental possibilities. Had it been as stable as common salt, for example, the water could simply have been boiled away, just as table salt is prepared from brine. Such exposure to heat would have destroyed the penicillin altogether, however. In Fleming's laboratory Ridley and Craddock (p. 67) resorted to the fact that at very low pressures water boils at a much lower temperature than normal; even so, a good deal of activity is lost and the end product is sticky and intractable. At Oxford, advantage was taken of a new method—freeze-drying—which had been developed in the meantime. It is based on the familiar observation that under suitable conditions ice will turn directly into water vapour without first liquefying; in freezing weather, for example, snow slowly disappears in sunshine without melting. During the 1930s this phenomenon had been utilized in Sweden for making dry preparations of sensitive biological fluids such as blood plasma and the semen used for artificial insemination in animal breeding. In effect the aqueous product to be dried is first frozen hard, usually by immersing it, in a globular flask, in a mixture of solid carbon dioxide and acetone. The contents of the flask are swirled gently during freezing so that the ice forms a thin film on the inside of the flask. The latter is then connected to a vacuum pump, which steadily pumps off the water as vapour. This process had two advantages. Firstly, the very low temperature eliminated the risk of destroying labile substances by heat. Secondly, the product was left as a fluffy porous powder which redissolves very easily. Today, of course, freeze-dried products—such as instant coffee— are so familiar as to excite no comment, but in 1939 the technique had not advanced beyond the laboratory. Although it was a Swedish development, Chain appears first to have heard about freeze-drying from its use by R. T. N. Greaves in Cambridge for drying blood serum. While the biological work depended on sterile solutions despensed by Heatley, the freeze-dried solid material was important for the chemical work of Chain and Abraham.

By a combination of back extraction and freeze-drying a stable soluble brown powder was produced early in 1940 which had an activity of about 5 units per g. Its exceptionally high antibacterial activity—a dilution of one part in several hundred thousand was lethal to a variety of test organisms—suggested that it must be fairly pure. It was already about twenty times as active as any sulphonamide. It later became clear that at this stage it was, in fact, only 0.3 per cent pure. Nevertheless, it provided manageable material that could be used for the biological experiments which were Florey's province. Unfortunately, these, too, were to be a source of friction with Chain.

Although based on two simple principles, the production of penicillin in this way was a very laborious process. By March 1940 Chain had managed to accumulate only one-tenth of a gram of this brown powder and on the morning of Tuesday 19 March he committed one-third of this to a single biological experiment. The work on pyocyanase had been proceeding in parallel and material prepared by Regine Schoental had been submitted for mouse toxicity tests to Dr. J. M. Barnes, working in the department, or to Professor Joseph Trueta. The latter was a distinguished Spanish surgeon, with much experience of war wounds during the recent Spanish Civil War, who had found a home in Florey's laboratory; in 1949 he was to become Nuffield Professor of Orthopaedic Surgery. These tests had been disappointing: all the pyocyanase preparations proved very toxic. When Chain brought along his sample of crude penicillin for testing—he had no licence to perform such experiments himself—the result was very different. An intravenous injection of 40 mg doses into two mice, made by Barnes with Trueta as an interested spectator, proved innocuous. According to Chain, this experiment was the turning-point in the whole penicillin project:

I remember very well the great surprise of both Trueta and Barnes when the injection . . . proved to be entirely innocuous. I consider this the most crucial observation in the whole development of the discovery of the chemotherapeutic properties of penicillin. . . . Why this simple extraction and toxicity experiment had not been done before it is difficult to say.[29]

Chain's claim is, however, open to question for the sample used was not assayed and thus the quantity of penicillin injected—which is crucial for an assessment of toxicity—is not known. All that this experiment could show was that the dose of that particular preparation was non-toxic.

Now it was Florey who felt that there had been a breach of their tacit agreement; an important biological experiment such as this should have been carried out by him and not by Barnes at Chain's instigation. Chain's justification for this was that over the past few weeks he had brought several samples to Florey, asking him to carry out toxicity tests, but the latter had put him off with the plea of pressure of other experimental work. Indeed, Chain is very specific about this, and again it remained a sore point for the rest of his life. According to him, his fourth request to Florey was made in the presence of Gordon Sanders, when they were engaged in extirpating lymph nodes from rats: Margaret Jennings was also there. Florey allegedly accused Chain of 'pestering' him with his samples, and Chain was annoyed. In 1979 he wrote:

After these rather humiliating remarks in front of others not involved in the project it became clear to me that Florey was not very interested in penicillin and I decided to ask my friend Barnes to do the first preliminary toxicity experiments. These were done during a morning and some one—I do not know who—certainly not myself, must have informed Florey about the outcome of the experiment for he turned up in my laboratory early in the afternoon saying 'I thought that we were going to do the penicillin work together'. I replied 'We were indeed, but as you remember on several occasions I could not get you to carry out the necessary tests as you were far too busy with other work'. He said 'This will be different in the future', and from that day he began to take a greater interest in the penicillin work. . . . [30]

It is difficult to know what to make of this episode, again indicative of personal friction at the very start of the project. Chain certainly seems to have given Florey a fair opportunity of making the toxicity test before going to Barnes, who was already doing similar tests for him in connection with pyocyanase. On the other hand, it is easy to see that Florey—preoccupied with running a large department needing reorganization to put it on a wartime footing and committed also to other lines of research—could not accord penicillin the high priority it had with Chain, who had no other responsibilities. Nevertheless, Chain claimed that it convinced him that Florey was not seriously interested in penicillin and it undoubtedly coloured his future relationship with Florey. The fact that Florey frequently discussed penicillin with Heatley at this time is at variance with the view that he was not interested.[31]

The lymph node extirpation experiments to which Chain referred were in fact part of a major project which had long engaged Florey's attention. These nodes were known to be the main centres of activity in the general lymphatic system, and appeared to have two main functions. Firstly, they generated lymphocytes, which constitute about one-fifth of the white cells in the blood. They were remarkable in seeming to have a very brief lifespan of no more than a few hours. Secondly, they appeared to play an important part in the body's natural defences against infection. Thus, bacteria injected into the lymphatic system became trapped in the nodes; so, too, do stray cells from cancerous growths, which may there become the source of secondaries. In the 1930s it was evident that the role of the lymphatic system was very important but remarkably little was known about it. Such a major problem in pathology would have a natural appeal for Florey and he had embarked on a serious investigation of it while still at Sheffield. There his main collaborator had been Dr. Beatrice Pullinger, who was already interested in the histology of lymph nodes and cancer cells and had acquired considerable skill in the experimental techniques involved. As we have noted (p. 47) she had shortly joined him in Oxford to continue the work.

Florey's approach had been novel and energetic. Briefly, he sought to extirpate all the lymph nodes in experimental animals and then observe the effects. The novelty did not lie in this—for it was a recognized method for determining the function of a variety of organs—but in applying it to so complex a system as the lymphatic system. It involved the injection of the system with dye to reveal the position of the nodes and then their systematic excision. The method was laborious and demanded long hours of delicate surgical work. Such conditions would be no deterrent to Florey, who regarded long hours of patient work as an essential ingredient for success in research. Sanders, with a natural gift for fine manipulative work, was originally brought in to master this new technique and did much of the work. In the event, the results were inconclusive, because the effects of removal of the nodes were confused by the traumatic effects of the surgery.

But this was not Florey's only string to this particular bow. From his early days at Oxford under Sherrington he had been interested in the microcirculation of the blood: that is to say, its movement in fine capillary vessels. Initially this involved no more than observing under the microscope the flow of blood in the capillaries in the thin web of a frog's foot, but he had gone on to make transparent windows to enable him to observe blood flow in the cerebral cortex under the highest powers of the microscope. In the 1920s this kind of technique had been developed as the Sandison-Clark ear-chamber, which consisted essentially of two glass (later perspex) discs applied to the rabbit's ear in such a way that vascularized tissue grows between them. The rabbit suffers no pain or inconvenience, and blood flow in the capillaries can be observed, and if necessary photographed, for long periods and the effects of various stimuli noted.

Misgivings about the practicality of the node extirpation experiments led Dr. Pullinger to turn her attention to the possibilities of the ear-chamber, especially for observation of the lymphocytes, whose nature and function was obscure. Although the principle was simple, the device was delicate and its construction difficult; it was in such circumstances that the value of the departmental workshop under Bush became particularly apparent. Sanders' ingenuity, too, made an important contribution to improvements in the device. Although not losing faith in extirpation, Florey himself became interested and this led to two important publications in 1939, involving also the American Rhodes Scholar, Robert Ebert.[32] Other research workers in the department were also involved in this project—Peter Medawar, Jean Taylor (who later became Mrs. Medawar), and J. M. Barnes. In all, Florey was directing the research work of a team of eight. Direction in this context meant exactly that, as Dr. Pullinger has made clear:

> Those on the staff who had their own personal grants were free to pursue their own investigations. Those of us who were dependent on, or sponsored by, Florey were not given the smallest corner of freedom to follow ideas of our own, unrelated to what we were doing with him.[33]

That Chain should have found it difficult to get his toxicity test done quickly is thus not altogether surprising. Nor is it surprising that Florey, informed of the result, should at once have seen its possible significance and taken a greater interest.

From this point rapid progress was in fact made. Florey went immediately to see J. H. Burn, Professor of Pharmacology. The reason was that so little penicillin was then available that a mouse had to be used and the solution had to be injected into the vein in its tail (Plate 5). This was a technique with which Florey was not familiar and he wanted Burn to demonstrate it to him. In retrospect, Burn appears[34] to have assumed that what he injected was a solution of penicillin but Kent has cast doubt on this.[35] Within his experience, Florey always wanted to carry out personally the first of any crucial tests; he never minded who carried out subsequent ones. It may well have been, therefore, that what Florey gave Burn was simply some bland solution; this would not conflict with Burn's comment that 'they did not explain what it was or why they wanted it done'.[36] Having learnt the trick of tail-vein injection, Florey would then have carried out a similar experiment in his own laboratory. However, it was a month before enough material could be accumulated for the purpose. The result was the same: the mouse showed no symptoms of distress. Nevertheless, the same doubt persisted: there was at that stage no means of telling, in absolute terms, what quantity of penicillin had been injected.

Whatever Chain may have thought of Florey's earlier attitude, he had no cause for complaint about the flurry of activity that immediately followed. The next highly significant experiment was to investigate the urine of a mouse injected with a solution of Heatley's brown powder. After a short time it was apparent that the urine had become dark brown, indicating that the pigment causing the coloration had passed unchanged through the animal's system. Far more dramatically, an assay of the urine by Heatley's method showed high penicillin activity. Thus three major points had quickly been established. Firstly, penicillin had a much higher activity against a range of pathogenic bacteria than any known sulphonamide. Secondly, it had no immediate toxic effects. Thirdly, when injected in the blood stream it was not inactivated but was excreted unchanged in the urine. Taken together, these results gave a strong presumption—though by no means proof—that penicillin could be a very powerful chemotherapeutic agent of a completely novel character. Much more remained to be done, however, before this could be argued with sufficient conviction to justify publication of the results.

The first toxicity test was not conclusive; the mouse showed no obvious reaction but there might nevertheless have been hidden effects that could militate against the clinical use of penicillin, especially if, as would be usual in chemotherapy, it was to be used over a period. Two important discoveries were quickly made. Firstly, it was shown by Margaret Jennings that penicillin had no apparent effect on leucocytes, the white blood cells that engulf and destroy invading bacteria; it would, therefore, reinforce rather than substitute for the body's natural resources. Medawar showed that penicillin did not affect the growth of tissue cultures, encouraging the hope that living cells generally would not be damaged by it. With new drugs there is always the possibility that while generally non-toxic they will damage cells of a particular organ, such as the liver. In the kinds of dose that would be appropriate for chemotherapy animal experiments showed no significant effect on blood-pressure, heart-beat, or respiration. Additionally, Margaret Jennings showed that, in contrast to the sulphonamides, penicillin is not inactivated by pus.

Florey himself, in collaboration with Margaret Jennings, immediately started an intensive investigation of factors involved in the possible use of penicillin in chemotherapy. Here, the ultimate objective would be to maintain a sufficiently high concentration of penicillin in the blood for long enough for all the invading bacteria to be destroyed; if a residue were left behind after penicillin administration was stopped the infection could simply burst out again. In a series of animal experiments it was quickly established that this was in fact a real problem: after injection, blood levels fell quite rapidly and could be maintained only by repeated topping up. As Florey used to put it, it was like trying to fill a bath with the plug out. While some loss could possibly be attributed to decomposition of penicillin in the blood—not unlikely in view of its known instability—it was clear from assays, set up by Heatley, that most of it was due to excretion unchanged in the urine. Attempts to administer penicillin by mouth—in the hope that it would be absorbed into the blood through the wall of the stomach and intestine—were not successful, apparently because of its sensitivity to the acid normally present in the stomach. There was, however, evidence of absorption from the duodenum if penicillin was administered by a tube bypassing the stomach.

Concurrently, A. D. Gardner and Jean Orr-Ewing were making a thorough survey of the principal pathogenic bacteria and their sensitivity to penicillin. Hitherto, information on this important point had been of a rather general nature. They confirmed the particularly high sensitivity of streptococci and staphylococci. As these are the commonest sources of sepsis in war wounds this was of very particular significance at that time: the so-called Cold War had ended with the invasion of Norway and Denmark on 9 April and the fall of France on 22 June. The gas gangrene organism (*Clostridium welchii*), another serious source of wound infection, was also sensitive; it was of particular interest because it was an anaerobe—that is, an organism that grows in the absence of oxygen. Among other bacteria sensitive enough to seem open to successful chemotherapy were those responsible for pneumonia, meningitis, diphtheria, and gonorrhoea. Mistakenly, it was supposed that syphilis was not sensitive and it was left to the Americans (p. 181) to demonstrate the high efficiency of penicillin in treating this form of venereal disease. It became clear, however, that even penicillin could not be an all-powerful 'magic bullet'; the bacillus of tuberculosis seemed entirely resistant to it, and the organisms causing enteric fevers such as typhoid were at best only marginally sensitive.

By this time, sufficient evidence had accumulated to indicate that penicillin could prove highly effective in treating a wide range of pathogenic infections of major medical importance. However, all this remained supposition until there was incontrovertible experimental evidence that bacterial infections could be controlled in laboratory animals and then in man.

The crucial experiment was carried out on Saturday 25 May 1940, as the German armies swept through northern France. On the morning of that day Florey, assisted by Kent, injected eight mice with a virulent strain of streptococci supplied by Gardner. Four mice were set aside as controls. The others were treated with penicillin: two with a single dose of 10 mg of Heatley's brown powder in solution and two with five 5 mg doses given at 2-hourly intervals. After that there was nothing to do but wait and see. Kent stayed until the early evening, when Heatley arrived to help Florey keep watch. By then the control animals were showing evident signs of distress; by the time Heatley finally left in the early hours of Sunday morning all were dead. The next morning, when Florey, Heatley, and Chain all came into the laboratory a dramatic outcome was apparent. Three of the treated mice were as lively as usual: the fourth was what Florey was apt to call 'a little *piano*', and in fact it died two days later. The term *pianissimo* he applied to mice *in extremis*.

The statistical odds against such an outcome being a matter of chance were enormous but Florey immediately embarked on more tests. That very Sunday morning he telephoned Margaret Jennings and summoned her to the laboratory: she recalls his saying 'It looks like a miracle'. (Years later she mentioned this to Dr. Sherwood Taylor, Director of the Science Museum and a staunch Catholic, who remarked: 'How surprised he would have been if it had been one!'). Then and there more trials were planned, using varying doses of penicillin, and carried out on the following Monday and Tuesday. Although the results cast no doubt on the original conclusions, the mortality among the treated animals was such as to indicate that careful control of dosage was essential for success and that more extensive trials would be necessary to work out a satisfactory regimen. In particular, it was evident that to prevent relapse treatment needed to be continued for a time after apparent recovery.

The immediate difficulty in stepping-up the scale of animal experiments was the supply of penicillin, yields of which were tiny. Here Heatley's inventive genius proved invaluable. Among the different kinds of culture vessel he pressed into service were ordinary bedpans—perhaps not altogether surprising in view of the medical milieu in which he worked. These proved so successful that basically similar vessels were later specially made for them by a firm in Burslem. This, however, lay six months in the future and for the moment whatever vessels came to hand had to be used. One way and another sufficient penicillin became available to carry out more extensive trials—though still only with mice—but the supply of raw material was still the limiting factor. That the work progressed as quickly as it did owes much to the devotion and resource of Heatley, who was almost entirely responsible for the production and extraction of penicillin for chemical and clinical experiments until June 1941, when he accompanied Florey on a visit to North America (see Chapter IV).

By this time sufficient progress had been made to justify publication and on 24 August 1940 the first paper from Oxford on penicillin appeared in the *Lancet*. This was no doubt chosen in preference to, say, the *British Journal of Experimental Pathology* because as a weekly it could offer much speedier publication. There were seven joint authors, listed alphabetically—Chain, Florey, Gardner, Heatley, Jennings, Orr-Ewing, and Sanders. It described therapeutic tests using three specific organisms— *Strep. pyogenes, Staph. aureus,* and *Clostridium septique.* Including the controls, some 300 mice were involved. In the streptococcus experiment 25 out of 25 control animals died, whereas 24 out of 25 animals treated with penicillin survived. With the staphylococci 24 out of 24 controls died and 21 out of 24 treated mice survived. Finally, with *Cl. septique*—where rather larger doses were used—24 out of 24 controls died and 21 out of 24 treated animals lived.

The conclusions are clear cut, and show that penicillin is active in vivo against at least three of the organisms inhibited in vitro. It would seem a reasonable hope that all organisms inhibited in high dilution in vitro will be found to be dealt with in vivo. Penicillin does not appear to be related to any chemotherapeutic substance at present in use and is particularly remarkable for its activity against the anaerobic organisms associated with gas gangrene.[36]

This publication had two immediate consequences. Following normal practice Florey had acknowledged the financial support he had had from the Rockefeller Foundation and the Medical

Research Council, in that order. Mellanby, in ignorance of the size of the grant from Rockefeller, felt that the MRC had been slighted. When Florey informed him of the facts Mellanby was in no way mollified. The penicillin work, he maintained, was 'as pure a piece of medical research as can be imagined'. Florey, he implied, had been deceitful in applying to the Natural Sciences Division of Rockefeller and he supposed that the Medical Research Division—for contact with whom he was the proper intermediary— would be aggrieved.

The second consequence was the appearance of Fleming in Oxford. According to Chain this was 'The day after he had read our first publication on penicillin as a chemotherapeutic agent which was published in June 1940'.[37] Here, as on some other points, Chain's memory is somewhat at fault. The paper in the *Lancet* appeared on 24 August and it was a week later (2 September) that Fleming turned up, having telephoned on the previous day. Florey and Chain showed him round the department but he spent most of his time with Heatley: he returned to London with a small sample of their precious brown powder. Later, in mid-November, Fleming sent eight cultures of *Penicillium notatum* which, he claimed, produced relatively little pigment. In fact, they produced plenty of pigment. Several routine batches were made up from one of these strains, but to no advantage.

The experiments published in the *Lancet* were a turning-point in the history of penicillin. The possibility of a momentous advance in medicine had been convincingly demonstrated but proof positive depended on clinical trials with human patients. This immediately raised an urgent question of supply; as Florey wryly remarked on that dramatic Sunday morning, a man weighs 3000 times as much as a mouse! His next immediate objective was to obtain enough penicillin to permit rigorous clinical trials with human patients. This demanded production facilities on quite a different scale from those he had.

Initially he had high hopes that the *Lancet* paper would stimulate interest in some of the chemical and drug companies who had facilities for working on the kind of scale necessary, but in this he was disappointed. The reasons for this were complex, and we will consider them later, but so far as Britain was concerned a major factor was that the war had entered a new phase. Continental Europe had fallen to the Nazis and for the moment Britain stood alone: in mid-August the Battle of Britain gained her a temporary respite but on 23 August the Blitz on London began, a prelude to heavy air raids on a number of other industrial centres. The war at sea was intensified: some 3½ million tonnes of British and Allied shipping was lost in 1940 alone. Industry was in no state or mood to turn its attention to what many would have seen as a speculative venture demanding new techniques and skills.

To Florey, whose faith was never shaken, it became clear that outside help would be forthcoming only if he took the initiative and actively sought it. There thus began a new phase in which work on penicillin and its production was increasingly undertaken outside the Sir William Dunn School of Pathology in Oxford and eventually grew into a huge international enterprise.

4

THE AMERICAN VENTURE

Florey's immediate needs in the early summer of 1940 were epitomized in his comment that a man weighs 3000 times as much as a mouse. The carefully controlled experiments published in the *Lancet* in August, and others performed under rather less rigorous conditions, gave very good grounds for hoping that in penicillin a totally new kind of chemotherapeutic agent had been found that outclassed even the sulphonamides, themselves still regarded as revolutionary. Nevertheless, it was impossible to equate results obtained in mice with those obtainable in man. The physiological processes of all mammals are broadly similar, but the existence of specific differences was well known. For example, the human body might produce enzymes that destroy penicillin: the existence of such enzymes had already been discovered in the course of the mould culture work. Again, there was the possibility that in man penicillin might evoke toxic effects, long or short term, that would preclude or seriously limit its clinical use. Thus it was established at an early date that rabbits and cats differed markedly in their absorption and excretion of penicillin. There was only one certain way of resolving these doubts: to prepare sufficient penicillin for adequate clinical trials. What adequate means in this context is not easily defined, but looking ahead a little we may note that when the Oxford team published their first clinical observations in the *Lancet* in August 1941, they described ten cases: even on the strength of these they were guarded and ready to say no more than that:

Enough evidence, we consider, has now been assembled to show that penicillin is a new and effective type of chemotherapeutic agent, and possesses some properties unknown in any antibacterial substance hitherto described.[1]

Not until March 1943, when Howard and Ethel jointly published in the *Lancet* a description of the treatment of nearly 200 cases could proof positive be claimed by them.

To go back to the situation as it existed in Oxford when the first successful mouse protection experiments were carried out, it had been shown that to protect a mouse 10 mg was barely sufficient. An equivalent dose for a human would be 30 g, for which at least 100 litres of the crude culture fluid would have to be set up. The weekly harvest, though increasing, was at that time probably less than 10 litres. On the basis that a satisfactory clinical trial would involve the treatment of, at the very least, a couple of dozen patients it seemed likely that it would take at least two years to prepare sufficient material with the unaided resources of the Sir William Dunn School of Pathology.

Such calculations are necessarily tentative and subject to changing circumstances: for example, the efficiency of the production and extraction process might be improved or new strains of the mould might be found which produced substantially higher yields of penicillin. Nevertheless, they were the sort of estimate on which Florey had to base his future strategy after the dramatic success of the first of the mouse protection experiments at the end of May 1940. From that moment his goal was to accumulate as quickly as possible sufficient material for a rigorous clinical trial. Briefly, three options were open to him. Firstly, he could further stretch the resources of his own laboratory and at least have a source of supply, however meagre, under his own control. Secondly, he could enlist outside help in brewing penicillin and process it himself. Thirdly, he might find some suitably equipped chemical manufacturer with sufficient faith in the prospects of penicillin to set up a pilot plant to prepare it and supply it to him for clinical evaluation. It must be emphasized that at this stage he visualized collaboration with industry as no more than a small-scale exercise to enable him to take his own research through the next crucial stage. There was no thought in his mind, at this stage, of seeking to promote large-scale industrial production. Despite his growing enthusiasm and confidence, the first person he had to satisfy that penicillin was as good as it appeared to be was himself. If for no other reason, professional caution would have held him back. He was well aware of the number of reputations which had been damaged, sometimes fatally, by premature claims which could not subsequently be fulfilled; among them was that of Georges Dreyer, his immediate predecessor at Oxford (p. 46).

In the event, Florey pursued all three possibilities simultaneously, but for convenience it is easier to consider separately what we may term the domestic and the external sources of supply.

On the domestic front, Florey was exceedingly fortunate in having in Heatley a man who was not only a first-rate scientist in his own field but possessed also a great manipulative ingenuity and skill. Under his guidance, a penicillin process plant was improvised which was capable of processing relatively large batches of crude penicillin broth, and it is to the production of the latter that we must first turn our attention.

As we have noted, the early batches of penicillin were prepared in whatever vessels came to hand. Thus Heatley's diary for 3 June 1940 records that he tried to collect biscuit tins from grocers in the city; the following day he obtained 100 from Huntley and Palmer's biscuit factory in Reading. In the latter part of 1940 the work was simplified by the adoption of standard culture vessels. A full description of these was given in the August 1941 paper in the *Lancet* but they were in use at the very end of 1940; the first were seeded over Christmas itself, a clear indication of the enthusiasm and sense of urgency with which all were now infected. They were made of pottery, glazed only on the inside, partly to save cost and partly to make them less slippery to handle. They were rectangular in shape (approximately 9 " × 11 ", 22.5 × 27.5 cm) and 2½ " (6 cm) deep; at one corner was a spout for filling, seeding, and removing the active fluid when fermentation was complete. A feature of this design was that they stacked close together, which was important when space was at a premium, especially in the sterilizer. They were made by J. Macintyre and Company of Burslem, who also made the porcelain assay cylinders. The initial order was for 150, at about 40p (8 shillings) each. By this time the Medical Research Council had realized that something potentially very important was afoot and paid for the new vessels. In use they were laid flat on shelves in the incubation room, the converted animal operating theatre, maintained at a constant 24°C. It was with these vessels that an attempt was made to increase production by introducing fresh medium under the floating mould felt when the first had been harvested (p. 100), but contamination became so frequent that this eventually had to be abandoned. It was hoped that when this new system was working, laboratory production would run at about 500 litres a week, though probably this was never quite attained.

The basic principles of extraction have already been described. First, the filtered medium was cooled, made slightly acid, and extracted within a few seconds with amyl acetate—replacing ether, at Chain's suggestion—to minimize decomposition. In Heatley's original experiment to test the feasibility of this the acidified medium had been shaken with solvent in a separating funnel, but for the relatively large quantities now involved this was not satisfactory and the funnels were replaced by 1-gallon (4.5-litre) screw-capped jars. The process was uncomfortably carried out in a cold-store in the basement, the low temperature diminishing the rate of inactivation of penicillin. Later, a counter-current process was used (Plate 6). In this, the penicillin-containing culture medium was sprayed into an ascending column of amyl acetate; the volumes were so arranged that something like a ten-fold reduction in volume was achieved in this stage. The amyl acetate solution was then back-extracted into very slightly alkaline water, a further halving of volume being achieved. The aqueous extract was then shaken with activated charcoal—similar to that then being used in civilian gasmasks—to decolorize it as far as possible, and the filtered solution was then back-extracted yet again, this time into ether. The ethereal solution was finally processed by chromatographic absorption on alumina, a method first used by Abraham in 1940, despite scepticism by Chain. The section of the alumina column containing most of the penicillin (p. 101) was then separated and washed with an aqueous solution. Finally, this solution was back-extracted yet again into ether and back into water. This final aqueous solution showed none of the great instability which had deterred the original investigators, though it still needed to be treated with respect. Much of the instability reported earlier was probably simple bacterial destruction. If stored in an ice-chest it lost no activity even after three months. If freeze-dried (normally as the barium salt of penicillin if required for chemical work) it kept almost indefinitely at room temperature provided all access of water was prevented; it could conveniently be stored in a standard laboratory dessicator.

The above is a somewhat oversimplified account of the process. Thus practical problems arose through the formation of troublesome emulsions between solvent and water. In practice, there was an accumulation of low-activity fractions, which were carefully collected and fed back into the system. Even so, some loss occurred at every stage and assays indicated that no more than one-third of the penicillin originally present in the crude culture medium was finally recovered.

The construction of Heatley's original solvent-extraction plant —used until November 1941—itself showed much ingenuity, and it is sad that no part of it has survived. Historically, it would rank with, for example, Roentgen's original X-ray tube or Lister's first air-sterilization plant designed to effect asepsis in the operating theatre. This original plant was followed by another built by Sanders, with Kent's help, in the animal house post-mortem room. At the time of its construction, many materials were in short supply because of the war, and standard items of dairy equipment, such as churns and milk-coolers had to be used instead. Large volumes of flammable amyl acetate were required and ether, apart from its soporific effect, is a dangerous explosive hazard. Certainly, the plant would fall far short of modern health and safety regulations and, in retrospect, it is perhaps surprising that no serious mishap occurred. The working conditions were unpleasant, and not improved by the need to wear overgowns, caps, and masks to reduce the risk of contaminations. The technicians concerned were all subjected to regular blood tests. By its nature, the work was what economists call labour-intensive and Florey successfully applied to the Medical Research Council for more technicians; in the end he had six girls working on the project under George Glister as senior penicillin technician. In the spring of 1942 the routine tests showed anaemia in Glister and five of his girls. Florey immediately took them off the extraction work and he and Kent worked the process between them. On 13 April he wrote to Heatley telling him of this and asked him to pass the information on to Merck (p. 143) in America.

Chain was not directly concerned with the construction and operation of this plant but in later life he passed some adverse comment on it:

I have always felt (and said) that a little less improvisation and more professionalism would have profited our work. For instance, counter-current extraction was the standard procedure in chemical industry for a process like the one we used for penicillin production, and if we had turned to industry for a commercial centrifugal machine when I asked for it, very soon after we began the extraction process we would have fared much better, and would have saved time. It took a couple of years before I could persuade Florey to buy a Sharpless [sic] milk separator centrifuge which eventually was installed by Sanders.[2]

No doubt there was some truth in this, but in fact Chain himself had no chemical engineering qualifications. There had, in fact, been a Sharples centrifuge in the laboratory since the mid-1930s, but Heatley found it of little value. In any case, Chain's reference to 'a couple of years' is an exaggeration, as Sanders' plant was constructed between April and July 1942. It was unfortunate that Oxford University then had no department of chemical engineering from which advice might have been sought—nor, surprisingly, has it one to this day.

As we now know, the therapeutic material being obtained at this stage was no more than 2 or 3 per cent pure. Florey and his colleagues assumed the purity to be a great deal higher—largely but illogically on the strength of its already extraordinarily high antibacterial activity—but they were well aware that impurities were still present. In particular, some samples contained so-called pyrogens, substances liable to produce an acute febrile reaction on injection. The consistent elimination of these required much care in the later stages of the extraction process.

While the Oxford workers were thus laboriously accumulating sufficient penicillin for Florey to carry out his first trial with a human patient (in February 1941) he had not neglected the possibility of enlisting outside aid to enable him to attain his immediate objective more quickly. His first approach was to the Wellcome Foundation, established in 1924 by the American medical and scientific philanthropist Sir Henry Wellcome, who had made a large fortune through his wide interests in the pharmaceutical industry. On his death he left most of his wealth to the promotion of scientific research and education, to be administered by the Wellcome Trust. The contact seems to have been made by Sir Henry Dale, the distinguished Cambridge physiologist who was shortly to become (1940-45) President of the Royal Society. He and a member of the Burroughs Wellcome staff spent two days with Florey in March 1941. Dale was then Director of the National Institute for Medical Research, but he had close contacts with Wellcome. From 1904 to 1914 he had been Director of the Wellcome Physiological Research Laboratories at Beckenham and when the Wellcome Trust was set up in 1936 he was appointed its first Chairman.

In mid-July 1940 Dr. J. W. Trevan, then Director at Beckenham, visited Florey in Oxford with his chief biochemist and expressed some interest. Some experimental work was done at Beckenham, but no significant results were achieved. At that time, Wellcome were heavily engaged in the manufacture of a variety of biological products essential for the war effort, notably vaccines, antitoxins, and blood plasma. Two years later, however, the situation had changed and they were able to collaborate.

At that stage of the war there appeared a very real possibility that Hitler might succeed in his threat to invade Britain and immediate needs necessarily took precedence over new ventures. It is not very surprising, therefore, that nothing substantial came of the Wellcome contact at that particular time. It was not wholly fruitless, however, for early in 1941 Wellcome approached the firm of Kemball, Bishop Ltd., of the Crown Chemical Works at Bromley-by-Bow, with the proposal that they should undertake large-scale production of penicillin brew, to be processed at Oxford. As they were thinking in terms of some 10 000 gallons (45 000 litres)—nearly six months output for Oxford—this would have been an exceptionally welcome accretion to the supply of raw material. At that time, however, it was not to be, for Kemball, Bishop were situated in one of the worst devastated parts of the East End of London and a new commitment of this kind was impossible. Later, however, when the situation was easier they did undertake the task and became important collaborators. It is, therefore, timely to say something about the firm and its background at this stage.

Kemball, Bishop were one of the relatively few firms in Britain in the fermentation industry. Since 1927 they had been associated with the American firm of Pfizer.[3] The latter were particularly concerned with the manufacture of citric and gluconic acids by fermentation with *Aspergillus niger* and *Acetobacter suboxydans* respectively. Curiously enough, one of Pfizer's early problems in citric acid fermentation was contamination with *Penicillium* moulds. The manufacture of citric acid by mould fermentation was a response to an attempt by the Italian government to monopolize sales in Europe of acid made from citrus fruit. Kemball, Bishop made citric acid for the European market and Pfizer shipped lime citrate to them. In 1935 a closer relationship was established when the two firms collaborated in building a new citric acid fermentation unit in London. Among British firms Kemball, Bishop thus had exceptional experience in carrying out large-scale fermentations of just the kind in which Florey was interested.

Kemball, Bishop once again exemplifies the curious way in which different aspects of the penicillin pattern interlock. Professor Harold Raistrick, as an expert on moulds, reappears in a different capacity—as consultant to Kemball, Bishop and, later, to Pfizers Ltd., who acquired them in 1958 and established themselves as manufacturers of pharmaceuticals, including penicillin, in a new works at Sandwich. In the United States, Pfizer—with whom Florey later established independent contact—became one of the earliest and biggest penicillin manufacturers. Yet another link was forged through Sir Robert Robinson, Florey's neighbour in the science area at Oxford. He, too, was a consultant to Kemball, Bishop and took a leading part in later research which established the chemical constitution of penicillin.

For the moment, however, we must go back on our tracks, for effective collaboration with Kemball, Bishop did not begin until early 1942, and in the meantime there had been other important developments. Not the least of these had been in the Florey's family life. Under the threat of invasion, a number of academic families in Oxford had decided to send their children to Canada for safety. After much heartsearching, they decided that Paquita and Charles should join the party which left for Montreal in July 1940. A factor which influenced them was that Florey's old friend John Fulton and his wife—who had no children of their own—offered to make a home for them in New Haven, Connecticut. As for all families in such a situation, the separation was traumatic and Paquita, then almost 11 years of age, seems to have felt it acutely. In the event, the separation was shorter than for some of the other children, because Florey was able to visit them in America in 1941 and bring them back in 1944 on his way home from a long visit to Australia. Any resentment they may have had at thus being summarily sent away, as it might have seemed to them, would scarcely have been mitigated by the fate of Oxford in the meantime. The dangers they had been sent away to avoid never materialized: there was no invasion, not even a single air-raid. The Oxford they came back to was identical with the one they had left but this was, of course, not foreseeable when they went away. In that summer Florey made plans to destroy everything relating to penicillin should the Germans arrive. The only exception was the mould itself; this he and Heatley and some others smeared on their clothes, from which it could be readily subcultured should they themselves escape.

In 1941 the possibility of collaboration with Kemball, Bishop proved shortlived, and two other industrial contacts had no immediate results. In June representatives of ICI, to whom also Robinson was a consultant, visited Oxford to discuss possible collaboration but the speculative nature of the venture, as it then appeared to them, and the great pressure of immediate wartime needs, precluded any constructive arrangement being made. Nevertheless ICI, like Kemball, Bishop, showed renewed interest later and produced valuable quantities of clinical material for use at Oxford. Interest by Boots, too, proved transitory at that time.

These successive disappointments persuaded Florey that no active support would be forthcoming from British industry at that time and his thoughts turned to the possibilities of North America. There the situation was very different. The United States was not then at war—the attack on Pearl Harbor did not take place until December 1941—and there were pharmaceutical firms (such as Pfizer) well able to produce penicillin in the quanitities he required if they were so minded. Although Canada was already involved, she was far from the scene of action and her industry not under the severe duress of British industry.

Having in mind the circumstances, and Florey's familiarity with the American scene, it would be surprising rather than otherwise if the possibility of American collaboration should not have occurred to him. Again, however, Chain strikes a discordant note. According to him:

. . . it was I who suggested to Florey insistently and repeatedly, as early as 1940, that the only possibility to get the production of penicillin going on an industrial scale was to try to persuade some American firm to get interested in such a project. He seemed to listen with interest though he provided plenty of counter-arguments why such initiative need not be necessarily successful.[4]

Chain does not enlarge on the nature of these counter-arguments, but several come readily to mind. First and foremost, of course, was the fact the proof of penicillin's chemotherapeutic value was yet to be established: what worked for mice might not work for men. Secondly, the mould was capricious: yields of penicillin were variable and sometimes non-existent. Thirdly, yields were at best miniscule: of the carbon present in the culture medium, less than 0.0001 per cent was incorporated into penicillin molecules. Operators of industrial fermentation processes were accustomed to think in thousands of tonnes; in the United States, for example, Pfizer made more than 6000 tonnes of citric acid in 1938. Finally, there was the possibility of synthesis. If penicillin could be isolated and its chemical constitution established, it might then be made synthetically without recourse to the mould at all. In that case, investment in large-scale fermentation and extraction plant for penicillin might be wiped out overnight. There were plenty of precedents for such an eventuality; thus the synthesis of alizarin and indigo respectively in the latter half of the nineteenth century had effectively destroyed the European madder growers and the Indian indigo growers.

Florey is quite explicit about his views on the likely reactions of industry at that stage:

. . . it was clearly realized that unless results could be obtained in man as striking as those in the animals experiments, it was highly improbable that any firm would embark on production on a sufficiently large scale.[5]

That the two men should have viewed the prospects so differently is scarcely surprising. For Chain, with his industrial chemical background and enthusiastic optimism it must have seemed surprising if American industry, without the wartime constraints operative in Britain, did not leap at so attractive a proposition. Florey, with his matter-of-fact approach and understanding of human reactions in practical affairs, could see the other side of the coin. Nevertheless, despite their differing degrees of optimism, it became clear that if penicillin was to be obtained quickly and in sufficient quantity to organize convincing clinical trials, the American chemical industry was the only real hope. On 14 April an opportunity arose to make such an approach. Warren Weaver, who had provided such timely aid through the Rockefeller Foundation in 1939, was visiting England from New York and Florey discussed the matter with him. The very satisfactory outcome was that the Rockefeller Foundation offered to fund a three-month visit to the United States by Florey and one of his colleagues.

In ordinary times such an offer could have been accepted without reservation, but those were not ordinary times. Travel in and out of Britain was uncertain and hazardous and high priority was essential to get the necessary clearance. For a start, Florey immediately went to see Mellanby, who shortly wrote to say that he fully concurred that this was the best course.[6] The precise wording of Mellanby's letter is significant, for it specifically mentions Heatley as his companion on the trip; Florey must, therefore, very quickly have made up his mind that he was the most suitable person.

The intervening waiting time was not wasted. Production and extraction had gone on continuously in the laboratory and enough penicillin collected for a limited number of clinical trials to be conducted. Bearing in mind the unfavourable circumstances the results were very encouraging. The unfavourable circumstances lay mainly in the fact that as a drug whose safety was still suspect general systemic administration of penicillin was reserved for desperate cases. Additionally, the scarcity of penicillin demanded that the quantities administered (by intravenous drip) were kept as low as was thought prudent; larger doses for longer periods might well have produced different results. Because of their small size, children were chosen for treatment when possible. Out of five cases of septicaemia two died and three survived; in the case of one death post-mortem examination showed that the infection had been subdued and death resulted from a cerebral aneurysm— the infection had been controlled. The first death, of a 43-year-old policeman, whose treatment began on 12 February, was particularly tragic. Virtually moribund from combined streptococcal and straphylococcal infection, he showed a striking improvement after receiving 4 g or penicillin in five days—then the supply of penicillin was exhausted, despite the drastic expedient of taking the patient's urine back to the Sir William Dunn School of Pathology to extract the excreted penicillin from it. The patient relapsed and died. However, in a sixth case, a severe urinary infection in a six-month-old boy was cured by penicillin orally administered. Finally, four infected eyes were cured by local application.

These results could certainly be described as promising, but Florey was content to claim no more than that:

During the course of some therapeutic trials in human infections it has proved possible to secure and maintain a bacteriostatic concentration of penicillin in the blood without causing any toxic symptoms.[7]

Nevertheless, they gave him some important confirmatory evidence to put before possible supporters in America. They were contained in a long paper in the *Lancet* which additionally described in considerable detail the way in which the mould was grown and harvested at Oxford and the penicillin extracted from it. Historically, this is a matter of some consequence. When the full importance of penicillin was finally recognized, and its production became a major wartime project, all further chemical publication was banned and the whole project became top secret. It is interesting to reflect that, had they been so minded, any rivals could go a long way on the road to producing their own penicillin on the strength of this paper alone. At that time there was, of course, no direct transmission of scientific (or any other) publications to enemy countries, but copies of the *Lancet* would have been available to Germany through Switzerland or Sweden at least up to 1943. As we shall see later, the Swiss pharmaceutical firm CIBA as early as 1942 did in fact instigate research at the Swiss Federal Institute of Technology, largely on the basis of this very paper in the *Lancet*. Through Switzerland, Florey learned of German interest in the spring of 1941 and he urged Mellanby,[8] unsuccessfully, to try to ensure that no cultures of *Penicillium notatum* reached enemy hands from Britain.

The authors of the second paper in the *Lancet* were different from those of the first. The names of Sanders and Jean Orr-Ewing did not appear, as they had not been involved in its preparation, but those of E. P. Abraham and C. M. Fletcher were added. The former—who had joined Chain to work on the chemical and biochemical aspects—needs no introduction at this stage, but Fletcher appears for the first time. He was the son of Sir Walter Morley Fletcher, Mellanby's predecessor as Secretary of the Medical Research Council, and had been recommended to Florey by L J. Witts, then Nuffield Professor of Medicine at Oxford, as a very suitable person to collaborate with him on any clinical trials that were made. It proved an admirable choice and Fletcher's quality is indicated by his later career: he went on to be Physician to Hammersmith Hospital and Professor of Clinical Epidemiology at the Royal Postgraduate Medical School in London. To many, no doubt, he will be better known through his association with such highly successful medical television programmes as 'Your Life in Their Hands' and 'Television Doctor'.

In the spring of 1941 Florey thus had plenty on his hands, and it must therefore have been a particular satisfaction to him to learn in March that he had been elected a Fellow of the Royal Society. Of this august body we shall have much to say later, for Florey later became its President—the highest office open to a British scientist. For the moment we will content ourselves with observing that it is a conservative body, not given to bestowing its accolade until the candidate's contribution to research has been firmly established. It is clear, therefore, that his penicillin work had little, if anything, to do with his election, for at that time he had published only the one short paper on it in the *Lancet* in the previous August. His election was thus essentially a measure of the esteem in which his research in other fields was held by his peers.

The formalities concerned with the American visit took a long time to complete and not until 26 June did they leave Oxford. The departure was marred by an unhappy encounter with Chain at the last moment. Chain's version is as follows:

He did not tell me of any action he took to arrange a journey to the U.S.A. and the first time I heard that he was going, accompanied by Heatley, was when I entered his office one day (I think in the spring) of 1941 for a routine talk and found his suitcases standing on the floor packed for a journey. When I asked him where he was going he told me that Heatley and he were leaving for the U.S.A. in half an hour. No other word of explanation came from him. I left his room silently but shattered by the experience of this underhand trick and act of bad faith, the worst so far in my experience of Florey. It spoiled my initially good relations with this man for ever. . . . This is, of course, a grossly insulting behaviour, particularly as the penicillin work was a joint venture between Florey and myself in which we were equal partners.[9]

This is very forthright and vehement comment, the more so as it was made forty years after the event. That Chain was upset by the incident and bore a lasting grudge is beyond doubt, and understandable, but there are mitigating circumstances to be taken into account. Of the three concerned, only Heatley is now alive to comment, and he is emphatic that in view of the special nature of the trip at a particularly anxious moment in the war they had both been strictly enjoined to say nothing about it to anybody.[10] For Florey at least, never given to confidences, this would normally have been no problem but another incident that occurred at about the time the trip was being planned had already widened the rift between him and Chain and did not predispose him to avoidable confidences.

This incident concerned the matter of patents. To Chain, with a family background of industry and commercial practice, it seemed logical that their research on penicillin should be protected by patents—not for their private benefit, but to provide urgently needed funds to support further research. Florey was not enthusiastic but Chain persisted and he put the matter to Dale, by then President of the Royal Society, and Mellanby. Both reacted vehemently; they thought the proposal that medical reseach workers should profit in any way from the commercial exploitation of their discoveries was entirely unethical. Chain was still unpersuaded and Florey, exasperated, sent him off to discuss it personally with Mellanby, who remained adamant. Chain had perforce to accept this but he was still not convinced.

We shall examine the whole question of penicillin patents later (Chapter 9) for after the war they became a matter of political dispute between Britain and the United States and for a time feelings ran high. For the moment we will comment only briefly. Firstly, it is doubtful whether at that time the work on penicillin provided the basis for a patentable invention. If it ever did, the disclosures in the 1941 paper in the *Lancet* surely removed it. Secondly, we must have regard to the professional ethics of the day, and not those that pertain now. At that time individual research workers in this country or corporate bodies such as universities, which sought to protect their discoveries by patents rather than publishing them freely to the world would have been looked at askance. The prevailing view was still that succinctly expressed a century and a half earlier by Sir Joseph Banks, one of the most illustrious Presidents of the Royal Society:

The keeping of secrets among men of science is not the custom here; and those who enter into it cannot be considered as holding the same situation in the scientific world as those who are open and communicative. . . . [11]

Today, in a totally different social and economic climate, the situation is reversed; for universities not to protect their interests and profit from their discoveries is regarded as a dereliction of duty. In 1948 the National Research Development Corporation was set up to secure 'where the public interest requires' the development and exploitation of inventions derived from publicly supported research and from other sources. As we shall see, one of the major projects it supported was the development of another very successful antibiotic, cephalosporin, at Oxford (p. 301).

So, somewhat inauspiciously, began the visit to North America on which their immediate hopes rested. That Heatley should have gone with Florey, and not himself does not seem to have worried Chain; the issue was that he had been kept in ignorance of the facts. The choice was, in fact, a perfectly logical one. The paper for the *Lancet*, which they had all approved, stated that 'N. G. Heatley devised the assay method and developed and supervised the production of penicillin'. Since the production of penicillin in quantities sufficient for a rigorous clinical trail was their sole objective at this stage, Heatley—besides being Florey's personal assistant—was the natural choice. The target was 1 kg of immediately usable material.

Ethel drove them to Bristol, where they stayed the night at the Royal Hotel, and they left Whitchurch aerodrome on 27 June, with Lisbon their first destination. Once there, their immediate problems were over as they were then put into the charge of a representative of the Rockefeller Foundation. Impatient though they were to get on their way, an enforced delay of four days in Lisbon—with its bright lights and well-stocked shops—must have been welcome after the austerity and blackout of wartime Britain. Then they went on to New York—a long flight via the Azores and Bermuda—and called without delay on Warren Weaver and, shortly after, on Dr. Alan Gregg, head of the Natural Sciences Division; this Division, it will be recalled, had been Florey's immediate sponsor. To the latter, Florey gave a long and lucid account of the stage they had reached with penicillin, including the results of their limited clinical trial, just about to be published in the *Lancet*. He carried with him a typescript version of this paper. Heatley's memorandum on this first meeting notes that the vexations question of patents was one of the topics discussed. So far as the Rockefeller Foundation was concerned Gregg was opposed to patenting on both moral and practical grounds.

For the moment they had no further need of hotel accommodation, as they were made welcome by the Fultons at New

Haven, on the coast some 100 miles (160 km) north-east of New York. For Florey, it was a home in more senses than one, for there he was reunited with Paquita and Charles. As their arrival coincided with the 4 July celebrations they could all relax briefly together. Mrs. Fulton has recorded that 'they talked and talked and got on famously. I don't know when they went to bed.' More to the immediate purpose, John Fulton had become Professor of Physiology at Yale University and a man of wide acquaintance in circles of immediate interest to them. In particular, he was able to introduce them to Ross Harrison, a medical man who had carried out important research on tissue culture and on the physiology of the nervous system, and who thus spoke Florey's professional language. He was also a man with great influence in the scientific establishment in America: he was Chairman of the National Research Council; a member of the Council of the National Academy of Sciences, roughly the counterpart of the Royal Society in London; Vice-President of the Board of Scientific Directors of the Rockefeller Institute of Medical Research; and since 1938 had been a member of the Natural Resources Planning Board. Thus within days of arrival Florey had found a powerful ally, whose introductions would carry much weight. Through him they were directed to C. Thom—the mycologist at the Bureau of Plant Industry at Beltsville, Maryland—who had first correctly identified Fleming's mould as *Penicillium notatum* rather than *P. rubrum*. Thom was greatly interested and took them to Washington on 9 July to call on P. A. Wells, acting assistant chief of the Bureau of Agricultural Chemistry and Engineering (BACE), of the Department of Agriculture. It is interesting that even at this early stage the question of patents again arose. Thom explained to Wells that

A forthcoming publication in *The Lancet* will describe the experimental results and should settle the patent question. These men are not particularly patent-minded . . . interested in seeing that no one commercial concern secures a monopoly on this material, which is an extremely valuable aid in the treatment of wounds.[12]

Thence they set off once again, this time to call on Dr. Orville May, Director of the Department's Northern Regional Research Laboratory (NRRL) at Peoria. This lies on the Illinois River, some 150 miles (240 km) south of Chicago, in the heart of a great maize-growing area—the latter a circumstance that was to prove unexpectedly relevant to the history of penicillin. Peoria is about 700 miles (1125 km) west of Washington, and while they were en route Wells and May had time to exchange brief telegrams. Wells referred to his visitors' interest in a bacteriostatic substance from Fleming's *Penicillium*, and requested experimental facilities; although the names of Florey and Heatley then meant nothing to him, May assured Wells that his laboratory would cooperate. Significantly, Wells replied to this:

I know it will occur to you . . . to try out the production of this bacteriostatic agent in submerged culture. . . . This would most certainly facilitate its commerical preparation.[13]

May had ample time to consider how best he could satisfy this unexpected request, and decided that the member of his staff most likely to be helpful was Dr. Robert D. Coghill who, with a staff of about twenty, was director of the Fermentation Division.

Florey and Heatley presented themselves themselves at Peoria on 14 July and on that very first day Coghill, after listening carefully to all that Florey had to tell him, repeated the suggestion that was to prove of crucial importance to the industrial production of penicillin. Florey records[14] that Coghill

inquired whether deep fermentation on the lines of that used for the production of glucuronic acid had been tried and suggested that this might be the key to successful commercial production.

At the end of the day, Coghill promised to make a number of his staff available for experimental work immediately, but only on condition that Heatley remained in Peoria to give his advice on the techniques used in Oxford and on his assay method in particular.

Florey, never averse to a sudden change of plan if useful results were to be obtained, agreed immediately. It was agreed informally, and subsequently confirmed in writing at the end of September, that:

in the event any patentable inventions are made concerning the production of penicillin in this preliminary cooperative investigation, such patents will be obtained under the usual Department of Agriculture procedure and will be assigned to the Secretary of Agriculture.

He himself left the following day to pursue other possibilities, mainly among leading pharmaceutical manufacturers. He left behind not only Heatley but a culture of the mould used at Oxford and a small quantity of their penicillin standard. He did not return for a month. Coghill honoured his promise to make one of his best research workers available for work on pencillin, but, in the circumstances, his choice was not a happy one. Dr. A. J. Moyer was unquestionably a first-rate and knowledgeable investigator of fermentation processes but he was overtly anti-British and isolationist, as were many others in that part of America; at a time when it seemed clear to most people that America was moving rapidly towards involvement with Britain in the European war such a man was not likely to be an easy companion for any visiting British research worker. It says much for Heatley's patience and forbearance that a tolerable working relationship was established. However, undercurrents were already beginning to appear that became much more serious later. As their collaboration developed Heatley suspected that Moyer was not being entirely frank with him. Although they agreed on the text of a joint paper, it appeared a year later under Moyer's name alone. Moyer also had an eye to personal patents; as a government employee he could not file patents in the United States but was free to do so abroad.

Nevertheless, important results were quickly achieved at Peoria, even though Moyer was away on holiday from mid-August to mid-September. The most important of these was that the yield of penicillin could be very greatly increased if the Oxford (Czapek—Dox) medium was replaced by one based on lactose and corn steep liquor. The latter was a sticky waste product, rather like molasses, left after extracting starch from corn. One of the objectives of the Peoria laboratory, in the heart of the corn-belt, was to find a use for it. There was no lucky chance about their investigating its possible use for penicillin production; as a matter of course they tried it for virtually every fermentation that came their way. The luck lay in the fact that for penicillin its effect was dramatic—in experiments by Moyer and Heatley the yield was multiplied tenfold.[15] After Heatley left Peoria in December 1941 attention was also directed to finding new and more productive strains of *Penicillium*, especially among the large collection already held by the NRRL. No less important, in the longer term, was the investigation of deep fermentation processes such as were widely used for the production of gluconic acid and citric acids. This necessarily involved investigation of new mould strains, for those that grow well in surface culture, like Fleming's, do not usually do so when submerged. The search for such a new strain was directed by Dr. Kenneth Raper. Initial results were disappointing; penicillin yields in submerged culture were much lower than in surface cultures. Even in November when surface culture could be made to yield 20 units per cubic centimetre, submerged culture gave no more than three to four units.

Although it was by no means immediately apparent, the visit by Florey and Heatley to the NRRL on 14 July 1941 was crucial for the development of penicillin on a worldwide scale. From that focus the ripples took time to spread, but they did so with decisive effect. To Florey, however, it was at that time by no means clear that he had triggered off an unstoppable chain reaction and he left Peoria with a list of introductions, on what he later referred to as a 'carpetbagging' tour of the American chemical industry. Like most carpetbaggers he got a mixed reception. Nevertheless, some of those who politely showed him the door were very soon anxious to climb on the bandwagon he had set in motion.

Florey had one other important appointment to keep. This was with A. N. Richards, Professor of Pharmacology at the University of Pennsylvania, Philadelphia, on 7 August (p. 27). Once again one of Florey's early contacts was, like Fulton, to be invaluable at a critical moment; Richards, with whom he had worked briefly in 1925, had been appointed Chairman of the Medical Research Committee of the Office of Scientific Research and Development, established only a few weeks previously. From him he received an assurance that he would give all possible support to the production of penicillin. The importance of his office promised that such support would be effective; as we shall shortly see, this promise was fulfilled.

He returned to Peoria on 23 August to collect Heatley, and was heartened to know that his visitors had included three representatives from Lederle who announced that their company was to invest $40 000 immediately in research on antibiosis. They resumed their carpetbagging tour, with Toronto as their first port of call. Their immediate objective was the Connaught

Laboratories, nominally part of the University of Toronto. Effectively, however, it was an independent institution, which prospered on the sale of biological products such as insulin and vaccines; it employed nearly a thousand people. In this respect it resembled, though on a much larger scale, St. Mary's at Paddington so it is not wholly surprising that Ronald Hare, Fleming's former colleague, should have taken up an appointment there in 1936. Nevertheless, it was a considerable surprise to Hare to be summoned by his Director, Dr. R. D. Defries, to meet Florey and Heatley and discuss with them penicillin 'of which I might possibly have heard'.[16] In the event, however, nothing was achieved. Defries argued that he lacked space and the necessary reorganization could not be effected; that they would do no more than duplicate work done elsewhere; and, particularly, that it would all be to no purpose because penicillin was bound to be synthesized quite quickly. Florey was not convinced, but had to put the best face he could on it. Nevertheless the possibility of synthesis was a most important consideration. Albert Elder, who became director of penicillin production in the United States under the War Production Board, recalls that he was ridiculed by some of his closest scientific friends for allowing himself to become associated with what 'obviously was to be a flop'—namely, the commerical production of penicillin by a fermentation process.[17]

However, Defries and the Connaught Laboratories redeemed themselves later. In August 1943, at the request of the Dominion Government, an old college building, the Spadina Building which had been used as military hospital in the First World War but had then been empty since 1936, was rehabilitated to make penicillin, first in surface (bottle) culture and later (November 1945) in submerged cultures. The conversion was completed in seven months, at a cost of $1.2 million; it could handle 250 000 bottles weekly. In this project Ronald Hare played an important part.

Disappointed at this cool reception in Toronto, they returned to America and started a round of visits to pharmaceutical firms in the mid-Atlantic States. These included largely abortive calls on Eastman Kodak, Distillation Products, and Johnson and Johnson. Later, they tried with Kodak to develop a cellulose-based penicillin capsule that would carry the drug safely through the acid gastric juices and so permit oral administration. As the tour progressed they became increasingly aware that, as we have briefly noted (p. 84), there was already some active interest in penicillin generated quite independently of their visit. At Rahway, they found research had been in progress at Merck since 1940 and had a useful exchange of views with the medical and scientific staff concerned. The Merck programme was part of a broader one—a general study of antibacterial substances produced by micro-organisms—launched in 1939 with Selman Waksman of Rutgers University (p. 83). At the time of the visit by Florey and Heatley they were already producing and processing 180 litres of mould medium every ten days. E. R. Squibb of New Brunswick, not discouraged by an adverse internal report on the prospect for penicillin in 1937, were not only actively engaged but had prepared a small quantity of material several times more active than the best then produced at Oxford. Squibb's renewed interest dated from October 1940.[18] Lederle had been interested in penicillin for nearly a year, as they had told Heatley at Peoria, but to protect their legitimate commercial interests were uncommunicative. Pfizer had followed the work closely for some months and were on the point of launching a production programme.

Nor was active interest limited to the pharmaceutical industry. In the summer of 1941 Perrin H. Long, Chairman of the National Academy of Sciences, had written to several medical centres in England inquiring about penicillin. In New York, Florey met René Dubos (p. 83), whose work on gramicidin had stimulated wider interest in antibiotic chemotherapy, and was introduced by him to a research group under M. H. Dawson working at the Presbyterian Hospital; his chief co-workers were Gladys Hobby, Karl Meyer, and E. Chaffee.[19] His particular interest was the treatment of bacterial endocarditis. Their enthusiasm was fired by the Oxford paper of August 1940, and they began fermentation, in hundreds of flasks, in September. Their initial culture of Fleming's *Penicillium* they obtained from Roger Reid (p. 71) who had done some experimental work at Pennsylvania State University in 1935. In October Dawson wrote to Chain, asking for more information and requesting a specimen of the Oxford mould culture; he even sent an international postal order for $5 to cover postage. The culture duly arrived on 28 October 1940, but unfortunately subcultures failed. Laboriously, they accumulated enough material to treat four cases of subacute bacterial endocarditis by injection and eight of chronic staphylococcal blepharitis (eye infection). As became apparent later the quantities of penicillin available were insufficient for effective treatment of the heart conditions, but Dawson was satisfied that there were no detectable toxic effects. The local treatments of eye infections, including one resistant to sulphathiazole, were satisfactory. Although inconclusive, these clinical trials are of great historical interest, for they antedate the first (February 1941) intravenous administration of penicillin in Oxford. Dawson, with Hobby and Meyer as co-authors, presented these results in a paper to the Society for Clinical Investigation on 5 May 1941. A handwritten comment on the summary says: '. . . it would appear that penicillin is a chemotherapeutic agent of great potential significance'.[20] Sadly, Dawson could not pursue this work; he was already a victim of myasthenia gravis and died early in 1945.

At the end of September Florey returned to Oxford for the start of the Michaelmas Term, but Heatley went back to Peoria, whence he made various sorties to sustain interest in the pharmaceutical firms, among them Squibb, and help them with their production problems. For the moment he was at the scene of action. His letters home were a great stimulus: in February 1942 Margaret Jennings wrote: 'I wonder if you realise that a letter from you is one of the great events of the week in the department? It passes from hand to hand with chuckles (for the incidentals) and excitement (for the major themes).'

For Florey the tour was at once a success and a failure. It was a success in that it happened to coincide with an emergent interest at various centres in America and this was greatly stimulated by his enthusiastic and circumstantial accounts of what had been achieved at Oxford, especially of his very encouraging, if not conclusive, clinical trials. His visit coincided also with a conviction in government circles that involvement in the war was inevitable, and this led to the establishment of various powerful agencies which, once convinced, could inaugurate major projects judged to be in the national interest. It was a failure, from his personal point of view, in that it failed to provide the kilo of penicillin he desperately wanted for his own clinical trials. Although still a speculative venture so far as chemotherapy was concerned the Americans, with their natural instinct to push

ahead fast on a large and expensive scale once they were committed, put their money on penicillin not to assist a relatively
tiny group working far away across the Atlantic but to supply
future battle casualties in their armed forces. This need became
real rather than apparent almost as soon as Florey had departed,
with the attack on Pearl Harbor in December. All he ever received
was half a million units from Merck; all other American penicillin
was appropriated by the Committee on Medical Research for
clinical trials in America. Writing to Heatley on 13 April 1942,
Florey said that this came in 'a damn great box which looked as
though it might have a kilo in it. . . . It was the sort of package in
which you might expect to have the Kohinoor diamond!' Alas, it
was nearly all wrapping: *parturient montes, nascetur ridiculus mus.*
However, the end result was to establish penicillin manufacture
on a large enough scale to treat all severe casualties, British and
American, by D-Day in Normandy less than three years hence.
Florey himself was to play an important part in working out the
most effective methods of using penicillin in warfare.

The importance of Florey's American visit has been succinctly
stated by Harry L. Yale of Squibb:

Howard Florey is generally recognized as the individual whose conviction regarding the potential of penicillin led him on a one-man crusade
that resulted in the launching of penicillin towards its unexpected
meteoric career as the first and most widely used antibiotic in the
history of modern medicine.[21]

For the moment we must leave Florey in Oxford, still hopeful
of American supplies but as a safeguard energetically—and not
without success—renewing his attempt to involve the British
pharmaceutical industry. In America, where Heatley was the
linkman, events were moving very rapidly and at a high level. On
2 October, only a week after Florey's departure, the Committee
on Medical Research approved Richards' request that he should:

. . . suggest to interested persons the desirability of a concerned program of research on penicillin involving the pooling of information
and results; and if the results are favourable, to proceed to arrange for a
conference on the subject.

The phrase 'pooling of information' has a significance not
immediately apparent to many British readers. Such an arrange-

ment might put individual firms in violation of the strict antitrust laws and the proposal that they might be overridden in the national interest is a measure of the importance the penicillin programme had already attained at government level. It is also a measure of the desire of most of the firms to cooperate that they went ahead without formal safeguard, an acknowledgement of their complete confidence in Richards' integrity. Not until 7 December 1943 was the exchange of information on penicillin formally legalized. The Attorney-General's exemption was very specifically restricted to penicillin and covered no other drug.[22] Not the least important consequence of Florey's visit was that a sporadic interest in penicillin at various centres—which might have taken a long time to produce results—was surprisingly rapidly translated into a major concerted national enterprise.

Having got his authority, Richards lost no time in calling a powerful group together in Washington on 8 October. Among those at this historic meeting was Vannevar Bush, appointed Director of the Office of Scientific Research and Development that summer. He held this office throughout the war and in matters of scientific policy wielded great influence at Presidential level; his political status was comparable with that of Lord Cherwell in Britain. Thom represented Peoria. There were high-level representatives of four major pharmaceutical firms already interested: Squibb, Merck, Pfizer, and Lederle. The last of these was cautious at this stage, ostensibly because of fears that there might be a risk of contaminating their sera operations, but they had from the outset indicated that their interest was 'strictly commercial'. George A. Harrop, Director of the Squibb Institute of Medical Research, indicated that they were well advanced towards being able to supply the material required for clinical testing; Dr. Geoffrey Rake, head of their Division of Microbiology, had already given Heatley material much more active than the best Oxford penicillin then available. At that time, it seemed possible that Squibb alone might satisfy Florey's immediate needs[23], and it is clear that they were anxious to secure a strong, even dominant, position in penicillin production. In a letter of 15 September, addressed to Florey at the Rockefeller Foundation in New York shortly before his return to England, Rake claimed:

We have every reason to believe that our total yield of activity is at least 10 times and closer to 25 times that which you and your group have been able to obtain. The reason for this is at present quite beyond me and I must confess is a matter of some surprise to me. Nevertheless, it should make the preparation of large amounts of active material somewhat simpler than we had at first believed would be the case . . . it seems probable that we shall be able to satisfy all of your needs and thus save you the trouble of trying to interest other Biological Companies.[24]

Two topics of major importance were raised informally even at this early meeting. One was again the patent position; the industrial representatives were given copies of the NDRC (National Defense Research Committee) and CMR patent forms. The other was the possibility of enlisting research support in the universities: Merck was already allied with Rutgers.

In December, Florey wrote from Oxford to confirm the productivity of the Squibb culture. He also informed Rake that he was sending Richards an abbreviated version of the extraction process used at Oxford and that a brief account of this would shortly be published in the British weekly scientific journal *Nature*, with a longer account elsewhere. In the event, this paper had to be withdrawn as a result of an embargo placed on all publication in Britain on chemical aspects of pencillin.

Unfortunately, Rake's hopes were not fulfilled and on 21 January 1942 he had to write:

we have had nothing but one trouble after another with our large scale production and have no material at all at the present time.

This admission of setback was particularly disappointing to Heatley who had written to Rake on 8 October saying:

It appears that you are a long way ahead of everyone else, and your results have rather taken the edge off my keenness in trying to push up the yield here. No one here knows of your results and I naturally intend to keep them secret unless you give permission for them to be divulged.

This last sentence indicates a dilemma in which he frequently found himself. With his central position he was the recipient of many confidences and at times it must have been difficult to recall what information he could disclose, and to whom. His central position also encouraged the belief that he could make penicillin available for desperate cases—something he could not then have done however much he might have wished to. Thus in November 1941 Professor E. D. G. Murray of McGill University appealed on behalf of a young colleague with a serious chronic infection, and he replied:

As far as I know there is not sufficient penicillin in this country (or in England) to treat one human case. . . . There is no question of withholding the material—it is simply not there.

Unexpectedly, Heatley was also in touch again with Leslie Epstein, Chain's co-worker on lysozyme at Oxford. He was just taking up an appointment at Johns Hopkins University, Baltimore, with Professor Longcope and Dr. Tom Brown. The latter had contacts with the pharmaceutical company Smith, Kline and French, who were anxious that Epstein should work on penicillin. When Heatley visited this company at the end of October they suggested—though with some diffidence, with the thought that in Oxford it might not be regarded as ethical—the possibility of offering Florey a research grant with no commercial strings attached. It does not seem, however, that this generous suggestion was pursued.

Yet another aspect of Heatley's activities at this time was to locate a source of supply of corn-steep liquor for Florey. The A. E. Stanley Manfacturing Co. dispatched a 5-gallon (22-litre) drum by sea, without charge, at the beginning of January 1942. He also learned, through the Corn Products Refining Co. that the liquor was available in England from an associate at Paisley, near Glasgow.

In consequence of their problems Squibb had to revise their policy of independent action and sought collaboration with Merck, which—in view of existing friendly relations—was readily agreed in February 1942. Since it was just such arrangements Richards had been hoping for this had his immediate approval. The terms of the agreement covered not only full exchange of information on research and development but joint ownership of inventions. The possiblity of admitting other companies to the partnership was also provided for, and in the event Pfizer, where John L. Smith was in charge of operations, joined on 30 September 1942, though apparently on slightly restricted terms.[25] For a time, this powerful combination dominated penicillin production in the United States. By contrast, work on the chemistry of penicillin remained under the strict control of the Council for Medical Research.

This display of strong interest by major companies led to the

War Production Board being inundated with inquiries from other firms: by the end of 1943 nearly 200 had expressed interest. By no means all had the necessary facilities and experience, however, and ultimately no more than twenty were approved. These enjoyed special facilities, which included not only priority in the allocation of materials, equipment, and manpower, all in increasingly short supply, but special tax relief to offset the risk of plant being made rapidly obsolete by the advent of synthetic penicillin. Their activities were coordinated through monthly meetings with the Board. As a measure of the government support forthcoming it may be remarked that it provided $75 million for the construction of penicillin plants by six companies—Abbot, American Cyanamid, Ben Venue, Bristol, Cutter, and Heyden. At the end of the war they were able to purchase these plants at rather less than half the cost.[26]

Before rejoining Florey in Oxford it is necessary to follow up the further repercussions of his visit, the more so as Heatley, his personal assistant, remained in the United States until the summer of 1942—arriving back in England on 17 July—and played an active part in developments there. Initially he remained based in Peoria but kept up his industrial contacts, although he and Florey were already—conscious that the policy of complete freedom of disclosure of information that they had deliberately adopted was not being reciprocated. Writing to Heatley in the spring of 1942, Florey expressed his disenchantment forcibly:

no-one in the States has taken the trouble to inform us about what is going on, though all here would be quite willing to do anything that was asked of them if good reasons could be produced for it. If this is an example of inter-allied cooperation God help us!

Thus in a letter to Coghill addressed from the Rockefeller Foundation and dated 25 October 1941, Heatley remarks:

I have had quite an interesting time since I left Peioria [sic], but I have not come across any developments as far as the yield of penicillin by the mould is concerned (If there had been any striking improvements it is unlikely that I should have been told about them anyway!) . . .[27]

He had devoted particular attention to Merck and Company where their meeting on 4 September had been very fruitful. According to W. H. Helfand they gave Merck 'immeasurably valuable assistance'[28]. Heatley was invited by them to take up a short-term appointment from the beginning of December 1941 to advise them on production techniques. One reason, no doubt, was that at a meeting in the University Club in New York in December George Merck had stated that if Heatley and Moyer's claims for corn-steep liquor could be confirmed—which, of course, they were—it would be possible for industry to produce the kilo of penicillin Florey so desperately wanted.[29] Heatley's departure was a disappointment to Peoria. G. E. Hilbert, the acting Director, told May—then acting assistant chief of BACE in Washington—that 'unless we can get some outside support for more personnel, the work . . . on this project will have to be very limited after Dr. Heatley's departure'. At Merck, Heatley found the penicillin programme very professionally organized under its Chemical Research Committee, working closely with their Medical Research Committee. He worked with H. Boyd Woodruff who was in charge of yield enhancement research, in which his assay method was invaluable. The industrial atmosphere was clearly not uncongenial to him, for in a letter to Florey in mid-December he mentioned that he might seek employment with an English firm when he finished at Merck. After he returned to Oxford he wrote to Merck saying:

of the time I was lucky enough to spend in America I think the six months I spent with Merck and Co. Inc. were the most interesting, the most agreeable and the most instructive, and I am very thankful to have had the opportunity of working for the firm.

The attack on Pearl Harbor on 7 December 1941 transformed the American situation overnight. Penicillin production for military needs was accorded high priority and Richards called another meeting of industrial representatives for 13 December. Apart from the National Research Council and US Department of Agriculture, there were representatives of Merck, Squibb, Pfizer, and Lederle. In a report on the meeting Coghill stated:

Dr. Richards . . . now looks upon the four commercial companies . . . as something in the nature of a closed corporation to which some others would be admitted . . . only if they had something to contribute . . . quite apparent that the commerical companies were still not desirous of throwing all their information into a pool . . . within a short time 400 to 500 grams of penicillin concentrates will be available per week.[30]

Coghill took the opportunity to point out that whereas the

NRRL had made all their information available 'so far [they] had received absolutely no information from others working in the field.' The complaint was noted and he shortly received invitations to visit all the commercial companies.

By that time America was rapidly getting on a war footing and this inevitably involved a clamp-down in the release of information on all projects of major national importance. On 19 December the President set up an Office of Censorship and although the penicillin project was not immediately affected a cautionary note was immediately struck. The following day Richards wrote to Coghill offering OSRD funds for technical assistance at the NRRL and adding:

. . . information which you are getting may be of potential importance to the enemy. I suggest that broad distribution may be unwise. . . . I should be glad to have you consider . . . distribution of that information through this Committee.

This was followed on 6 February by a letter from James Conant—President of Harvard University but then acting director of the Office for Emergency Management—urging him 'to use the utmost discretion in all forms of communication'. In March restricted access to information on every aspect of penicillin was formally introduced and this inevitably limited the amount of information sent to England. The Committee on Medical Research set up an office in the American Embassy in London under Dr. Joseph Ferrebee to coordinate American and British research and production efforts. This 'Top Secret' attitude in America—which, however, never approached that in which the Manhattan Project was shrouded—was in marked contrast to the more relaxed approach in Britain, which had then been at war for more than two years. Mellanby, it will be recalled, had not taken seriously Florey's concern that the Germans might enter the field. In 1944 it was learnt that the Reich Patent Office had granted patent rights for the production of penicillin in Germany to Dr. T. Morell and the I.G. Farbenindustrie. Morell, who had been awarded the Knights Cross of the German Merit Order was Hitler's personal physician. Fortunately he was also a charlatan and in the event no serious move was made to make penicillin in Germany. In Britain there was no restriction on the publication of clinical results; for example, in 1944 a special issue of the

British Journal of Surgery was devoted to 'Penicillin in warfare', to which Florey, Heatley, and Margaret Jennings all contributed.

The entry of the United States into the war had far-reaching economic repercussions, not least of which was the introduction of an 85 per cent excess profits tax. According to Coghill this was of crucial importance:

Early yields and recovery, however, were very discouraging and I am convinced that without our wartime 85 percent excess profits tax, enabling industry to carry on research and development with fifteen-cent dollars, we never would have had penicillin at all. Penicillin is thus a more-or-less direct result of World War II. One might call it a by-product of the war. It has probably saved many more lives and eased much more suffering than the whole war cost us. . . .[31]

In an admirable study of the wartime development of penicillin W. H. Helfand and his colleagues acknowledge the importance of such economic considerations but rightly draw attention to the fact that a great deal more than money was at stake among industrial leaders:

Under the American system, they were not obliged to accede to a good deal of this [government] authority, and some in the drug industry did not choose to allow themselves to be tied into an arrangement that would place them under such obligation. But the fact that men of the calibre of Merck, Smith, and Major were particularly anxious to cooperate, says much for the higher motives of which they were capable.[32]

In the case of Pfizer, at least, the economic risk was certainly real rather than hypothetical. Apart from other considerations, penicillin could be developed only at the cost of cutting back on riboflavin, the company's most profitable line. Selling at around $6 per gram, it represented more than one-third of the company's earnings at the time.[33]

The pooling of industrial information, in advance of government approval, was an unusual departure but it is not quite clear how fully it was effective. Albert Elder, who as Co-ordinator of the Penicillin Program 1943-44 was as well placed as anybody to know, remarked later:

Progress could have been more rapid with a free exchange of information. One industry man said that as he saw my job, I was to go from one plant to another collecting honey, but I was not to distribute pollen along the way. Years ago I destroyed my little black book containing secret information garnered as the honey from the plants.[34]

This apparent anomaly could be quite plausibly explained simply on the basis that in the course of such a massive crash programme, launched under wartime conditions, it would be virtually impossible to establish a completely smooth-running system. However, it is probably nearer the truth to say that individual firms were keeping an eye on their own interests.

As it got organized, several distinct lines of research and development emerged in America which roughly paralleled— though on a vastly greater scale—what Florey and his colleagues had pursued in Oxford. Firstly, more productive *Penicillium* strains were sought. Secondly, a chemical research programme was launched with the hope that the molecular structure of penicillin could be elucidated as a prelude to synthesis. Thirdly, much attention was directed to the extraction process with the object of producing purer, and ultimately pure, penicillin.

Responsibility for the search for more productive mould strains was entrusted to Kenneth Raper, Curator of the Culture Collection at Peoria. Apart from other sources, he was able to enlist the help of the Army Air Command with the result that hundreds of specimens flooded into his laboratory from places as far apart as Calcutta, Chungking, and North Africa. Ironically, the best producer of all, coded NRRL 1951, was cultured from a mouldy melon picked up in a Peoria fruit market. It is tempting to speculate that this derived ultimately from a spore that escaped from the NRRL, much as Fleming's strain most probably escaped from a laboratory near his own (p. 65). From this, a superior mutant (X-1612) was produced at the Carnegie Institute by irradiation with X-rays and another (Q-176) by ultraviolet irradiation of this at the University of Wisconsin. The results were dramatic. With Q-176, using improved culture media, the activity of the brew was increased to around 1500 units per cc, compared with one to two units for the earliest material prepared at Oxford.

As has been mentioned earlier, BACE at Washington had directed their thoughts to submerged culture even before Florey and Heatley set foot in their office (p. 131). Although confidence in this process proved completely justified, there was at that time no absolute certainty that it would succeed—just as Florey had no certainty that what was true of mice was true also of men. For this reason the War Production Board, whose target became the provision of ample stocks of penicillin for the invasion of Europe in 1944, set up a number of bottle plants very similar to that in use at Oxford. These were capable of handling up to 100 000 1-litre bottles—each containing 200 cc of medium—daily. Commenting on this, Coghill remarked:

I am aware that many people in the United States and England have asked, 'Why did we ever build bottle plants?' The answer is that it was the quickest way to life saving penicillin and the only *sure* way, *at that time*, to assure production for the military. The Wyeth bottle plant, operated by C. Raymond Rettew, was for several months the largest penicillin producer in the country.[35]

Reliance on bottle plants alone was a daunting prospect, however, for it was calculated that with the yields then available, and the stockpile of penicillin called for, the programme might require a row of bottles stretching from New York to San Francisco. In some instances a compromise solution was reached. Merck, for example, developed a tray-culture plant in which the trays were enclosed in large steel vessels: the latter were in due course converted to 750-gallon (3400-litre) fermenters.

Briefly, two other production processes were tested. In the so-called trickle process the inoculated broth flowed over sterile wood chips or stones; explored particularly by the Harrower Laboratories in California, it was an adaptation of a process used for vinegar manufacture. The other, in which Parke Davis and Schenley took a particular interest, involved growing the mould on sterile bran. Both processes proved troublesome and expensive and were soon abandoned. In the case of bran the main problem lay in its low thermal conductivity which made it difficult both to sterilize satisfactorily and to keep at the optimum temperature for mould growth.

Even as it became clear that submerged culture was feasible, major policy decisions had to be taken on the basis of calculated risk. In the summer of 1943 Elder, the newly appointed Coordinator, faced the difficult task of deciding what size fermenters should be adopted. By that time tanks up to 1000 gallon (4545 litre) were known to work, but 10 000-gallon (45 450-litre) tanks were much more attractive. By that time, all sorts of equipment was in short supply—tanks, piping, pumps, valves, and the like: the bigger the tanks the less ancillary equipment was needed. An essential feature of the fermentation process was, for example, strict control of acidity and for this instruments known as pH meters were required in large numbers. They were also in demand in large numbers for the Manhattan Project. Rightly, as it proved, Elder plumped for the larger vessels.

As the organized production programme developed and the original 'club' of three manufacturers expanded, the availablity of penicillin soared dramatically. The first patient to receive commercially produced penicillin in America (manufactured by Merck) was successfully treated for streptococcal septicaemia on 14 March 1942. This case is of particular interest, for it was Mrs. Ogden Miller, wife of a Yale professor and a close friend of the Fultons, who had contracted puerperal sepsis and was very gravely ill. Fulton sought Heatley's aid in obtaining penicillin from Merck. At first this was declined but shortly the company made available 5 g of their precious stock. The immediate result was dramatic and the patient eventually made a full recovery, though further treatment was necessary to counter subsequent flareups of the infection. Years later, Fleming was to cause great offence by posing for a photograph with Mrs. Miller, claiming her 'as his most important patient'. By June, ten more cases had been treated; between that time and February 1943 enough was available to treat 100 patients. In August 1943 the results of treating 500 cases were published and fully confirmed earlier expectations. The system of dosage used accorded closely with that found satisfactory in Oxford—10 000 units every three hours initially. On 22 May 1943 the chairman of CMR published in the *Journal of the American Medical Association* an authorized statement indicating the status of penicillin production and its therapeutic effectiveness. This fully endorsed Florey's expectations. Thereafter production accelerated so much that it had to be measured in billions of units. The annual rate of production was 2 billion units (one billion equals one thousand million) in the first half of 1943, 41 billion in the second half, 684 billion in the first half of 1944, and 2489 in the second half (after D-Day).[36] Production for the second half of 1944 exactly matched the target set by the War Production Board, yet in the following year it was trebled, thanks to greatly improved technology.

Coghill has dramatically described his excitment at seeing this huge rate of production:

One morning, in early 1944, after being shown through the Pfizer plant in Brooklyn, with its many multithousand gallon fermenters, I stood at the end of the finishing line and saw 100 000-unit vials of penicillin coming out faster than I could count them.[37]

At the same time the price dropped fantastically. A penicillin voucher from Reichel Laboratories dated 3 August 1943 quoted a price of $200 per million units, for penicillin made in a basically uneconomic bottle plant. By April 1944, just before D-Day, the price had fallen to around $35 per million units—by 1950 it was to be no more than 50 cents. The first priority was to ensure that the expected needs of the armed forces were fully met, but as early as 1 May 1944—when public pressure was mounting—a Civilian Penicillin Distribution Unit was established. Earlier, civilian use had been restricted to patients involved in clinical trials; the unenviable task of controlling this use was entrusted to Dr. Chester B. Keefer of the Evans Memorial Hospital, Boston.

One of the few exceptions to this restriction occurred after a disastrous fire in the Cocoanut Grove nightclub in Boston on the night of 11 November 1942. The death toll eventually reached 500, and even against the background of wartime casualties horrified the nation. In the early hours of the following morning the area was put under martial law and, by special dispensation, penicillin was rushed under police escort from Merck at Rahway, nearly 400 miles (640 km) away, to treat some of the worst casualties.

By that time the American public had become well aware through the media of penicillin and its unique properties, though great care was still taken to keep secret key details of the processes used to produce it. Inevitably many accounts were inaccurate and sensational, and laid much emphasis on harrowing descriptions of individual cases; typical headlines in 1943 were 'Stricken Girl Begs First Lady for Penicillin' and 'Penicillin Helps Boy; Is Denied Woman'. In this welter of popular publicity the vital contribution of the small research group across the Atlantic in Oxford was largely overlooked; to many Americans it was an American discovery.

In February 1944 Albert Elder resigned as Penicillin Coordinator, to join Corn Products Company, and not in the happiest circumstances:

For some months I had burned the candle at both ends trying to speed up the programme. I was bushed. I was broke because I had traveled so much and the government allowance did not take care of normal travel expenses.[38]

Few people were better informed than he about the American penicillin project and he was able to dispel some misunderstandings in an article which appeared shortly afterwards in the authoritative *Scientific Monthly*.[39] Among the interesting facts disclosed was that 50 per cent of the penicillin was still being lost in the recovery process; clearly the Oxford workers, with their makeshift plant, had done well to recover one-third.

Elder also touched briefly on the controversial question of synthesis, which he described as 'clothed in deep veils of secrecy'. Initially, in October 1942, Merck was of the opinion that prospects for synthetic penicillin were too tenuous for any hopes to be pinned to them in the short term, and they advised Squibb accordingly. When Squibb succeeded in crystallizing penicillin in the summer of 1943, however, Richards believed that penicillin synthesis had been brought much nearer and advised Vannevar Bush that it might be possible within a year. Bush appointed a committee of inquiry under Dr. Hans T. Clarke, a chemist at Columbia University, who reached the conclusion that six months might suffice to develop a workable process. On the strength of this, the Committee on Medical Research promptly launched a massive penicillin synthesis programme, initially with Merck, Squibb and Pfizer but later involving at least ten other American chemical companies. Additional liaison was established with British investigators through the Therapeutic Research Corporation (p. 158).

It was a far-reaching, but, in the short, term, unrewarding programme, costing overall some $5 million, and involving several hundred chemists.[40] Synthetic penicillin never became a commercial reality though the detailed knowledge gained of its complex chemistry was essential for the later development of the therapeutically effective semisynthetic penicillins.

With the end of the war, the official American penicillin programme was wound up almost as quickly as it had been begun.

In September 1945 Coghill was writing to Dr. Otto Behrens of Eli Lilly, saying:

I am very sorry that we shall not be able to cooperate with you as closely in the future as we have in the past, because we have discontinued our work on penicillin at this laboratory . . . penicillin production being what it is, the whole problem has lost any sense of urgency.

Later that year OSRD began to close down, and Coghill formally offered his resignation at Peoria to Vannevar Bush, saying that he was to become Associate Director of Research for Abbott Laboratories. Various accounts of the wartime development of penicillin in the United States have been published but one that is authoritative, concise, and readily available is that of A. N. Richards.[41] Another recently (1982) published account is that by J. C. Sheehan.[42] This is more sympathetic than most to the claims of Fleming and emphasizes the extent of American interest in penicillin before Florey and Heatley arrived on the scene.

After this digression into the early history of industrial penicillin production in America we must return to Florey and his activities in Oxford after his return. Though a digression, it is for three reasons one highly relevant to an understanding of his later career. Although the centre of action was the United States, the success of penicillin immensely boosted his scientific stature and opened up many new avenues of achievement. Secondly, although it was the Americans who made the running, useful channels were eventually established for the exchange of information between America and Britain, and with these Florey was intimately concerned. Thirdly, it had important political repercussions when allegations were later made in Britain that American industry had taken an unfair advantage in the patent field.

5

THE ADVENT OF
BRITISH PENICILLIN

It was as well that Florey was fond of travelling, for a tremendous amount, including two transatlantic flights under wartime conditions, had been crowded into his three-month trip. The journey home was uneventful and included a day in Bermuda. On his return, the situation at the laboratory did little to cheer him. As he wrote to Heatley on 9 October 1941:

Arrived back intact on 6th October. . . . As far as I can see things are much the same here, though the production of penicillin is apparently in a complete state of chaos. . . . I have not yet had sufficient courage to put my head inside the theatre. . . . I have superseded Chain in the brewing department and told the girls to go on just making one brew and then starting again. When this is going there should at least be some supplies of material. As far as I can see at present practically nothing has been produced during the last three months . . . the department seems to be semi-moribund as far as I can see.[1]

The criticism, of course, was of Chain, who had taken charge of penicillin production in Florey's absence. In later (1979) recollections Chain denied all knowledge of any such situation: '. . . I cannot recollect such incident. As far as I remember, we did not encounter any particular difficulty.'[2] Nevertheless, the fact of the matter was that very little penicillin was available and the recollection of others concerned is that some innovation introduced by Chain, with the best intentions, had not been successful. In particular, difficulties had arisen from an attempt to prevent the drift of spores in the incubation room by oiling all exposed surfaces to make them tacky. To the same end the spouts of the culture vessels had been fitted with caps instead of cottonwool plugs; unfortunately these excluded also the access of oxygen necessary for penicillin production. Soon after his return, Florey modified Heatley's original countercurrent extraction plant to include much longer tubes, running down the stairwell from the roof to the first floor. This considerably improved the yield, up to 80 per cent, which was as much as American industry was getting.

It is very characteristic of Florey that although he had at that time good reason to hope that American manufacturers, especially Squibb, would quickly solve his supply problem he immediately turned his attention to developing sources in Britain. It was as well that he did so for, as we have seen, virtually none of the penicillin produced in the early days of the American crash programme found its way to Oxford. Although it was some months before this unpalatable fact had to be accepted, he was in fact no better off than he was before his visit in respect of material for the clinical trials which he personally wished to conduct. In cynical mood, he wrote to Heatley in March 1942 to say that Lord Cherwell had importuned him for some penicillin ointment for Churchill's daughter: 'What we really need is some big shot in the Government to get really ill, and then I dare say the thing could be made to move. However, there it is.' The lack was frustrating. On 2 August 1942 he wrote to Sherrington '. . . if the price of two bombers was sunk into the project we could really get enough to do a considerable amount.'

The extent of Florey's disillusionment by that time is clear from a letter he wrote to Mellanby on 11 December 1942. The lack of American material had been explained on the grounds that its instability made it necessary to transport it refrigerated in dry ice. Florey dismissed this as a transparent excuse; he himself had sent material to Merck and it had arrived with little or no loss of potency. He added:

I have now had a very thorough lesson with all these commercial firms. They have been of practically no help to us and I could give you a very snappy judgment on the incompetence we have met almost everywhere. However, I can do nothing about that.[3]

In fact, this judgement was too harsh as far as Merck was concerned. In the autumn of 1948 Heatley visited Merck on his way back from California, where he had been a Rockefeller Fellow. He was surprised to be told that George Merck wished to see him personally. It proved that Merck wished him to convey his personal apology to Florey for not having fulfilled their promise to send him penicillin. The reason was that their total output was commandeered by the armed services.

For the processing of home-brewed material Florey had in the past relied heavily on Heatley, but the latter had remained behind in America and, in the event, did not return to Oxford until July 1942, after an absence of nearly a year. In the meantime he kept Florey informed as best he could of developments in North America. Fortunately, Florey found an able substitute in Sanders, with the technical assistance of Kent, who also had a natural gift for improvisation, and a local plumber, Jack Mascall (Plate 7). As long as the brewing went satisfactorily, the extraction plant could cope with it. Indeed, he had a certain amount of overcapacity on this side, and this led him to explore again the possibility of getting outside assistance to undertake fermentation alone and having the crude material shipped to Oxford for working up. In pursuit of this he was able to enlist the support of two firms—Kemball, Bishop and ICI—who had been unable to help at an earlier stage.

On 23 February 1942 he received a letter from J. E. Whitehall, joint managing director of Kemball, Bishop, saying that he understood from Sir Robert Robinson that Florey would disclose to them the Oxford method of producing penicillin and let them have a specimen culture. The letter had a proper sense of urgency that must have appealed to Florey; Whitehall said he had heard from Robinson only that day and he would send two of his colleagues to Oxford on the first day convenient to Florey—one of them, he mentioned, was not only an organic chemist but the possessor of an Oxford Blue for running. He was in fact J. G. Barnes, who had come up to Trinity as a scholar in 1938. Whitehall went on to recall the earlier request from the Wellcome Foundation for 10 000 gallons (45 450 litres) (p. 122) and explained that although he still could not consider work on this scale Robinson had assured him that a more modest contribution would be welcome, as indeed it was. Thus began a constructive and friendly relationship that extended over more than two years. It is recorded in correspondence that survives, partly in the archives of Pfizer Ltd at Sandwich, which took over Kemball, Bishop in 1958. While always very much to the point, Whitehall's letters have an old-fashioned turn of phrase, in contrast to Florey's brisk and down to earth approach.

Despite Kemball, Bishop's eagerness to go ahead delays were inevitable while they mastered techniques of culture and assaying by Heatley's method. The latter involved the use of pathogenic organisms (staphylococci) with which they were not familiar. On this Florey had to sound a cautionary note, for Kemball, Bishop wrote on 13 March to say that 'they understood that . . . this culture could be handled by unskilled girls without any harmful results'. By return of post Florey sent a cautionary reply:

I also enclose a culture of the staphylococcus. I think I should say that this should be approached and handled with the usual bacteriological precautions, that is it should in no way be slopped about and should not be allowed to get on hands. Girls can be easily trained to deal with it and, in fact, are doing so here.[4]

With the same letter he sent a new subculture of the *Penicillium* strain used at Oxford. An earlier one had failed to grow and Kemball, Bishop had obtained an alternative—but less productive—one from the type collection at the Lister Institute.

By chance, Florey himself was at that time involved in correspondence about the Lister Institute, but on a very different matter. Sir John Ledingham, the Director, was nearing retirement and Sir Henry Dale—who was about to be appointed a Governor—wrote to Florey to inquire whether he would be interested in being nominated as his successor.[5] Florey considered the matter carefully but quickly decided that he did not want his name to go forward. Apart from other considerations, and his reluctance to undertake a largely administrative job, there would have been great difficulties in transferring the penicillin project, on which all his hopes were then centred. In the event, Alan Drury was appointed from the staff of the Medical Research Council; he later became associated with the British penicillin project (p. 159).

Under wartime conditions what now seem trivial difficulties were of major consequence. Florey even found it difficult to feed his laboratory animals, and in 1941 the MRC had to supply him with a letter to take to the local War Agricultural Committee to ensure continuity of supply. The Oxford plant was designed to operate with standard 12-gallon (54-litre) milk churns, but these were then in short supply. For the first batch from Kemball, Bishop two empty ones were sent to London from Oxford by passenger train. Delivery of the brew by road was considered but thwarted by lack of severely rationed petrol: a lorry would require about 12 gallons (54 litres) for the double journey. It was necessary to set up a cumbersome arrangement by which the churns were taken by road to Paddington Station, loaded on to a passenger train to Oxford, and finally collected at the station there and taken to the laboratory.

By 11 September 1942 all these preliminaries were past, and the following historic telegram was dispatched:

Milk churn arriving Oxford Great Western today 5.45 you may collect tonight or railway will deliver in the morning Kemball.[6]

Meanwhile, however, things had been moving at government level and on the 23 September Florey was able to tell J. E. Whitehall that the Ministry of Supply was calling a meeting of interested parties to see how it could help to promote penicillin production: Florey had recommended that Kemball, Bishop should be represented. On 28 September he again wrote, encouragingly:

As you will know, the Ministry of Supply is prepared to help in any way possible with the production of penicillin. As I have told you before, I consider your firm quite the most likely to be able to produce penicillin in quantity in the near future. Others have 'plans' but translation of these 'plans' into action is quite a different matter. I have the impression that now we have the backing of the Ministry of Supply and the Army as well, and they are not prepared to stand about and have the work held up for lack of material etc., we shall be alright. For the immediate future it can be said that if you apply to Mr. Denston of the Ministry of Supply for the milk churns to send us 200 gallons every 10 days you will have no difficulty in getting them. With regard to the petrol Mr. Denston will have to activate the Ministry of War Transport. Again, I think that they should have no difficulty in getting it for you.[7]

So far as Kemball, Bishop were concerned the 'plans' involved the building of their own extraction plant at a cost of £3000; the sending of raw material to Oxford for processing was only an interim measure for which no charge was made. However, it was to be a rather long interim as their plant did not become operative until 24 November 1943.

The closeness of the collaboration between Florey and Kemball, Bishop is indicated by an internal office memorandum prepared by V. J. Ward on 22 September 1942:

My visit to Oxford has given me invaluable experience in the working up of the fermentation liquor—experience which would have cost me many weeks of trial and error. . . . I was given every facility by Prof.

Florey to enquire into the working of the process and the assay methods employed.[8]

At the Ministry meeting on 28 September Kemball, Bishop was represented by E. C. Quill, a director, but they did not attend a second one on 13 October. The reason was that collaboration might involve disclosure of details of their citric acid process and it was necessary to clear this with New York.

Whitehall's letter to John L. Smith of Pfizer (14 October 1942) is worth quoting as it pinpoints the conflicts of interest that collaboration involved:

We are keenly anxious to assist the country in any way we can but to be quite frank with you I am very doubtful when a body of men meet with competitive interests as to what is their intention of collaboration. Does it mean an absolute thing without mental reservation or is it a disclosure of so much information which you have no objection to convey to other interests? I ask that question, not only in respect of British firms but also U.S.A. firms. If, as Professor Florey says, and of course, he is acquainted with the progress of others in this country, we are the most likely people to successfully produce Penicillin it is not from friendship—I have only met him once—but from a knowledge that our liquor is at least equal and possibly better than that of other producers. Are we then to go to these meetings disclosing all our techniques and knowledge and if so what are we to get in return? Our present policy is quite clear. Penicillin must be produced, and no private interests, not even our own, must interfere, but if we can successfully produce it without collaboration then we are fulfilling the intention of the first point.[9]

The other main industrial representative at the Ministry of Supply meeting was ICI. The visit to Oxford by senior representatives of their Dyestuffs Division, Blackley, in May 1941 was not without result, for an informal arrangement on an exchange of information and material was concluded. Almost at once experimental cultures were made and a small production unit was established at Blackley, using essentially the production and extraction techniques developed at Oxford. In December 1941 they let Florey have 3 g of crude barium salt. In May 1942, production was transferred to a small specially designed plant at Trafford Park, using tray cultures: this had a rated capacity of 2 mega-units* per week, but was gradually worked up to 60 mega-units

---

* 1 mega-unit = 1 million Oxford units.

per week before it was closed down in March 1944 and incorporated in a 300 mega-unit plant.[10] After their initial preoccupation with other urgent matters Burroughs Wellcome were able to start small-scale production, and after a visit there in June 1942 Florey reported that 'they had done some very nice work'.

In establishing this important relationship with ICI the connecting link was Robert Robinson. He was highly regarded by them as a consultant and for a brief spell in 1920 had been Research Director of the British Dyestuffs Corporation, parent of ICI Dyestuffs Division. For penicillin production it was not an ideal relationship, in that they had no experience of fermentation processes, like Kemball, Bishop, nor even of biological products generally, like Wellcome. At that time, they had no Pharmaceuticals Division as such. Nevertheless, they were a powerful company with great knowledge and experience of a wide variety of industrial chemical processes. Their greatest strength lay in synthetic organic chemistry and they played an important role in the elucidation of the chemical structure of penicillin, in which Robinson took an increasingly active part.

Meanwhile, there had been two other important developments in the British pharmaceutical industry. Five major firms had reached an agreement in 1941 to pool their research resources to avoid wasteful duplication of research. This combined venture was known as the Therapeutic Research Corporation of Great Britain Limited and the participating firms were Boots, British Drug Houses, Glaxo, May and Baker, and the Wellcome Foundation; it did not include ICI, however. At an early stage this consortium realized that penicillin was a suitable subject for joint investigation. At the same time it was realized that there was need for collaboration, so far as practicable, with the American firms cooperating with the US Government in penicillin production. This collaboration was effected through the Office of Scientific Research and Development in America and the Medical Research Council in Britain. It was, however, restricted to work on the chemical nature of penicillin and did not include production. Additionally, as we have noted, the Ministry of Supply intervened to take penicillin production under its wing as a major wartime project. Thus on both sides of the Atlantic production and supply were now firmly in the hands of the professionals. Nevertheless, Florey had still to lay his hands on sufficient penicillin to conduct the extensive clinical trial that had been his personal objective for the past 18 months.

A meeting convened at the instigation of the Minister of Supply, Sir Andrew Duncan, on 25 September 1942, was pitched at a high level. As Florey looked round the table he must have felt that at last things were on the move, though what his private thoughts may have been at the presence of Fleming must be a matter for speculation. He was certainly seriously concerned at the thought that Duncan was a friend of Fleming, and the latter had, indeed, been concerned in getting the committee set up. He was concerned, too, about the bureaucracy he saw raising its head. The chair was taken by Sir Cecil Weir, Director-General of Equipment and Stores. The Director of Medical Supplies, Mr. F. Warburton, was absent only because he was in America investigating penicillin production at first hand. The armed services, who would have the first call on penicillin as it became available, were represented by Major-General L. T. Poole, of the Pathological Department of the Army Medical Directorate. Raistrick, of the London School of Hygiene, was there to give expert advice on mould metabolites generally although he had, of course, done a little work on penicillin ten years earlier (p. 68). The Therapeutic Research Corporation was represented in force, as were ICI and Kemball, Bishop. While the potential producers outlined their plans, Florey made a strong plea for the distribution of penicillin to be 'conducted with great strictness . . . he hoped the material would be handed out only to units which were under strict biological control.'

Out of this first meeting grew a formally constituted General Penicillin Committee under the chairmanship of Arthur Mortimer, Deputy Director of Medical Supplies. It met roughly quarterly, at the office of the Wellcome Foundation in Euston Road—for the first time on 13 October 1942—and Florey made a point of being there when he could. Later members included Robert Robinson; Professor I. M. Heilbron, a distinguished organic chemist from Imperial College; and A. N. Drury, newly appointed Director of the Lister Institute, representing the Medical Research Council. The Lister was important because of its expert knowledge of biological products such as vaccines and serums. Its general terms of reference were 'to increase and accelerate the production of Penicillin, to effect the pooling of tech-

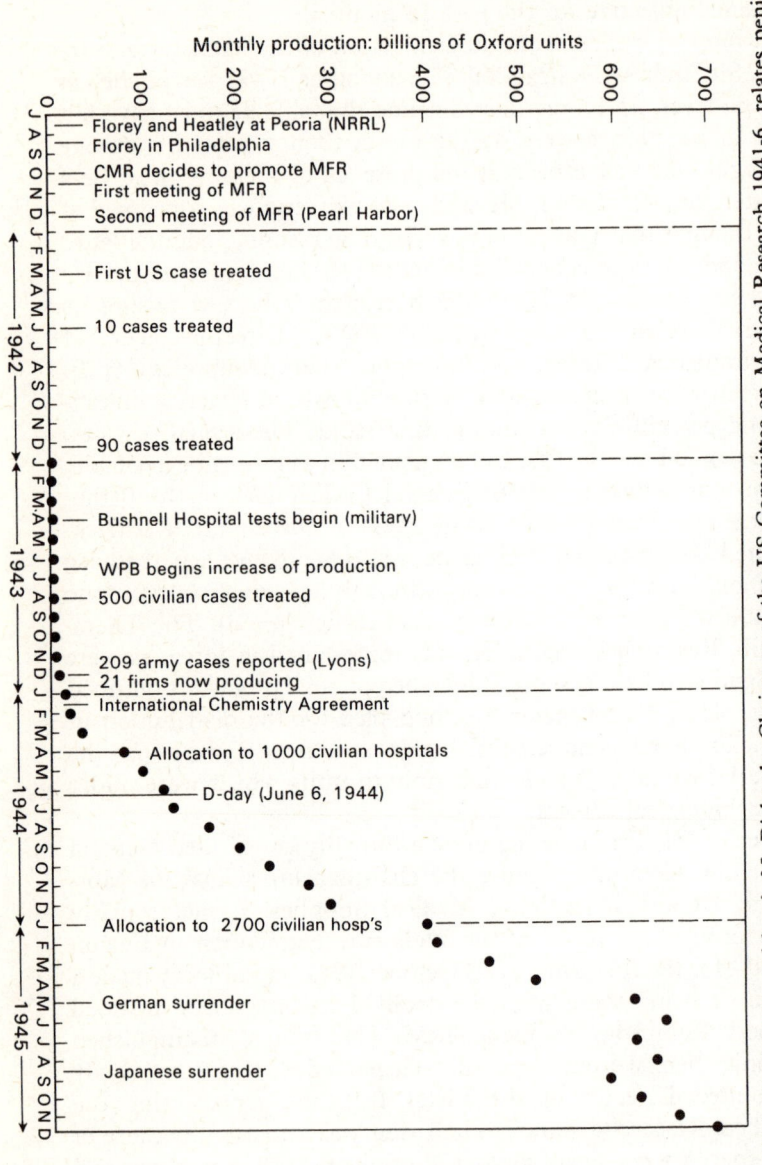

Fig. 2. This chart, prepared by A. N. Richards, Chairman of the US Committee on Medical Research 1941-6, relates penicillin production in the United States to the visit of Florey and Huntley in 1941.

nical information and to ensure that material produced was put to the best possible use.' It requested the Medical Research Council to set up a Clinical Trials Committee; this was pretty well autonomous, and reported to the General Committee only on matters relevant to production and the chemistry of penicillin. Florey viewed this committee with considerable suspicion, believing that it would deprive him of penicillin necessary for his own clinical trials (p. 164).

At this stage the future of penicillin was assured: Florey's 'one-man crusade' had achieved its objective in a surprisingly short space of time. In North America a massive crash programme of production had been launched; although Britain's contribution was necessarily planned on a smaller scale, the programme had powerful industrial support and the assurance of high priority in support from the Ministry of Supply. He was conscious that progress no longer depended upon his own drive, though his special knowledge and experience—and above all his enthusiasm—meant that his personal contribution was far from over. Indeed, his role as an international advocate for penicillin was only just beginning.

The matter of clinical trials, however, was very much a personal issue. That these would be rigorously conducted in North America and Britain as material became available was not in question. Nevertheless, it went entirely against his nature that in this final test he should not personally satisfy himself that his confidence in penicillin was wholly justified—however many people did similar tests elsewhere was immaterial.

By the beginning of 1942 enough penicillin had been accumulated from Oxford—where half had to be diverted for chemical research—and from ICI—who sent a further 5 g in February (which Florey referred to as 'derisory' in a letter to Heatley)—to make it possible to think of further clinical trials even in the absence of the hoped-for supply from America. At that stage the ICI material was of low purity. In a memorandum dated even some six months later Ward, of Kemball, Bishop, noted:

The I.C.I. are producing some penicillin and while I was at Oxford two lots of dried material containing each a million units arrived. This material is not received with great enthusiasm as it is very dirty and requires considerable processing before it can be used.[11]

However, this is somewhat at variance with Florey's view. His opinion of ICI had improved, and in April 1942 he wrote to tell Heatley that they were supplying six or seven hundred thousand units per week—'It is quite good stuff'.

With still pitifully small resources he had to plan his campaign carefully, concentrating on cases requiring only local application by relatively small doses. Even at this stage his task was not easy. Clinical staff, of whose conservatism he had so often complained, were still suspicious of penicillin and tended to make available to him only difficult cases which had failed to respond to conventional treatment, especially chronic cases where the infection was well entrenched. Later, Florey reached a firm conclusion about this:

> I was once optimistic enough to believe that penicillin correctly used would be fully effective even in the presence of much slough and pus, for it is not apparently inactivated by them. Extended experience has shown that this is not the case and that the more chronic the inflammation the greater is the difficulty of removing the infecting bacteria.

However, success under such adverse conditions was more impressive than in acute conditions. A further difficulty was the departure of Fletcher to be Assistant Physician to the Emergency Medical Service. This gap was most happily—and efficiently— filled by Ethel who, after a lot of essentially administrative work with the blood transfusion service, was delighted to be once again back into hospital work—the more so as it was work of such particular importance and personal interest.

Four local hospitals were used for these important trials: the Radcliffe Infirmary, the Wingfield-Morris Orthopaedic Hospital, and the 101st General Hospital of the Royal Army Medical Corps—all in Oxford—and the Princess Mary's Royal Air Force Hospital nearby at Holton. The last two were important in fostering contact with military surgery. The trials were designed not only to demonstrate the overall efficiency of penicillin in chemotherapy but to work out satisfactory but economical systems of application and dosage. In systemic use it was necessary to monitor the level of penicillin in samples of the patient's blood. For this Heatley's plate-and-cylinder method was not sufficiently sensitive and a simple dilution technique (p. 97) was devised.

In all nearly 200 cases were treated—15 systemically (by mouth or by intravenous or intramuscular injection) and 172 by local administration. The systemically treated ones were diverse and included an infection of the orbit of the eye, acute and chronic osteomyelitis, and a cavernous sinus thrombosis. All recovered, on the basis of three-hourly injections of 15 000 Oxford units. Among the local infections very successfully treated, 22 mastoid infections were of particular interest because, being infected cavities, they had much in common with many war wounds:

It is useless to apply penicillin unless the whole infected area can be reached, and local application must therefore be accompanied by suitable surgery. For this purpose 'suitable surgery' may not be orthodox surgery; free drainage is undesirable because the penicillin drains away with the exudate. In our view it is best to establish a closed cavity where possible into which penicillin can be instilled and from which exudate can be sucked away periodically, if necessary. We are particularly indebted to Mr. R. G. Macbeth and Mr. G. H. Livingstone [Oxford surgeons] who have modified their usual mastoidectomy operations to fulfil this condition. This type of infected cavity may be considered as a model for other situations. . . .

This approach was typical of Florey, to gain the greatest possible amount of information from every experiment. As we shall see, this unorthodox closed cavity technique was later widely adopted in the treatment of battle casualties.

One of the systemically treated cases was of special interest, for it concerned a friend of Fleming who was gravely ill in St. Mary's with streptococcal meningitis. Fleming appealed personally to Florey, who immediately came up by train with all the penicillin he could muster. The response was disappointing and after consultation it was decided, as a measure of desperation, to inject penicillin into the spinal fluid, something which had never before been attempted. The result was a dramatic recovery, not surprisingly held at St. Mary's to Fleming's credit.

A full report of these trials was submitted by the Floreys to the *Lancet* for publication and appeared in March 1943;[12] by then Florey was on the point of leaving for North Africa to put his radical ideas into practice. Ethel's interest in clinical chemotherapy was sustained and over the period 1952-60 she published four large volumes—1800 pages in all—on the clinical application of antibiotics.[14] Between 1944 and 1956 she contributed to fourteen papers on the clinical use of penicillin.

The organization of extended clinical trials had been the cause of a brush with the Medical Research Council. On 15 February 1943 Florey wrote to Mellanby:

Hartley [Sir Percival Hartley of the National Institute for Medical Research] is coming to see me on Tuesday about penicillin standards. I am afraid someone must have misinformed you that I wanted the Council to carry out clinical trials on my behalf with penicillin made here. Our difficulty has been to obtain enough material to carry out all the work we should have liked to do. Of course if I should ever have a surplus I should be very glad to add it to your pool, but I have no doubt you will obtain all you need for your trials from some of the drug firms. . . . I am quite confident that the Council would not wish to interfere in any way with work being done under my supervision, work which has been going on satisfactorily now for a long time. . . . I enclose a first draft of a report on the cases already treated. This is not for circulation yet as several emendations are required.[15]

Florey goes on to suggest that the committee should not meet until his report (the paper for the *Lancet* referred to above) could be studied, and he expresses his readiness to make available all his knowledge and experience. Nevertheless, he is quite clear that he is not going to restrict his own freedom of action.

On the same day he wrote to Ethel expressing great misgivings over the affair:

I have had a letter from the MRC which looks as though they are trying to take penicillin out of my hands. I have seen Buzzard [Regius Professor of Medicine] and Cairns, who are quite annoyed. It is too long to write about, in any case there is going to be a lot of unpleasantness and perhaps a bloody good row.[13]

Mellanby sent a temporizing reply a week later, saying that there had been pressure from the Ministry of Supply since the previous October for the Medical Research Council to coordinate all clinical trials:

It has been very difficult to start this work and I have had more trouble over it than with any other committee I have formed. . . . Naturally I am disturbed at the idea that the work of this committee might interfere in any way with your own investigations. . . . I want you to realise how important I think it is that your own work should continue, if you so wish. On the other hand, from the draft paper which you have just sent me on the subject, it appears to me that you have taken the cream off the investigation and I think you may be quite prepared now to let others have some experience in this form of treatment with your guidance.[15]

Mellanby goes on to make a vague and rather unconvincing suggestion that Florey should direct his attention to making a new 'discovery'—such as something to knock out the tubercle bacillus or viruses, or perhaps a modified penicillin that would not pass through the kidneys so quickly. Florey went to see him a week later and made it clear that although he was prepared to give the committee all the information and advice he could—and would even attend its meetings if Mellanby thought it necessary—he intended in any case to continue his own clinical trials, especially in the Army and in the RAF at Holton. At the same time, he indicated to Mellanby that:

he was tired of his many external contacts on this subject, both with manufacturing firms and others and would prefer to continue his work independently.[15]

By the end of the year he wrote even more dispiritedly:

I must confess that we are all getting very tired of the manoeuvring going on about penicillin and are anxious to quit the field now as soon as the chemistry is cleared up.[16]

Again, six months later, he wrote to J. C. Herrald of the MRC:

We are very anxious now to be relieved as completely as possible of all routine type of investigation associated with clinical work. I do not feel there is very much more to be got out of this sort of thing except perhaps a dotting of the i's here and there.[17]

This comment was made *apropos* of a proposal that Dr. A. H. T. Robb-Smith should have an assistant at the Radcliffe to look after routine clinical work; 'it is very dull stuff anyway', said Florey.

Before considering the visit to the North African theatre of war, the next major episode in Florey's life, we must consider a change of emphasis in the laboratory's research programme. In the broad sense, production of penicillin was no longer part of this. Although still of great immediate importance, as the sole source of penicillin under his direct control, it was perfectly clear —with so much industrial activity on both sides of the Atlantic—that it would soon be unnecessary and it was, therefore, continued as essentially a routine stopgap operation. Heatley returned in the summer of 1942, but, paradoxically, was temporarily unable to impart any of the useful information on production that he had gained with Merck because of the nature of his contract with them; he had, therefore, to turn his attention for the time being to other matters. With characteristic thoughtfulness, Heatley had asked Florey if there was anything he could bring back from America. Florey's reply (4 May 1942) throws an interesting light on the prevailing situation:

At the moment we are able to secure all the necessary laboratory supplies if the chits and so on are filled in, but I should be glad if you would slip in your pocket some pipe cleaners and flints for lighters, as these things are almost completely unobtainable here.

Roughly half the penicillin produced in Oxford was set aside for chemical investigation in which Chain and Abraham were making important progress, in close collaboration with Robinson and Dr. Wilson Baker in the Dyson Perrins Laboratory; their work became merged in the major Anglo-American cooperative project already noted (p. 150).

It was, therefore, timely for Florey to reconsider his departmental research strategy, and a number of major factors had to be taken into account. First and foremost, thanks to his own initiative, penicillin had become part of a major international venture and Oxford could no longer expect to have a decisive influence on the main course of events; there was no point in duplicating research—whether medical or scientific—that was being effectively done elsewhere. With his relatively limited resources it was essential for him to break new ground if impetus was to be maintained. On penicillin itself there was still no lack of problems even though the major obstacle of bulk production was in process of being overcome; indeed the rapid increase in the number of cases treated constantly revealed new ones. There was, for example, the problem of penicillin resistance—later to be of major worldwide consequence. The existence of penicillin-resistant strains of pathogenic organisms among species normally very sensitive had been discovered at an early date. More disconcerting, it was discovered that other strains could acquire resistance, and pass it down to their descendants, simply by exposure to penicillin—a natural bacterial defence mechanism. This resistance was especially liable to develop if treatment was insufficiently intensive and prolonged; if too small a dose was used and it was stopped prematurely the infection would flare up again and perhaps be insusceptible to renewed treatment. Moreover, these resistant strains could be transmitted to other people by the normal processes of infection. Apart from this, many important pathogens—such as those responsible for tuberculosis —were almost insensitive to penicillin; for this reason it later came to be called a 'narrow-spectrum' antibiotic. It was also becoming evident that although penicillin was virtually non-toxic a few individuals were naturally hypersensitive to it and responded so violently that they could not be treated with it at all. It was clear, therefore, that although penicillin had enormously extended the field of chemotherapy it was by no means a magic bullet that would harmlessly destroy every human infection.

There was, therefore, a powerful incentive to find new agents which would complement penicillin. So far as antibiotics were concerned there were two obvious lines of progress. Firstly, it might be possible to manipulate the penicillin molecule chemically to produce substances with different ranges of antibacterial activity, just as the changes had been rung on the sulphonamide molecule in the 1930s (p. 73). This was not feasible at that time, however, because the chemistry of penicillin itself was still too little understood. Later this approach was to yield dramatic results: the semisynthetic penicillins, particularly identified with Chain and the Beecham Group, and the cephalosporins which were to be, in the late 1950s, another triumph for the Sir William Dunn School of Pathology. The second choice was to take another lucky dip in the existing antibiosis bag in the hope of finding another antibiotic with properties generally similar to penicillin but having a different antibacterial spectrum. As has been emphasized, literally scores of different examples of antibiosis had been recorded in the literature but never investigated: some at least appeared promising. An up-to-date survey had recently been published by Waksman[18] of Rutgers University, but a systematic investigation was being carried out much nearer at hand—by Dr. W. H. Wilkins and his research assistant G. C. M. Harris in the Mycology Laboratory at Oxford. As early as the spring of 1940 they had started, in collaboration with Florey, a study of the antibacterial activity of cultures of 100 fungi, tested against three species of bacteria—*Bact. coli, Staph. aureus*, and *Pseudomonas pyocyanea*. They reported activity in nine species of *Penicillia*, 18 of *Aspergilli*, and three of *Fungi imperfecti*.[19] A year later they followed this up with a description of another 100 species and reported that 800 more were being investigated. As a general conclusion they reported that the *Aspergilli* were relatively more productive (40 per cent) of antibiotics than *Penicillia* (25 per cent).

These investigations, and those previously reported, revealed a vein of ore well worth pursuing; it seemed scarely conceivable that penicillin, their first choice, should be the only clinically effective anitbiotic, or even the best. Yet this improbability was in fact not far from the truth; penicillin has few equals and, overall, has not really been surpassed. Florey was always very conscious of this and less than a year before his death recorded the following:

We had a bit of luck with penicillin—a great deal of luck. . . . We happened to hit on an antibiotic that worked in man.[20]

In 1942, however, this plethora of examples of antibiosis seemed full of chemotherapeutic promise—the main problem was to select one, or a few, for the detailed investigation necessary to establish whether it had clinical promise or not. In the event, leaving aside the pyocyanase research already in hand, an early choice was a fungus named *Aspergillus fumigatus mut. helvola Yuill*, originally obtained by Wilkins from the Lister Institute, but several other possibilities were also explored. For those new lines of research additional workers were recruited; F. J. Philpot was supported by the Agricultural Research Council and T. I. Williams held a Nuffield Research Scholarship. Heatley, temporarily tied over penicillin by his agreement with Merck, also joined in this research on other antibiotics. An early approach by Florey to Nuffield had proved fruitless, as the latter had apparently been advised that nothing would come of the penicillin work. A little later (1943-45) money was forthcoming from the Nuffield Provincial Hospitals Trust after intervention by Sir Farquhar Buzzard, Regius Professor of Medicine, who persuaded Nuffield to visit the laboratory and see at first hand the work in progress. Generally speaking, Florey's finanicial problems were now much less.

The investigation of *Aspergillus fumigatus* yielded quick results, largely because immediate use could be made of the techniques developed for penicillin: the porcelain brewing vessels; Heatley's assay method; the chemical techiques of adsorption on charcoal and chromatographic analysis. A contributory factor was that the antibiotic substance was chemically robust and survived most ordinary laboratory manipulations: it was thus evidently different chemically from penicillin.

From the culture medium a crystalline substance was obtained at the satisfactory rate of 0.4 g per 100 litres of crude brew; after the full name of the parent mould it was named helvolic acid.[21] Preliminary tests showed that its range of activity was similar to that of penicillin, though its potency was less; nevertheless it was still far more active than any sulphonamide. Moreover, it was active against penicillin-resistant strains of pathogenic bacteria. It was not significantly deactivated by pus or whole blood, and leucocytes were not affected at concentrations much higher than those necessary to inhibit bacterial growth. Florey was guardedly optimistic and on 18 November 1943 wrote to the MRC saying: 'This substance has much of interest as it appears to come nearer to becoming a chemotherapeutic agent than any other antibiotic but penicillin'.

The Distillers Company—large-scale producers of fermentation alcohol whose thoughts were turning to getting involved in penicillin production—undertook to make at their Commercial Solvents works at Bromborough, near Liverpool, sufficient helvolic acid for proper evaluation. This would have been a useful introduction to the production of antibiotics generally: in fact, they went on to operate a Government penicillin factory at Speke. They failed to produce any helvolic acid, however, because of technical difficulties due to contamination, but in the event this was of no consequence. Although mouse-protection experiments carried out by Florey and Margaret Jennings with staphylococci gave an encouraging prolongation of life, helvolic acid proved to have one literally fatal defect—it played havoc with the liver. Biological work was therefore abandoned, though the rather surprising descrepancy between the high antibacterial level in the blood and the feeble degree of protection led Florey and Jennings to have another look at it in 1946. Its overall properties made it of sufficient interest to continue the chemical investigation. This included an examination by the distinguished X-ray crystallographer Dorothy Crowfoot (or Crowfoot Hodgkin —she married Thomas Hodgkin, son of the Provost of Queen's College, in 1937) who made important contributions to the chemistry of penicillin,[22] and in 1964 became a Nobel Laureate.

By chance Waksman and his co-workers were also looking at the antibiotic activity of cultures of *A. fumigatus* and isolated an active substance which he called fumigacin.[23] At first this seemed identical with helvolic acid but their purification was imperfect and it proved to be a mixture of this and another antibiotic named gliotoxin, which had been isolated as early as 1936. This example is indicative of the confusion prevalent at the time. By then groups all over the world were isolating antibacterial substances from a variety of moulds and bacteria and giving them instant baptism with new names; in many cases the same substance proved to have been given several quite different names. Additionally, individual moulds might produce more than one antibiotic. Thus Flora Philpot at Oxford isolated from *A. giganteus* an antibiotic, claviformin,[24] which Florey and Jennings had obtained two years earlier from *Penicillium claviforme*. To complicate matters futher, the same substance had been obtained in 1943 from *Penicillium patulum*, and named patulin; it also appeared in the literature variously as expansine, clavacin, clavatin, and penicidin. As patulin, this antibiotic had a shortlived fame in 1943 when W. E. Gye claimed that it was the long-awaited cure for the common cold.[25] The medical world was sceptical but the affair attracted so much publicity that the Medical Research Council had to organize a definitive trial in 1944; this showed the claim to be quite without foundation. Florey commented caustically:

No better example could be found of the necessity for the meticulous biological examination of antibiotics before their use in the clinic is recommended.[26]

In the early summer of 1943 this complexity of antibiotics was dramatically illustrated within the penicillin field itself—American penicillin was different from British penicillin (p. 173)! Throughout 1942 the purity of penicillin had been steadily increased by improved extraction techniques. Early in 1943, in the Squibb laboratories, the ultimate goal was reached; H. B. MacPhillamy and O. Wintersteiner produced pure crystalline penicillin (as its sodium salt.) (Plate 8). In accordance with the Anglo-American agreement on the exchange of information, this news immediately passed by telegram to the representative at the American Embassy in London of the Committee on Medical Research, Dr. Joseph Ferrebee, together with some important data on the physical properties and composition of the crystalline material. Coghill happened to be there at the time and together they went down to Oxford to tell Chain. According to a circumstantial account by Coghill Chain was disappointed at not achieving this crucial step himself, for by that time he himself had material which he regarded as pure—but he had been unable to crystallize it. He was also mystified, for the scientific data from Squibb was in some important respects at variance with his own results. Coghill has described what then happened in the following terms:

Chain placed his amorphous preparation on a microscope slide and we each had a good look at it. No crystals! We discussed the whole perplexing situation for the better part of the afternoon, Chain meanwhile pacing his laboratory. Every once in a while he would stop and look through the microscope. At one of these stops he took a mere glance and shouted, "Its crystalline!" We each took another look, and sure enough, long beautiful needle crystals had taken the place of the amorphous powder of an hour or two ago.[27]

There is no doubt at all that Coghill gave this account in good faith, but the facts of the matter are very different.[28] Chain and Abraham learned the contents of the telegram immediately, probably through Robinson. Abraham promptly converted a little of his best barium salt to the sodium salt and took a small sample to Dorothy Crowfoot Hodgkin for examination. She placed it on a microscope slide and shortly afterwards observed that it had crystallized, as a result of taking up water from the atmosphere. Abraham went back to his laboratory and repeated the experiment; he then showed the result to Chain, who clearly had not made the observation himself.

It is clear, therefore, that what Coghill witnessed was not an original experiment but a rerun of one carried out by Abraham a few days earlier by Abraham and Dorothy Crowfoot Hodgkin. The reason for this must be a matter for speculation, but possibly it was simply Chain indulging his taste for the dramatic. This is quite consistent with the pacing about and looking from time to time down the microscope; he would know that after a certain lapse of time there would be a sudden dramatic transformation of the amorphous brown material into shining crystals. Whatever the reason, the Americans were suitably impressed. Ferrebee remarked, *apropos* of Chain's typically restless pacing: 'I guess if I was working with him I would want to have him under a bell jar'. The episode is of interest also as underlining the fact that the American production process—using deep fermentation with corn-steep liquor—produced a penicillin (G) slightly different in chemical composition from that (penicillin F) resulting from the Oxford method of surface culture. These slight differences were reflected in the fact that one crystallized under dry conditions whereas the other required the presence of water vapour. In Britain these penicillins were known as penicillin I and penicillin II.

The matter was clinched when ICI chemists mixed American and British penicillins, subjected the mixture to chromatographic analysis, and isolated two chemically different products. In the event, it was shown that using different mould strains and different conditions of fermentation, several very closely related penicillins could be produced. This discovery was important for the chemical investigation as it quickly resolved some puzzling anomalies. In February 1944 the workers at Imperial College identified a third penicillin (III) identical with one obtained in July 1944 by workers at Peoria (X). In December of the same year Abbott workers obtained penicillin K (IV).[29]

An important development in the chemistry of penicillin was the belated discovery in July 1943—made independently by British and American workers—that the penicillin molecule contained sulphur, in addition to carbon, hydrogen, oxygen, and nitrogen. Rectification of this surprising oversight cleared up many chemical difficulties and in October 1943 the Oxford chemists (Abraham, Baker, Chain, and Robinson) put forward as one of two possibilities what is known as the 'β-lactam' formula, which, after much controversy, was finally accepted as correct in 1945 when Dorothy Crowfoot Hodgkin and her collaborators in the Department of Crystallography confirmed it by X-ray analysis.

The chemistry of penicillin is extremely complex and far beyond the scope of, and inappropriate to, a work such as this.

Moreover, although much of it was worked out in the Sir William Dunn School of Pathology and thus nominally under Florey's direction, he himself took no part in it. Specialists interested in the subject should consult the massive 1100-page Anglo-American publication which appeared after the war.[30] This described the work of 130 British scientists in eleven research groups and 299 Americans in 21 groups. It was appropriate that Robert Robinson,[31] perhaps the last of the great organic chemists in the classical tradition and with whom Florey had collaborated from the very beginnings of his return to Oxford, should have been chairman of the three editors. It is an interesting indication of the way in which science has advanced since the war that, given a few micrograms of pure material the best modern techniques would enable the structure of penicillin to be elucidated within a week.

We must, however, note one important practical implication of the chemical work. The β-lactam structure, which had not hitherto been encountered in any natural product, is unusual in containing a four-membered ring involving three carbon atoms and a nitrogen atom. For well-founded technical reasons, which need not concern us here, it was clear that to synthesize such a ring would be difficult and time-consuming, involving new chemical techniques of ring closure. The risk that heavy investment in fermentation plant might have to be written off at short notice thus became very much less worrying. Although synthetic penicillin was eventually made in the laboratory by J. C. Sheehan in 1959[32], all commercial penicillin is still basically made by fermentation.

These were heady times, with something new happening in the antibiotic field almost daily. In the Pathology Laboratory it was customary for those who were free to meet for tea in the library at 4 o'clock, sitting round the table for quarter of an hour or so; there was never any lack of interesting things to talk about. One enlivening item of news was that a buffalo had died at London Zoo and a post-mortem had shown its lungs to be choked with a green mass of *Aspergillus fumigatus* mould. As various strains of this were at the time front-runners in the antibiotic stakes at Oxford, and spores must have been drifting about pretty freely, this example of aspergillosis caused some consternation and a general tightening up of the culturing process, but happily, no ill-effects were ever noted. Florey himself, noticeably losing his reserve, came to these tea parties when he could and could be relied on for some stimulating and trenchant comment.

The chemical work on penicillin had one quite unexpected but —at least in retrospect—amusing consequence. Early in 1944 there was a suggestion, which proved to be without foundation, that the penicillin molecule and that of biotin (vitamin H) contained a common structural feature. This led to a request from the Editor of the *Lancet* for a short general article on biotin, not one of the best-known vitamins. With Florey's approval, this was prepared by the present writer. Later, a similar note was prepared for a very reputable British Council publication called *Monthly Science News*. Both were anonymous, and both referred very briefly to the fact that biotin deficiency may cause loss of hair; both also mentioned that biotin deficiency is almost unknown in man—since it is adequately synthesized by bacteria normally present in the intestine—unless the diet contains very large quantities of raw egg-white, which contains a protein that immobilizes biotin. All this was totally misconstrued by the *Daily Sketch* as meaning that biotin cured baldness, and on 26 April they published a news paragraph accordingly. Worse, they had managed to discover the writer's name and for good measure stated that vitamin H had been discovered in the Sir William Dunn School of Pathology; in fact it had been discovered by Fritz Kögel in Germany in 1935. As a result hundreds of desperate letters, from the bald and balding, arrived at the laboratory asking where this new miracle drug could be obtained. Florey, who disliked newspaper publicity intensely even when it was substantially correct, was predictably furious, but saw the funny side as soon as it became clear that no fault attached to anybody in his department. This, too, was good tea-party conversation.

Given the burgeoning interest in antibiotics in the late 1930s, it was inevitable that penicillin would be developed sooner or later. In the early 1940s, however, the emphasis was on sooner, for the only reason for the strong support given to it on both sides of the Atlantic was the expectation that it would contribute substantially to reducing mortality and disability from war wounds, especially those to be expected in the impending invasion of Europe; in the short-term, civilian use was of secondary importance. With its unique properties, it was to be expected that effective techniques for the treatment of battle casualties by penicillin would differ from those traditionally employed, even those using powerful new chemotherapeutic agents such as the sulphonamides. The development of these techniques was Florey's next concern, and the early summer of 1943 found him with the Army in North Africa.

Before he left, however, he had put in hand an important change in the running of his department. He had for some time been concerned that the Medical Research Council were able to support his key workers only on a year-to-year basis. This gave them no security, and he was conscious of having asked some of them to stay with him in order not to disrupt the penicillin work. At that time Nuffield was anxious to support the penicillin research substantially. It was agreed, therefore, that while the MRC would continue to provide funds for apparatus and general facilities, Nuffield would support five research workers—Abraham, Chain, Jennings, Heatley, and Sanders—on a five-year basis.[33]

6

NORTH AFRICA, RUSSIA, AND AUSTRALIA

By the spring of 1942 sufficient penicillin was available from Oxford—including raw material from Kemball, Bishop and ICI laboriously processed there—to think seriously of carrying out field trials on the control of infection associated with war wounds. At a meeting of the War Wounds Committee of the Medical Research Council in April Florey was able to offer the Army—through Major-General L. T. Poole, Director of Pathology at the War Office—some penicillin for trial in North Africa. It was a pathetically small amount and of low potency, assaying at around 30 to 40 Oxford units per mg. It was dispatched by air in July to Lt. Col. R. J. V. Pulvertaft, a Cambridge-trained pathologist who had joined the Royal Army Medical Corps from the National Institute of Medical Research in 1940 and was then in Cairo. At that time the military situation was confused; in June Rommel had driven British forces back to the Egyptian frontier and Tobruk had fallen. Not until November did Florey have any news and it was then no more than a brief message to say that 'it has been used on at least one case with some encouraging results'. It has been reported[1], though the evidence is not conclusive, that the first Allied soldier to be treated with penicillin was W. J. McGowan, son of Lord McGowan, then Chairman of ICI. He was serving with the Sherwood Rangers, and was wounded at El Alamein in October 1942. More material was sent in November 1942 and March 1943 and on the strength of this Pulvertaft was able to report that 15 cases of wound sepsis had been treated with very satisfactory results. By that time the military situation had been transformed; the British had resumed the offensive and linked up with the Americans and on 12 May the German Army in Tunisia surrendered. The next objective was Sicily and the Allied forces landed there on 10 July.

Transport was no longer a major problem and in May 1943 the War Office dispatched to Algiers what they called a Penicillin

1. Shoemaker's tools found in the roof of Saddler's, Standlake, the home of Florey's grandfather, Walter Florey, in the mid-nineteenth century.

2. Souvenir of Florey's Spitsbergen expedition of 1924, an experience which made a lasting impression on him. The drawing is on a scrap of oiled silk (artist unknown).

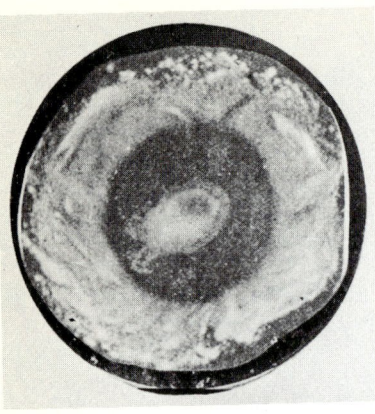

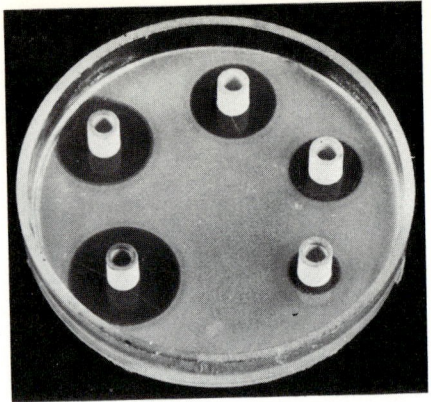

3. Florey's first experimental observation of antibiosis was in 1930. This example from his paper with N. E. Goldsworthy shows inhibition of bacterial growth by *B. coli* (central colony).

4. Heatley cylinder-plate assay method. The size of the zone of inhibition of bacterial growth round the cylinder is a measure of the activity of the solution tested.

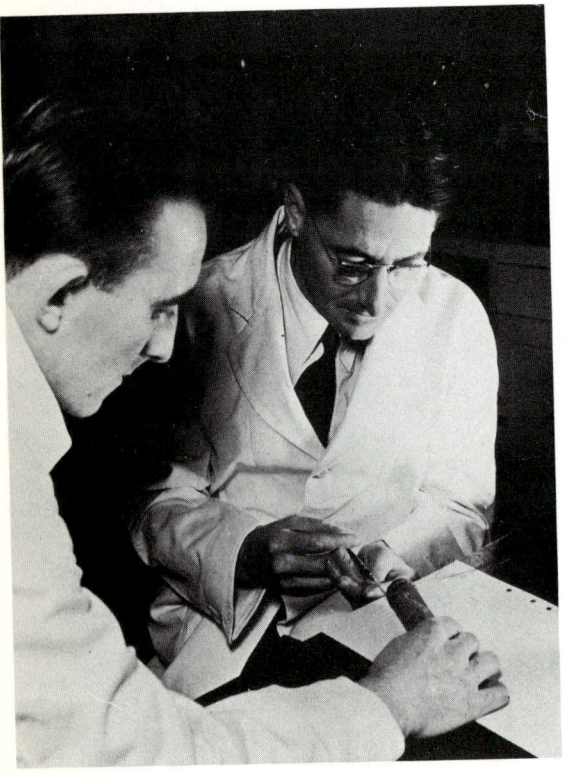

5. For almost the whole of his working life Florey's research was carried out with the technical assistance of J. H. D. Kent. Here they are shown injecting a solution into the tail of a mouse, a technique which Florey learnt from Professor J. H. Burn.

6. Heatley's original counter-current apparatus used at Oxford to extract penicillin from crude culture fluid.

7. Later penicillin extraction apparatus made at Oxford by A. G. Sanders (seen operating it), J. H. D. Kent, and J. Mascall in the first half of 1942.

8. The climax of the chemical investigation of penicillin came in the early summer of 1943, when pure crystalline penicillin was first isolated—penicillin G in the Squibb laboratories in America and penicillin F in Oxford.

9. Presentation of Nobel Prizes in Stockholm, 10 December 1945. From left to right: Artturi Virtanen, Alexander Fleming, Ernst Chain, Howard Florey, and Gabriela Mistral.

10. Mrs Mary Lasker, whom Florey first met in New York in 1946 on his way home from his South American tour: it was the beginning of a lasting and generous friendship with both Howard and Ethel.

11. The John Curtin School of Medical Research, Canberra, as it appeared at the time of Florey's resignation as adviser in the summer of 1955.

12. Dr Margaret Jennings on the steps of the Sir William Dunn School of Pathology, on the occasion of her taking her MD degree (June 1956).

13. Dr N. G. Heatley.

14. Florey officially opens the John Curtin School of Medical Research, Canberra, 27 March 1958.

15. Ethel Florey c.1960.

16. Florey's sister Anne outside the cottage at Corris Uchaf where she went to live in 1948 after retiring as school matron at Abingdon. She returned to Australia in 1953.

17. To many, Florey seemed a forbidding character but those who knew him well were aware of a warm and amusing side to his character. This picture shows him in relaxed and happy mood on the eightieth birthday of his old friend Paul Fildes in 1962.

18. Memorial unveiled in Westminster Abbey on 2 November 1982. It is adjacent to those of the astronomers John and William Herschel and the naturalist Charles Darwin.

19. Australian fifty-dollar banknote, commemorating Florey's contribution to the development of penicillin. It includes mice used in experiments; the mould inhibiting bacterial growth on a Petri dish; and Heatley's cylinder-plate assay method.

Team, taking ten million precious units of penicillin with them. The team was in fact no more than a trio, consisting of Lt. Col. Ian Fraser, surgeon; Major Scott Thomson, bacteriologist; and a technician. Later that year Florey was asked to go to North Africa to review the situation; he was joined by his old friend, compatriot, and colleague Hugh Cairns, then Consulting Neurosurgeon to the Army with the rank of Brigadier and in charge of the Military Hospital (Head Injuries) then located in St. Hugh's College, Oxford. In this last capacity he had already received small amounts of penicillin from Florey (p. 162) and they thus made a very effective combination.

North Africa 1943

Arrangements for the North African visit began to be made in November 1942. Writing to Ethel, who was busy with clinical trials with Leonard Colebrook in Birmingham, Florey wrote:

Cairns and I visited the Army bigshots. They agreed on the spot to provide a surgeon and bacteriologist and clerk full-time to come and learn for a week or two about penicillin . . . proceed by air to North Africa and get data on 100-200 cases in a couple of months. Possibly do a few gas gangrene cases but these are apparently very few.[2]

Nevertheless, it was April before arrangements could be finalized. The War Office wanted to give him military rank and send him out in uniform, but in the end he avoided this. He believed that he would be a freer agent if he went as a civilian. Florey arrived in Algiers in the hospital ship *Newfoundland* at the beginning of May, and Cairns joined him on 29 June. Thereafter he had a busy couple of months shuttling to-and-fro by air between Sousse and Tripoli, some 250 miles (400 km) apart—with a week in Cairo and finally arriving back in Britain by air on 1 September.

It was an interesting and constructive visit about which we have two main sources of information. On the purely medical side there is the confidential report to the War Office and the Medical Research Council which the two men prepared with impressive speed immediately after their return. Running to over 100 pages it was delivered on 13 October and, with remarkable dispatch, published the same month.[3] Much of the information in it was embodied in a special issue of the *British Journal of Surgery*,[4] in the following year when much more information was available. On the personal side there is some illuminating comment in letters[5] he wrote to Ethel between the beginning of June and the middle of August.

These letters are interesting not only because of the information they give about the trip itself but the light they throw on their personal relationship at that time. Bearing in mind that Howard's letters were not noticeably passionate even in the days of their postal courtship, and that they had now been married nearly twenty years, their tone seems fairly relaxed. As then, he always addressed her as 'My dear Girl'. That he wrote at least eight letters, under trying circumstances, between the beginning of June and mid-August indicates something more than duty. Unfortunately almost all Ethel's letters failed to catch up with him because he was moving about so much. A letter of 3 July is typical:

One can clearly see it is too late to get the casualties at the base hospital and the main work must be done nearer the scene of things. . . . Everything very scarce and dear but I have bought a pair of slippers for you. . . . If you don't want them send them to Paq. . . . Perhaps you will never get them anyway as I am posting them.

Again:

Hot as Hell. Sit all day in a bath of sweat and drink 9 to 10 pints per day. Nights good though. Only fly in the ointment is to have F . . . about—he talks more nonsense in a confident manner than anyone I have ever encountered. . . No sightseeing—but floating over the country a lot can be seen from the air.

From an earlier letter it is clear that he finds his surroundings agreeable. He was lodged temporarily in a school that was once a monastery, comfortable enough except for lack of a mosquito net. The countryside is well cared for and prosperous with colourful vegetation—bougainvillea, jacaranda, gum trees, and vineyards. He tells Ethel that it 'is very like Adelaide, indeed', a nostalgic note that often crept into his letters. Thus when he was in Uruguay in 1946 he wrote to her about a drive down a road planted with eucalyptus and gums—'just like Australia in wintertime'. He records his pleasure at meeting some fellow 'Aussies'. Clearly, Australia always meant a good deal to him and, as we shall see in a later chapter, he was at one time close to returning there permanently.

Medically, the situation had changed significantly since the first small supplies of penicillin had been sent to Pulvertaft. At that time there had been fierce fighting and he had seen many newly wounded men. By contrast, when Florey arrived the situation had stabilized and many of those he saw in hospital were suffering from infected wounds which had stubbornly refused to heal. At first he could do little but observe—'just footling about' as he described it to Ethel—for Cairns was bringing out their main supply of penicillin, some 40 million units. It arrived with a covering note from Heatley who, with his usual attention to detail, had checked the assays and noted certain discrepancies.

Today, with penicillin long established in routine use, it is difficult to realize that in the early days its application had to be justified. Just as Oxford clinicians had been reluctant to allow Florey to treat any but their most desperate cases—he wryly described himself as a corpse-reviver—so many army surgeons and doctors were suspicious of the new drug. For the most part they put their faith in the sulphonamides, though not all of them even did that. As he wrote home to Ethel, 'all surgeons have their opinions [about sulphonamides] ranging from being no use to they are the goods'. In this Report, Florey and Cairns reached a firm conclusion on this:

It is probably going much too far to say that sulphonamide applications by the present methods are of no value, but they certainly do not provide an answer to the treatment of septic wounds.

Without convincing demonstrations, Army doctors could not be expected to see eye-to-eye with Florey and Cairns, who started from the assumption that the clinical value of penicillin had already been proved and what was now necessary was to see what changes were necessary in medical procedure in the field to take the greatest advantage of its unique properties. Decisions on this were facilitated by the attachment of experienced American officers to British medical units.

Between them, they confirmed the important conclusion early reached by Florey that for the best results prophylactic treatment was desirable and should be commenced as early as possible:

One strong impression conveyed to all who followed these cases was that it was far too late to start penicillin treatment weeks or months after wounding at a Rear Base Hospital, and that its use should be tried much earlier, before the establishment of serious infection.

And again:

> There is a time period in the history of war wounds, up to about 10 days, when the wound is relatively clean and suture is possible. The tissues are fresh, the organisms have not become intractable and insensitive to chemotherapy, and the haemolytic streptococcus in particular is uncommon. There can be little doubt that infection with this latter organism is usually the result of 'hospital infection', and is seldom seen in a wound less than 10 days old.

They made the important recommendation that soft tissue wounds should be closed by suture at the earliest possible moment and treated with penicillin by a method similar to that which Florey had devised for mastoid. Fine rubber tubes were sewn into the wound and penicillin solution was instilled through them periodically. This was not only effective but appealed to the nurses, who found it easier than changing conventional dressings. That the surgeons agreed to this radical departure from accepted practice is a tribute to Florey's personal confidence and authority. As a concomitant to these recommendations it was necessary that forward area medical officers should have special training; this seemed to them desirable on general grounds:

> We saw some examples of forward operations on head wounds which suggested that the surgeons who performed them had not given serious thought to what they could expect to accomplish by their operations.

In all over 100 casualties were treated, including chronic septic wounds, recent fractures, gas gangrene infections, burns, and head wounds. With characteristic understatement he told Ethel half-way through the visit that 'results are beginning to mature—good, bad, and indifferent'. In fact, as the official Report shows they were on the whole very good considering the difficult circumstances, which included the inevitable disruption consequent on the invasion of Sicily and subsequently of the Italian mainland. Of necessity the work had to be done on an *ad hoc* basis without the careful controls that would normally be practised. Florey was very conscious of this, and urged Ethel to make the most of her opportunities at Birmingham: 'I hope you have got your Birmingham results in order as it is fairly certain they will be the only really controlled series for a long time to come'. It is interesting that even with so much urgent work on hand Florey found time to indulge his seemingly endless scientific curiosity. In the Report he speculates on the nature of the healing process, a subject on which, with Professor Paterson Ross, he had prepared a report for the MRC in 1940 and to which he was to direct his attention again in later years:

Seeing that nearly all wounds are infected, it is interesting to inquire why all of them do not assume a chronic inflammatory state. A proportion do, but the majority eventually heal, in spite of the continued presence of pus-producing organisms. Many are inclined to attribute the supervention of chronic sepsis to 'constitutional' or nutritional factors. This may well be true, and it seems remarkable that as far as we could ascertain no serious attempt has been made to investigate the nutritional state—used in a broad sense—of patients with septic and healing wounds.

While the strong government support given to penicillin production had humanitarian motives, it was also based on strictly practical considerations. It was of the first importance that men suffering wounds not involving permanent disability and discharge from duty should get back to their units as quickly as possible. In this context one naturally tends to think of casualites sustained in battle but in the stress of war venereal disease can frequently be as disabling as enemy fire. At Sousse, Florey and Cairns learned from Major W. H. D. Priest, Adviser in Venereoolgy for Tunisia, that gonorrhoea was prevalent in highly trained fighting troops, such as parachutists, shortly before they were due to fight and many cases did not respond to sulphonamide treatment. Accordingly, Priest was given sufficient penicillin to treat ten cases of gonorrhoea, mostly contracted in local brothels. The results were dramatic, both in nine cases which had failed to respond to one or more courses of sulphonamide and one not previously treated at all. They concluded that:

This treatment is so simple that there would appear to be no reason, if sufficient penicillin is available, why it should not be carried out in forward medical units, with no more than two days absence from duty.

In fact sufficient penicillin did quickly become available and a year later Major John N. Robinson, of the US Army described 95 per cent cures in 1000 cases of sulphonamide-resistant gonorrhoea.[6] By that time success was also being achieved with syphilis, another major military problem. Its extent can be judged from the fact that in April 1943 intensive arsenotherapy had been initiated in certain US Army hospitals in Europe. Over 2000 patients had been treated and although an 85-90 per cent cure was reported—not much less than that achieved with penicillin—it involved 25 days hospitalization and the availability of doctors with special training in syphilotherapy. The treatment could evoke very unpleasant symptons and, in unskilled hands, could even be fatal. In passing, it may be remarked that this use of penicillin was envisaged at an early stage; at the War Production Board in America, Elder displayed on his desk a notice reading: 'The goal—to make penicillin so cheaply that it costs less to cure than to get it!' However, in some quarters this was not thought amusing, and he had to remove it.

For successful military use of penicillin it was necessary not only to have sufficient quantity of the drug but also to train men in the new and unconventional techniques necessary to use it to the best advantage. Not the least important result of Florey and Cairn's mission was to build up a small team of surgeons and bacteriologists to work with forward troops in Italy. Additionally, Florey—in addition to all his other activities—gave lectures at Algiers, Sousse, Tripoli, and Cairo, to the Airborne Division, and even, on his way home, in Gibraltar.

Thereafter, progress was rapid. The War Office organized course of penicillin instruction for nearly 200 pathologists and over 500 clinicians at the Royal Herbert Hospital, Woolwich. In these courses much use was made of film, which Florey, with his keen interest in photography, shot in North Africa. This film was not for the squeamish, and on one occasion when he showed it in Oxford the projector went whirring on after it had finished —the operator was on the floor in a dead faint!

Looking ahead a little, the supply position improved so rapidly that it was eventually possible to fly 20 million units a day—an amount hardly credible at the start of the campaign—to the Italian theatre of war. This raised unforeseen transport difficulties. The freeze-dried penicillin was very light and fluffy and the bottles were relatively large and heavy. This problem was referred to Dr. J. W. Trevan of Wellcome, who immediately suggested tableting—a natural reaction as the original firm of Burroughs Wellcome had built up an important business in tableted chemicals of various kinds, especially for photography. This not only eased the transport problem but greatly simplified dispensing in the field.

Florey's visit was a success in more ways than one; he clearly enjoyed the experience and made an excellent impression on most of his military colleagues even though in his last letter home he expressed the fear that everyone would be glad to see the back of him because he had got them working so hard. On his return he received a very gratifying letter from Lt-Col. W. Brockbank of the 48th General Hospital, Middle East Forces:

Both you and Cairns left us with no doubt that you had enjoyed being with us. That seemed clear each day. Mind you, I credited a great deal of your obvious joie-de-vivre to a natural paternal pride in a flourishing and rapidly developing offspring, but when you had washed penicillin from your hands and joined us in the Mess there was never once any suggestion of 'My God, its bully again' or 'Only one egg today?' attitude. In fact you practically became the life and soul of the dining room and particularly you did us a world of good by stimulating scientific discussion and thought in a way that is foreign to army medicine. Rest assured we have missed you very much and if you are ever round this way again (visiting Russia or some other jaunt) you will be sure of a rousing welcome if you call in.[7]

This reveals a side of Florey's nature that was quite genuine when a social occasion called for it; he could be severe and forbidding, but it is a great mistake to think he was always so. However, one of his letters to Ethel shows him back in abrasive mood:

Brush with consulting orthopaedician who started giving raspberries. Had the outlook associated with orthopaedics. It was a very great advantage not being in the Army because I was able to give him a few home truths and seem to have been in form that day.

Florey leaves in an interim report a record of his own satisfaction with the trip:

Wherever we went we were treated with the greatest kindness and hospitality. We stayed always in hospitals as our work required that we should do so. This was fortunate for us as we learnt more, and more quickly, from daily contact with a large variety of MOs than would have been possible if we had been inspecting. We were most impressed by the attention the wounded from Sicily received . . . and above all with the morale and bearing of the wounded.

In another letter to Ethel he remarks that it was a relief to be 'out of the atmosphere of England and see some of the chaps here. It might do some of our colleagues good.' He never spared himself and it was a gruelling trip. He lost 10lb (4.5 kg) in weight but gained 'a slight figure again'.

The tide of war was now decisively changing. At the beginning of September the Italians surrendered unconditionally and a few weeks later declared war on Germany. German troops in Italy made a more stubborn defence than was expected and not until 1 May 1945 were they to surrender finally on that front, but nevertheless it was possible to make positive moves towards the long-awaited opening of a Second Front in northern Europe, for which the Russians were pressing. This demanded not only close military collaboration between all the Allies but also consideration of the immense political problems to be solved when at last the Nazi power was broken. On 28 November these great issues began to be debated between Churchill, Stalin, and Roosevelt at the Tehran Conference, at which a firm decision was taken to give priority to Overlord, the great military operation which opened with the D-Day landings in Normandy on 6 June 1944. Throughout the proceedings Churchill suffered from a sore throat and feverish cold but was kept going by Lord Moran, his personal physician. On his return journey he collapsed at Tunis with pneumonia and it is interesting that although penicillin was then available there from Pulvertaft, Moran and his colleague Dr. D. E. Bedford elected to play safe and use a sulphonamide. Fortunately it did the trick and Churchill was well satisfied:

The M and B, which I also called Moran and Bedford, did the work most effectively. There is no doubt that pneumonia is a very different illness from what it was before this marvellous drug was discovered. I did not at any time relinquish my part in the direction of affairs . . .[8]

A Churchillian statement, but somewhat behind the times, bearing in mind that this was written in 1951 when penicillin would have been the treatment of choice. Other accounts suggest that he was in fact more seriously ill than he was inclined to admit and Mrs. Churchill was flown out from England. Moran insisted on several weeks' convalescence at Marrakesh. During this enforced leisure he read Jane Austen, who 'seemed to go very well with M and B'. We are left to speculate on a literary accompaniment to penicillin. Possibly Jane Austen again, a writer of whom Florey, too, was fond; he used to compare Margaret Jennings with Anne Elliot.

North Africa was the turn of the tide in the war: it was also the turn of the tide in Florey's personal affairs. His passion for research was undiminished but his opportunity much less. Altough literally hundreds of other people were now involved with penicillin, for the moment he still had a unique role to play. His knowledge and experience of its properties, and his personal prestige, were such that it was to him that the highest authorities inevitably turned for guidance. This led to another long and arduous journey before the year was out, this time to Moscow.

Russia 1943-44

The Tehran conference had, of course, taken many months to set up and apart from the crucial political and strategic deliberations of the three leaders at the summit there was much activity at a lower level. Relationships between Russia and her two main allies were always uneasy at the best, with less trust on the British side than the American, but at that particular time, with firmer assurances about a Second Front—to which Russia attached immense importance for the relief of German pressure—there was something of a thaw. As one consequence of this the Russians in the summer of 1943 invited an Anglo-American scientific mission to visit Russia. Each country was to send two men, and Florey was selected to head the British team; his companion was A. G. Sanders. Brockbank's parenthetic reference in September to a 'visit to Russia or some other jaunt' suggests that Florey already had some hint of this while he was in North Africa. The choice was doubtless made on the basis that the production and use of penicillin was a major, though not the only, topic to be discussed. Others specifically included were chemical warfare, typhus, malaria, blood and plasma transfusion, wound healing, disinfestation, and air sterilization. Nevertheless, Mellanby advised Florey just before he left that it was his war experience that would be of the greatest interest to the Russians. The American team was similarly penicillin-orientated. It consisted of Dr. Baird Hastings, who had represented the National Research Council at the earliest penicillin meetings in America at the time of Florey and Heatley's visit in 1941, and Dr. Michael Shimkin, a fluent Russian speaker.[9]

Before considering Florey's personal role, it is useful to consider briefly the Russian background. There, as in America, Dubos' isolation of tyrothricin in 1939 (p. 83) had stimulated interest in antibiosis as a potential new source of chemotherapeutic agents, and this was further encouraged by the problems of treating tragically large numbers of war casualties. In January 1942 a laboratory for the study of antibiotics was set up in the Institute of Tropical Medicine in Moscow. This was under the direction of Dr. G. F. Gause, who later became head of the Institute of New Antibiotics of the Academy of Medical Sciences.

With N. Brazhnikova, Gause screened many hundreds of soil bacteria including a strain of *Bacillus brevis*, from which Dubos had obtained tyrothricin. From their strain they obtained a similar but chemically distinct and simpler antibiotic which they named gramicidin S(oviet). Unlike penicillin, this was too toxic for parenteral use but was quickly found to be useful in war surgery for the control of local infections. By early 1943 some 1500 cases had been treated in ten Russian hospitals and in July the Medical Research Council of the USSR formally admitted gramicidin S for general medical use. Large-scale industrial production was started and a handbook on its use was published in November. For several years gramicidin S was the Russian front-runner in antibiotics.[10] By contrast, although the various publications on penicillin had been followed with interest little had been done except small-scale laboratory cultures of a strain of *P. notatum*, which was wrongly identified as *P. crustosum*. Thus when the Anglo-American mission arrived they found the interesting situation that their hosts knew quite a lot about antibiosis and techniques associated with antibiotic production and use but virtually nothing about penicillin. To make good this deficiency was one of their principal tasks.

Florey and Sanders, taking with them in their briefcases phials of penicillin and reports on its production and use, left Oxford for London by train in the early hours of 23 December 1943. The account that follows is based on the detailed day-to-day account compiled by Sanders of what they did and whom they met.[11] It is typical of the two men that while Sanders' diary was a clothbound book Florey entered his notes in three government-issue notebooks. The weather was cold and foggy and the aeroplane that was to take them from Hendon to Prestwick was grounded. Instead they went to Scotland that night by sleeper and finally took off late on Christmas Eve. For the next stage of their journey Florey was on familiar ground that he had left only a few months previously. They landed at Marrakesh, where Churchill was convalescing, on Christmas Day and then flew on across the old North African battlefield to Cairo. There they found that their arrival was not expected and no transport had been organized. They were eventually met by a Third Secretary whose offhand and patronizing manner Florey found 'extremely irritating', as he remarked in the subsequent report he prepared for the Medical Research Council: 'he would be likely to do more harm to British interests in five minutes than could be repaired in six months'. Even a special letter of introduction written for them by Clement Attlee had no effect at first. After a day's rest, during which Florey renewed acquaintance with Pulvertaft, they continued by a circuitous route to Tehran, being joined by their two American colleagues at Abadan.

Tehran was to prove as unlucky to Florey as it had been to Churchill; he went down with influenza and had to be admitted to the American Hospital at Camp Amirabad with a high temperature. He convalesced pleasantly with the British ambassador, Sir Reader Bullard. He was a better patient than Churchill, however, and sensibly decided not to proceed until he felt really fit, and in fact it was 23 January—just a month after leaving Oxford—before they finally moved on to Moscow, where they were soon comfortably ensconced in a hotel suite and well looked after.

While officially an emissary of the British Government Florey was also a representative of the Royal Society and as such was hospitably received by its Russian equivalent, the Academy of Sciences; much later it was to award him its Lomonossov Medal and elect him a Foreign Member (1966). From Sir Henry Dale, President of the Royal Society, he brought two very valuable gifts. One was a copy of the first (1679) edition of Newton's *Principia*, one of the most important scientific works ever published and written by Dale's most illustrious predecessor as President. It is now a collector's piece of great value. The other was the draft of a letter from Newton to Prince Alexander de Menzicoff, chosen because the latter was the first Russian to be elected a Fellow of the Royal Society (1714).

During their month in Moscow the visitors were kept busy with visits to hospitals and clinics. Florey described the clinical use of penicillin—showing his North African film to appreciative audiences—and Sanders its production and assay by the Heatley method. Florey's gift for languages did not extend to Russian. As he remarked afterwards 'it is very exhausting trying to make contact with a vocabulary of about 100 words and some waving of arms, and one is never sure whether one has really understood the other'. Transliteration from cyrillic characters was also a considerable problem. Much time was spent at the Institute for the Biochemistry of Micro-organisms and Immunology. The Director was a woman, Professor Z. V. Yermolieva, and Florey clearly found her a welcome contrast to most of her more stolid colleagues: 'she is about 45 and is a vivacious woman of much charm. . . . I suspect her personal charm rather than any outstanding scientific ability has been a big factor in her scientific career': so he described her in the official report he submitted after his visit. Not all their time was devoted to penicillin, however. Sanders gave valuable information on British practice in blood transfusion and the use of plasma substitutes, drawing on his considerable experience in this field in Oxford (p. 92). They brought valuable knowledge of synthetic substitutes for the antimalarial drug, quinine, then very scarce because of the Japanese occupation of most of the East Indian cinchona plantations. Additionally, there was, of course, also the usual round of social occasions, including six visits to the Bolshoi Theatre where, among others, they saw the famous ballerina Ulanova. Apart from its scientific importance the mission had diplomatic overtones; both the British and the American governments were anxious to improve relations with Russia and the British Ambassador, Sir Archibald Clark Kerr, a friend of Cairns, made known his satisfaction with the way the visit had gone. Florey was losing the outspoken impetuosity of his younger days, that had branded him as a scientific Australian bushranger, and emerging as a more mature and urbane character.

This medical mission had two interesting consequences. The first was that Florey was given some ampoules of gramicidin S to take back to England, and in due course these found their way to

Dr. R. L. M. Synge, a biochemist then working at the Lister Institute. He obtained further quantities from the Soviet Red Cross and Red Cresent Societies in London and began an investigation of its chemical structure, later in collaboration with Dorothy Crowfoot Hodgkin at Oxford. This work showed that gramicidin S was a pentapeptide—that is, a combination of five amino acids; the interesting feature was that the same five acids were present in Dubos' tyrocidine, but differently arranged.

The second consequence was the result of a comment by Florey that the best way for the Russians to learn about penicillin would be for them to send a mission to Britain and the United States to visit appropriate laboratories and plants. This plan came to nothing, but in 1945 a Russian biologist, N. Borodin, came to work for a year in Oxford in Florey's department. In due course, Florey, Borodin, and Philpot published an account of an antibiotic, tardin, produced by *Penicillium tardum*.[12] This proved to have no clinical value. Borodin was to appear later in a different guise, as a member of the Soviet Trade Delegation in London at Highgate. In the summer of 1948 Chain was in formal correspondence with him about collaborating with the Soviet Government in setting up a penicillin factory in Russia with a capacity of 500 billion units per month. That, however, is another story, to which we will briefly return later.

Florey had hoped to return quietly to Oxford after his visit to Moscow, but Pulvertaft—whom he had met in Cairo on the way out—had been busy organizing a lecture tour for him. Heatley had sent him some slides he had asked for on the way out. He spoke in Tehran, Cairo, Beirut, and Jerusalem and visited the Weizmann Institute in Rehovoth. Returning finally to Cairo—encountering a considerably chastened Third Secretary—he and Sanders were able to enjoy three days of relaxation, and took the opportunity of sightseeing (and of course taking photographs) at Luxor. The Oxford influence proved far-reaching. Among those he met in Cairo was another Magdalen man of his own age, T. S. R. Boase, who was Professor of the History of Art in London University: at that time he was acting as the British Council representative in the Middle East, and was thus well placed to organize Florey's travels. After the war Boase came· back to Oxford as President of Magdalen College. Florey also met another old friend, Keith Murray (later Lord Murray) Fellow, and subsequently Rector, of his own college, Lincoln. Murray, an agricultural economist and historian, found himself in Cairo during the war as Director of Food and Agriculture of the Middle East Supply Centre. All these activities took up much time; he and Sanders did not get back to Oxford until the early hours of 29 March, more than three months after they set out. There, at 2 o'clock in the morning, Kent met them at the station and helped them home by loading their luggage on his bicycle. It had been a gruelling trip. They had been away 97 days, of which 42 had been spent in travel or hanging about waiting for transport. Only four days counted as holiday.

On his return Florey wrote a long official report on his mission. It was in two parts, both heavily stamped 'Secret'; the second part was additionally stamped 'Not to be sent to America'. This proviso was not designed to keep relevant information from the Americans but because Florey—with characteristic efficiency —took the opportunity of using his experience to offer some well-considered advice about the organization of any future missions and the desirability or otherwise (in his view otherwise) of keeping a senior British scientist resident in Moscow. He also made some exceedingly scathing remarks on the scientific press releases the Ministry of Information was making available in Tehran, especially a radio script on penicillin originating with the British Overseas Press Service in New York. The only embarrassment to the Americans of seeing the second part of the report would have been the high praise he gave to their organizational ability. In due course Baird Hastings, who had left Moscow before Florey, sent him a copy of his own report for information and comment.

Australia 1944

After his trips to North Africa and Moscow—both of them intellectually and physically demanding, especially under wartime conditions and with a spell of illness—even so inveterate a traveller as Florey might have been glad of a stay at home. If so, he was to be disappointed, for very soon another such demand was to be made of him, this time to visit Australia. Like those he had just made, the main purpose of this visit was to give urgently needed authoritative information on the production and use of penicillin for the treatment of war casualties. It was, therefore, a call that could not be ignored, especially as it was his own country that was calling for his services. Quite unexpectedly, this trip had important repercussions; it led to his close identification from the very outset with the project to set up an Australian National University in Canberra. As this greatly affected the whole course of his later life, and almost led to his permanent return to Australia, it will be the subject of a separate chapter. For the moment we will consider the trip only briefly and in the immediate context.

In May 1944 Churchill summoned an Imperial Conference in London. Among those who attended was John Curtin, the Australian Prime Minister, who asked Florey—supposedly at the instigation of General Blamey, the Australian commander-in-chief[13]—if he would visit Australia as an adviser on penicillin. He agreed to come as quickly as his commitments allowed and the necessary travel arrangements could be made through General MacArthur, but in the event it was July before he could get away. He went out with enhanced prestige, for the Birthday Honours of the summer announced that George VI had conferred the honour of knighthood on him. Fleming also received this honour in the same year. By that time the scope of the trip had been extended, as the American authorities also wanted to take advantage of his presence and had asked him to give lectures and visit hospitals in the Pacific theatre of war. He went out via the United States and then visited Madang, Alexishafen, and Lae before reaching Australia. There general responsibility for providing penicillin for the armed forces was in the hands of Colonel E. V. Keogh, who later had a distinguished medical career. Bottle-plant manufacture of penicillin had been established in the Commonwealth Serum Laboratories by Dr. Percival Bazeley, a veterinarian, who was later to become its director. Bazeley, hauled back from New Guinea, had gained the necessary knowledge and experience in the course of a quick visit to the United States in the latter part of 1943, accompanied by H. H. Kretchmar, a chemist who was also taken from military service. They brought back with them from Peoria a culture of the high-producing *Penicillium* isolated in the local market (p. 146). Independently, a firm of chemical manufacturers in Adelaide, F. H. Faulding and Co. Ltd. had begun manufacture in 1943 using the Oxford method of production and extraction; information about this, and a culture of the mould, had been obtained from Dr. Nancy Atkinson, a lecturer in bacteriology at Adelaide University.[14] This enterprise in his home town pleased Florey very much. Opportunities for doctors to gain experience in the clinical use of penicillin were arranged by Keogh at the Heidelberg Military Hospital in Melbourne. By such improvisation sufficient penicillin was made available to meet urgent military needs in the operations following the landing of the 9th Australian Division at Tarakan, in North Borneo, on 1 May.

It is said that Florey was upset to find that for advice on the production of penicillin Australia had relied wholly on the United States and not turned to him, as the Australian-born pioneer, at all. Allegedly, he said as much to Keogh.[15] If so, any feelings of rancour seem soon to have disappeared. It is understandable that, as they were situated, the Australians should turn to America. In the Pacific, Japan was the common enemy, as Churchill reminded his listeners in a sombre passage in a broadcast to the British people after VE Day:

We must never forget that beyond all lurks Japan, harassed and failing, but still a people of a hundred millions, for whose warriors death has few terrors. . . . We must remember that Australia and New Zealand and Canada were and are all directly menaced by this evil Power.[16]

It was a timely warning. In the euphoria of the defeat of Germany it was easy in Europe to forget that on the other side of the world the war still raged. The military need for penicillin in the Pacific area was as great as ever. This argument applied with equal force to the Japanese and it is not surprising that they had made a considerable effort to make penicillin for themselves. More surprising is the fact that Russia and Germany did so little.

Japan and penicillin

So far we have looked at the major projects started in Britain and the United States and noted very limited work on a laboratory scale in the other partner of the Grand Alliance, Russia. We have noted, too, a small joint programme started in 1942 in neutral Switzerland between the Swiss Federal Institute of Technology and CIBA, the industrial chemical firm located in Basle (p. 127). Florey had expressed fears that through Switzerland important published information might find its way to Germany.

These fears were justified, though fortunately no consequences damaging to the Allied cause resulted. At the Pharmacological Laboratory of Berlin University, Manfred Kiese made a detailed survey of publications on antibiotics, including those of the Oxford group. This was published[17] in August 1943 and by devious routes a copy of the journal reached Tokyo through an organized system set up to transmit newly published scientific information to Tokyo via the Japanese Embassy in Berlin. It was sent by whatever means were available under wartime conditions —by cable, by mail through Switzerland, or in the luggage of returning diplomats. The organization had a budget of about £10 000 per annum and nearly a thousand books and journals are known to have been transmitted between September 1943 and September 1944. By the time Kiese's article appeared communications had become exceedingly difficult and it seems that the journal was carried by one of a party of Japanese from their Embassy in Berlin who sailed from Brest on 5 October 1943 in the Japanese submarine I-8 and arrived at the naval base of Kure, near Hiroshima, on 21 December. By 5 January 1944 Kiese's article had been translated into Japanese and before the end of the month a proposal had been put to the Ministry of War for a £10 000 programme of research on the purification and synthesis of penicillin, to be completed by August. This was approved. A Penicillin Committee was set up and had its first meeting on 1 February.

On that very day the Committee had important confirmatory evidence of the importance the Allies attached to penicillin and the progress they had made. The popular newspaper *Asahi* completed publication of a long and circumstantial account of penicillin sent by cable from its correspondent in Buenos Aires. It gave much information about how penicillin was made and how it was used; it even reported large-scale production at Peoria. Substantially it was correct and the one major error it contained ironically strengthened rather than weakened its impact. This was a note to the effect that Winston Churchill's life had been saved by penicillin when he went down with pneumonia in North Africa; as we have noted, his physicians played safe and relied on a sulphonamide. This was to be the last cable from Buenos Aires, but during the summer of 1944 more useful publications on penicillin trickled through the system to Tokyo, despite a worsening war situation.

After a false start, when cultures of *Penicillium* showed no antibacterial activity, and it was rumoured that the whole affair was an elaborate hoax by the Allies, the Japanese made remarkable progress. By mid-May some 750 mould strains had been tested and 75 showed antibacterial activity. Inevitably, some of this activity was due to other antibiotics but efficient penicillin producers were quickly identified and grown in surface culture in flasks or trays. Penicillin was extracted mainly on the basis of the Oxford process, by absorption on charcoal and extraction with acetone. At a meeting on 30 October important progress was recorded. Using the best available material, mouse protection experiments similar to those carried out at Oxford at the end of 1939 had been carried out; the pathogen used was *Streptococcus pneumoniae*. A petient suffering from a purulent inflammation of the thigh had been successfully treated by intravenous injection. The purity of this material is difficult to assess as although the test organism was *Staphylococcus aureus*, as used in Britain and America, it was of a different (Terajima) strain; it is recorded as having been effective at a dilution of one part in 1 600 000. This is roughly comparable with the Oxford result of 1941. Much later, it was shown that the penicillin unit based on the Terajima strain was about five times greater than the Oxford unit.

It was also reported that the purification process had been so much improved that a crystalline barium salt of penicillin had been prepared. If correct, this is astonishing for it will be recalled that in the massive Anglo-American project this stage was not achieved until the early summer of 1943. There seems, however, to be some discrepancy, for analysis of the Japanese material showed the presence only of carbon, hydrogen, nitrogen, and oxygen; no sulphur was indicated. Early chemical work in Britain had been confused through failure to detect sulphur but the analyses were done on very impure material; it is harder to see how it could have been overlooked in pure crystalline material.

At this stage a decision was taken to initiate industrial production. In support of this the Japanese had not only the evidence of their own research and development programme but—no less important—abundant evidence from the world's press that the

Allies had such faith in penicillin that they had already started large-scale production and were plentifully supplying their forces in the field.

Unhappily, this decision was taken when Japan was in a situation similar to that of Britain in the autumn of 1940; increasingly heavy air-raids were severely disrupting industrial production. Nevertheless, the attempt was made, and once again the popular press provided inspiration. An article in the Egyptian science magazine *Parade* illustrated a penicillin plant utilizing some dairy equipment—itself reminiscent of the simple Oxford extraction plant—and an approach was made to the Morinaga Milk Company at Mishima; before the end of the year a small production unit was in operation. Using essentially the Oxford method of production and extraction they obtained yields of about 3 g of the calcium salt of penicillin from every 100 litres of crude mould broth. Early in January 1945 the Banyu Pharmaceutical Company set up a small penicillin plant at Okazaki, in a converted silk factory. By this time pencillin had been renamed nekiso (the blue principle) in accordance with Japanese reluctance to adopt western nomenclature.

By that time, however, conditions in Japan were deteriorating so rapidly that no major development was possible. For all practical purposes penicillin made no impact there until after the war, when large-scale production was achieved with the collaboration of American advisers. This story of Japan's wartime penicillin project is necessarily brief; those interested in a detailed account are referred to a recent paper by Yukimasa Yagisawa, Director of the Japan Antibiotics Research Foundation.[18] It is interesting to speculate why, when they all had equal opportunities, Russia and Germany virtually ignored penicillin while Japan forged ahead so rapidly, but that is outside the scope of this book.

7

THE TEMPO CHANGES

The following year, 1945, was one of changing fortunes for Florey, as for the world. For six years he had not only driven himself remorselessly in order to get penicillin established but had had to contend also with a multiplicity of other commitments inseparable from his duties as professor in Oxford responsible for the running of a large department carrying out both teaching and research. The visits to North Africa, Moscow, and Australasia had been stimulating but tiring. With success achieved, and responsibility for the production, distribution, and use of penicillin in other hands, some reaction was to be expected, yet real relaxation was not possible. All kinds of matters incidental to penicillin could not be ignored; the claims made by Fleming, controversy over the decision not to seek patent protection, constant demands for lectures and articles, official duties of various kinds, were all irritating and time-consuming even when set against the satisfaction of wide recognition of his pioneer work.

The tone of the letters he wrote to Ethel on his travels shows very clearly that while there had certainly been no belated blossoming of romance the tensions of the earlier years of the marriage had eased. His descriptions of his experiences are relaxed and laced with his own dry brand of humour; the sometimes inconsequential admixture of comments and inquiries on matters of joint professional interest are a tacit recognition of the independent importance of her clinical work. Her wellbeing was always very much in his mind and in later years, when her health began seriously to fail, the need to organize his finances to make adequate provision for support of an invalid wife weighed heavily on him. There is no reason to doubt his own statement that this was a factor, though certainly not the only one, in his decision to resign his professorship and accept the Provostship of Queen's College, which offered him longer tenure. To most people, even those who knew him well, Florey seemed supremely confident and self-sufficient, a highly efficient operator deferring to nobody; a man who knew exactly where he was going and how he would get there. As so often happens, however, this brave front concealed an inner need for reassurance and encouragement. Such a need Ethel, mindful though she always was of his wellbeing, had never been able to fulfil and the time was irrevocably past when the kind of warm relationship he craved might have been achieved. Increasingly, he found himself turning to Margaret Jennings not only as a very competent colleague in research but as a confidante with whom he could relax and unburden himself of problems and anxieties that others did not even realize were troubling him. Thus started a long and tender personal relationship that culminated, after Ethel's death in 1966, in their marriage only a few months before the end of his own life.

Following his visit to Australia in 1944, Florey gave much time to preparing the memorandum on a proposed school of medical research requested by the Australian government; this was completed and dispatched early in April 1945. It was to prove the start of a quite unexpectedly heavy commitment in which he was to be involved for the next ten years and, to a lesser extent, for the rest of his life. With its completion, however, domestic affairs for the moment largely claimed his attention. Not until the spring of 1947 did Florey become formally associated with the Australian National University, as a member of the Academic Advisory Committee.

By the beginning of 1945 the war in Europe was not over, but barring unforeseen developments the end was in sight. The Allies were relentlessly closing in on Germany from west, east, and south and Churchill, Roosevelt, and Stalin met again, at Yalta, to plan for unconditional surrender. There was a general easing of tension and a move towards relaxation of wartime restrictions. In February, an apparent misunderstanding about this led the Oxford workers into a sharp dispute with Glaxo and the *Biochemical Journal*. Chain was greatly incensed to see in that journal an account of the chemistry of penicillin which was offensive to him on several counts. After consultation with Florey and his chemical colleagues Chain wrote an angry letter[1] to the Editor. He complained, first and foremost, that the article contravened a security ban, backed with the authority of the Official Secrets Act, that nothing should be published on the purification and constitution of penicillin: even when the ban was lifted, the understanding was that nothing was to be published without the agreement of all concerned. Secondly, the Glaxo workers had claimed credit for chemical work done by Chain and Abraham and published in 1942, before the ban came into force. Thirdly, Glaxo had criticized the amyl acetate extraction process, which they said gave poor yields and troublesome emulsions. Chain pointed out that 90 per cent yields were obtainable; that the Oxford workers had found, and disclosed to Glaxo, that a Sharples centrifuge would deal with the emulsion; and that most commercial firms had adopted the use of amyl acetate. He concluded sourly that 'if the Glaxo workers obtain poor yields then this reflects only on their technique'. Later, Florey and Chain similarly complained through Mellanby about another article, by V. Du Vigneaud, that had appeared in the American journal *Science* on 9 November 1946. There was some embarrassment when it transpired that Robinson had given this his approval without consulting anybody. Eventually, of course, the whole story of the chemical investigation of penicillin during the war appeared in proper form in the collective work already mentioned (p. 174), and this brought to an end a period of desultory bickering between the workers concerned.

In the preparation of this massive work Florey had no direct part, although he got drawn into Anglo-American squabbles about delays in publication and breaches of the non-disclosure agreement. But he and his Oxford colleagues were embarked on what grew to be an even more considerable enterprise. This was a comprehensive review, to be published by the Oxford University Press, of the whole field of antibiotics—'a survey of penicillin, streptomycin and other antimicrobial substances from fungi, actinomycetes, bacteria, and plants—from the earliest observations in the latter part of the nineteenth century'. The reference to plants reflects the fact that Mrs. E. M. Osborn—wife of T. G. B. Osborn, also from Australia, who was Professor of Botany in Oxford—was carrying out in the laboratory a survey of antibacterial substances produced by plants. His co-authors, in addition to Ethel, were Chain, Heatley, Margaret Jennings, Sanders, and Abraham. As they remarked in their preface 'the book grew to dimensions not originally contemplated'. In the event it ran to nearly 1800 closely printed pages, in two volumes, and included some 3600 references to published books and papers. It is, of course, now quite outdated—for nobody had the strength to produce a second edition—but still an immensely valuable source of reference, especially for information on the history of antibiotics; Florey himself contributed a long opening chapter devoted entirely to the history of antibiosis. One purpose of this, it is said, was firmly to drive home the point that scores of examples of antibiosis were known—some even to the extent of clinical use—before Fleming discovered penicillin. He was also author or co-author of no less than twenty-one of the other forty-seven chapters.

The preparation of this *magnum opus* proved a considerable burden, and sometimes a cause for despair, to all concerned. Margaret Jennings was a great support in its preparation. Florey makes some amusing comment about his collaborators[2] in letters he wrote to Ethel in the summer of 1948, when she was visiting Australia, carrying out a programme of lectures and visits which he had organized for her there earlier in the year, and happily away from it all:

Mrs. Jennings' mother has just broken her leg and I suppose she will not get her stuff finished and Heatley has chosen this time to have his house decorated. Sanders' brain seems to be going as he stands gazing out of the window whenever he comes to see me, till I have to throw him out. Miss Collingwood has given a fortnight's notice and Chain is giving much trouble. We have had to rewrite a good deal of streptomycin. What a task! We now have to have completely new galleys. . . . Except for all these annoyances and a thoroughly bad summer and my hay fever all is going very well.

The trouble with Chain to which he refers arose from the latter's suspicion that he was not going to get in the book all the credit to which he believed he was entitled. A week later things are much the same:

The book is steadily wearing everyone out here and Miss Hedström [who had the onerous task of preparing the manuscript for press and correcting proofs] is very temperamental but I am managing to keep her on the job. Mrs. Jennings was in a rage this morning and Miss Poynton sits among a sea of paper with tight lips.

He wonders gloomily if it matters whether it is finished or not;

the international situation was then so grim that war with Russia seemed more than likely.

Ethel, however, was undaunted and not only produced herself a companion volume on the clinical applications of penicillin (1952) but three later ones (1957-61) on the application of other antibiotics which had by then found their way into clinical use. Originally the intention was that the first of these should be published under her and Howard's joint names, but in the end he decided that she had done so much of the work that her name alone ought to appear on the title-page. Her problems were not with collaborators, for she was sole author, but with the Oxford University Press, about whom Florey wrote irascibly from Melbourne in September 1951:[3]

I have written to Hollis to say I don't want my name in your book and telling him what I think of the Press taking 1¾ years to publish it. I told him I had urged you to write no more books as they were so slow.

Unfortunately, he omitted to tell Ethel about this and the first she knew about it was in a mystifying letter from the Press. However, her patience was greater than Howard's, and in due course her other books did appear under their imprint, with an acknowledgment of their courtesy and helpfulness; Howard remained disillusioned and took his literary custom elsewhere.

For the moment, however, we must go back to Oxford as it was in the summer of 1945. The war in Europe ended on 8 May, when Jodl surrendered unconditionally to Eisenhower. Amidst the general relief and jubilation it was easy for many to believe that life could resume where it left off in 1939. In fact, of course, immense problems of reconstruction and rehabilitation loomed large and life was never the same again. For Oxford, which in the physical sense had been untouched by the war, the main problem was the same at that of 1919: coping not only with the normal university intake but with large numbers of ex-servicemen— much more mature in their outlook—whose education had been interrupted. As in all teaching departments, this became a major preoccupation in the Sir William Dunn School of Pathology. Immediate academic prospects were depressing, however, with few opportunities for permanent—or even semi-permanent— appointments. Nearly twenty years were to elapse before the great university expansion programme adumbrated by the Robbins Report of 1963 took effect.

With the end of hostilities travel became generally easier, though there were severe currency restrictions. One consequence of this was that Chain was able to go abroad, and in the Long Vacation went off to the United States. For Florey this was a relief, for they were at odds over various matters, not least the future direction of research in the laboratory. Florey was anxious to devote a considerable effort to the preparation and evaluation of new antibiotics, but could see no prospect of acquiring the large-scale fermentation units that Chain was anxious to have. Nor was he anxious to encourage chemical investigation of new products; experience with penicillin had persuaded him that such specialized work was best done in chemical laboratories with more appropriate facilities. Furthermore, he made no bones of the fact that he was weary and disheartened about academic prospects in Britain, as is made clear in a letter of advice he wrote to Chain in America:

If someone liked to give enough money to endow decent salaries for the early penicillin workers that would be excellent but they will have to make the offer. I am not interested in any expansion here and now prefer to be left in peace. I strongly advise you to get a job in the States as I don't believe that there is any future here such as you would like.[4]

But correspondence between Chain and Duthie at the same time indicates clearly that while Chain was enjoying travelling round the States, and basking a little in the penicillin limelight, he did not want to spend the rest of his life there. Duthie had problems of his own. He needed more apparatus—especially as the Emergency Public Health Service was moving out of the Sir William Dunn School of Pathology completely in October and taking with them incubators and other items he had been allowed to use —but no money was available, and even if it had been supplies in Britain were desperately short and waiting-lists correspondingly long. A water-bath would take six months to deliver. In a postscript to one letter he asks Chain to bring from America a spare pair of blades for his animal clippers. On inquiring round, Duthie found that Oxford salary scales were likely to be even lower than those at provincial universities like Leeds and Sheffield. Florey, he had reason to believe, was greatly disheartened by the attitude of the University. He had decided to put in for a professorship at Liverpool, where Florey was going to be an adviser and in a position to be helpful. In the event, however, he took a job at the Lister Institute.

In the course of a long working life Florey published over 200 works,[5] including his contributions to the large book on antibiotics and a textbook on general pathology.[6] Most of these were original research papers, but towards the end of the war and in the years immediately after there was a preponderance of lectures and reviews, principally on penicillin. They include, for example, a Friday Evening Discourse to the Royal Institution (1943); the Cawthorn Lecture given to the Cawthorn Institute in New Zealand (1944); the Peter Le Neve Foster Lecture to the Royal Society of Arts (1944); and the Lister Memorial Lecture to the Royal College of Surgeons (1945). He was also much in demand for lectures abroad. Thus April 1945 found him in Sweden and he wrote home:

I have slept 4 nights in trains, one night or part of it in an aeroplane and have given 5 lectures—another tonight, two tomorrow, 2 Friday and so on. This makes the Australian trip look like a rest cure.[7]

Reviews appeared in such diverse journals as the *Oxford Magazine*, *British Medical Bulletin*, and *Endeavour*. There was nothing very original in any of them, for they presented the same sort of material in different ways, for different readerships, but they still had to be done with care and they were time-consuming.

In the autumn of that year, however, he had occasion to prepare a lecture of a very different kind. On 25 October it was announced that he was to share with Chain and Fleming the Nobel Prize for physiology and medicine (which we would now call biomedical research). The excitement in Oxford was enormous, for this was, of course, the supreme accolade; Florey and Chain were at once put in the same class as such giants as Adrian, Sherrington, Dale, Domagk, Doisy, and Dam (all of whom have been mentioned earlier in this book).

As may be imagined the annual selection of the prizewinners is an exceedingly difficult task. The administration is in the hands of the Nobel Foundation set up, after great legal problems, to administer the surprisingly loosely phrased will of the Swedish industrialist Alfred Nobel, who died in 1896. The first prizes were presented in 1901. Those for physics and chemistry are awarded by the Royal Swedish Academy of Science, those for physiology and medicine by the Caroline Medical Institute. The prize for literature is given by the Swedish Academy and that for peace by the Parliament of Norway, which in Nobel's day was part of Sweden. The selecting bodies accept nominations from many quarters—including former laureates—and they are subjected to highly persuasive arguments. While scientific merit is paramount other factors—especially national pride—are not immaterial. It is, for example, normal for nominators to put forward the names of their fellow countrymen. Much interesting light has been thrown on the nature of the complicated decision-making process in a recently published book.[8] Not the least of the difficulties was that of reconciling the nature of scientific research with Nobel's expressed wish that the prizes should go 'to those who, during the preceding year, shall have conferred the greatest benefit on mankind'. Great discoveries—penicillin among them—tend to be the fruits of labour over a much longer period.

The prizegiving ceremony in Stockholm is always a very grand affair, presided over by the King of Sweden, with all participants in formal evening dress with decorations. It takes place in the late afternoon of 10 December—the anniversary of Alfred Nobel's death in 1896—and is followed by a grand banquet, after which less formal drinking and conversation goes on until the small hours of the morning. That year's ceremony was a particularly splendid one, for it was the first to be held since the outbreak of war. Although few awards were made during the war, though it had been rumoured that it might have been given for penicillin in 1944, there were nevertheless some past Laureates who had yet to receive their awards. Thus the other 1945 Laureates—the Finnish biochemist Artturi Virtanen and the Chilian poetess Gabriela Mistral—were joined by Leopold Ruzicka and Corneille Heymans (1939), and H. S. Gasser and Johannes Jensen (1944) (Plate 9). Otto Hahn, who had been awarded the Chemistry Prize in 1944, would have been there too, but was still effectively under house arrest in a country house near Cambridge. He eventually got to Stockholm to receive it in 1946. All in all, it can fairly be described as a glittering occasion.[9]

On the day after the prizegiving Fleming and Florey each had to give the customary Nobel Lecture. By a piece of bad luck Fleming was suffering from a severe cold, a reminder that penicillin was not a panacea for all ills. Fleming gave a straightforward account of his discovery of penicillin and early experiments, with the implication that the work of Florey and Chain was somehow a direct continuation of it.[10] Florey decided to break new ground and gave an interesting account of the way in which research on antibiotics depended on the development of appropriate techniques and their co-ordination; this was, of course, very much a reaffirmation of his lifelong belief. He was at particular pains to stress the contributions of his Oxford colleagues. Chain, as might be expected, devoted his lecture—which was published separately because he could not deliver the final manuscript version until March 1946—to the chemistry of penicillin. It is an excellent account,[11] and includes a succinct summary of the arrangements made for the exchange of information between America and Britain from May 1944. He ended by confirming that although traces of synthetic penicillin had been found in various reaction products this had no industrial significance:

All attempts to improve the very small yield of synthetic penicillin (about 0.1%) have failed, and it appears improbable that a synthetic process will be evolved that could compete successfully with the cheap biological production of penicillin.

This was a prophecy that proved entirely correct.

The personal situation of the three Nobel Laureates in Stockholm prompts interesting speculation. They had to appear together on many occasions, including a dinner given by the British Ambassador on the day before the ceremony, and put on a show of mutual amiability. Yet the truth of the matter was that relations between Florey and Chain were strained, to say the least, and one of the few bonds between them was resentment at what they regarded as Fleming's immodest claims. Yet in later years Chain became very much better disposed towards Fleming:

[After Stockholm] I saw him more frequently during the last years of his life on various congresses and meetings which we both attended. He was a man of few words who found it difficult to express himself, but he gave the impression of a kind and warmhearted person though he did everything to appear unemotional and aloof. I thought we were brought nearer to each other through the intermediation of his charming second wife whom I knew since the war years when she worked in his Department at St Mary's Hospital. Being both of continental origin, she of Greek descent, I myself with a Russian-German-Jewish background, we understood each other very well and she was ideally suited to act as an interpreter between the temperamental continental and the restrained Scot. Though Fleming and I were as different as could be with regard to background, interests and character, I had the impression that he had feelings of sympathy towards me, and this was certainly mutual as far as I was concerned.[12]

Fleming's second wife was Amalia Voureka, a Greek bacteriologist who had come to work in Fleming's laboratory in 1946 (not during the war as Chain stated) with a bursary from the British Council. His first wife, Sareen, died in October 1949 and he married Amalia in 1953. Sadly, his second marriage—like Florey's—was shortlived: he died less than two years later, at the age of 73.

Florey, however, was never disposed to forgive Fleming, aided and abetted by St Mary's Hospital, for what he regarded as totally unwarranted claims in respect of penicillin. He felt the injustice as much on behalf of his colleagues as of himself. The extent of Fleming's contribution has been carefully evaluated in an earlier chapter (pp. 63-71). It was by no means inconsiderable but inconsistent with the claims he later made himself—and did nothing to discount when made by others on his behalf—after the Oxford workers had published their account of the unique chemotherapeutic properties of penicillin in the summer of 1940. Florey, for once, encountered a situation he could not handle and in June 1944 was driven to appeal to Mellanby for help and advice:

I am writing to you to see if it is possible for you to help me out of what has become an intolerable position. . . . It has long been a source of irritation to us all here to witness the unscrupulous campaign carried on from St Mary's calmly to credit Fleming with all the work done here. I have sufficient evidence of one sort and another that this is a deliberate and clever campaign. My policy here has been never to interview the Press or allow them to get any information from us even by telephone. This has been rigidly adhered to in spite of protests from some of my colleagues [especially Chain] from time to time. . . . In contrast, Fleming has been interviewd apparently without cease, photographed etc (we have complete 'archives' of this here) with the upshot that he is being

put over as the 'discoverer of penicillin' (which is true) with the implication that he did all the work leading to the discovery of its chemotherapeutic properties (which is not true). It is being put over that, at
most, we 'developed' the subject here. You, of course, know how dishonest this is and might reply 'why worry'. This has been our line and
would continue to be if it were not that my colleagues here feel things
are going much too far and, while for the most part do not want publicity
or special credit for themselves, are getting quite naturally restive at seeing so much of their work going to glorify and even financially enrich
someone else. . . . I have been emboldened to write to you by the fact
that during the last week several people—some non-scientists—have asked
me if there wasn't something a bit peculiar about the propaganda, and
one of them, who is in a good position to know, lays a good deal of it at
Lord Moran's door.[13]

Lord Moran was at that time a powerful figure in the medical
world. Since 1941 he had been President of the Royal College of
Physicians and, more immediately relevant to the issue, Dean of
St Mary's Hospital Medical School. Ever since the success of the
Oxford workers had been noted in a leading article in *The Times*
of 30 August 1942, there had been a consistent campaign from St
Mary's to apportion the lion's share of the credit to Fleming.
The opening shot was fired immediately by Sir Almroth Wright
who wrote to *The Times* on the following day. With his love of
the classical languages he included the phrase *palmam qui meruit
ferat*—'let him who won the palm bear it'—Nelson's motto derived
from some verses by John Jortin. Wright categorically stated that
the palm-bearer was Fleming, and that the citadel in which he
bore it was St Mary's Hospital. From Oxford, Robinson replied
with a further letter—which might have been more strongly
phrased—stressing the importance of the local contribution, but
irreparable damage had been done. The Fleming myth had been
created almost overnight and persists to this day. It has been per-
petuated as recently as 1974 in a biography of Fleming designed
for the general reader. The author was William Howard Hughes,
a medical graduate of London University, lately Reader in Bacteriology in the University of London and for many years Consulting Bacteriologist at St Mary's. By his own account he knew
Fleming well, and as the author of a book on *Concise Antibiotic
Treatment* he was particularly familiar with this aspect of
therapy. *A priori* one must assume that he was familiar with,
or could easily ascertain, the facts. Yet his book contains the

following extraordinary account of events at St Mary's after the publication of the successful mouse-protection experiments at Oxford:

Fleming's reaction to the new situation was at once to place the resources of St. Mary's Hospital at the disposal of the Oxford team. . . . We had a factory on the third floor of the building and in the basement, where vaccines were being produced for the Forces. We had the means of growing larger amounts of mould than Oxford could and our technicians had been making it every week since its discovery. The penicillin in its crude form in broth was poured off into large churns and put on to the passenger trains at Paddington to be collected at Oxford only about an hour later by their technicians.[14]

The facts of the matter are that the only penicillin made at St Mary's in the intervening years was in the routine subculturing of the mould and that the churns of crude culture medium (synthetic, not broth) dispatched from Paddington merely passed the front door of St Mary's en route from Kemball, Bishop (p. 156). Hughes goes on to say that:

Fleming also had access to patients in hospital . . . Florey sent him samples to try on human cases. The first patient whose life it saved was a police sergeant. Fleming had the satisfaction of being the first to see the drug used successfully.

Again errors abound. The police sergeant was a patient in the Radcliffe Infirmary in Oxford and, sadly, he died. Fleming's first experience of penicillin in action was when, in response to his urgent appeal on behalf of a friend, Florey generously brought all his available penicillin to St Mary's and instructed Fleming in its use (p. 163).

Later he implies that the Oxford workers sought to belittle Fleming's discovery, which they never did; their object was to keep it in perspective. Hughes states:

Oxford has never quite adjusted to this [the undisputed fact that Fleming was the first to observe and describe penicillin] and there has for many years been a plaque outside the Physic Garden which credits Florey and Chain with the entire discovery.

This is a reference to a rose garden endowed by the Lasker Foundation, and the wording of the plaque is unexceptional, and a plain statement of the truth:

This rose garden was given in honour of the research workers in this university who discovered the clinical importance of penicillin.

For saving of life, relief of suffering, and inspiration to further research, all mankind is in their debt.

Those who did the work were: E. P. Abraham, E. Chain, C. M. Fletcher, H. W. Florey, M. E. Florey, A. D. Gardner, N. G. Heatley, M. A. Jennings, J. Orr-Ewing, A. G. Sanders.

Unfortunately, Howard Hughes' seemingly authentic account was typical of many emanating from less informed sources. Sadly, it probably has to be accepted that the mischief caused will never be undone, and that Fleming will remain established as the folk hero of penicillin in the popular mind.*

Mellanby was sympathetic to Florey's appeal and wrote:

I want to assure you in writing, as I did orally, that I think the reticence as regards press interviews and the fairness and generosity in apportioning credit to Fleming of all in your laboratory have been excellent and above criticism, and whether judged from a short term or long term point of view are, I am convinced, the most desirable. You need have no doubt whatever in your mind that scientific men . . . have appraised the situation correctly and know that, from the point of view of scientific merit your work and that of your colleagues stands on a much higher level than that of Fleming. . . . In time, even the public will realise that in the development of this story of penicillin, the thing that has mattered most has been the persistent and meritorious work of your laboratory.[15]

With the benefit of hindsight it is easy to see that Mellanby's advice was wrong, and why it was wrong. Nevertheless, in the context of the time it was difficult to fault. Academic ethics were very different then from what they are now and it was potentially very damaging for either Florey or Mellanby to tangle with such outstanding public figures as Moran and Wright. Florey was very conscious that whatever the merits of his case he was likely to come off worst: 'I realise I am in great danger of being accused of trying to get "something for myself"'.

Florey's letter to Mellanby was written shortly before he left for his visit to Australia (Chapter VIII) when he travelled via the United States. He was so much incensed by an article in *Time*, which he considered gave excessive praise to Fleming, that

* Very recently, R. G. Macfarlane has published a critical assessment of Fleming's role in the history of penicillin under the appropriate title *Alexander Fleming: the man and the myth*. Chatto & Windus, 1984.

Fulton was moved to send a warning note to Chester Keefer, responsible for clinical trials in the United States, whom Florey was to meet in Washington:

I might warn you that he seems to be utterly infuriated by the recent account of penicillin in *Time*. . . . I protested vigorously when the editors consulted me prior to publication but they said that their story had been dictated from the top, and I somehow gained the impression that Norman Kirk's [Surgeon-General of the Army] office must have had a hand in it.

In reply, Keefer tried to defend the article but Fulton stuck firmly to his guns:

The paper [Fleming, 1929], as you say, has a great deal in it but he did not in 1929 or, as far as I can gather, in any of his subsequent papers, do a single critical experiment that would establish the clinical usefulness of penicillin. . . . It was the type of experiment that Fleming seemed not to have the imagination to carry out.[16]

Fleming clearly enjoyed the lionizing that resulted from his identification with penicillin, and it would be scarcely surprising if over a period of years he did not unconsciously ascribe to himself a role greater than it really was. The Nobel Prizegiving ceremony gave him a splendid opportunity to bask in the limelight of press interviews in Stockholm. By contrast, Florey avoided them as far as possible and with Ethel took himself off to the laboratories of Uppsala University. Their Oxford colleagues were not forgotten and they returned with numerous gifts of a kind not available in Britian immediately after the war.

Apart from their immense prestige, the Nobel Prizes were of considerable monetary value, being endowed from the estate of the wealthy Swedish industrialist Alfred Nobel. It has been said that as late as October the intention had been to give the entire medical prize to Fleming. Later it was proposed to give him half and to share the remainder equally between Florey and Chain, but in the end all three shared it equally. In later years Florey used to say ruefully that this was the only real capital he ever acquired in the course of an arduous life; in later years it helped to finance the buildings of his house at Marston and with the children's education.

Regardless of the apportionment of credit, the award of a Nobel Prize firmly set the seal on Florey's scientific and public reputation: scientific because there is no higher professional accolade, public because the annual award attracts worldwide notice. Public esteem is, of course, fickle. A brilliant discovery in mathematical physics may provoke no more than passing awe that a man's mind can grapple with such things, but identification with a medical discovery that affects the health of millions is something much more readily understood. Whether he liked it or not, Florey had become an internationally popular figure, and had to perform public functions of a kind and on a scale he had never previously contemplated. Among other things, he had, as it were, to perform the equivalent of the athlete's lap of honour, and in the summer of 1946 this took him on a long tour of South America, organized by a cultural body, the British Council. It was different from his earlier tours in North Africa, Russia, and Australia. Its purpose was not to promote the production and effective use of penicillin—for that stage was really past—but, in the aftermath of war, to remind the neutral world of Britain's inventive genius. To say that he was averse to such things would be an exaggeration, for few people really mind being made much of after a personal triumph; nevertheless, they were for him by no means an unmixed blessing. On the debit side they seriously interfered with his research and with many other preoccupations such as, at that time, his growing involvement with the Australian National University and its school of medical research. More particularly, they were intellectually demanding and physically exhausting. On the credit side, they provided an exceptional opportunity for him to indulge his lifelong passion for travel and photography. He himself tersely summarized the pros and cons in one of several letters[17] he wrote home to Ethel while on this tour: 'I never wish to give another lecture on penicillin, though on the whole it was probably worth it to see South America'.

The tour began inauspiciously. At Natal, in Brazil, his aeroplane punctured a tyre and a replacement had to be flown from Montevideo. The delay cost him two days and then fog at Rio, his first port of call, made it necessary for him to land elsewhere and be driven in. He finally arrived just after noon, to be told that he had to go immediately to the lunch organized in his honour—'unshaven and in a sticky shirt'. However, the occasion went off well and afterwards he had a session with the press.

Then, apparently, he dug his toes in and said he would do no more that day; this was a policy he was driven to follow throughout the tour—and on other occasions—not from any reluctance to please his helpful and generous hosts but simply in the interests of self-preservation. Apart from this, he was naturally anxious to see something of these (to him) new countries; as he confided to Ethel 'I didn't really come all this way to meet Brazilians!' He was both amused (in retrospect) and exasperated (at the time) by the theatricality of his hosts; the comings and goings during his lectures; the breakdown of slide projectors; the endless flashbulbs of the press. By his own account he bore it all with exemplary patience, simply waiting for things to be put right before going on.

Although at Buenos Aires, where it was hot and humid (they 'really beat hell out of me') his hosts made it a memorable occasion. They gave him an honorary degree; three of the largest volumes he had ever seen, a classical work on the flowers of Argentina; and presents for Ethel which the British Council sent back to Oxford. The 36-hour rail journey through the Andes to Chile, in brilliant weather, gave him a great deal of pleasure and he exposed a lot of film which he sent back to Sanders for processing, with strict instructions to show it to Ethel. By the time he got to Lima in Peru he was getting into the swing of things. To Ethel he wrote:

I am less tired. I am now unbelievably tough in refusing to do things. . . . Only 3 lectures instead of 4. Usual degree, elogias, etc.

From Lima he went to Bogota in Colombia; by then the timetable had gone awry through bad flying weather on earlier legs of the trip, and it was hard to get air tickets. Eventually he reached Mexico, which he enjoyed and to which he had particularly been looking forward, and then a 24-hour flight took him to New York.

Several times in his letters home to Ethel he expresses his wish to get back to Oxford. He is concerned about Paquita's college entrance examination results and about Charles' illness; even the thought of resuming contention with Chain does not depress him. It is an amiable, rather rambling, correspondence typical of a long-married husband away from home—news of his own progress mixed with concern for domestic details, and remarks of medical interest. Thus in his last letter, from New York, he comments unfavourably on rumours that Waksman's streptomycin was to be released to hospitals; he had no great opinion of the antibiotic, which has disturbing side-effects, nor of its discoverer. Relations were clearly less strained.

On arrival in New York on 10 September he did not proceed straight to London but stayed until 20 September to undertake some private business; not surprisingly this included a quick visit to the Fultons at Newhaven, and he gave two lectures at Yale. He also made contact with a charitable foundation, the Albert and Mary Lasker Foundation, which over the years gave him considerable support—to the tune of around $30 000—for a variety of purposes. This included not only $16 000 over the period 1946-48 to support three biochemists to work on antibiotics in Oxford but donations for quite different matters such as secretarial help for Ethel while she worked on the book; later research on arteriosclerosis; and, much later again, a contribution to the Florey Appeal Fund of Queen's College.[19] Mary Lasker also endowed the rose garden in Oxford to be a permanent memorial to the penicillin research team there (Plate 10). While he was in New York on this occasion she took him off to meet a director of Squibb, who promised some support for his research.

It was the first time Florey had met Mrs. Lasker and in his last letter home he confided to Ethel his pleasurable surprise at finding that she was quite young. It was to prove the beginning of a lasting and generous friendship with the Floreys. In 1957, when Ethel fell ill on a visit to America, Mary Lasker paid her heavy hospital expenses. At this first meeting she undertook to pay the expenses of a visit by Ethel to America to study the use of penicillin at the Mayo Clinic and elsewhere: 'don't say I don't look after your interests', Howard told Ethel in his last letter home. This visit proved very valuable to her, as she acknowledges in the preface to her book on the clinical application of penicillin. In the same letter he told her, too, that he still had two lectures to give and also a broadcast; however, as the latter would produce some much needed dollars he thought it worth the trouble.

Mary Lasker and other friends in New York were able to bring Florey up to date on a development which had thrust penicillin into the political limelight. The end of the war found an ambivalent attitude towards Russia in America. On the one hand there were those who regarded her as a gallant ally who had suffered grievously in the common cause, to whom the west owed a considerable debt. On the other, were those who recalled Russia's invasion of Poland in 1939; and her subsequent conclusion of a pact of non-aggression with Germany enabling the latter to turn her full force on the west; and how she had been drawn into the war not through any sympathy with the western world but because in spite of everything she had been invaded by Germany. Regardless of opinion, however, it was indisputable that the devastation and loss of life in Russia had been prodigious and aid in reconstruction was urgently needed. If huge sums were to be spent to rehabilitate former enemy countries it was surely logical to do something for a former ally.

It was in this atmosphere that a group of eminent American scientists launched, in January 1946, a fund to provide Russia with a penicillin plant capable of producing 80 billion Oxford units monthly, roughly the output of one of the largest American plants then in operation. It was named the Hugh Cabot Memorial Fund, after Hugh Cabot, descendant of the Bristol merchant venturer Sebastian Cabot, who had worked throughout the war to raise funds for Russian relief. He had died on 14 August 1945, the day Japan capitulated. The prime mover was the very distinguished astronomer Harlow Shapley, director of the Harvard Observatory, who had lately returned from a mission to Russia. His reputation attracted some powerful supporters to the Executive Committee, including the medical historian Henry Sigerist and Elliot Cutler, who had been Chief Surgical Consultant with the American forces in Europe; in this capacity he had come to see Florey in Oxford during the war. As sponsors they found such eminent supporters as Eleanor Roosevelt; Charles Kettering, Vice-President of General Motors and founder of the famous Sloan-Kettering Institute for Cancer Research; Robert Oppenheimer, who had been in charge of the atomic bomb project at Los Alamos and was at that time still in favour; and Igor Sikorsky, the helicopter pioneer. The press gave strong support, especially through such well-known scientific journalists as Watson Davies, David Dietz, and Gerald Wendt. The *New York Times* of 29 January was enthusiastic and thought that there could well be reciprocal benefits:

It will not be surprising if the Russian researchers . . . succeed in producing penicillin at a rate heretofore unattained. If they do this, Russian doctors and Russian patients will be immediate gainers, but the benefit will be shared by medical science the world over.

On 13 February a grand banquet for 500 guests was held in Boston's Copley Plaza Hotel formally to launch the fund, the scope of which had by then been extended to cover not only penicillin but the exchange of medical knowledge generally. Three more impressive figures had joined the Committee: Joseph E. Davies, Roosevelt's special wartime envoy to Stalin; Thomas Parran, Surgeon-General of the US Public Health Service; and Allan Forbes, President of the State Street Trust Company of Boston. More and more public figures lent their names, from the universities, industry, learned societies, the judiciary, organized labour, and the world of entertainment. Among them was the ambitious actor-politican Ronald Reagan who, as President of the United States, was to be identified more than thirty years later with a hard policy against Russia.[20]

With so much support and so much goodwill throughout the United States it seemed impossible that the target would not be reached, if not substantially surpassed. Yet by September, when Florey arrived in New York, the whole enterprise was collapsing. The cause was a rapid deterioration in political relations between the United States and the USSR. One of the first dissonant notes was struck by Churchill's famous 'Iron Curtain' speech delivered at Fulton, Missouri in March—but adumbrated in the same terms in a telegram to Truman in May 1945.

An iron curtain is drawn down upon their front. We do not know what is going on behind . . . this issue of settlement with Russia before our strength has gone seems to me to dwarf all others.

Churchill felt strongly about this; in his memoirs he says that 'of all the public documents I have written on this issue I would rather be judged by this [telegram]'.

In America a similar distrust of Russia developed at the official level in the summer of 1946 and a fickle press changed from enthusiasm to hostility. Suddenly, there was a reluctance to provide Russia with useful information of any kind, though through the Soviet-American Medical Society a high-yielding *Penicillium* strain was traded for the Bogomoletz cancer serum, which was worthless. After the Presidential election in November, Harry Truman introduced his Temporary Commission on Employee Loyalty, prelude to a period of near-hysterical anticommunism. Sensing this change in political climate in Washington most supporters of the Memorial Fund quietly dissociated themselves from it.

For Florey, this was at the time no more than very interesting talk-of-the-town news, but it was to have its repercussions in Oxford a couple of years later. So far as there was logic in it, the anti-Soviet feeling that grew up in America in 1946 had two bases. Firstly, there was a fear that subversive communist elements constituted a serious internal political threat. Secondly, there was a desire to maintain the established technological advantage over Russia; there was a belief that this could be effected by strict security measures designed to deny her access to all important technical information. There was a touching faith in high political echelons that the atomic bomb was based on some secret formula, and that as long as this could be preserved no Russian bomb need be feared. It was not generally realized that not only were the basic principles of the bomb published to the world just before war broke out in September 1939 but that the Russians—unlike the Americans and British at the beginning of the Manhattan Project—knew from the outset that an atomic bomb was not only theoretically possible but technically achievable. It was to be a very great shock to American public opinion when the Russians exploded their first atomic bomb as early as 1949: somehow, it seemed, the genie had been allowed to escape from the bottle. It was a still greater shock when Russia outstripped America and achieved the first manned space flight in April 1961.

Similar reasoning seems to have inspired the proposal to provide Russia not with large quantities of penicillin, not with blueprints for the construction and operation of a plant, but with a prefabricated factory to be shipped to Russia and erected there with the help of American advisers. The tacit assumption was that the Russians were not capable of designing, building, and operating a plant without assistance. This was simply not true, for the same arguments applied as to the atomb bomb; not only had the basic principles and much operational information already been disclosed in one way or another, but the immense value of the product had been proved beyond question.

It was, therefore, inevitable that when the Memorial Fund collapsed the Russians should continue to go ahead on their own initiative, but at the same time they sought as much authoritative advice as they could find. With America virtually closed to them for political reasons, it was natural that they should turn to Britain, where the whole penicillin project had been initiated, and it was not surprising that in Britain they should turn to Chain, a neglected figure. Not only was he one of the original prime movers, who had shared a Nobel Prize with Florey and Fleming, but he was of Russian descent and wrote and spoke the language fluently; he was, indeed, a gifted linguist, and was familiar also with German, English, and French and later also Italian. While in Moscow, Florey in his forthright way had suggested that if the Russians wanted to learn how to make and use penicillin their best course was to come and see for themselves. As a result of this Dr. Borodin had spent a year in the Sir William Dunn School of Pathology as a research worker (p. 189). He reappeared early in 1948 in a different guise, this time as representative of Technopromemport, part of the Soviet Trade Delegation in London. He was accompanied by two colleagues, Dr. V. I. Zeifman and Mr. V. A. Chernyarski. The three had long discussions with Chain in his laboratory on the purification, crystallization, and assay of penicillin. In July he entered into a formal agreement with Technopromemport to prepare by October memoranda on the industrial production of penicillin and streptomycin. The target, based on the best American and British practice, was a very large plant producing 600 billion units of amorphous or 250 billion units of crystalline penicillin per month. The longer-term intention was that, for a substantial consideration, Chain should visit Russia from time to time to advise on the building of the plant and thereafter act as a consultant on an annual basis.[21] There was no objection in principle to such an agreement. Chain had satisfied himself that no British regulations were an impediment to an arrangement of this kind; so far as Oxford University was concerned there would be no conflict with his obligations as he was shortly to leave England, with leave of absence, to take up an appointment in Rome at the Istituto Superiore di Sanita. The Americans, however, took a different view and for some years Chain's trafficking with the Eastern bloc countries cost him his America visa. Florey heard this news from Waksman, to whom he did not take, while on a visit to America in 1951. Writing to Margaret Jennings from New York he said:

However, I learnt one thing of some interest and that is that Chain has been refused a visa to visit the U.S.—presumably because of his visits to Czecho Slovakia.[22]

However, Chain was at that time in quite distinguished company in this respect, including that of P.M.S. Blackett (later Lord Blackett), Florey's successor as President of the Royal Society in 1965. In the event, Borodin fell from grace and did not return to Russia, and this particular proposition came to nothing.

After completing his business in New York, the afternoon of 20 September found Florey back in Oxford. It had been a strenuous three-month trip in which he had travelled about 15 000 miles (24 000 km); given some 20 set lectures and innumerable impromptu talks; been principal guest at many formal occasions and obliged to perform accordingly; visited hospitals; and done a great deal of organized sightseeing. Sometimes he spoke in Spanish from a prepared translation, an additional strain though he was gratified at the results. He wrote and told Ethel:

Apparently my Spanish is quite understandable and I was told it was better pronunciation than the Professor of Spanish at Oxford but I can't understand the locals at all.

This one-way system of communication is all too familiar to travellers abroad! Typically, he had prepared himself for these excursions into Spanish by brushing up his knowledge of the language with the help of a Linguaphone course. This was to stand him in good stead later when in 1950 and 1958 he visited Madrid to lecture. His host on these visits was Professor Florencio Bustinza, an ardent admirer of him and his research. Florey was asked, in a broadcast interview from Bustinza's home, what he regarded as the most exciting moment in the penicillin work:

It is difficult to say, but for me probably the most exciting experiment was that in which it was definitely shown that penicillin would definitely protect mice against certain death caused by streptococci.[23]

In his travels in Europe he gained also a good command of French and a little Italian. The trip had had its compensations of course; travel in new countries and a chance to see and photograph the magnificent scenery of the Andes. Nevertheless, it is not surprising that halfway round the course he privately resolved that it would be a long time before he lectured on penicillin again—a resolve that proved easier to make than to keep in his new role of elder statesman.

8

THE AUSTRALIAN CONNECTION

Up to the Second World War Florey had visited Australia only once since his arrival at Hull on that bleak January morning in 1922. That visit—in the Long Vacation of 1936—was a sad one, to see his dying mother. In 1944, however, an opportunity arose for him to revisit Australia in very different circumstances. By that time his scientific reputation had been doubly endorsed. Election to Fellowship of the Royal Society in 1941 was in itself an acknowledgment of outstanding achievement. But, as we have noted, it can have had little to do with penicillin (p. 128), for the paper on 'Penicillin as a chemotherapeutic agent' had appeared in the *Lancet* only in the summer of 1940. By 1944, however, the penicillin work would have been justification in itself, for only a year later it was to merit the supreme accolade of a Nobel Prize. The unique value of the drug was established beyond doubt and the United States had given top priority to a massive crash-programme for its manufacture, primarily for military purposes. A leading article in *The Times* in the summer of 1942 loosed a flood of publicity that Florey could not stem; willy-nilly he had become nor merely a distinguished academic but a public figure whose impact on the health of the world was incalculable. In 1943 he had visited North Africa with Cairns and gone with Sanders to Russia as part of an Anglo-American mission. It was no matter for surprise, therefore, that Australia should claim his advice and help in 1944. It was to prove a visit of great consequence, for it affected the whole pattern of the rest of his life, and came within a whisker of completely changing its course.

This tour was initiated by John Curtin, then the Prime Minister of Australia and the Australian Government arranged the passage. The Nuffield Trustees gave financial support and he went out as Nuffield Visiting Professor to Australia and New Zealand. Not surprisingly, the tour had important military overtones, for the war was still far from won and the Australian army was much concerned with the supply and use of penicillin. At their request, he travelled out via the United States and spent two weeks there—visiting Washington, New York, New Haven, and Boston—inquiring into developments in penicillin therapy and the treatment of shock and burns. Thence he went to New Guinea—making several hazardous journeys to the interior in light aircraft—and on to all the major centres in Australia—Brisbane, Sydney, Melbourne, Canberra, Adelaide, Perth, North Queensland, Central Australia, and the Northern Territory. In New Zealand he visited Auckland, Wellington, Christchurch, Dunedin, and Nelson. It was a gruelling tour, occupying the last six months of the year, during which he gave more than forty lectures and gave much practical advice on the manufacture and use of penicillin. As Florey remarked in his subsequent Report to the Trustees:[1] 'The distances involved were very considerable, and this necessitated a great deal of travel by air. Even so, I had relatively very little time in one place.' The military aspects were to have an unexpected consequence, but they were by no means paramount at the time; Florey had an exceptional opportunity of visiting universities and research institutes, primarily to discuss on behalf of the Trustees possible changes in the terms of the Nuffield Dominions Travelling Fellowships. What he saw and heard of medical research in Australia depressed him greatly, and he made some typically outspoken and pungent comments in his Report, concluding that

the research facilities and conditions in Australia fall far below the standards necessary in a civilised community. . . . Australia has during the last 12 months lost a considerable number of really good people to appointments abroad, and they have nearly all of them pulled out owing to the unfavourable conditions of work.

Of the Research Institutes, only the Walter and Eliza Hall Institute in Melbourne earned his approbation. He was critical, too, of the National Health and Medical Research Council of Australia, of whose members he says bluntly that 'with the greatest good will one can only credit two of these people with knowing the slightest thing about research'. As over the years in Britain, he had no faith in the ability of the clinical medical profession to organize research; in this he ran contrary to Australian opinion. He advocated the setting up of a medical research council similar to that in Britain.

As a visiting celebrity, Florey had plenty of opportunities for making his views known, particularly to an audience of businessmen at the Constitutional Club in Melbourne and in an address on the future of medical research at Adelaide University. He got a good press and there was much editorial advice to the Government to heed his words. Even the clinicians took his criticisms in good part. In Melbourne, where he was made an Honorary Fellow of the Royal Australasian College of Physicians, Sir Alan Newton, President of the Royal Australasian College of Surgeons, remarked:

I hope it is not invidious on this occasion to point out that these men [such as Florey] have not done their work in Australia and New Zealand. Scientific work done here has been comparatively insignificant. We have consistently exported our best scientific brains and we have been unable to attract men of equivalent quality from overseas to replace those we have lost. The reason is not far to seek. We do not offer adequate facilities for research in this country.[2]

Many Australians were conscious of the backwardness of their country not only in medicine but in the universities generally. These were few in number—six universities and two university colleges—and poorly endowed; the prewar grant to the University of Sydney was no more than £100 000. They had no concerted policy nor could they have pursued it if they had. P. H. Partridge, professor of social philosophy at the Australian National University 1951-75, recalled in 1978 that 'many people . . . have no conception of what very narrow little parochial oligarchies our universities in many respects were until after World War II'.[3] This view of the state of affairs up to the Second World War is similar to that expressed by Donald Fleming;[4] research was negligible and native and imported talent took itself off to better places overseas. As late as 1957 the Report of the Committee on Australian Universities (the Murray Report) said:

At the present time it is hardly an exaggeration to say that no way exists for the universities to form or express a concerted policy, or even to give, in answer to questions from government or from any other source, agreed general advice.

For young and ambitious men the academic prospect was dismal and it is not surprising that many, like Florey, left to seek their fortunes abroad either in Britain, with which Australia's ties were then closest, or in the United States, where prospects were even better. Because of the poor research facilities few returned. Nevertheless, apathy and complacency were by no means universal and Australia did not lack men anxious to bring about improvements.

The conditions of the competition for the original design for the capital city of Canberra (1908) required the allocation of a university site. The winner, Walter Burley Griffin, assigned it to a position beneath Black Mountain where in fact it was eventually built. In the 1920s the need for a national university had been powerfully argued by such men as Sir Mungo MacCallum, first Vice-Chancellor of the University of Sydney, and Professor T. H. Laby[5] of Melbourne, famous to generations of scientists throughout the world as the co-compiler of Kaye and Laby's tables of physical and chemical constants. Whatever hopes there may have been for realizing these dreams were dashed by the depression of the 1930s.

The desire for reform had a twofold purpose. Firstly, improved academic prospects at home would staunch the flow of graduates abroad which—like Britain's brain-drain to America in the 1950s —was damaging Australia's national interest by siphoning off her ablest young men. Secondly and no less important, the creation of better facilities in Australia would make it feasible to attract back some older men, enriched by their experience overseas.

Florey's visit and forthright comments were timely in catalysing public and private discussion of the whole question of university reform. Among those who happened to be in Melbourne at the time of Florey's address to the Constitutional Club was Professor R. D. Wright, who had been appointed to the Chair of Physiology in the University of Melbourne in 1939. At that time, however, he was a colonel on the staff of Alfred Conlon, Director of Research and Civil Affairs in the Australian Military Forces. Conlon had direct access to General Sir Thomas Blamey, Commander-in-Chief of the Australian Military Forces, and Blamey —who had been instrumental in inviting Florey to Australia (p. 191)—had direct access to John Curtin, the Prime Minister. Thus was forged a chain of communication that was to have a profound effect on the Australian university system and was powerfully to influence the remaining twenty-four years of Florey's life.

'Pansy' Wright we have already encountered; Florey had met him in Melbourne during his visit in the summer of 1936 and had been so impressed that he had invited him to spend the academic year 1936-37 with him in Oxford. They were thus old friends and accordingly on the day after Florey's address Wright set off for the Melbourne Club, where Florey was staying, and invited himself to breakfast. We must suppose that the conversation was lively and uninhibited; Florey had a great capacity for relaxing and enjoying himself when the opportunity arose and Pansy Wright—now Sir R. Douglas Wright, Chancellor of the University of Melbourne—even then had an established reputation for forthright expression in the Australian vernacular. However, the talk was not without its serious side and Wright became very conscious of Florey's deep personal interest in Australian universities and their problems. This led him to suggest a meeting with Alfred Conlon and as, by rare chance, Florey had no immediate engagement, this was arranged for the same day.

Conlon appears only transitorily in our story, but he was such a remarkable character and played so important a role at this particular period, that he deserves more than passing mention. Prewar he had read both medicine and law—although he did not complete his medical studies until 1951—and at that time he was only 36 years of age. He had had a meteoric military career, first on the staff of the Adjutant-General and then on that of the Commander-in-Chief, with the rank of colonel. He was a highly controversial character, variously regarded as a demigod or a charlatan. There is no question, however, but that he was a powerful backstage operator, with a remarkable flair for persuading people at the very top to listen to his ideas and, very often, accept them. It is said, for example, that the big manpower scheme put into effect by the Labour Government after the Pacific War had started was Conlon's concept which he put direct to Curtin.

After his death in 1961, a number of Conlon's friends and associates contributed to a memorial volume[6] and it is perhaps pertinent to quote two of them. One was Herbert Coombs, whom we shall meet again later as Chancellor of the Australian National University:

his influence was perhaps too great for good results because it did tend to be resented by the more regular focal points of authority and also because, frankly, I think it did give Alf a distorted impression of what could be achieved by the sort of personal influence he exercised.

John Kerr, a lawyer who was Conlon's righthand man in the Directorate of Research, and later became Governor-General of Australia, wrote:

It would be quite wrong to think of Alf as a universally accepted wise pundit of the wartime years. . . . In terms of the great centres of national power Alf's writ ceased to run with the termination of the war.

Be this as it may, Conlon's writ ran strong in the autumn of 1944 and on the afternoon of 19 September he took Florey in to see Blamey. Clearly they got on well from the outset and the meeting lasted several hours. Afterwards, Conlon and Wright sat down and drafted a letter proposing a national centre for medical research—in what they supposed to be language suitable for a Commander-in-Chief—for Blamey to send to Curtin. The possibility of this quick concerted action reflects the intimacy between Wright and Conlon. They were used to discussing all manner of things, including the possibility that Australia might be 'the new Constantinople' if the northern hemisphere really wrecked itself. Blamey went to see Curtin the next day and subsequently had several informal talks with him. A letter was finally sent formally on 24 October 1944. The powerful impression Florey had made on Blamey was clear:

I am deeply impressed with his sagacity and wisdom, apart from the undoubted gifts that he possesses. I feel that he is undoubtedly the person to be entrusted with the development of a project of such far-reaching national importance. Apart from his world standing and his maturity, the pre-eminent authority that he would enjoy among Australian scientists, I feel that he is capable of infusing inspiration into the technical direction of research programs.[7]

The letter went on to formulate concrete proposals for a National Medical Research Institute, probably to be located in Canberra—'in the front garden of the Commonwealth Government'—and, by implication, with Florey at its head. The cost was tentatively set at £200 000 p.a.—a figure literally snatched from the air, but one that was to create difficulties later when proper estimates came to be made. The Prime Minister responded quickly; within a week he called for the preparation of a cabinet agendum recommending the setting up of an institute of the kind Blamey had proposed. Indeed, he was so enthusiastic that he wanted to make a firm proposal to Florey before he returned to England. This quick response reflects the timeliness of Florey's proposal; in 1943 the government had set up an interdepartmental committee to review the whole system of Commonwealth educa-tion. In the event, Curtin fell ill and was unable to fulfil his offic-ial duties; in particular, a meeting arranged with Florey had to be cancelled and the two never met. Florey had to content himself with writing on his return to Oxford. Curtin died in July 1945 and was succeeded by J. B. Chifley.

Florey was clearly keenly interested in the possibility. On 2 October he wrote to Ethel from Perth:

I have received suggestions that I should come back here and do something. This is quite confidential, but very large sums of money would be forthcoming—more than the MRC had in England before the war. I have temporised—the country looks lovely and for children ideal. I think we have forgotten what it was like. Keep all this to yourself.[8]

From Perth he returned home by way of the United States. By that time the tide of war had turned. American and British forces had landed in Italy and Normandy and made substantial pro-gress; in the east, the Russian offensive was going well. Though the flying-bomb attacks on London had caused much loss of life, the impending defeat of Germany was clear. In the circumstances it seemed safe for Paquita and Charles to come home to Oxford and Florey returned by way of the United States to collect them from the Fulton's en route and travel back with them on board a ship sailing in convoy to Britain.

With Curtin's illness, momentum was lost and opportunity given for reactionary forces to marshall their strength; there were many vested interests which were by no means favourably inclined to the proposed new institute. Back in Oxford Florey was kept reasonably well informed of what was going on, at two levels. Firstly, he was getting official letters from the various bodies and individuals concerned. Secondly, he was getting long and highly unofficial letters from Conlon; these tended to be written in cryptic terms to avoid censorship.

At the official level, the Minister of Health set up a committee of three to investigate the financial and scientific aspects involved, and the implication of the proposal in relation to existing and projected institutions, and to our policy with regard to medical and social services in which medical research forms an integral part.[9]

The members were Sir David Rivett, then Chief Executive (and shortly Chairman) of the Commonwealth Council for Scientific and Industrial Research (CSIRO); J. H. L. Cumpston, Director-General of Health; and A. J. Goodes, a senior Treasury official.

Rivett was a good choice. Like Florey, he had spent three years at Oxford as a Rhodes Scholar, and then worked at the Nobel Institute in Stockholm before returning to Australia in 1924 as Professor of Chemistry at Melbourne. He had been elected a Fellow of the Royal Society in 1941. Professionally he was a chemist; he made no bones about his ignorance of the special needs of medical research, but he took steps to dispel this. For a start, he got in touch with Florey, asking his views; in return, he got a long memorandum to which we will turn later. He also got in touch with Dr. F. M. B. Burnet (later Sir Macfarlane Burnet), director of the Walter and Eliza Hall Institute in Melbourne; this, it will be recalled, was the only medical research institute in Australia that had earned Florey's approbation. (Burnet was a first-rate scientist, and went on to receive a Nobel Prize for Medicine in 1966.) Burnet's reply to Florey was lukewarm. He himself, he said, had never suffered from lack of support by the National Health and Medical Research Council and he believed it would be a mistake to set up a new institute embracing all disciplines relevant to medical research; he thought it better to support nuclei of one or two good men at existing centres.[10] Possibly this view was not wholly dispassionate; Burnet was entitled to think that the high cost of the proposed new institute would not only diminish support for existing ones but draw away highly qualified staff. Conscious no doubt of his own administrative problems, Rivett was from the outset opposed to public service control of the new institute; it should be run, he thought, by men with personal knowledge of research. He and Florey thought along similar lines, and until he retired in 1949 he was helpful in an official capacity not only in giving encouragement and support but, no less important, in keeping Florey posted on what was going on in Australia.

Cumpston, however, was unsympathetic to the proposal and

counselled delay while the whole issue was re-examined. In his opinion, the National Health and Medical Research Council, set up in 1937, was doing a good job in supporting medical research in Australia; one may suppose that he had seen—or at least been told of—Florey's scathing comments on the Council made in his Report to the Nuffield Trustees.

Meanwhile, Florey had not let the grass grow under his feet. Back in Oxford he had applied himself energetically to preparing the memorandum[11] that Rivett had asked for. It was dispatched on 7 April 1945, and was a detailed and thoughtful study, running to 19 typewritten pages. Rivett immediately gave it wide circulation, wider indeed than Florey had visualized. Writing to Florey in June, he says that it had been copied and sent to Ministers and officials concerned and widely distributed to senior members of the medical profession. Not all medical men had received it favourably, he warned; to many, what seemed no more than common sense to him and Florey seemed idealistic and unattainable. He also gave news of a possible rival: the Queensland Government was seriously thinking of setting up a medical research institute. Rivett had seen the draft bill and was highly critical; the proposed institute would be run by a council consisting largely of medical practioners. The Queensland Institute of Medical Research was in fact established in 1947 at Herston.

For several reasons this memorandum deserves careful consideration. Firstly, it was in essence the blueprint for what later became the John Curtin School of Medical Research in the Australian National University at Canberra, with which Florey's fortunes were to be closely linked for the rest of his life. Secondly, Florey had by then completed some 25 years of highly successful medical research, and this represents his considered views of what a first-class medical research institute should consist. It embodied several proposals to which he had not been able to give effect at Oxford. Last, but not least, it was a project in which he might have a strong personal stake. Although, as he said to Ethel, he had temporized about giving any firm commitment, this might well be the building in which he would spend the rest of his working life; he thus had every incentive to make as good a job of it as he could.

Florey begins by again summarizing his views on the then current state of affairs in Australia, and time for reflection had done nothing to moderate his views.

Burnet, after his return from America, could make the observation that if all the medical research in Australia stopped tomorrow no-one would notice the difference, and I fear this somewhat depressing situation is not a great exaggeration. I think everyone I have talked to, both in Australia and here, is agreed that among the fundamental reasons is the unsatisfactory state of the overall conditions for medical research.

A variety of reasons had contributed to this situation. The professors were overburdened with routine work and underfinanced; some were incapable of research 'no matter what the conditions were'; and control lay too much in the hands of medical practitioners. This last view was, of course, one that Florey had always held strongly: it had come to the surface even in his courtship letters to Ethel, not always too tactfully. In the present context he emphasizes the point by remarking that to his knowledge two first-class scientists had lately left Australia for this very reason.

Australia should have no illusions that the situation would right itself. In fact it would become worse; in Britain, the natural goal for ambitious Australians, the government was going to give much more support to science in the universities, with more and better paid jobs. A large new medical research institute was to open at Mill Hill, on the outskirts of London. Various trusts were planning to use their funds to support research. In his emphatic view there was only one solution:

How can these circumstances be circumvented? In only one way in my opinion, and that is to make research conditions in Australia not only equal to those here, but superior. This I am quite certain could be done and no one should allow the argument that Australia has a small population and therefore cannot aim so high to influence them for one moment. I always mention Holland and Denmark in this connection. The medical research in these countries (population about 3 000 000 in the case of Denmark) was first class and they had many first-class scientists working in good conditions.

This was a theme to which he was to return time and again over the years. As an Australian, he had deep affection and loyalty for his country, but with his wide experience he did not allow this to blind him to the realities of life. He had no patience with those of his countrymen who thought that makeshift facilities would be sufficient to attract back, let alone retain, really able scientists.

Having delivered this dire warning of the penalties of inaction, he proceeds to specify in some detail the minimum requirements for an institute prestigious enough to turn the tide. Characteristically, he first addressed himself briefly but emphatically to the administrative system. Despite his brushes with the Medical Research Council in Britain, he believed a similar, but simpler, body should be set up in Australia. Its basic role would be the same: to concern itself with the scientific aspects of research policy and stand as a buffer between the director and government, relieving him of political pressures. Not least, it should protect him from pressure to produce quick and dramatic results, always alluring to politicians with their short terms in office. Nevertheless, he did not propose that time should be wasted while the institute was being built, which would be at least three years from approval being given. In the interim, staff should be trained at research centres in Britain, the United States, or anywhere else that a 'cell' could be established with adequate facilities.

On the personal side, the key appointment would obviously be that of director, who would play a dual role. His primary duty would be to run a first-class laboratory with the highest research standards, but in addition he would help to foster research at other centres. While the establishment should be clearly defined, he should be under no obligation to fill posts unless he was absolutely satisfied that he had got the right man. As the director would have social responsibilities, such as entertaining visiting scientists, it would be appropriate for him to have a house, as was provided at Mill Hill and at the leading European centres. It would be understandable if at this point he was not unmindful of his own possible future requirements; domestic accommodation had always been a problem with him. Under the director would be five division leaders of professorial calibre, and capable of formulating and conducting original work. Each would be assisted by four or five hewers of wood and drawers of water—skilled professional research workers but lacking the originality to work independently. Finally, there would be up to a score of trainees, young graduates serving, as it were, their apprenticeship in research. This was an ambitious scheme, envisaging over fifty qualified research workers. If one adds to this the necessary staff of technicians, secretaries, administrative officer, laboratory manager, librarian, and so on the total rises to near a hundred. In a thoroughly businesslike way Florey costs all this on the basis of current academic salaries, reaching an impressive total—for that time—of about £100 000 p.a.

On the building itself he is rather less explicit, though he indicates that laboratory accommodation must be provided for five main divisions—microbiology and tropical medicine; experimental pathology; pharmacology, physiology, and nutrition; biochemistry and chemistry; and biophysics. The crucial importance of this needs stressing. Much of Florey's success in Britain had been due to his recognition, in the face of established tradition, that medical research thrives when a variety of scientific skills can be deployed. In Australia, the idea was still prevalent that the right people for the job were medical men.

His estimate of the cost of the building was to prove less than fortunate. On the basis that his own laboratory in Oxford had cost £80 000 to build in 1926 to accommodate 20 research workers, he thought that this might be scaled up threefold, to £240 000, for the 60-odd research workers he eventually visualized for Australia. It is true that he qualified this by saying that there would have to be 'appropriate adjustment for present costs and Australian conditions' but unfortunately it came to be regarded as a carefully considered estimate; in the event the cost was nearly four times as much, and this naturally led to trouble.

Up to this time the location of the new institute, should it be approved, was still being argued but the balance was in favour of Canberra. Florey saw the force of this argument, especially if the Government were to expand the educational facilities there by the creation of a postgraduate university. On the other hand, he saw arguments in having it near a great city such as Sydney, though not so near the centre that there was insufficient room for expansion. Presciently, he concludes:

I do not feel you would wish me to debate these points, but clearly the decision is one of crucial importance and might affect developments for very many years to come.

In the event Canberra was chosen—partly no doubt because it was situated in national rather than state territory, thus eliminating problems arising from interstate rivalry—and they did include the institute within a national postgraduate university, but it is debatable whether the choice was a good one. A relatively small community of politicians, civil servants, and academics living in isolation from a major centre of population creates obvious problems.

Characteristically, Florey ends his memorandum on a shrewd tactical note. When he wrote it he would have been aware of misgivings such as those expressed by Burnet—which no doubt would have been conveyed to the government—that what was good for the new institute would be correspondingly bad for the old ones.

. . . it is clear that the Director and staff would have a great opportunity not only to get scientific work done under excellent conditions but also perhaps to make some lasting impression on the scientific and intellectual thought of Australia . . . the establishment of the Institute does not diminish the importance or opportunities of any existing institute but on the contrary greatly improves their position if they co-operate.

There, for the moment the matter rested as far as Florey was concerned. Curtin's ill-health and the consequent lack of his personal interest delayed matters considerably. In June, Conlon, who claimed to have his ear very close to the ground, wrote, in a typically convoluted letter, that the matter was still very much alive; that Florey was the man they wanted; that the money would be forthcoming; and that a concrete proposal could be expected before long. He wrote again in August, after Curtin's death, to say that things were on the move again, and steps were being taken to brief the new Prime Minister, Chifley; Florey's memorandum was proving most useful for this purpose. Firm ideas had emerged about finance, on the basis of £250 000 capital outlay over a period of years and £125 000 p.a. for running costs when established; these figures were very much in line with those in Florey's memorandum and presumably based on it. The director might expect a salary of £3000 p.a., plus £500 p.a. for entertainment, and a house—again in line with Florey's suggestion.

All this was indicative of activity at the Australian end but Florey in Oxford was far from clear what was going on. In March 1946, however, he had an encouraging letter from Pansy Wright to say that despite its long dormancy the project was far from fizzling out but was on the point of blossoming fully; Florey might expect a formal proposal via the diplomatic bag within a few weeks. In his reply (20 March 1946) Florey expresses pleasurable surprise:

My last information from somebody I thought probably knew, as he sits on various committees, was framed to the effect that I would be much better employed teaching people here and not meddling in the little affairs of Australia. I took this as a hint, or more than a hint.[12]

He adds that the delay had made more difficult his acceptance of a firm proposal. Since visiting Australia he had become deeply committed to reorganizing his laboratory in Oxford, having raised a lot of money and turned the building inside out: 'I merely mention this so that you will not expect me to be able to give an answer by return of post'. This letter concludes with his thanks to Wright for a parcel of 'eatables', a reminder that postwar difficulties were being superimposed on an intrinsically complicated project.

Wright showed Florey's letter to Conlon, who wrote back immediately, with apologies for not having been in touch again earlier. The reason, he says, is that it was difficult to compose a progress report when progress was so very slow. He acknowledged that when the matter had first been mooted Florey had said that delay might lead him to accept other commitments that would make acceptance impossible. That difficulty might in any case be averted, he suggests, on the basis that Florey need not actually come to Australia for a couple of years, except for short visits; he would want time to travel extensively and select staff.

Generally speaking, his long letter radiated optimism. The Prime Minister would be coming to London shortly and with him, as his principal economic adviser, would be Dr. H. C. (Nugget) Coombs, an economist. At that time Coombs was Director-General of Post-War Reconstruction and already a man of great influence. Conlon clearly thought highly of him and—with his usual flair—predicted a brilliant career for him, including the Governorship of the Commonwealth Bank of Australia (to which he was in fact appointed in 1949). Coombs, to whom Conlon had just spoken, would try to see Florey during his London visit and negotiate a firm arrangement. In Conlon's view, however, there need be little in the way of negotiation; if Florey would indicate exactly what he wanted, there was no doubt that he would get it.

As it turned out, Coomb's visit fell short of Conlon's rather euphoric expectations, as is apparent from a long letter Florey wrote to Pansy Wright on 4 June.[13] He had had lunch with Coombs, been given some documents, including a draft of the proposed Act to establish the University; and had a general talk. His main concern is that the concept was still much too woolly, with far too many loose ends.

What I have suggested to Coombs is that those who are involved in framing this should get down to brass tacks and see what they really mean by this proposed university and how it actually would function. . . . I warned Coombs and I may as well warn you that I believe more harm will be done by thrashing about trying to do things in a hurry than by going about it calmly and making good foundations.

Among the brass tacks he had in mind was the fact that it would take at least four years to get a laboratory built in Canberra; he gathered that 'it is next door to impossible at the moment even to think of getting a house'. There were great staffing problems, too. He reiterated his early warning that if too many good people were lifted from existing Australian institutes, the whole purpose of the new University would be stultified. Young Australians would have to be trained, and a considered campaign launched to persuade overseas workers that it was worthwhile to come to Canberra. Nevertheless, he ends on an optimistic note:

I think in the years to come, if the thing were really started on straight lines with all the obvious causes of friction eliminated from the start, that you might find there would be a surprising number of people willing to go from this country, provided the conditions were right.

The question of his own participation remained unresolved. He had explained to Coombs that a decision on this was impossible unless he could be certain that 'a substantial body' of first-rate scientists could in one way or another be attracted to Canberra.

In the course of this same letter to Wright he mentions an awkward personal complication; he was committed to a tour of South America (p. 210) from early June until the end of September. This accounted for most of his long vacation, when he might have had a little additional time to devote to the affairs of Canberra, but it also coincided with the forthcoming Empire Scientific Conference in London, organized by the Royal Society.

Apart from providing an opportunity to meet Rivett and Burnet (whom he did in fact see briefly before he left), this could have been a timely occasion to indicate that it should not be looked on as 'committing scientific hara-kiri to go to places like Australia and *a fortiori* Canberra'.

In the meantime, however, cautionary words had not inhibited political action in Australia, where the original concept of a medical research institute had been subsumed within the much more ambitious one of a new postgraduate university. It was the draft Bill to establish this that Coombs had left with Florey in May for his comments. The new University was to include, besides the original medical institute, departments of physical sciences, social sciences, and political studies. Before replying to Coombs on 1 June, 1946, Florey had some discreet consultations with colleagues, among whom was Sir Henry Tizard, then one of the elder statesmen of science in Britain, formerly Rector of Imperial College, London. In his letter[14] to Coombs he makes some pertinent suggestions, some—but not all—of which were included in the final Act. The substance of his advice, as it was to Wright, was to proceed cautiously, leaving as much freedom of action as possible to deal with a developing situation.

Could you not frame your Bill in a more general way and leave a good deal of the detail to be accomplished by regulation? . . . Decisions which are arrived at now are going to affect the Institution for very many years to come. . . . In my opinion it would be far more desirable and in the long run would produce better results if you could get a broadly based Enabling Bill, after which the preliminary arrangements and plans could be thought out in great detail before any decisive steps were taken to implement the Bill.[14]

Earlier in this letter Florey seizes on a point that was to prove of fundamental importance.

For the satisfactory running of any of these schools [of physical sciences] it seems to me that it would be necessary to be quite clear as to what the respective functions of the Vice-Chancellor and the Director of these Schools are going to be, to avoid any subsequent difficulties. . . . I think you would have to make it very clear as to who does and who does not appoint staff to your Research Institutes and where the financial control lies.

Cautiously, he remarks that these matters would have to be taken a good deal further before his own possible relationship to the Medical Research Institute could be decided. In the event, his caution was justified; over the years the problems of division of responsibility were to prove of serious consequence.

This correspondence is very significant in relation to Florey's association with the new University, which was to influence the rest of his life. It makes it crystal clear that from the very outset— even before the Act establishing the Australian National University was passed by the House of Representatives—Florey's advice was being sought not only on the Medical Research Institute but on University matters in general. He was to continue in this role until his death, at which time he held the office of Chancellor.

Assent was given to the Australian University Act on 1 August 1946, and note had been taken of some of Florey's comments. It is interesting, in view of his own final role, that it provided for a Chancellor to be its titular head. This office had not been mentioned in the draft, and Florey had remarked drily that if there was no Chancellor 'a Vice-Chancellor would seem to be something of an anomaly'.

While Florey's advice on the drafting of the Bill was actively sought, others directly concerned felt slighted. Among these was Rivett. In a letter to Florey[15] written on 20 November 1946, he says that while the proposal was still at the Bill stage, he had asked that copies should be supplied to him and certain others who had been invited to act on special committees, so that they might offer constructive criticism. This was refused on what he called the 'utterly stupid' ground that its contents were secret until Parliament had dealt with it. Probably he knew that it had been shown to Florey by Coombs when they met in England in May.

As A. P. Herbert once remarked, there is no fun in any Act of Parliament and the Australian National University Act was no exception. Dry reading though it is, it made certain provisions which were of fundamental importance to our present story. To an extent it was drafted in accordance with Florey's advice not to be too specific at the outset. In the long run, the University was to be governed by a Council of not more than thirty, of whom up to twelve could be political nominees. Initially, however, its affairs were to be ordered by an Interim Committee nominated by the Governor-General. A final choice of site was made; it was to be at Canberra in the Australian Capital Territory. Here there already existed Canberra University College, established in 1929 as a teaching institution whose students were prepared for degrees of the University of Melbourne. The Act provided that this College might be incorporated within the new University. This option was taken up in 1960 but in the interval the arguments for and against were a matter for serious controversy.

On 20 August Wright wrote to Oxford, giving an informal progress report. The Interim Council had been established and was to have its first meeting three weeks hence. Its eleven members included Wright himself, Rivett, Coombs, and Eric Ashby. Ashby (later Lord Ashby) was then Professor of Botany at Sydney, but he returned to England shortly to become Professor of Botany at Manchester. The Chairman was a distinguished economist Professor R. C. Mills, of the University of Sydney; who later became Director of the Commonwealth Office of Education. In 1949 R. G. Menzies, shortly after his election success, appointed him Chairman of the Commonwealth Committee on the Needs of Universities. Initially, Rivett seems to have been fairly happy with the Interim Council, writing to tell Florey in October that it had 'some quite reasonable people on it' and that he would find it 'a very sympathetic body'. By February 1947, however, he is evidently disenchanted, writing about its 'vagueness' in attending to the affairs of 'the so-called National University'.

Back in Oxford from his South American tour, Florey, too, was getting restless. Coombs had been over again and come down to Oxford for a few hours but, as he wrote to Rivett[16] on 27 January 1947, 'he seemed extremely vague and I concluded he did not know much about what was going on or what was required'. Another reason for discontent was that Mills had been in England and had not attempted to contact Florey: 'I must confess that Mill's omission to get into contact with me while he was over here has left a rather poor impression on me'. This was not the last time Florey was to be annoyed by the failure of senior officers of the University to pay a normal courtesy call while in England. However, Wright had visited England at the instigation of the Interim Council and had helped to clarify matters. He was to go on to the United States to make a study tour of medical research laboratories there.

In his letter telling Florey of the setting up of the Interim

Council and of its composition, Wright had expressed the view that it needed knowledgeable guidance; he suggested that a person with Florey's experience should be appointed to act as an adviser to it. As we shall see, the Interim Council did in due course take this formal step, but meanwhile Florey had not been inactive in his isolation.

From the outset almost all those concerned with the setting up of the Medical Research Institute—or the Australian National University that shortly emerged as a broader concept—were conscious that its success depended upon its ability to attract a nucleus of outstanding men; once established, they would be a powerful magnet for others. Florey, of course, was the prime target when medical research alone was in question, and his stature had been enhanced by the award of a Nobel Prize. But with the decision to proceed on a broader basis, with other research schools than medicine, the net had to be more widely cast. For the proposed Research School of Physical Sciences it was inevitable that there should be a special interest in M. L. E. Oliphant. Like Florey he was an Adelaide man, born there in 1901, and had made his way to Cambridge in 1927 with the help of an 1851 Exhibition Scholarship. He had worked at the Cavendish Laboratory as Assistant Director of Research (1935) and since 1937 had been Poynting Professor of Physics in the University of Birmingham. The high quality of his research had been recognized by his election as a Fellow of the Royal Society in 1937. He and Florey were thus much of an age and had a good deal in common. It was, therefore, natural that Florey should get in touch with him when the concept of the Australian National University began to take shape. This project was to draw them close together and over the years they had a profuse and frank correspondence about the University's affairs.

On 19 September 1946 Florey received a brief personal letter from Rivett saying that Oliphant was going out to Canberra in the following month; from this he gained the impression— apparently for the first time—that Oliphant seriously contemplated moving to Australia. He wrote at once to Oliphant inquiring if this were so, saying that it was the first intimation he had had there was to be a meeting in Canberra; on the contrary, he had gathered from Wright that Coombs was coming to London. A meeting was arranged in Oxford but Oliphant could not manage it as he was feverish in reaction to the vaccination he had had before his journey. He wrote to say that he had seen Coombs in London in early October but, like Florey, had found him vague about University affairs. He himself was off to Canberra in January (1947) and could not change his date as, apart from other commitments, he was then on the Council of the Royal Society. Equally, Florey was still unable to get away before March at earliest, so they had reluctantly to conclude that they could not go together. This was a particular disappointment to Rivett, who rightly felt that the two of them together could have more than twice the effect of either singly. He was convinced that unless both Florey and Oliphant could be brought out on satisfactory terms the project would be suffocated at birth and he, for one, would lose all interest in it.

Florey and Oliphant contrived to meet in Oxford before the latter left for Canberra and this was the start of a long and fruitful cooperation. At Oliphant's suggestion Sir Raymond Priestley, then Vice-Chancellor of the University of Birmingham and well versed in academic matters, was consulted. His main concern was the possible incorporation of Canberra University College, which catered almost entirely for local boys and girls from the families of civil servants in the city. This Priestley thought would cause a great imbalance, which he suggested might be adjusted by insisting that at least half the students should in future be drawn from outside the Capital Territory.

With this informal alliance of Florey and Oliphant sound advice on the development of the research schools of medicine and physical sciences was assured, but there remained the schools of social sciences and of Pacific Studies. For the former, advice was to hand in Oxford in the person of W. K. Hancock, Chichele Professor of Economic History since 1944. Another Australian, he was born in Melbourne in 1898, and thus was also a contemporary of Florey: they had been friends since Florey's first arrival in Oxford in 1922. Before being appointed Professor of History in the University of Birmingham—thus overlapping with Oliphant there—he had been Professor of Modern History in the University of Adelaide and knew the Australian academic scene well. Finally, for Pacific Studies, there was available R. W. Firth, who had been appointed Professor of Anthropology in the University of London in 1944. He, too, was of much the same age as the other three. He was a New Zealander, born in 1901, and a graduate of Auckland University College. He had done research in the Solomon Islands and had been a lecturer, and later Acting Professor, in the University of Sydney.

This informal arrangement was regularized in April 1947 when each of the four received an invitation from Mills, as Chairman of the Interim Council, to constitute themselves as an Academic Advisory Committee. They were each to receive an honorarium of £250 p.a. and an expense allowance of £200 p.a. They were invited to come to Canberra for consultation during December 1947 and January 1948. The hope and intention, in those early days, was that all four would eventually end up in Canberra as directors of the proposed research schools. This was, indeed, expressly stated in a Cabinet Memorandum of February 1948.[17] As we shall see, however, things were destined to turn out otherwise. For the moment, however, a viable Canberra/Oxford axis had been established; even if at times if manifestly did not rotate at the same speed at either end, it organized some very considerable talent. The Committee met roughly once a month in Oxford, members taking it in turn to take the chair. While what may be called the Oxford Group turned their thoughts to academic organization, those in Australia concentrated on getting buildings and administration going. Collaboration over such a distance was inevitably difficult. With communications a great deal worse than they are now, there was plenty of room for misunderstanding and frustration. The existence of two widely separated centres of activity, one not always at all clear what the other was doing, makes more difficult the historian's task of disentangling the course of events. The opening of a London office of the University facilitated liaison.

Within little more than two years the whole tenor of Florey's life had changed. A suggestion made in a hastily contrived talk with Blamey during his Australian tour in 1944 had blossomed into a major enterprise to which he now had a substantial commitment. How he viewed this we can only surmise, but clearly he must have done so with mixed feelings. On the one hand, as an academic of Australian origin he must have derived great satisfaction from the fact that he had become a prime architect of a uniquely constituted new university in his homeland. Even though he was by now a public figure—with Fellowship of the

Royal Society, a knighthood, and a Nobel Prize behind him—he can scarcely fail to have been flattered to find the Prime Minister, Cabinet Ministers, the Commander-in-Chief, and others of great consequence deferring to his views. At the same time he saw very clearly—perhaps more so than anybody else concerned—that an enormous amount of work would be necessary to translate the concept into a successful reality and that a substantial proportion of this was going to fall on his shoulders. All this would be in addition to the incessant demands on his time arising from the spectacular success of penicillin, the need to keep his own large laboratory in Oxford running smoothly, and his intense desire to do his own research.

His own position, too, must have given him pause for thought. He was well aware that the hope, and indeed expectation, in Australia was that he would return there permanently to be director of the new medical research institute. Should he fail to do so there was bound to be disappointment, even though he had been scrupulously careful to reserve his position on this point. Nor, even if things turned out well—which was still open to doubt—can he have been sure in his own mind that he wanted to leave Britain for a relatively small and isolated city in Australia. Canberra might be the capital, but its population was then less than 20 000—about the same as Penzance—and it was relatively remote from the bustling centres of population such as Sydney and Melbourne; nothing much went on there except government. Even if the new University was a success it would be glowing in a vacuum for, as we have noted earlier, research activity in the rest of Australia was minimal.

In the event, Florey never went permanently to Canberra, although he contributed greatly to its success. Just possibly things might have been different had Curtin not fallen ill. His intention had been to put a firm proposition to Florey before he left Australia. Had he done so, while interest and excitement ran high, Florey might for once have allowed his heart to rule his head and agreed on the spot. But the psychological moment passed. Florey went home and not only had time to reflect but went through a period of doubt in which it seemed that the whole project had been shelved. When this was resolved it was difficult to rekindle the original fervour.

For the moment, therefore, the issue was left open and

whether he himself eventually went or not there was no lack of immediate work. The Academic Advisory Committee began to meet regularly, often on a Sunday morning in Florey's room at the Sir William Dunn School of Pathology. As we have seen each member had a special field of interest, but all were aware that the Research Schools they were helping to shape had to fit within the framework of the new University as a whole. Florey's immediate concern was the medical school, which in the 1946 Act had been formally entitled the John Curtin School of Medical Research; for convenience it is usually called simply the John Curtin School. Here he had two immediate tasks.

Firstly, a suitable building had to be designed and erected, and this in itself was a major undertaking. Such buildings are highly specialized and outside the experience of any ordinary architect. Even those who have some experience need much guidance from those familiar with the needs of the kind of research to be undertaken. In this case the situation was complicated by the fact that Florey visualized what were really five cooperative laboratories working under one roof. They required elaborate services to support them, ranging from fume cupboards to sterilizers, from animal houses to chemical laboratories, from cold rooms to incubators. It was evident from the outset that under postwar conditions pertaining in Australia merely to build the shell of the building, especially in a relatively remote place like Canberra, would present considerable practical difficulties. Several years at least would be required for this stage of the operation. But the building alone was insufficient. It would have to be stocked with a mass of specialized scientific equipment, much of it in short supply in the postwar world generally. Where available, it might have to be purchased with dollars, not easily acquired. Last, but by no means least, an adequate library had to be built up: library facilities in Australia generally were then poor.

Building and the provision of equipment were at least manageable problems, even if difficult and time-consuming; given sufficient money and time they would materialize. But the buildings and equipment alone were insufficient; they required staff—including research workers, technicians, and animal house attendants—if any useful work was to be done with them. From the very outset Florey had laid it down that the recruitment of first-rate people was an essential condition for success, and he had expressed very clearly indeed his opinion that it would be exceed-ingly difficult to get them. People of all nationalities would be welcome; indeed, if he himself came out as Director he would hope to persuade some of his Oxford colleagues to come out with him. Nevertheless, in the main they would have to pin their hopes to Australians, either indigenous or expatriate, and of those there simply were not enough of the calibre needed for the various specialities. This problem was aggravated by the self-denying ordinance that Canberra should not be stocked at the cost of depriving existing institutions of their relatively few able staff; this would be neither in the national interest nor con-ducive to good future relations. To have any hope of attracting the people essential for success the John Curtin School had to be at least as good as, and preferably better than, any comparable insti-tution in the world. He had difficulty in persuading his com-patriots of this, some of whom had no understanding of world standards of excellence, but he was quite inflexible in his insist-ence.

In the absence of a sufficiency of suitably qualified people, the alternative was to create them. For this purpose a scheme of fel-lowships and studentships was quickly devised to provide research opportunities for those who appeared to have the talent but lacked experience. In the absence of any facilities at all in Canberra at this stage it was, of course, necessary to find accom-modation for them elsewhere. Here Florey's status and powers of persuasion were invaluable; he was able to establish 'cells' for his potential recruits in first-rate laboratories in various parts of the world. Although some permanent top-level appointments were made at a very early date, the fellows and scholars were on a short-term basis. Although they had reasonable expectations of appoint-ments in Canberra in due course, there was no guarantee of this. Not all might fulfil their promise to fit into the research pattern that finally emerged; equally, not all would have wanted to com-mit themselves at so early a stage. It was considered that in any event the investment would not be lost, in that the scheme added to the pool of highly skilled manpower.

Although Florey was given considerable freedom to enlist whomever he thought appropriate, those he chose had of course to be formally appointed by the University on properly defined terms. The Academic Advisory Committee had to work closely with the University authorities in Canberra, and for the moment we must divert our attention to what was going on there. Control was vested in the Interim Council. This had been enlarged but not, if we may believe a letter sent by Rivett to Florey in February 1947, with advantage. The members were, Rivett maintained, essentially adminstrators and professional organizers with whom he found it difficult to communicate. His simplistic view was that they should hand the whole of the scientific side over to Florey and Oliphant; he had even suggested this at a Council meeting and been thought 'a bit daft'. Worse was to come, for the Minister proposed to enlarge the Interim Council by appointing some Members of Parliment to it 'to comply with the spirit of the Act'.

One of the most important duties laid on the Interim Council was to make a recommendation for the appointment of a Vice-Chancellor, to be formally endorsed by the Government-General. In accordance with the Act, the appointment would be for five years in the first instance. As he would be *ex officio* the chief executive officer of the new University all concerned recognized the crucial importance of choosing the right man. Many names were canvassed, both in Australia and overseas, and the final choice was D. B. Copland. On paper, his qualifications were impeccable: he was a distinguished Australian scholar with an international reputation; he had been Professor of Economics in Tasmania and of Commerce in Melbourne; and visiting professor in the Universities of Cambridge and Harvard; he had also had administrative experience as Commonwealth Prices Commissioner during the war. Additionally, the Interim Council was persuaded that he possessed the qualities of foresight and decision essential for the job. The appointment was important to the University; it was also very important to Florey personally, for it was with the Vice-Chancellor that he would have to deal in future.

At the time of his appointment Copland was Australian Minister in China, at Nanking, and difficulties in communication raised some problems, Mills' letter of appointment (though technically asking Copland if he would consent to his name being submitted to the Commonwealth Government) was dated 8 December 1947, but various circumstances occasioned delay. Copland raised questions about being provided with a house and car, and about a retirement allowance, which aroused sufficient hostility for the question of his appointment to go back to Council instead of direct to government. He also raised the question of his acceptance with Mr. H. V. Evatt, the Minister for External Affairs, and the latter's staff apparently talked too freely; the correspondent of the Chinese Central News prematurely published a story that the Australian Government had invited Copland to take the post. As a consequence of all this, Council's recommendation did not formally go to the Minister until mid-February. Then difficulties arose about transport, as he was reluctant to travel without his family, and he announced that he could not be in Canberra until the middle of May. He knew that the Academic Advisory Committee were coming out from England at Easter, and supposed that he ought to meet them. Could not their visit be postponed? Meanwhile, Council were getting restive and a cable was sent saying that his presence at the conference with the Academic Advisory Committee was 'regarded as vital'. Eventually he compromised, cabling to say that he could not arrive for the opening of the conference but would be in Canberra for the second part of it. Even then he was disappointed—a final cable said that his flight had been rescheduled and he would not arrive in Sydney until late on 6 April, the day on which the conference was to end. None of these difficulties were of much consequence in themselves but collectively they made for an inauspicious start. The Academic Advisory Committee were making the long journey from England at considerable inconvenience, they had had long discussions about research policy, and they doubtless felt that the new Vice-Chancellor had not matched their own diligence.

At this stage Florey felt himself to have given no more than 'a very conditional "yes"'—as he put it to Ethel in a letter home—about going to Canberra as Director. On this basis, he thought she could accept with propriety an invitation to visit Canberra that he had organized during his own stay.

Once arrived Copland applied himself energetically to his duties. Six weeks later, in a memorandum prepared for the Academic Advisory Committee summarizing the present state of play, he expressed his optimism about establishing the kind of university they had been aiming at during the previous year. They must have been less well pleased, however, at his statement that he was keeping the Prime Minister and other Ministers fully informed of what was going on; from the outset one of their fears had been political domination of academic affairs and a traditional Civil Service approach. A week later he wrote personally to Florey expressing Council's appreciation of his offer, made in a memorandum discussed during the Easter conference, 'to carry on getting staff and buildings together for the Medical Research Institute'. He proceeds to make a detailed proposition to Florey for his participation. Briefly, Council expressed itself honoured if Florey would accept responsibility for directing the establishment of the John Curtin School for the next five years. He was to come occasionally to Canberra for consultation and perhaps spend a year there on special leave from Oxford. As this went well beyond his current role of membership of the Academic Advisory Committee, he was asked to consider taking the formal title of Acting Director. He would be assisted by a Medical Advisory Committee. In consideration of these services he would receive an honorarium of £750 p.a., plus basic expense allowance of £150. Copland hoped that if this proposal was acceptable, Florey would agree to a public announcement being made.

The last two paragraphs of this letter are important. Firstly, Copland stressed that Council was anxious that this five-year arrangement should in no way prejudice a decision by Florey to accept the Directorship in the meantime if he wished. Secondly, he reiterated the hope that he will have 'the advantage also of [his] wise counsel on general academic policy'.

Florey lost no time in replying at length to this letter, which was dated 24 May. He wrote back on 8 June, falling in readily with almost everything that Copland suggested. The only major point is that while his responsibilities should be defined, no specific title should be conferred on him.

I have had a word with the University authorities here, and there would be very considerable difficulties in giving me any title, such as 'Acting Director'. There is no objection to my doing the work for you as long as I perform my duties here properly, but the introduction of any title is undesirable. . . . I think it would be as well not to mention my proposed year's leave of absence. I do not anticipate any difficulty in obtaining it, but I do not wish to apply for it now when it is not wanted at present. I can always come out to Australia during a vacation without consulting anyone.

The only additional request he makes is that an allowance of £75 per annum should be made available to his secretary, Miss W. M. Poynton, in consideration of the additional work she did for the University. Might he also buy a filing cabinet? The modesty of these requests is typical.

For the moment, Florey must have viewed the situation with satisfaction. So far as the John Curtin School was concerned he was firmly in the driving seat for the next five years, and for the same period he had preserved his options with regard to the Directorship. He was to have a say in University policy generally. He had secured his position with regard to Canberra without upsetting the authorities at Oxford. Last, but not necessarily least, a substantial increment had been added to his Oxford salary. His relationship with Copland was good: he ends his letter of acceptance (8 June 1948) thus:

> May I say in conclusion how much I appreciate being allowed to take part in the great experiment and that I have every confidence that you will be able to 'put it over'.

The greater part of this letter is, however, devoted to summarizing the immediate needs of the new School; basically these related to buildings and staff. The first had still to be planned; much thought was required to make it 'one of the best designed and ultimately best equipped in the world'. He proposed that Council should enlist the help of Dr. A. G. Sanders, his colleague at Oxford since 1936, and his companion on the wartime visit to Moscow, who had been responsible for planning postwar alterations in the Sir William Dunn School of Pathology. He proposed an annual honorarium of £250. This proposal was agreed and Sanders later paid three long visits to Canberra and contributed substantially to the planning of the new building. At the most optimistic estimate the completion of this lay several years in the future—it was, in fact, not formally opened until 1958—and in the absence of any sort of suitable alternative accommodation in Canberra, no research of any kind could be undertaken there. But the recruiting of staff could not wait on the availability of laboratory accommodation in Canberra. It was abundantly clear, at least to Florey and those cognisant of the realities of the situation, that senior staff would be very difficult to attract and no opportunity should be missed of making firm proposals to them.

The same applied to more junior staff, with the added complication that some at least would need additional training and experience if they were to reach the very high standards set for the Australian National University.

To circumvent these difficulties it had been decided in principle that key people should be offered immediate appointments and found alternative research accommodation until Canberra was ready to receive them. One of Florey's major contributions to the Austalian National University was that his high personal standing made it possible for his protégés to be found accommodation in first-rate laboratories. Fellowships and scholarships were to be offered on a similar basis but in the short term and with no guarantee of the offer of a permanent job by the Australian National University; only those of demonstrable promise would be chosen. All this Florey spelled out in detail in his letter of acceptance to Copland and he even at this early stage puts forward some specific names, some of which, at least, we shall encounter later. He also stresses the importance of technical staff and, in particular, of a really competent laboratory manager. It is evident that he has a very clear understanding of the realities of the situation and the problems ahead.

Copland also sent Florey a copy of a formal letter from the University to Oliphant inviting him to become Director of the Research School of Physical Sciences, an appointment which he took up in 1950. In this[18] Copland expresses misgivings about the general building programme:

My friends in Canberra appear to have become quite unconscious of time and in some ways remind me of the Chinese. They will readily promise things beyond their capacity, and they seem able to do it without any sense of humour. In that respect they differ from the Chinese, who are always quite charming about promises they make, and still more charming about their inability to fulfil them.

This comment deserves more than passing notice. There were in fact to be great delays, which exasperated Florey—never the most patient of men—and led to friction. It is interesting, therefore, to note that even at this early date (May 1948) those on the spot recognized them as inherent in the Australian situation at that time.

Although permanent accommodation was even further away

than was then supposed, Florey was determined to get a few troops into the field. In particular he was anxious to make an immediate offer of the Professorship of Biochemistry to A. H. Ennor. An Australian, then 37 years of age, he was a graduate of Melbourne University, whence he had been appointed research biochemist in the Baker Institute of Medical Research, Melbourne. During the war he had done government research and afterwards came to Oxford for two years (1946-48) as Wellcome Research Fellow in the Department of Biochemistry. Florey had, therefore, had an opportunity of assessing both his personal and research qualifications for the job and had obviously been greatly impressed, for he had in mind that he should be 'Temporary Assistant Director of the whole school (without prejudice to later arrangements)'. This proposal was not, however, endorsed by Council.

Council moved swiftly, and on 21 July 1948 Ennor told Florey that he had in principle accepted their invitation. He wrote from the Commonwealth Serum Laboratories (CSL) at Parkville, Melbourne—a government institution—where he had just taken up an appointment. He added the good news that CSL could provide adequate accommodation for the building up of a biochemical unit prior to the move to Canberra. Florey replied expressing his pleasure:

I look upon the Department of Biochemistry as quite the most important in the School, one which will have to be organised, not only to do its own work but to integrate with and assist work done in other departments—in particular microbiology.[19]

Thus began a close association which extended over some seven years, during which the John Curtin School was shaped. Over this period Ennor and Florey exchanged scores of letters with complete mutual confidence, often running to several pages, and Ennor became very much Florey's man in Canberra. These letters, largely still extant, throw much light on the development of the School and are an important source of information on its history. Additionally, Florey and Ennor also exchanged views by what they called 'shouting' at each other across the world by means of recorded discs, flexible enough to be rolled up into tubes for posting. Unfortunately, many of these have been mislaid; even if found, it is doubtful whether they would now be playable.

Two other key appointments were made almost at once. The first was Adrien Albert, professor of medical chemistry, in October 1948. He was an Australian, then 43 years of age, and a chemistry graduate of Sydney, and before the war had worked for his PhD degree in London University. From 1938 to 1947 he was back in Sydney, building up an international reputation for his work in chemotherapy. In 1949 he was back in London, working at the Wellcome Institute, but his appointment there was nearing its end. Many shared Florey's high opinion of him. Sir Paul Fildes, a member of the staff of the Medical Research Council and an old friend of Florey from his London Hospital days, regarded him as 'one of the few chemists who could talk to biologists in language they could understand'. Sir Robert Robinson, the President of the Royal Society and perhaps the greatest organic chemist of his generation, thought so well of him that he offered to find space for Albert and his unit in his own laboratory in Oxford, next door to Florey's. Briefly, it seemed that the arrangement might founder over the question of accommodation. Less than a month after his acceptance Copland suggested to Albert that he should return to Australia in 1949 and work in the government's Munition Supply Laboratories in Maribyrnong, Victoria. Albert reacted strongly, saying that he knew the laboratories well and thought them quite unsuitable; they were an hour's tramride out of town, academically they were isolated, and the security regulations were irksome. If the requirement were enforced he would resign. Out of the blue, Florey found himself involved in a major row. Ennor supported Copland, arguing at length that Maribyrnong was no worse than the Commonwealth Serum Laboratories where he was. Council debated the matter in November and referred the matter to Florey for a ruling. Florey put the matter to the Advisory Committee in Oxford in December—preferring not to make a personal decision —and Albert was summoned to state his case. In the end a compromise was found; Albert should remain in England—in fact, at the Wellcome Institute—until the 'roofed shell' of the John Curtin School had been erected, which it was thought would be some three years ahead. In January 1949, the news of Albert's appointment was formally released to the press. In retrospect, it seems clear that Albert was right in insisting that he remain in a place where he had daily contact with academic colleagues of similar interests. The episode is interesting as exemplifying the Council's reliance on Florey at this stage. They were content to leave a major decision to his personal judgement, but it all took up an inordinate amount of his time.

The third of the early appointments (1949) was that of Frank Fenner to the chair of microbiology. Another Australian, he had worked under F. M. Burnet at the Walter and Eliza Hall Institute. In 1948 he had gone to America to work under the distinguished microbiologist René Dubos. In December 1948 he was startled to receive, quite unexpectedly, a cable offering him the chair of bacteriology (later designated microbiology) at Canberra. That this preceded a formal letter from the University indicates how free a hand Florey was given in building up the staff of his School. Fenner returned to Australia in 1950, and temporarily resumed his research at the Hall Institute, where two laboratories were made available to him.

While Florey and his colleagues were beginning to form a clear idea of the kind of laboratory they wanted, they were still a long way from achieving it. An architect had to be appointed, contractors engaged, and—above all—finance had to be available to match the design. The latter was to prove a source of anxiety for a long time; although liberal promises had been made on the basis of what would now be called 'guestimates', no firm costing was possible in the absence of detailed plans. Moreover the political and economic situation is never stable, especially in the aftermath of war, and promises made in good faith could not necessarily be redeemed. In fact, in October 1949 Chifley appointed a committee to look into the financial needs of all the Australian universities. The University was well represented: the Chairman was R. C. Mills, chairman of the Interim Council, and Copland was a member.

The architectural design of the John Curtin School was under the general direction of Professor B. L. Lewis, who had been appointed Architect to the University. He was Professor of Architecture in the University of Melbourne and also had an extensive private practice. Florey's relationship with him was not a happy one. By the spring of 1948 he had reached the conclusion that if progress was to be made he needed architectural advice from another source and one with which he could communicate more easily. After consultation with Copland he approached a friend from his Sheffield days, Stephen Welsh, who had just been appointed Professor of Architecture there. Between them they devised, tentatively, a scheme by which, in effect, Welsh would design the building in collaboration with Florey and his colleagues, particularly Sanders, leaving Lewis to do little more than produce the working drawings. When this proposal became known in Canberra, where it was submitted to the Buildings and Grounds Committee in July, the sparks flew. The Committee refused to support it, saying that the University was already committed to Lewis as architect and could not employ another architect except in an advisory capacity; if Welsh wished to accept this role, he might be paid £50. Lewis, predictably, was furious, especially as he discovered that the intention was to pay Welsh's fees by deductions from his own. Welsh, he claimed, had been unethical and committed a breach of professional etiquette; he had been impertinent; he would lay the matter before the Royal British Institute of Architects [sic] (whom Welsh had in fact consulted) and the Royal Australian Institute. Rather oddly, this last threat was to be carried out only with Florey's permission; he can scarcely have imagined it would be forthcoming. Finally, if the University did not retract, he threatened to resign.

Acquainted with all this furore by Copland, Florey wrote a temperate and reasoned reply, but he did not for a moment concede that Lewis should have any hand in designing the scientific aspects of the building. He and Sanders would consult with Albert, Ennor, Wright, and others who knew what they were talking about where medical research was concerned and Lewis could confine himself strictly to the building:

Professor Lewis's reaction seems to be somewhat violent, but as I do not wish to start designing a building with a professional altercation I should be glad if you can persuade him to drop the matter.

I think it may clarify matters and put Professor Lewis's function in perspective if I say a few words about the designing of this building from my point of view. . . . The architect must be entirely subordinated to the scientific requirements of those who are to inhabit it. . . . If the School of Medicine is a bad design Sanders and I and any other scientists intimately concerned will have to take a great deal of the blame, and not the architect. As Professor Lewis has had no previous experience of constructing laboratories he may not be aware of this point of view.

When this initial plan [i.e. Lewis's general concept] is received I will arrange to have it seen by those in this country with recent experience of building laboratories (scientists, not architects!).[20]

In the same letter he reiterates his inflexible determination that the Medical School shall be 'a building which will be recognized the world over as being a first class laboratory'.

Lewis back-pedalled in turn:

... I trust that Sir Howard does not feel that [my] violence was directed towards himself. . . . I well know my deficiencies and trust that they can be made good by assistance from scientists, including Sir Howard. . . . I also realise that my experience of laboratory building is slight and remote in time but I trust that with . . . the advantage of the overseas studies taken at Sir Howard's directions that these deficiencies can be made good.[21]

Happily, Welsh took it all in good part, and the University authorized a payment to him of up to 150 guineas. Thus the dust settled, but it was an inauspicious beginning; Lewis never regained Florey's confidence.

The episode at least served to show both parties where they stood and Florey was free to go ahead with the design of the laboratory as a massive research tool, leaving Lewis to propose how this should be translated into bricks and mortar. His chief aide was, of course, Sanders who was officially involved but he sought assistance in many quarters. For example, ICI—to whom he was a consultant for many years—had sent one of their senior staff to the United States for six months in 1948 simply to study new ideas about laboratory design there. It was very helpful to have the direct benefit of his advice. In Europe and Australia few laboratories had been built since before the war, and these had been designed and built on austerity lines. Meanwhile, however, science had advanced very rapidly and new ideas were at a premium.

The summer of 1949 provided, for the first time, an opportunity for the three newly appointed professors—Ennor, Albert, and Fenner—to meet in Oxford with Florey and Sanders. The opportunity was taken to complete the outline design of an H-shaped building, conceived by Florey and Sanders, in which each wing was to have service rooms on the north side and laboratories on the south. The cross-link was to accommodate service facilities such as library, lecture and seminar rooms, and administrative offices. There was also provision for an animal house—essential for experimental work of this kind—and for a very large and well-equipped workshop. In insisting on the latter Florey no doubt had in mind the importance to his own research in Oxford of the departmental workshop presided over by S. W. Bush. At Canberra a first-rate workshop would be doubly important; apart from making specialist research equipment it would be invaluable, with limited local facilities, for making and maintaining standard apparatus.

Almost immediately after this meeting, with the decisions fresh in mind, Sanders left for the first of his visits to Canberra, returning to Oxford for the start of term in October. It was not an easy one as financial difficulties—which he had no remit to discuss—loomed large. Briefly, the Cabinet had in 1947 approved a cost of £150 000 for a building of 50 000 square feet, based on £3 per square foot: the Florey/Sanders plan was for a building of about 235 000 square feet (21 620 square metres), costing according to Lewis's estimate £1 million at £4 per square foot. The two differed by a factor of six. Not altogether surprisingly, Sanders was asked if they were still talking of the original concept. The best he could say was that

the very great discrepancy arose from the difficulty of visualising the ultimate provision that has to be made for scientific work at a high level . . . the School at present envisaged was substantially the same as that which had been discussed by Sir Howard Florey in Oxford and in Australia over a number of years.[22]

Goodes, the man from the Treasury, began to wonder whether Canberra would do no more than 'duplicate facilities and work already available or being carried out elsewhere in Australia'.

Sanders clearly had a rough time and no doubt was glad to escape, even though he went down with infective hepatitis on his return. Lewis wrote to him: 'by this time Australia probably seems like a bad dream'. Nevertheless, the new estimates were eventually accepted as a realistic target. Plans were made for Sanders to go back to Australia again in July 1950 for another three months, coinciding with a visit by Florey, accompanied by Albert. All concerned went ahead with detailed planning on the basis that finance would be available at the new level. Florey was still unhappy about Lewis's interpretation of his concept. In a memo to Sanders in January 1950 he wrote 'The plans seem to me to have nearly all the faults which we have struggled to avoid'. Presumably Sanders concurred, for Florey again took Lewis to task:

You will already have had some severe criticisms of your proposals. . . . There are so many factors involved, with which you are not so conversant as those who live in laboratories, that if you alter one thing there are a lot of consequential alterations to be made, and it is now far simpler in my opinion to go on with what you agreed with Sanders and with the suggestions we have made for cutting down the size than to start all over again.[23]

About this time, Florey gained two important new recruits. He had been giving thought to an appropriate person for the unfilled Chair of Physiology, and concluded that J. C. Eccles was the right person. A medical graduate of Melbourne, he had come to Oxford as a Rhodes Scholar in 1925 and worked with Sherrington. He had returned to Australia in 1937 as director of the Kanematsu Institute of Pathology in Sydney, gaining his FRS in 1941, and then moved on in 1944 as Professor of Physiology in the University of Otago, New Zealand. Florey had no doubts about his suitability but thought it unlikely that he would be interested. Nevertheless, he wrote to Eccles:

I have been assured by various people in Australia that I am wasting my time writing to you, but my own view of this matter is that if you don't ask you will never know. I shall not be surprised if you tell me not to be silly as you are well dug in at Dunedin and do not wish to move.[24]

To his pleasurable surprise, Eccles was not only interested but in a surprisingly short time, and with minimum fuss, the appointment was made; the main problem seems to have been to provide a house big enough for Eccles' family of nine children. The appointment dated from 1951 (though he did not move to Canberra until 1952) and he remained until 1966. Once again Florey's have-a-go attitude had paid a dividend. Again, too, his flair for scientific talent-spotting was apparent; in 1963 Eccles was to be awarded a Nobel Prize for Medicine for his work on the electrical phenomena involved in nerve impulses. The appointment was a great relief to Florey; as he remarked to Margaret Jennings, 'I now have no worry about academic standards'.

No less important, in its way, was the appointment of a Laboratory Manager. In November 1949, R. A. Hohnen, the Registrar, had sent Florey a draft of an advertisement for the post. He replied characteristically:

I am afraid the person you envisage . . . would be qualified for a seat with the archangels. I have reworded the advertisement to bring it down to something more realistic, as it is quite certain that no individual exists who would fit your requirements.

Equally firmly he increased the offered salary to £1200, saying he saw no reason why the General Manager of his School should be paid less than that of Oliphant's Research School of Physical Sciences. The advertisement did not materialize an archangel, but it did ultimately lead to the appointment of A. F. Bunker, a qualified engineer, who arrived in Canberra from England in September 1950. Again he had made an admirable choice. Apart from being professionally very competent, Bunker literally devoted himself to the task of establishing the new laboratory, working prodigiously long hours. Moreover, he established an excellent rapport with Florey and proved an important independent source of information about what was really going on in Canberra.

In the Spring of 1950 Florey was laid low with bronchial trouble but April brought heartening news. The Cabinet had approved £810 000, plus £200 000 for equipment, plus provision for the animal establishment and the laundry. All was set for 'crucial' talks in Canberra in August/September. Florey, Sanders, and Albert were coming out from England; Eccles from New Zealand; and Ennor and Fenner would join them. It would be a golden opportunity to clarify matters. In a letter to Copland, in March, Florey confessed:

Sanders and I have got a bit hazy with the various proposals and counter-proposals which have been made since we last saw the plans. I think the thing to aim at is that the final OK should be given to the plans when I come out in August. I do not believe that we are going to clear up some of these points by correspondence.[25]

Into these comparatively placid waters Lewis now threw a considerable pebble. In May he wrote to Florey to say that he wished —for 'reasons of personal prestige'—to accept an invitation from the British Council to lecture in Turkey, and this would mean leaving before Florey's visit was over. To Lewis, Florey sent an icily cold reply, telling him that it was a matter for the Vice-Chancellor. To Copland, however, he expressed himself much more bluntly:

I must confess that neither Sanders nor I are greatly interested in raising his prestige, and I think perhaps it might be as well to impress on him that he is the architect for a building which is going to cost £800 000 and that the University is paying a considerable sum of money in fares etc. to have three of us come out in connection with the plans. I for one shall be extremely annoyed if I am kept hopping about by the architect because he is leaving within a few days of any final discussion. . . . My own feeling is that on a project of this kind the architect really should hold himself entirely at the disposal of the University for as long as the University wants. I imagine his fee would be a pretty fat figure. . . . His lack of experience in the building makes it much more difficult for us all . . . if we don't stand over him he will alter something at the last moment which will cause further trouble.[26]

Copland concurred, and added for good measure:

It is not merely the Medical School, but he has under way a large contract for University House, the Physics Laboratory, and other housing. He should not be writing to you at all about this matter.[27]

The matter was eventually settled, but it did not improve personal relationships. In a letter to Copland of 15 June 1950 Florey comments 'I gather he [Lewis] will be on the job when we are all out in Australia'.

This same letter[28] is of interest in quite a different context. About this time Florey was beginning to suffer from the heart trouble that was eventually to prove fatal, and he would have a natural desire—but one that he was not anxious to expose—to take things a little more easily. There is, therefore, perhaps some special significance in a plea somewhat at variance with his usual buoyancy:

I thought if I could keep up with the schedule I should probably be pretty well done in by the end of it. . . . You very kindly suggested that a friend of yours would look after me in Brisbane. What I really had in mind was to retire to the seaside for a couple of days and just sit about. . . . I would very much like to meet your friend but he might want to entertain me and I doubt if I should be feeling up to that.

Many outstanding points were indeed settled during this Canberra meeting and Florey returned to Oxford in an optimistic frame of mind, leaving Sanders to wind things up. One decision taken was to keep the Academic Advisory Committee still in being, Oliphant remaining a member, even though the centre of gravity had decisively moved to Australia. But when Sanders returned to England on 1 October he brought disquieting news. When he had gone down to Melbourne for further talks on the plans with Lewis he found only one man working on them. Sanders got the impression that Lewis wanted to get out of the job, but would have to be bought out. To Copland Florey wrote:

It seems a deplorable situation, but I would ask you to consider whether some drastic action cannot be taken to get much more architectural help for Lewis, and if he refuses explore the possibility of breaking his contract. . . . We have all put a great deal of time and thought into [the plans] and I can say that the architect has contributed practically nothing to this job. . . . I trust you are still strong enough to keep on battling with the forces of darkness. There seem to be quite a number of these at work.[29]

So affairs lurched on, not assisted by political developments. The government had embarked on a remarmament programme coupled with an anti-inflationary policy, in pursuit of which the allocation of scarce resources such as steel was assigned to various new authorities, with all the bureaucratic consequences. As an economist Copland welcomed it as a retreat from what he contemptuously called the Australian 'milk-bar' economy: as a Vice-Chancellor with a major building programme it made his task more difficult.

In February 1951 Florey sent an urgent plea to Ennor:

. . . we run the risk of having all work on the Medical School stopped . . . keep the ball in play until I come out in September, as we really must try in the event of a refusal of supplies to save something. . . .[30]

By June estimated costs had risen to £1.6 million, not including equipment, and it was not known if Cabinet would agree this. Back in Oxford Florey was despondent; seven years after the scheme had been proposed, and so enthusiastically endorsed at the highest level, it seemed to him as though it might yet founder. Writing again to Ennor in June he confessed

I can't make head or tail of all this building business. All that is quite certain is that nobody has signed on the dotted line as yet that the Medical School will be put up.

That summer Oliphant could offer no solace, except the gloomy one that Australian affairs were so bad that they could change only for the better. In Canberra rumours were rife that the scheme was to be abandoned; morale was low.

Only Copland still radiated optimism. In June he had arrived in Oxford fresh from political lobbying, including a talk with the Prime Minister: 'The Medical School will go ahead if what the Prime Minister told me on Saturday morning has any meaning at all'. Nevertheless, in July the Cabinet was calling for a new appraisal of the building programme and the annual cost. To many the constant direct intervention of Government in University affairs was not favourably regarded; a neutral intervening body, like the University Grants Committee in Britain, would have been welcome. Apart from the question of principle, some critics in Canberra were saying that Copland was getting himself far too involved in politics, making public pronouncements on the cure of Australia's economic ills, to the detriment of his duties as Vice-Chancellor. Writing to Oliphant in February 1952, Florey said:

I was a little startled to see in 'The Times' the other day that Spender [Sir Percy Spender, Australian Minister for External Affairs 1949-51, later President of the International Court of Justice at The Hague] and Copland have been exchanging abuse in the press to such an extent that it secured about 6 to 9 inches of the main foreign page of 'The Times'.[31]

How much truth there was in this criticism of Copland and how much it was the fruit of idle gossip in an isolated and frustrated academic community is difficult to discern. There is, however, no doubt of his political ambitions, which were shortly (1953) to be fulfilled with his appointment as High Commissioner to Canada; he had already been awarded his KBE in 1950.

Florey was out again in August for more talks. Whatever else was doubtful, it was clear that the completion of the Medical School still lay some years ahead. It could not be surprising if in the meantime some of the widely dispersed staff lost heart and tried their luck elsewhere. In certain instances this was a real and not a potential danger. To counter it, it was decided to erect temporary buildings for research in Canberra. There was, of course, an element of risk in this, for there is much truth in the saying that there is nothing more permanent than a temporary building.

However, Council approved the proposal and some temporary laboratories were available for occupation by Ennor and Fenner in November 1952; Eccles also worked in these temporary buildings. So also did George Mackaness, an experimental pathologist who had gone to Oxford as an ANU Scholar in 1947 to work with Florey. He later became President of the Squibb Institute of Medical Research in the United States. Albert was not among those who moved into them, preferring to remain in London until permanent accommodation was ready.

It is clear that by now Florey was beginning to have serious thoughts of abandoning Canberra to its own devices. Writing to Margaret Jennings in Oxford he says:

I look forward to getting away from all the talk here. . . . I am gratified to say that everyone seems very pleased with the Medical School appointments, and would be nonplussed if I said I was fed up with being an adviser owing to the slow progress. If they only knew.[32]

Nevertheless, these visits to Australia were not without their compensations. With Oliphant and other congenial company there were excursions to the country and sea. In Melbourne he was able to visit his sister Hilda and his niece Dr. Joan Gardner, who had worked in the Biochemistry Department at Oxford. On such occasions he was able to leave aside the cares which made him seem, to many, a forbidding and rather cold person. There is ample evidence that given the opportunity—though unhappily he was not given it very often—he could be relaxed and light-hearted and thoroughly enjoy himself. The climate was a welcome relief from that of Oxford and, as he often remarked, was ideal for children. The relief of his hay fever was also a great advantage. But, as he wrote to Ethel at this time, Australia was all the same 'a young man's country' and he no longer felt young.

By that time the Interim Council had been dissolved and a permanent Council established. The office of Chancellor—on whose absence in the original draft Act Florey had commented—went to a distinguished Australian, Lord Bruce. He was a former Prime Minister, a former High Commissioner in London, and at that time Chairman of the Finance Corporation for Industry. Although Florey found his understanding of academic affairs very limited, and it was difficult to pin him down to their discussion, the two got on very well and he was a useful ally while in London, where the Corporation had offices in Lombard Street. Florey said, 'he is very sympathetic to the idea [of the ANU], and is a man of sufficient age, and good presence, to be able to put things over'.

While the affair of the Medical School ground on in this frustrating and time-consuming way, Florey was still dispensing advice on many other University matters—the chair of history, the Wardenship of University House, the foundation of an Australian Academy of Sciences. But with his greater wisdom and wider experience he found the limited vision of some of his compatriots exceedingly irritating. As so often, he unburdened himself to Oliphant, who had his own share of problems, writing in April 1952:

I live in a semi-vacuum with regard to the A.N.U. Ennor writes me a chatty letter from time to time. . . . I don't think people in Canberra really realise, as you and I do, that it is not looked upon as the intellectual mecca of the world, and that people are not falling over themselves to take jobs there. In fact, there is a serious loss of good A.N.U. scholars and other Australians to this country at the present time.[33]

If he could write thus in April, he must have been considerably astonished at a proposition put to him, albeit informally, in October. At that time Copland was on the point of resigning to go to Canada as High Commissioner and it would, therefore, be necessary to appoint a new Vice-Chancellor. The suggestion was made that Florey should take the appointment temporarily, with the option of either continuing in it or taking up the Directorship of the Medical School when the permanent buildings were completed. An added inducement was that he would be on the spot to urge on the building programme. The underlying thought was that after two or three years Coombs could decently detach himself from his Bank and take on the Vice-Chancellorship.

In his reply to this proposal Florey said that after weighing the pros and cons for a week he had decided that if a formal offer were made he would have to decline it. He had no taste for administration, he said, and had 'already refused two good administrative jobs in this country, one of which is paid at least double the rate that I get now'. One of these jobs was presumably the Directorship of the Lister Institute and the other the Secretaryship of the Medical Research Council. In November 1948 John Fulton had written to inquire if he would be interested in a post at the Graduate School of Public Health in Pittsburgh or in a Chair of Pathology at Yale. Florey replied very firmly:

I am afraid, tempting though both these suggestions are, that I could not as things are, lead you to suppose that I could accept either of them if made. As you know, I like America and Americans, and there are very strong urges to come to your country but there are many difficulties. . . . As you know, Mellanby will be retiring next year and the Medical Research Council earlier this year recommended that I should be his successor (without asking me, I may say). As it is a job I should dislike very much I have refused it, but it does mean that if I should go to the U.S.A. I should never be able to set foot again here. In addition, I have virtually promised that if I leave Oxford I shall go to Australia where I am at the moment helping them to establish their new University.[34]

Although he turned down the proposal for the Vice-Chancellorship there exists the draft of a long letter to Oliphant—the heavy correction of the original showing the care with which it was composed—indicating that he almost took the fly thus unexpectedly cast over him. He suggests that he might serve as Vice-Chancellor from March to December 1953. This might give him the opportunity to 'see that the Medical School is well on its way to being built':

So far as I am aware no definite decision has been taken to build it and the sole visible manifestation of these buildings is some concrete slabs for what is to be the permanent workshop. This work-shop, which is of a rather temporary structure, will, I understand, take eighteen months to construct.

But his real objective was very much more ambitious—to rescue the University from the 'administrative morass' into which, in his view, it had fallen. As so often in the past Florey sought to impose conditions, even in the face of what to many would have seemed a tempting proposal:

Council would have to agree that I could bring with me somebody with extensive knowledge of the organisation of Universities, their finances and all the rest, who would act as my personal adviser. I know of two first-rate possibilities in this direction . . . my 'mission', horrible word, would be to review the workings of the University which has now been "going" 5 years.

The basis of his contention is that research—supposedly the main objective of the University and the activity always nearest his own heart—was being subordinated not only to administration, but to an inefficient administration:

I consider that a number of blunders were made in setting up the University. . . . Although I still think parts of [it] will function very well it is clear that the time-scale for setting it up has been greatly extended from that originally contemplated. . . . If I had been on the spot I should probably be in a madhouse now from all the futilities which must occur locally almost daily. . . . I consider the machinery of the central administration is of poor quality. . . . The University seems to have made quite ridiculous contracts for its buildings. It does not seem able to get them finished and as far as my information goes temporary buildings of the Medical School owe their very existence to the great energy expended on them by Bunker.

Rather suprisingly, for he might well have been singled out as the arch administrator, Copland escaped his strictures:

I have never had any difficulties in dealing with Copland for the simple reason that I have never got hopping mad at the lack of progress nor felt violent about some of the administrative incompetence. The reason is quite simple:- Delay did not interfere with my experimental work and scientific activities.

The situation was indeed paradoxical. He was officially adviser for the establishment of the Medical School and as such was paid a substantial annual retainer; it was still expected that he would in due course become Director; his advice was being constantly sought on all sorts of other matters relating to the ANU; and, last but not least, he commanded respect at the highest level as one of Australia's most distinguished sons. To W. R. Crocker, Professor of International Relations (shortly to embark on a distinguished diplomatic career as High Commissioner in India) he confided:

There have been great flappings going on in Canberra consequent on Copland's resignation and I must have dictated about a quarter of a million words of one sort or another in the last month or so.

Yet he was kept in ignorance of matters of crucial importance—for example, he knew of Copland's pending departure only a day before he saw it in the newspapers in England—and relied for information on private correspondence and visitors to Oxford. For Florey, there was only one explanation: it was 'bureaucracy gone mad'. How far this stricture was justified is another matter, to be examined when an official history of the University comes to be written. What matters in the present context is that it was Florey's deeply held conviction, and it coloured his thoughts and actions.

Florey's next visit to Canberra was scheduled for the early part of 1953, and he deliberately timed it for the end of March to avoid troubling Copland, who was departing in February, with 'embarrassing questions' just as he was leaving. Sanders received an invitation to be there again at the same time. Florey went out determined to bring matters to a head, mainly from sheer exasperation, but in a letter to Oliphant he hints again at another reason: 'I shall be fifty-five next year and I already begin to feel feeble—in fact I don't feel at all well from time to time.[35] As always, Oliphant was understanding and sympathetic:

I do hope you will not come out on your visit if it is going to place a great strain on you. After all, there is a limited amount which any individual can do in this world, and it is better for you to apply a stimulus from that side than to risk cracking up as a result of trying to be here too.[36]

He, too, had known his moments of despondency, as he records in his contribution to the Conlon memorial volume:

I used to say to him [Conlon], if I felt downhaearted, 'Look here, I think I'll go back to England; its no good trying to carry on here. The atmosphere's all alien and wrong.' He helped me through those early years here [he had arrived in 1950] when one felt like dropping one's bundle and going back to where things were easier.[37]

The 1953 visit was a turning-point in Florey's relationship with the Australian National University. First and foremost he made it clear that he did not wish to continue as adviser. In theory there was no reason why he should not bow out; his original appointment, in May 1948, was for five years. In practice, this caused such consternation that he reluctantly agreed on a compromise. He would continue as adviser provided he had nothing more to do with the building and a Dean was appointed to the Medical School to deputize for him; their long and friendly relationship made Ennor a natural choice. He indicated, too, that he could not—'for personal reasons'—take the Directorship of the School. Nevertheless, it was not easy to disengage himself. On 28 April he wrote to Margaret Jennings: 'Today I spent 4 hours designing the damned building here. . . . I am heartily sick of the whole thing and long to get away.'[38] This additional work was largely occasioned by the fact that on the previous day the arrangement with Lewis as architect had finally been terminated, an event that Florey recorded with great satisfaction. Fortunately, it had proved possible to do so on agreed terms without recourse to arbitration. His place was taken by the Melbourne architectural firm of Mussen, McKay and Potter; the senior partner (Norman Mussen) immediately opened an office on the University site. This change so effectively got things on the move again that Sanders obtained a term's leave of absence from Oxford so that he could stay in Canberra until the end of August. Nevertheless Florey's relationship with some of those on the spot was not an easy one, and his view of long-term prospects not optimistic; to Margaret Jennings he confided 'It will be a miracle if this place can be given a real University atmosphere'. His misgivings were shared elsewhere, but for different reasons. Within the Cabinet the Prime Minister had to contend with a faction, led by R. G. Casey and Kent Hughes (Minister of the Interior), who wanted to abandon the project altogether. Their reasons were partly financial—understandable enough in the economic circumstances of the day—and partly trivial. They disliked, for example, the inclusion of John Curtin's name in the title. They disapproved, too, of the word School in the context of an institution which did not train doctors. Council debated this at length in October 1953 but decided no change in the title was necessary, especially as this would require amendment of the ANU Act. There was adverse comment, too, in some sections of the press, notably the *Melbourne Herald*. One of Florey's tasks during this visit was to speak at a dinner for Menzies, Casey, and Kent Hughes and give a carefully considered review of the history and objectives of the School. This was followed up with an Open Night for Parliamentarians in November, when the Opposition was apparently more in evidence than the Government.

The situation was not improved on the occasion of the election of a new Vice-Chancellor on 31 May. Although Florey had turned down the possibility of taking the job himself—though it was never formally offered to him—he had given much thought to other possible candidates and had had considerable confidential discussions on the subject at a very high level. The Chairman

had invited him to attend the meeting of Council at which the
new appointment was to be made and he went fully expecting to
be able to express his opinion. To his intense irritation he was
not only excluded from the discussion but asked to withdraw
from the meeting, apparently at the instigation of Roland Wilson,
Secretary to the Treasury. He gave a pithy account of this in
another letter to Margaret Jennings:

It is very significant that [a] faction succeeded in preventing me giving
my views. I was asked to the Council by the Chairman and then thrown
out. I thought this very flattering to the influence they thought I might
wield.[39]

Strictly speaking the Council seems to have been within its
rights, for Florey was not a member and highly confidential
business was to be transacted. Nevertheless, in view of his quite
exceptional status, it would have been sensible, and possible, to
have made a special dispensation allowing him to stay. Thereafter, he was not sent the minutes of Council and Board of
Graduate studies.[40] It was an affront he neither forgot nor
forgave. Afterwards Florey remarked to Oliphant:

What matter could be of greater concern to me, as the potential Director
of a Research School, than the choice of the man under whom I would
serve administratively. If that is Council's attitude towards those who
will do the real work in the University, it can count me out.

The new Vice-Chancellor, Leslie Melville, was another economist. A graduate of Sydney, he had been the first Professor of
Economics at Adelaide and was currently Assistant Governor of
the Commonwealth Bank. Melville made an unfortunate start
with Florey by returning to Australia via England but making no
attempt to contact him in Oxford. It has been said that Florey
was considerably offended by this oversight but in writing, at
least, he was philosophical about the matter. Writing to Oliphant,
he merely said:

I dare say the fact that he did not call on me while he was here was due,
probably, to his lack of knowledge that I had anything to do with the
University.

In fact, this was substantially correct. A year later Ennor wrote to
Florey to say that he had just discovered that Melville's secretary
had omitted Florey's name from a list of people he ought to see
in England.

Whatever the reason, Oliphant was not surprised; even by the end of January 1954 he himself had had no discussion with Melville, despite a memo which, as Acting Vice-Chancellor, he had given him on his arrival some three months earlier. In this, Florey saw the hand of Roland Wilson, to whom he attributed the belief 'that the natural scientists needed severe handling and curbing'. Nevertheless, things were moving; November 1953 brought the welcome news that the Medical School could go ahead substantially as planned.

In Canberra, 1954 opened auspiciously. The Queen and the Duke of Edinburgh paid a State Visit to Australia in February, during the course of which University House was formally opened and the newly created Australian Academy of Science—located on the fringe of the University site—received its Royal Charter. It was a memorable occasion for Oliphant, for he had been a very active promoter of the Academy and had encountered many obstacles, not least of which was the prior existence of the Australian National Research Council, founded in 1923. Although not strictly a national academy, it enjoyed considerable prestige in Australia, and understandably many members were reluctant to see the establishment of a more august and more select body to which relatively few of them could expect to be elected. With Dr. D. F. Martyn, of the Mount Stromlo Observatory in Canberra, Oliphant had worked hard to create the Academy and it was appropriate that he should serve as its first President (1954-57).

Florey, too, played a part in the creation of the new Academy, mainly as an informal intermediary between its sponsors and the Royal Society, on which it was closely modelled. Initially, Oliphant and his collaborators had hoped that the Royal Society would actively support its plea for a Charter. In 1952-53 Florey was a member of the Council and had informal discussions with, among others, the then President, Sir Cyril Hinshelwood, and the Biological Secretary, Sir Edward Salisbury, Director of Kew Gardens. As a result, he advised Oliphant privately that the Royal Society would not support the foundation of a sister academy in Australia. This was not due to any lack of sympathy with the proposal—though it must have been aware of some degree of local opposition—but simply that it had to be punctilious in observing the conditions of its own Charter. As always, he went to great trouble to get the position clear:

Salisbury expressed great anxiety about the possibility of the Royal Society being put in the position of being accused of interfering in Australian matters . . . by the terms of its Charter it is precluded from expressing any views as a body on controversial matters. I do not think there is the slightest chance of the Royal Society expressing public support for the proposed Academy of Sciences. In Salisbury's view, which I think is quite reasonable, the Society can be of real assistance later. The procedure would seem to be this: for you and others in Australia to get your petition in giving reasons; give opportunities for the A.R.N.C. and others to object if they wish; and for the Privy Council to make a decision. What is very likely to happen is that the President of the Royal Society would be asked his views about the petition as a private individual. Salisbury thought there would be no difficulty in conveying the impression to those granting the Charter that the Royal Society thought it desirable that Australia should have a fully representative high-class Academy . . . then it would be a practicable proposition to go to the Royal Society and ask for recognition as a Corresponding body—recognition such as is given to the National Academy of Sciences in the U.S.A., and so on.

I have shown this letter Salisbury, who will reply in a more formal way as Secretary of the Royal Society, if you so desire, but perhaps under the circumstances this informal intimation of the position is more appropriate. I would emphasise that any lack of action at the present time should not be interpreted as "bloody-mindedness".[41]

This was in fact a pretty accurate prediction of the course of events. There were 23 Foundation Fellows, including Eccles. The Charter provided for two classes of members—Fellows and Corresponding Members. The latter comprised 'persons, not normally resident in Australia, who are eminent in some branch of natural knowledge'. This latter category was indeed eminent, for in the first 25 years of the Academy's history only ten elections were made. These included Florey (1958), in such distinguished company as Lord Adrian (1955), Sir Robert Robinson (1955), and Lord Todd (1960).

Florey had planned a further visit to Canberra in 1954 but thought he 'detected a slight sales-resistance in Melville's quarter to my coming out'. Oliphant replied that while there was some truth in this, Florey should regard it as no more than a sympton of Melville's native caution. Reassured, Florey replied:

I am looking forward to coming out this time. Last time, as you know, it didn't look a very pleasant prospect, but with University House in operation and no gross worries about the general set-up things should look a great deal better.[42]

Melville was, in fact, quite happy to meet Florey and get the benefit of his advice, for the Australian Vice-Chancellors had to prepare a forecast of the development of each university for two successive quinquennia commencing in 1955. Apart from general considerations, he was anxious to see the matter of the Medical School settled.

The major development was that the new architects had moved ahead fast enough to call for tenders and these were considered by the Council in September, after Florey had returned to Oxford. Melville was at pains to send all the details to Florey and in particular to explain why the Council had decided to accept the tender of Karl Schreiner of Canberra. There were considerable arguments for and against this decision. In favour was the fact that Schreiner's tender was quite substantially lower than that of his three rivals: he was prepared to accept a penalty clause if completion exceeded 15 months; as a builder he was generally considered good; and it was thought that his relationship with the unions was particularly good. On the other hand rumour had it that he was on the verge of bankruptcy, and inquiry had shown that his financial resources were 'slender', and there were doubts whether his health would stand up to the strain of such a substantial contract. As a precaution, a medical examination was to be conducted and the Council took comfort in the fact that if Schreiner was unable to continue Mrs. Schreiner, too, was very competent in the building business.

We can only surmise what Florey made of the news that a contract for nearly a million pounds for the buidling of the Medical School had been let to a contractor whose financial stability was in doubt and whose health, too, was open to question. He must at least have been relieved that he was no longer concerned with the building. He reminded Ennor that far from thinking Schreiner a good builder Bunker had been 'thoroughly dissatisfied' with the construction of the temporary buildings, and that Ennor himself had had trouble with the building of his own house. To Melville he contented himself with saying: 'I expect he will drive you all mad before he is finished, or anyway the building will.'[43] In the event, doubts about Schreiner proved not ill-founded. In March 1956 he was taken into the custody of the ACT Supreme Court, where claims by Supersteel Pty Ltd. and others were pending against him. The case attracted wide publicity and the University was marginally involved, as the plaintiffs contended that Schreiner's big contract for the Medical School had led them to suppose that he had adequate funds at his disposal. In the end, his wife had to find a surety of nearly £10 000 before he was released to go on a business trip to Austria, allegedly to look at various types of machinery and improve his knowledge for finishing the university job. In fairness, however, it should be recorded that in the end Schreiner did successfully complete the Medical School. By the time, however, Florey's relationship with the University had changed yet again.

The year 1954 had ended auspiciously. The building programme was going so well that in November Melville was able to write, on behalf of the Council, inviting Florey to come to Canberra for about eighteen months from March 1957, with his wife, to act as Director of the School. Florey temporized, saying that it might take as long as twelve months for him to see whether such an arrangement could be contrived, but certainly implying that he was not averse to the proposal. The main difficulty, he thought, might lie in raising funds for fellowships etc. so that he would have an adequate supporting staff.

Over the next months a querulous but polite correspondence ensued on a variety of topics. The most important topic arose from Florey's suggestion that it might be possible to attract to Canberra a very eminent Australian chemist, A. J. Birch, then Professor of Organic Chemistry at Sydney. Apart from Birch's own views on the subject, a number of factors had to be considered. Although the ultimate aim was a Research School of Chemistry, available funds permitted only a modest start and the proposal was that initially Birch should be found room in Albert's section of the John Curtin School. While Florey thought that Albert might be persuaded to accept this arrangement, he was adamant that Albert should be properly consulted and not faced with a *fait accompli*. It was necessary, too, to ensure that no offence was caused at Sydney. The budget of the John Curtin School was moving into the red and a new development could be financed only by economizing elsewhere. The whole matter was delicate and supposedly restricted to Melville, Oliphant, and Ennor in Canberra, and Florey in Oxford. Birch was interested enough to come to Canberra in January 1955 and to submit a memorandum indicating the kind of arrangement which would be acceptable to him. Unfortunately, just as it began to look as though something might be achieved, there was some breach of confidence. In mid-February, Ennor—in a handwritten letter to Florey—said that wild rumours were rampant on the campus, including one that Albert had resigned in protest:

Quite a garbled account but containing the odd grain of truth which indicates that someone has talked unwisely. . . . This place is quite the worst I have known in dealing with confidential information, and there are v. few people I would trust but these shall be nameless.[44]

An awkward situation was aggravated because Oliphant took the opportunity of a visit to England to discuss the matter personally with Florey, but on the basis that he (Oliphant) had not been shown Birch's memorandum. Taxed with this by Florey, Melville replied irritably that Oliphant's memory was at fault; Birch had given Oliphant a copy of the memorandum, and Oliphant had passed it on to him with the Physics School stamp on it. He complained justifiably that Florey and Oliphant had not told him what they thought Birch should do nor given him any proposal to put forward: 'I cannot ask Council to make a blind appointment without being able to say what is involved'.

They were at odds, too, over finance. Florey accepted that while strict budgetary control was necessary, there should be some system by which a supplementary grant might be made available to take advantage of special circumstances.

. . . I think you and Council will be subjected to very severe criticism if you allow one of the most distinguished chemists in Australia, and one who Sir Robert Robinson maintains is one of the two best pupils he ever had, to leave without a serious effort being made to find out whether the A.N.U. could meet his immediate requirements and make him reasonably happy about the future. . . . It would be very humiliating, I think, for the University to have to turn away really good people because it had tied its hands for many years to come by itself suggesting a ceiling [of expenditure]. . . . If you yourself suggest freezing expenditure for an indefinite time, then the possibility of the build-up of the Medical School is in my opinion seriously jeopardised.[45]

This exchange reflected an important difference of opinion on academic policy. Melville defended himself by saying that there was no question of freezing expenditure indefinitely and in fact the government grant to the ANU would treble between 1951 and 1956. He hoped for more funds for the Medical School but

this will, of course, be dependent on the University maintaining good relations with the Government. I am not happy about the way in which we are going about this at the moment.[46]

One can sympathize with both parties. Florey had always been dubious about the amount of direct government intervention in the affairs of the University; whatever Melville might think, as chief executive he had to deal with the situation as it existed and not as he might wish it to be.

In the event, the question of providing an acceptable position for Birch resolved itself when, rather reluctantly, he accepted a firm invitation to occupy the prestigious chair of organic chemistry at Manchester, once occupied by Robinson himself. Happily, this was not the end of the matter for in 1967, when circumstances had changed, he did go to Canberra first as Dean of the Research School of Chemistry and later (1970) as Professor of Organic Chemistry, a position he held for ten years; this, however, is beyond the limit of our present history.

This exchange had again raised serious doubts in Florey's mind. So far as he was concerned, the interesting figures were those for the Medical School and not for the University as a whole. In June he wrote to Melville:

I can only go on the documents that come before me. The Long Term Estimates compiled on the 27th April 1955 show that in the years 1957-8 and 1958-9 the amount of money to be put into the John Curtin School is held steady at £245,829. The Department of Experimental Pathology seems to be frozen at £15,002 from 1955-56 to 1958-59, which covers the period of the invitation from Council for my visit in 1957. Now that this matter has been raised it will be necessary for me to consider the invitation in more detail. I have never had, nor asked for, detailed proposals, but perhaps the time has now come to consider the matter in detail. I wonder if you would be so good as to let me know what Council had in mind.[47]

To this Melville sent a cool reply on 16 June, agreeing that it would indeed be desirable to consider detailed proposals for visit in 1957. He pointed out that in his original letter of invitation in the previous November he had specifically invited Florey to 'prepare a proposal with a view to securing the service of other distinguished scientists in the School during the period of your visit'.

A pencilled note shows that this letter was never acknowledged but in the following weeks Florey gave careful thought to his position, and reached the conclusion that it was untenable. On 24 August he sent a formal letter of resignation. It was brief and to the point:

> It has become increasingly apparent to me that I can no longer undertake the dual task of looking after a fairly large department in this University and acting as Adviser to the J.C.S.—an occupation which has, in fact, taken a good deal of time and energy for several years. After very considerable thought, I should be glad if you would ask Council to accept my resignation as from December 31, 1955. . . . This will mean that, as far as I am concerned, I shall not be able to undertake the arduous organisation of bringing out a number of people in 1957, as was at one time proposed.
>
> I need hardly say that it is with very considerable regret that I have to sever my formal connection with the Australian National University but I can feel moderately happy in that I think the Medical School is now on its way to being firmly established, though I have little doubt that great efforts will still have to be put into its elaboration.[48]

He mentioned in the letter that he had had an opportunity of discussing his resignation with Ennor, Eccles, and Wright in Oxford and it was they who had urged him to continue until the end of the year. The implication was that, left to his own devices, he would have finished then and there.

This letter created considerable consternation in Canberra; nobody was disposed to take it at its face value. Melville cabled Wright and Ennor in Oxford to seek enlightenment before putting the matter formally before the Council on 9 September. How should he explain matters to the Prime Minister; was Bruce aware of the situation? He was worried that the grant for the Medical School would be reduced. At the Council Meeting both Coombs and Oliphant sought to provide some background information 'but this only made the Council more uneasy about the reason behind your decision'. The upshot was that the Council cabled an invitation to him to visit Canberra at the earliest possible moment to discuss the future of the Medical School, but 'not (repeat not) to urge you to reconsider resignation which you may not wish to do'. Florey was not to be drawn, however, and immediately declined. He reiterated that he had not resigned over any particular issue and certainly not over 'the imposition of what has been called "ceilings".

I fully sympathise with the Government in wanting to know now and at regular intervals what they are committed to in supporting the National University. This is a system which works in this country through the Government [i.e. University] Grants Committee and we are all familiar with it.[49]

He announced, however, that it was his intention to prepare two papers. The first would 'put down on paper some reflections and views about the Medical School'. The second was to be 'on general University policy and conduct'; this was to be submitted direct to the Chancellor, who could make what use he liked of it. Private correspondence shows very clearly that his purpose in this was to ensure that this second paper was not quietly shelved by the Council or subjected to 'jiggery-pokery in the central office'. Meanwhile

I am sure I can give Council a not too gloomy picture of the present position of the Medical School. Its future will be determined by Council's sagacity. They can look upon me as dead, if they like, and then they would be faced with exactly the same position as they are now.[50]

At its next meeting Council expressed its regret that Florey could not come to Canberra and state his views in person; confirmed that the wished him to continue until the end of the year; and 'would be honoured if [he] would consent to visit [them] later and officially open the new medical school building'. This continuation he took very seriously; for example, he had a very long and detailed correspondence with Fenner about the future of the School after he had ceased to have any responsibility for it.

Coombs had intervened personally urging him to pay an immediate visit and to him, too, Florey tried to make it clear that his resignation was simply because things had become too much for him:

I cannot any longer attend to a department here which has more people in it than the whole of the John Curtin School, and try to influence things 12 000 miles away.

Anticipating Coombs' possible reply that he could control events if he came to Canberra, he said:

I have watched the development of the University from time to time with considerable dis-quiet . . . as yet it has not established itself as a place to which I could whole-heartedly recommend any but the young to go.

To Ennor, by then returning by sea to Australia on a ship calling at Colombo where he would collect mail, he gave the same reasons and adding those of 'increasing age and cynicism'.

In a long letter, Oliphant made no secret of his dismay, which he knew would be shared by many in the John Curtin School, at Florey's decision. He had very much looked forward to the stimulus of having Florey in Canberra, if only for the proposed 18 months' visit. He added his own strong plea that Florey should, if at all possible, make at least a quick visit to Canberra then and there. In any event he welcomed Florey's proposal for a statement of his views—the blunter the better. In an equally long reply Florey adduced another reason for his reluctance to come to Canberra: 'I should be spending my whole time on administrative matters because of my lack of confidence in the general set-up'.

By coincidence, as it happened, Florey was not the only man who had decided the time had come to break with Canberra. Bunker, the Laboratory Manager, was disenchanted for a variety of reasons: the stagnation of Canberra and the difficulty of getting leave to be away from it for even a day; a downgrading in status and salary relative to other grades of staff; no appreciation of his services; an absurdly elaborate stores control system. The last straw, it seems, had been when Ennor had asked the Finance Committee that Bunker might be paid for leave he had been unable to take because of his work for the Medical School. This had been refused; the Committee told him that the accumulated leave could be taken when he had completed ten years service. Florey replied to Bunker immediately and sympathetically:

I am extremely glad to hear what has been going on. It is of course considerably worse than I had anticipated. I have been kept completely uninformed about your alteration in status, and your letter is the first I have hear of it, but it is in line with the development of a steady diminution of control at the periphery to central control. I fully sympathise with your wish to get another job. . . . If I have a chance I shall certainly keep an eye open for something for you . . .[51]

Florey was always loyal to his friends, and was as good as his word. Bunker gave his name as a referee and Florey wrote what serves also as an epitome of his services to the Medical School:

I cannot imagine why the Australian National University has not made sufficient efforts to keep one of its best servants. He has been the mainstay in the building of the Medical School, both in temporary and permanent quarters, the latter of which are not yet complete. . . . I could go on enumerating the admirable services which, to my certain knowledge, Mr. Bunker has given the Australian National University. If you are fortunate enough to get him I am sure you will be more than satisfied with his energy and organising ability.[52]

In the end, Bunker left a year later to take up an appointment in Melbourne. As we shall see, what Florey regarded as shabby treatment of Bunker was still very much in his mind when he wrote the first of his two memoranda. He had gone to considerable trouble to check the facts of the matter as far as he could with Ennor.

In Canberra, Melville was very much in the eye of the storm. As Vice-Chancellor, he had to explain an embarrassing situation to various important people—the Prime Minister, the Chancellor, and the Council among others. He had intended coming to England in November to see Hancock and thought that this would provide also an opportunity to talk things over with Florey. In the event he postponed his visit to January, when he would be travelling through en route for America, but Florey was evasive —he pleaded that he would by then no longer be Adviser and January was a particularly busy time for Royal Society committee work and his own teaching. Understandably, he was reluctant to have any discussion until he had completed and dispatched his two memoranda. Nevertheless, Melville was insistent and Florey invited him to have dinner with him in Oxford and stay the night in Lincoln College.

The meeting was something of an anticlimax as Melville was suffering from an attack of asthma, which delayed by several days his departure for America and from which he was still suffering when he finally got back to Canberra, and Florey was determined not to be drawn. Surprisingly, however, he did drop a hint that all was not lost, for in the course of a long letter to Oliphant he confided that:

I did mutter to Melville that perhaps it would be better if I came out at some later date and spent a year or so doing some research, but this of course is somewhat of a pipe dream.[53]

Even more surprisingly, he even went so far as to change his mind and give Melville a copy of his memorandum for Council. The preparation of this had occupied him until just before Christmas, for as he explained to Oliphant 'the contents of my documents . . . must of course by very carefully composed and contain nothing which is not defensible. I do not, therefore, propose to write them hurriedly.' He did, in fact, go to great trouble in the matter and sought advice in many quarters:

[It] has taken a lot of time and energy and has been successively refined and most of the insulting passages removed by one person or another . . . this present version bears to the original one the same relationship as a rather pale pink to the best vermilion.[54]

It was not a task to his liking; early in November he wrote to Ennor 'I find it very hard work and am heartily sick of it'. In spite of this cooling-off period the memorandum to the Council was a very forthright document; many of his friends had urged him that it should be. Florey was astonished to find that it was issued in printed form under the imprint of the Government printer; he was concerned that this meant that it was to be given much wider circulation than he had expected. The explanation was exactly the opposite. It was thought to be the best means of keeping it confidential; duplication by the administration was, allegedly, then equivalent to a press release. In fact, it remained officially confidential unitl 1980, when it was declassified so that carefully selected extracts from it could be included in the Annual Report of the John Curtin School. Florey's Report runs to some 8000 words, so only salient points can be noted here. It is of interest not only in the context of the Australian National University but because it represents Florey's mature judgement—he was then nearing his 60th birthday—on how research should be conducted within a University framework.

He begins, however, with a personal and somewhat tendentious account of his reasons for resigning as Adviser. He reiterated that the burden of trying to run two research establishments on opposite sides of the world was becoming almost intolerable. He might have summoned up the necessary enthusiasm if the financial situation had been more certain and the general trend of the University's affairs more promising than in fact they were. He had been astonished to learn of the Council's dismay at his decision. It had never been 'almost certain' that he would come to Canberra as the first Director of the John Curtin School; on the contrary, from the beginning he had tried to make it clear that he was unlikely to do so:

I do not think I deceive myself over this matter as Sir Keith Hancock has told me that this was the impression that he had when he was closely associated with the University.

In the same paragraph he complains bitterly of what he regarded as offhand treatment by the Council:

I cannot believe that Council thought it a serious possibility, for on two decisions of crucial importance to the University, and to me if I was to be a Director, neither my advice nor my opinion was asked, and, indeed, on one occasion they were somewhat ostentatiously avoided. I cannot conceive that I should have been treated in this way if Council had really hoped and believed that I should leave this country [Britain].

Here he clearly had in mind the occasion when he was excluded from the Council while the new Vice-Chancellor was being selected. The second occasion was probably when the University began an investigation into the political affiliations of a research worker whose appointment he was supporting. Having loosed this broadside he proceeds to review the present state of the Medical School; its future; and University policy.

On the credit side he praises the high quality of the staff; where a suitable person was not available no appointment had been made. He went out of his way to praise Ennor:

Professor Ennor and his wife have put in prodigious efforts to bring it about and, as he can tell you, much care has been taken to try to secure agreeable as well as scientifically capable individuals . . .

He flies to the defence of Bunker, holding him up as a shining example of the way in which research staff can be complemented by a good laboratory manager:

It should be absolutely understood that the first call on the professor's energies should be to undertake and direct research. . . . Mr. Bunker . . .

has done much more than I had ever thought a laboratory manager could do. . . . I myself have seen how good his work was and on every occasion when I visited Canberra tried to impress on the central administration how great was his value and how necessary it was that they should take steps to ensure that he was satisfied with his conditions. . . . It appears to me that this key man has not been handled very well and his departure . . . will certainly divert to administration, at least for some time, highly qualified people who should be doing research.

He refutes criticism that the building is too large; it was never intended to be fully staffed at once but to be 'full of active research workers in 25 years—the declared aim'. The JCS *must* be big, otherwise one of the prime requirements of successful research in Canberra would not be met, i.e. the establishment of a stable scientific community in a geographically isolated place. Once again he states his absolute conviction that successful medical research demands the collaboration in close propinquity (within a coo-ee) of a range of specialists—chemists, biochemists, physicists, and biologists. 'A narrow interpretation of "medical research" must be avoided at all costs. In the present age it is nonsensical.'

But it is to overzealous administrators in general, and those responsible for the John Curtin School in particular, that his fiercest salvo is delivered.

The only excuse for administration is that it subserves constructive work. Far too many think that there is some particular merit in administration *per se*. . . . Difficulties over the type of staff that should be employed occupied much time when Sir Douglas Copland was Vice-Chancellor. Professor Oliphant and I struggled for a long time to get him, and through him Council, to understand that departments devoted to experimental science must have a strong nucleus of permanent staff. He conceived of departments being like sausage machines, spewing out graduates in a steady stream. It took an enormous amount of energy to persuade him of what was obvious to those who knew about the organization of scientific work. . . . It is a misconception to suppose that the primary function of the J.C.S is to train post-graduate students. Its primary function is to do research. . . . For many years I have watched the gestation of an administrative monster. Relentlessly the University has encompassed itself in a complicated administrative machine, perhaps fitter for an undergraduate University but largely out of place in an institution founded expressly to foster the acquisition of new knowledge. This monster no doubt was conceived with best intention but rather hastily and without much thought.

Leaving aside personal considerations, he criticizes the conditions under with a Director whould have to operate and compares it adversely with that of any science professor at Oxford who—within agreed budgeting limits—was master in his own house. The Director would have virtually no freedom in the selection of even relatively junior staff—'equivalent to or perhaps less than Departmental Demonstrators in Oxford'—and an 'administrative Moloch' seemed to have gained control of the supply system.

In Canberra the principle seems to be that everyone is a crook. . . . On one of my visits to Canberra Professor Oliphant and I spent much time trying to convince Sir Douglas Copland that complicated supply systems were inappropriate to scientific departments. . . . an assistant remarked that it worked quite well in libraries and I was forced to point out that the J.C.S was a laboratory and not a library.

The Council would have to reconsider the running of the School:

In my view, the first thing to be determined is, does the University want a Scientific Director or some one who would attend to the many chores that seem to have piled up owing to administrative complexities.

Turning to University policy in general he is no less trenchant. In his view, the Act of Incorporation was

an attempt from the armchair to devise a government for a type of institution unknown to Australia and indeed, as far as I am aware, without a direct parallel elsewhere. To call its establishment "a great intellectual adventure" is too gradiloquent. It was an essay in organization . . . defects in the originally proposed organization have become apparent— defects which may be sufficiently serious to defeat the objects for which the University was started.

He proceeds to examine ways in which he believes things have gone wrong. He points to an antagonism within the University between Natural Sciences and Social Studies; the administrative system might be appropriate for the latter but not for the former. Politicians and civil servants had far too much say in policy and the selection of personnel, a potential danger to which he had drawn attention as early as 1945. The composition of Council was inappropriate for the task it had to perform:

Its composition may in some senses be "representative" but of what I am not sure. I have the impression that it is dominated by the ideas of those who are primarily administrators and not by the ideas of people who understand the very delicate task of protecting the goose that lays the golden eggs, i.e. the research worker, from needless worries and complexities.

He believed that a major omission by the Council was failure 'to determine what are the functions of a Vice-Chancellor in a very particular type of institution'.

Some members of Council may look on a Vice-Chancellor as a managing director. Nothing could be further from the truth. He occupies a difficult position in which he has to deal with his intellectual equals who may be turbulent and emotional people. . . . He has to convince research workers that he knows what research is about and his overriding interest should be to forward research by all possible means. In the long run he will be judged only by how successful he is in this. . . . At present the functions of the Vice-Chancellor in relation to the Schools are nebulous. The whole position needs rethinking.

Finally, he raises a major issue to which we have previously referred only briefly. In 1950 Senator Joseph McCarthy had advised President Truman that the State Department was riddled with communists and communist sympathizers. This ushered in a period of intensive witch-hunting in which careers were wrecked or frustrated by any evidence of communist contact, even in adolescence. In America, Robert Oppenheimer was one of its most famous victims; in Britain Blackett, who was to be Florey's successor as President of the Royal Society, was for several years denied entry to the United States. Chain, too, had been similarly penalized. The contagion spread widely, though less severely, and Australia was not immune. In Canberra trouble broke out in 1954 over an appointment of an Oxford graduate in the Medical School whom Florey supported; the candidate undeniably had had communist sympathies as a young man but there was no evidence that he was still actively concerned. Florey thought it was immaterial whether he had or not; provided the man's research was sound, he cared nothing for his political views unless they were so actively ventilated as to be a source of trouble. He was furious over the whole matter—particularly as he had not been consulted—and found wide support for his views. He consulted among others the man's former tutor, the head of his College, the vice-chancellor of a provincial university, and the Director of the National Institute for Medical

Research. All concurred that they would have no part in inquiries into people's political past. He wrote emphatically to Ennor in December 1955:

> If the Vice-Chancellor and the General Board want to do the University the maximum of harm they are proceeding in the right way. . . . I asked a distinguished man who might in certain circumstances have taken a job in Canberra what his reaction would be if he knew that political investigations were being made and he at once said he would not touch it with a barge pole.[55]

He wrote equally emphatically in his Report:

> . . . as soon as it is known, at least in scientific circles, that the A.N.U. has taken to investigating political or religious beliefs in its appoint-ments it will lose stature. . . . It may be supposed in Canberra that extreme Left Wing sympathizers are greater nuisances in laboratories than others. This has not been my experience. The one person I have had in my department whom I knew to be a member of the Communist Party never gave trouble but some of the worst difficulties have come from people on the extreme Right.

He went on to state that at that time he himself voted Conserva-tive, one of the few glimpses we get of his own political leanings. In the event the man concerned was offered the appointment but declined it, presumably because of the criticism.

So far as his second promised memorandum was concerned, Florey's dealings with Lord Bruce had not been very satisfactory. When Wright was in England in the summer of 1955 he had seen Bruce and expressed his misgivings about the imposition of finan-cial ceilings in Canberra. As Chancellor, Bruce had reacted strongly and written at length to Menzies, as Prime Minister; he sent a copy of the letter to Florey for comment. Unfortunately, he dealt almost entirely with financial matters—which for a banker was natural—and urged a reassessment of the needs of all the Australian universities. He suggested that a Royal Commission should be set up to examine the situation. What Florey's reactions were we do not know, but he must have been disappointed at the limited scope of Bruce's proposals. Nevertheless, he persevered and prepared the promised second memorandum for Bruce's own use. This concentrated on the special needs of the research schools and was in line with that submitted to the Council: decen-tralization and simplification of administration and devolvement of responsibility on each director. He particularly stressed the need for some buffer oganization—akin to the University Grants Committee in London—to stand between Government and University. He ends on a pungent note:

I am convinced that the University, if it continued to be governed in the present manner and on the present principles (if there are any) can only end by being second rate and it will achieve this distinction with the maximum of effort.

Florey gave Bruce this memorandum in the belief that he might shortly be able to discuss it with the Prime Minister in person, but unfortunately Bruce's business trip was cancelled. Moreover, Bruce had already intimated to Menzies that he thought he should resign as Chancellor in favour of somebody resident in Australia, so his influence was on the wane so far as the University was concerned. Bruce invited Florey to talk to him over lunch at the Athenaeum in mid-February but afterwards Florey wrote and told Oliphant that he was doubtful about any useful outcome; other possible routes to the political ear should be explored. Nevertheless, Bruce did send a copy of the short memorandum to Menzies and suggested that the latter should get a copy of the full Report from the University.

Florey's clear desire at the end of 1955 was to end what had become a frustrating and wearisome relationship with the Australian National University, and at first sight the highly critical tone of his Report, and its forthright phraseology, might have been expected to have fulfilled his wishes quite smartly. That it did not do so can be attributed to a variety of factors. Firstly, Florey was addressing himself to an Australian audience which was accustomed to an abrasive approach; doubtless he would have chosen his words differently if he had been submitting a report to, for example, the Hebdomadal Council in Oxford. In a letter to Margaret Jennings he once wrote that in Canberra everybody shouted at each other, and he found himself doing the same. Secondly, Florey's name was one to be conjured with, and his very carefully considered advice could not be lightly set aside. Thirdly, he had been urged to express himself very freely. Last, but by no means least, his total withdrawal might well have serious practical consequences; financial support for the Medical School tacitly assumed that it would be, as it were, under his patronage. Within the School itself there were particular grounds for disquiet; without Florey's decisive influence and leadership, and in the absence of any comparable figure as Director, they might well lose ground to the competitive social sciences. Apart from all this, there were those who hoped—not without reason as it turned out—that Florey might yet be persuaded to change his mind. It is surely significant that his resignation was not reported in the ANU News; the issue for February 1956 contains a long account of progress with the building of the School but not a hint that Florey had resigned as from the end of the previous year. Surprisingly, indeed, in view of rumours rife on the campus, news of his resignation did not become public knowledge until June 1956, when the States Grant Bill—concerned with financial aid to universities, was debated in the House of Representatives. Dr. Evatt, the Leader of the Opposition, sought to make political capital out of it. The press referred at length to 'ugly rumours' that he had resigned because of threats to academic freedom at the National University. In fact, of course, only a small part of the Report had dealt with this; other aspects were of much greater importance.

Meanwhile, however, there had been a surprising turn of events. Far from having severed his connection with the Medical School, Florey was once again giving serious consideration to coming out as its Director.

As is not unusual in academic institutions, events had moved at a leisurely pace in Canberra. Although the Report had been received in January and circulated to the Council, it did not come up for formal consideration until the March meeting, when its discussion was deferred until a later date. Meanwhile, Melville, Wright, Ennor, Oliphant, and a few others intimately concerned had met privately to discuss the situation. As a result, Oliphant was able to write assuring Florey that his Report had been taken in good part and had generated no illwill. So much so, indeed, that Oliphant was able to give him a warm assurance that if he were able to come to Canberra in due course to open the Medical School he would be welcomed and honoured. Florey wrote suitably to Melville and September 1957 was tentatively agreed for the visit.

The resignation proved more apparent than real. Florey's advice was sought on candidates for the Chair of Experimental

Pathology; he was invited to serve on the selection committee; they wanted to commission a portrait of him in oils to hang in the School if he could find time for the necessary sittings. Ennor kept him posted on the progress of the School. Oliphant was in Oxford in May and gave him the latest news and gossip. In June, Florey went off to Canada on the start of a tour that kept him abroad until September; in New York he learnt that he had been proposed as an Honorary Fellow of University House. He kept in close touch with Ennor and in August intimated that the possibility of coming out as Director was once again appealing to him. Why this should be is not clear, but one reason he gave to Ennor was the imminent demolition of his house in Parks Road to make way for a new engineering laboratory. It so happened that Coombs was to be in England late in September and this gave him an opportunity to discuss Florey's requirements for the visit in detail, and on his return to Australia he wrote to say that there seemed to be no remaining obstacles.[56] He hoped that Florey might pay a quick visit to Canberra to settle the details. Another Council member, Warren McDonald, also visited Florey in Oxford to say how pleased he was at the prospect and later wrote to say that Bruce was enthusiastic.

For Melville and Ennor, however, this volte-face had created many problems. On the assumption that they lacked both a Director and a Professor of Experimental Pathology they had had discussions in Canberra with a very senior British academic who had expressed interest in the Chair; in the new situation this could not be pursued. There was also the perennial question of money but here chance—no doubt a contrived chance—had played a part. In April the Prime Minister—who by then had received a copy of the memorandum sent by Bruce—had been the guest of the Dining Club of the John Curtin School and this had provided an opportunity for some special pleading. Protocol would have to be observed, however, if the visit was to go ahead. It would be necessary to contrive that Council should formally ask Florey to reconsider his former decision—which in September they had resolved not to do—and present him with a new invitation. In view of the drubbing that the Council had received in his Report this might seem to present some difficulty, but Ennor and Melville were confident—and, as it proved, rightly so —that this could be managed.

By the end of the year the necessary preliminaries had been concluded and a crucial meeting of Council was held on 14 December. The Vice-Chancellor explained that Florey had been in correspondence with the Dean of the Medical School (Ennor) and indicated that he was ready to consider an invitation to the Directorship; he would want to develop Experimental Pathology and establish the study of Cytology and of Pharmacology. The Prime Minister had indicated that additional funds could be made available and—despite normal University practice — specifically earmarked for this purpose. At the end of a long discussion it was formally agreed:

That the Vice-Chancellor be authorized to negotiate with Sir Howard Florey and to invite him to accept appointment as Director of the John Curtin School of Medical Research and as Professor of Experimental Pathology.

It was hoped that these negotiations might place in Canberra, but if Florey could not pay them a visit Ennor—accompanied if possible by Melville—was to go to Oxford.

On the very same day Melville wrote two letters to Florey. One was essentially a confirmation of the Council's invitation and a statement of salary: £A4524 p.a. as Director and £A350 p.a. entertainment allowance. The second contained various assurances about the development of the School generally and the financial arrangements in particular. He stressed that he had discussed the latter personally with the Prime Minister and added that the latter was anxious to see Florey in Canberra as soon as possible. He followed this with another letter confirming that the Board of Graduate Studies would agree to a relaxation of normal appointment procedures to enable him to recruit staff in England. There was thus good reason to suppose that the die was cast and that at last Florey would return permanently to Australia.

Florey wrote to Melville early in January to congratulate him on the award of a KBE in the New Year's Honours List, but not until 21 January did he reply to the invitation to accept the Directorship. He did so at length, in a nine-page letter which must have caused considerable dismay in Canberra, for he was once again qualifying his acceptance. The tacit understanding had been that he would come out as full-time permanent Director.

Now he pleaded the difficulty of persuading his key colleagues in Oxford, without whom the continuation of his research would be extremely difficult, to join him on this basis; indeed, in a long letter to Ennor in November—before the matter was formally put to the Council—he expressly raised the question

> whether they (the Council) would like me to pursue the matter with the possibility that some of the arrangements might be of short duration. . . . It is perhaps hard for people in Australia to realise that the attractions of Canberra are not immediately obvious to the denizens of the Thames Valley. . . . I feel fairly sure that of those people who came on a 2-year basis, or at least for a limited time, some would stay on.[57]

There was, however, no suggestion of impermanence, so far as he himself was concerned. Had there been it is inconceivable that the Vice-Chancellor—if only to protect his own credibility—would not have brought this to the notice of the Prime Minister and the Council in view of the special and considerable financial provision required.

Nevertheless, this is what Florey now proposed; he would apply for leave of absence from Oxford University to come out for a sabbatical year and act as Director during that time. He expected to be able to bring with him on a short-term basis two of his senior research colleagues (Margaret Jennings and Gordon Sanders); two very experienced technicians, one of whom was James Kent, who by then had been with him for nearly thirty years; and his secretary Miss W. M. Poynton, who from the very outset had been intimately acquainted with the build-up at Canberra. Additionally it might be possible, with the approval of the Royal Society, to persuade Dr. J. C. F. Poole—a Locke Research Fellow of the Royal Society working in his department at Oxford—to come for a short time. If a senior appointment could be found for him he might also be able to bring with him a young Australian research worker Dr. Henry Harris, to whose elegant experimental work—carried out in both Britain and America—he gave high praise. Harris had held an ANU Travelling Scholarship at Oxford in 1952 and was currently Director of Research, British Empire Cancer Campaign, in the Sir William Dunn School of Pathology. If he were willing to go to Canberra it would be convincing evidence that the ANU could succeed in its purpose of attracting back really able Australian research workers.

The remainder of the letter confirms the seriousness of his intent. He inquires in detail about pensions and removal costs, return fares for those who came on a short-term basis, and the purchase of apparatus. All this suggests that the matter of the Directorship is settled in principle, though not in detail. Thus he writes:

I should like authority, when I have submitted a list and you have agreed to it, to order the equipment so as to have it in Australia as soon as possible. There is nothing more frustrating than having to wait for tools to work with.

Yet he is clearly uneasy that his proposal for a short-time Directorship might not be acceptable. He brushes aside a suggestion that Melville and Ennor should come to see him in Oxford with the excuse that:

I am extremely occupied and in addition to everything else I have a heavy undergraduate teaching programme for the next few weeks. I am afraid I should be able to give little connected thought to any matters you might raise.

More significant are the last two sentences of this long communication:

You have done me the honour to ask me to open the J.C.S. and I have also had a letter from the Registrar about an Honorary Degree. In the changed circumstances I can well believe that both these suggestions would be an embarrassment to you, and I should not be at all offended if you wish to make new arrangements about both proposals.

In spite of all this he formally applied to Oxford University for a year's leave of absence without pay for himself, Margaret Jennings, and Gordon Sanders, and this was granted on 8 February.

Melville put Florey's new proposals to the Council at a special meeting on 18 February 1957 and wrote at length to Florey on the same day. His letter was friendly and conciliatory, but he spelled out very clearly the difficulty in which the University had been placed. The academic staff had welcomed the possibility of his coming as Director even though the diversion of funds might prejudice the development of other Schools. If Florey came out for a year and then decided not to stay it would reflect adversely on the University, who might seem to have been tried and found wanting. Within the Medical School there might well be opposition to the research policy of a Director who might be transient and not necessarily supported by his successor. Most particularly, he stressed that the additional funds made available for the Medical School by the Prime Minister were conditional on his accepting the Directorship. If he delayed a final decision on this until after a trial period of a year the money might be lost. As Melville sagely remarked, Governments and Prime Ministers come and go and the promises of present incumbents may not necessarily be fulfilled by their successors. He urged Florey definitely to accept the Directorship, as this would make the Government's present financial undertaking operative. Ennor, too, wrote in similar terms pointing out the problems that would arise if a short-term conditional appointment were made.

As the minutes of the special meeting show, Melville represented the views of the Council very fairly, but on one crucial point these views were quite definite. If Florey accepted the Directorship they would agree to virtually everything he had asked, including the creation of a Professorship of Cytology to which he might appoint whom he pleased. Indeed they were prepared to delegate to him responsibility for other appointments he might wish to make—a very remarkable concession. The one thing it would not agree to was keeping the offer open for a period during which he was working in the University. If this condition was not acceptable, they would still be very happy for him to come as a visitor on the terms proposed in the last letter. Finally, Council reiterated its wish that there should be personal discussion—in either Canberra or Oxford—with the Vice-Chancellor and the Dean of the School.

In the event Ennor alone came to Oxford and after various preliminary discussions with both Florey and some of his senior colleagues—in the course of which Oliphant tried unsuccessfully to be a mediator—there was a crucial meeting in Florey's room on 19 March, following long hours of discussion between the two principals. In addition Margaret Jennings, Gordon Sanders, and Miss Poynton were present. There are various versions of what took place but there is no doubt that it was a stormy and unhappy meeting. Two short written memoranda survive—probably prepared by Florey and Miss Poynton respectively[58]—but they are brief and uninformative. We have also Florey's subsequent letter to Melville and a much more forthright one to 'Pansy' Wright.

The version current in Oxford is that Ennor, having been dispatched by Council as an ambassador to find some formula by which Florey might yet be persuaded to accept the Directorship, was in fact unfriendly, even hostile. It is asserted, too, that in private talks he had indicated to members of the group who might come out temporarily that they would not be made welcome in Canberra. This led to suspicion of duplicity; that Ennor, who as Dean was in practice running the School, did not like the thought of being supplanted and outshone and nor did some of his colleagues.

For his part, Florey was clearly in an abrasive mood, and raised various difficult questions. He demanded to know what he was expected to do if he came out almost immediately with neither professional colleagues nor properly trained technicians. Had the Council some other Director in mind? If he refused, what alternative plans did the University have? On what grounds had it been suggested that if he came out for a year he might orientate research in directions not acceptable to the School after he had gone?

In his letter to Wright of 27 April[59], Florey's main complaint is that Ennor was not prepared to make any concessions; that he and some of his colleagues thought that he was scientifically finished and fit only to be an administrator; and that he had been very disparaging about some of the colleagues whom he proposed to bring with him from Oxford for a sabbatical year. The letter is too long to quote in full but as it concerns the crux of the whole dispute with the University some passages deserve quotation in Florey's own words, especially as he clearly chose them very carefully:

It was perhaps a pity that Council did not give me enough rope to hang myself by but there it is. I cannot quite make out why Ennor was sent over by Council but his visit was quite revealing to us all here. He seemed to arrive with a "take it or leave it" attitude not very well covered by boisterous bonhomie . . . no real attempt was made to see if current difficulties could be overcome except in so far as I solved them myself. I sensed a feeling of hostility but kept on boring away for several rather exhausting days. Finally Oliphant arrived and, as I said to him, we could have arranged the matter in the course of the afternoon. After I had talked with Oliphant, Ennor was had in to talk with us both, but it was clear that he wished to do nothing except extract a 'yes" or 'no" from me about coming as Director, regardless of the position in which I found myself at the moment. Those he said were Council's instructions, and no doubt this was true. I knew there was something behind all this and I suggested to Sanders that he take Ennor out to dinner and see if anything emerged. It did—Ennor and possibly others in the School think I am scientifically finished and would only be useful as an administrator and figurehead and for attracting people into the net— though how I am to do that if I am finished escapes me, but whether I did any experimental work or not did not matter. This explains why Ennor made it apparent that he at least was not prepared to be helpful about my coming out with colleagues and technicians for a year. . . . I was astounded at the freedom with which he was prepared to offer the services of, among others, Fenner's head technician and so on, as if he controlled everything. He has no idea of what is involved in experimental work of the type we do here. But then he seemed to think it did not matter whether we did experiments or not.

As far as the colleagues whom he might bring with him were concerned Henry Harris emerged as a particular bone of contention. Florey was staunch in his defence:

I was accused of going to do the School harm by starting work of which members of the School did not approve. Stripped of its verbiage this meant Harris. The Harris situation I regard as very serious as Australia has now lost a good scientist and the main purpose of the J.C.S. has in this case been frustrated . . . at one time or another it was made clear that Ennor—and perhaps others—were not going to have Harris at any price. It appeared to make no difference that others besides myself considered Harris to be the best brain that I have had for many years. No impression was made by the fact that Abraham could speak strongly in favour of Harris, that Gowans, a critical chap [later Secretary of the MRC] who had occupied the same room for two years at least, said that he would be glad to serve under Harris as professor, that Fildes supported him and that my enquiries had elicited no complaints about Harris being difficult. . . . I have no hesitation in saying that Harris would have built up an active department, in its way as good as Fenner's, in a subject badly need at Canberra. . . . Ennor made it plain that he would be unwelcome and naturally I told Harris not to go. . . . The upshot of all this is that none of us want to come to Canberra even for the year.

In the fullness of time Harris was to become Florey's successor as Professor of Pathology at Oxford, an appointment which he warmly approved.

As on previous occasions, Florey takes the opportunity of expressing his sympathy for Melville in the difficult position in which he was placed:

I have now had a cordial letter from Melville for whom I am sorry. . . . I thought I had better give you this background or you might think I am mad. I do not want any fuss of any sort made but for the first time I believe that the J.C.S. can now go seriously wrong.

Ennor, 12 000 miles from home and facing such an inquisition on his own, must have had an uncomfortable day. Florey reacted strongly to the demand that he must immediately accept the Directorship before any other matters could be discussed. But this was not Ennor's demand but that of the Council; of this he was not even a member, although he had attended meetings by invitation. He was not authorized to negotiate on this point even had he wished to do so. So far as research facilities—as opposed to research staff—were concerned they would have been the same in September whether Florey had then come out for a year or permanently.

It was the end of the month before Florey wrote formally to the Vice-Chancellor finally declining the Council's invitation:

. . . if I accepted Council's invitation now I cannot see how I could make any serious impact on the scientific activities of the John Curtin School. I should be a figurehead and an administrator and, as I have all my life struggled against becoming merely an administrator, because I like doing experiments, this would be very distasteful. . . . I am afraid, therefore, that my answer, since you have asked that it should be categorical, must he "No" . . . with the progress of the conversation [with Ennor] I was unable to convince myself that such a [one year] visit woud serve any useful purpose. My colleagues involved also received this impression and so I have decided with their concurrence to give up any thought of spending a year in Canberra. . . . I am asking Oxford University to cancel the leave of absence it has given me.[60]

The Council took this refusal surprisingly well. It not only reaffirmed its invitation to Florey to open the John Curtin School and accept an honourary degree but offered to provide a £A5000 to meet travel expenses and salary supplements if he was able to spend a sabbatical year in Canberra with a small group from Oxford.

Meanwhile Florey had been in correspondence again with Melville and only then (23 April) did he express, though in understanding terms, his misgivings about Ennor.

I am afraid I shall have to be rather frank about Professor Ennor's visit or you will fail to understand why neither my colleagues nor I now wish to spend a sabbatical year in Canberra, though preparations for this were quite advanced. I have on all occasions, as far as I am aware, backed Professor Ennor and therefore was somewhat non-plussed by his consistently somewhat reserved and even slightly hostile air. I should think that during the last few years his patience has been sorely taxed in many ways and he may have been exasperated at trying to solve the difficulties in what seem to him to be simple matters. I may have annoyed him by trying to find out what was behind it all. In any event, all of us concerned concluded that Professor Ennor, at least was indifferent to whether or not we came on sabbatical leave. The prospects of our doing anything useful with the technical help available in Canberra seemed somewhat remote. . . . Professor Ennor's visit has left a painful impression in this department in more ways than one, but of this we can perhaps talk later.[61]

To this Melville replied only briefly, expressing his disquiet. About Ennor, he would only say that in his experience he had been absolutely loyal to Florey and his enthusiastic admirer.

In April 1957 Crocker—who by then had moved on to be High Commissioner in Canada—wrote as a result of a talk he had had with Oliphant in Ottawa. He assured Florey that though his past hesitations might have offended some people in the University, those who really mattered still genuinely wanted him. In his reply he again attributes his final decision to the attitude of Ennor:

The final difficulty, quite frankly, was caused by a visit here of Ennor who, as you know, is Dean of the Medical School. He succeeded in upsetting everybody in my department. There is no evidence that Melville was in any way concerned in this, as I am fairly convinced that he would like to have had us out there.[62]

In view of this final sentence, it was perhaps unfortunate that Melville was not able to accompany Ennor to Oxford, as the Council had hoped.

Thus, on an unhappy note, ended a dream that had lasted thirteen years; there was no further prospect of Florey returning permanently to Australia. Nevertheless, it was not the end of his association with the University; before the summer was over he was even back in correspondence with Ennor about candidates for the Chair of Experimental Pathology. In March 1958 he finally fulfilled his undertaking to open the John Curtin School and received an honorary degree. In the last years of his life he once again had a formal and very important relationship with the University; in 1965 he was elected Chancellor and held this office until his death in 1968. To this later, and much happier, connection we shall return briefly later (p. 368). For the moment we shall simply remind ourselves that the University was a major factor in his life for almost the whole of the period with which this biography is concerned. It made great demands on his time and attention—as well as on his affection and loyalty as an Australian—and it was by only the narrowest of margins that it failed to change the whole course of the latter part of his life.

But this long relationship had another important significance. Medical research was his greatest single interest in life and he had strong, and at that time radical, ideas on how it should be organized. To him Canberra must have seemed initially a golden opportunity to put his ideas into practice untrammelled by existing traditions, buildings, and equipment and with resources sufficient to attract research workers of the highest quality. Though the dream never came true so far as he was concerned, the history of the John Curtin School of Medical Research (Plate 14) gives us a remarkable insight into his ideas on the nature of research.

9

A NEW ANTIBIOTIC TRIUMPH

For some ten years after his crucial decision to join with Chain in a thorough investigation of penicillin this remained Florey's chief research preoccupation. As we have seen, however, the heavy demands made on him by the spectacular success of this project, and his close involvement with the Australian National University, severely limited the time he personally could give to research of any kind. Nevertheless he was responsible for a large research department which by then had become the leading centre for experimental pathology in Europe and which he still personally directed.

Additionally, of course, with the return of Paquita and Charles he had new family responsibilities to face. On his way home from Australia in December 1944 he had collected them from the Fultons at New Haven and travelled with them on board a ship sailing in a convoy to Britain. Their return raised immediate problems of schooling, for the Floreys had not entered their names for any schools, then as now a rather necessary precaution when private education is in prospect. When he had left home Charles was only five years old but he came back a boy of ten. Very fortunately, the Dragon School was able to find a place for him. Not only was it one of the best preparatory schools in the country, but it was very close to the house in Parks Road. Paquita, then 15, went to the Oxford High School for Girls, a member of the Girls' Public Day School Trust; this, too, was only a short distance from home. There was no question about anything other than private education, and in due course Charles went on to Rugby, presumably on the recommendation of the Dragon School and certainly with the help of N. V. Sidgwick, Chemistry Tutor at Lincoln, who was himself an Old Rugbeian and at that time a School Governor. He, too, was bent on a medical career and trained first at Cambridge and later at University College Hospital in London. It is an interesting sidelight on Florey's ability as a teacher that in later life Charles acknowledged how much he owed to him for his tuition in physiology at home. He was known at Caius as a crack physiology tutor, with a special flare for forecasting Tripos questions.

For Charles, only five years old when he arrived, the Fulton's house on Mill Rock became very much a second home and in 1961 he was fortunate enough to be able to make his way back there when he embarked on a course in public health at Yale, later working with John R. Paul in the WHO Serum Bank there. In 1966 he was married from the Fulton's house to an English girl who was working in New Haven; three years later he and his wife went off to Jamaica to work with an MRC Epidemiology Unit. Paquita went to Edinburgh to study first history and then psychology, a subject at which Florey looked askance in his younger days but later was to endorse in his capacity as President of the Royal Society. There she met and married a young science teacher, John McMichael, the son of an Oxford doctor, who eventually became head of the science department at Edinburgh Academy. She herself took advanced degrees in psychology and embarked upon a very active career in teaching and research in this field.

With the return of the children, family holidays had to be reckoned with. In the years immediately after the war holidays abroad were difficult, particularly because of currency restrictions, but some happy family vacations were spent in Cornwall and additionally a pleasant retreat was offered by Howard's sister Anne. She had given up her job as school matron at Abingdon and gone to live in the remote Welsh village of Corris Uchaf, close under the south side of Cader Idris. (Plate 17). These pleasant excursions ended in 1953, when Anne decided to return to Australia. Howard was confident that he would be seeing her again in the course of his visits to the Australian National University (Chapter VIII) but he was sufficiently concerned about her departure to cry off a lunch engagement with Lord Bruce, then Chancellor of the University, in order to see her safely off at St Pancras. No doubt he recalled her solicitude in meeting him in London on that cold winter day in 1922.

Despite the plethora of new antibiotics described in the years immediately after the war only one had become of medical importance by 1950. This was streptomycin, discovered in 1943 by Selman Waksman at Rutgers University, New Brunswick.

This was of particular interest because it possessed antitubercular activity, which penicillin lacked; it proved, however, to have potentially serious side-effects, especially on the sense of hearing and in some circumstances on kidney function, and its use had to be carefully monitored. In 1950 Waksman became the central figure in a major antibiotic lawsuit in the United States. Florey was in no way involved—and indeed had no liking for Waksman—but he followed the case with particular interest as an object lession in the possible consequences of university—industrial agreements involving patents, such as had been urged on him in some quarters at home.

The facts were widely reported in the press, and a well-documented account has been published elsewhere;[1] briefly, they are as follows. In 1939, Merck's interest in the chemotherapeutic possibilities of antibiosis (p. 83) led to an agreement to support Waksman's work in this field. The question of patents was specifically considered. It was agreed that in return for an exclusive licence to manufacture any useful new products Merck, as patent owners, would pay a 2½ per cent royalty to the Rutgers Research and Endowment Foundation; of this, Waksman was personally to receive 50 per cent. With the benefit of hindsight, this generous allocation to Wakesman suggests that in 1939 no large financial returns were expected.

By 1945, however, the situation had radically changed. Waksman clearly realised that in streptomycin he had a potentially valuable new chemotherapeutic agent—as well as some other antibiotic possibilities in prospect—and he was unhappy about the exclusive rights granted to Merck. He was doubtful about Merck's ability to produce the necessary quantity and believed that without the stimulus of competition the price might be unnecessarily high. More particularly, no doubt, he was conscious that in 1945 Rutgers University—a very old foundation dating from 1766, as Queen's College—was designated State University of New Jersey. Under this new flag an exclusive arrangement with a single industrial firm could be an embarrassment. Merck recognized the difficulties and generously agreed to forego their exclusive licence in respect of streptomycin and other possible new antibiotics; the Foundation then made non-exclusive licence agreements with half a dozen other companies. In the long run, the decision was greatly to the disadvantage of

Rutgers. As competition mounted in the antibiotic field after the war it became increasingly difficult for any pharmaceutical company to market new products without the initial advantage of an exclusive licence. The search for new antibiotics at Rutgers was consequently severely curtailed.

Initially, however, all seemed satisfactory and Merck proceeded to manufacture streptomycin on a non-exclusive basis. It was at this stage that the legal dispute arose. The first published account of streptomycin carried, in addition to that of Waksman, the names of Albert Schatz and E. Bugi.[2] Schatz's name appeared also on the Memorandum of Invention filed with Merck in November 1943, and on the US Patent issued in 1948. Schatz had every reason to regard himself as a co-discoverer of streptomycin, and consequently entitled to a share of the substantial royalties beginning to accrue. However, when he raised the matter with Waksman at the beginning of 1949 he got no satisfaction and so resorted to litigation, in which he was entirely successful. A settlement was reached in December 1950 and the President of Rutgers, Dr. R. C. Clothier, announced the terms of agreement. Schatz was unequivocally recognized as a co-discoverer of streptomycin; he was to be paid 3 per cent of the royalties paid to the Foundation, and another 7 per cent was to be distributed among the other research workers concerned. The magnitude of the sums involved is indicated by the fact that up to 1978 Rutgers received royalties on streptomycin totalling $12 million.

From the outset, Florey acknowledged that they had an extraordinary amount of luck in selecting penicillin for special study when embarking on a general investigation of the widely reported phenomenon of antibiosis. The paucity of medically useful antibiotics among those previously and subsequently discovered confirmed this judgement—though Florey himself was to be surprised when a second winner in this field, cephalosporin (p. 301), subsequently came his way in 1948 although it was many years before it was introduced into medical practice. In the immediate postwar years his opinion was sought on the clinical potential of a variety of new products—erythromycin, terramycin, vivicillin, and flavoryzine to name only a few—but none had real promise and some he labelled as frankly bogus.

In contrast to potential rivals, penicillin had by 1950 come into such universal use that the word had even found its way into children's rhymes. The popular magazine *Lilliput* quoted (September 1952) a new version of an old skipping song:

> Mother, mother I am ill,
> Send for the doctor from over the hill.
> In comes the doctor,
> In comes the nurse,
> In comes the lady with the alligator purse.
> Penicillin says the doctor,
> Penicillin says the nurse,
> Penicillin says the lady with the alligator purse.

In passing, it may be remarked that this verse scans best if the word is accentuated as penicill'in rather than peni'cillin. The latter variant was often used up to 1943, when it was solemnly abjured as part of the Anglo-American agreement.

While penicillin and other potentially useful antibiotics still posed many challenging problems—most particularly their mode of action, which in turn related to the acquiring of resistance—certain aspects of research on them no longer seemed appropriate for a biologically oriented laboratory such as the Sir William Dunn School of Pathology. For example, the screening of large numbers of micro-organisms in a systematic search for new products was more suitable for large industrial laboratories than small university ones. Large-scale fermenters—which Chain hankered after, and subsequently acquired in Rome—could not easily be accommodated. Chemical investigations, increasingly dependent on sophisticated new techniques and apparatus, were best conducted in laboratories designed, staffed, and equipped for such work.

In revising his research strategy to meet a new situation it would be natural for Florey to be influenced by the evident consequences of the international availability of penicillin, one of which was a general prolongation of life. This was desirable in itself, but inevitably resulted in a corresponding increase in the incidence of diseases to which older people are particularly prone. Among these is atherosclerosis, a degenerative disease of the arteries characterized by deposition of fatty substances in the intima, accompanied by fibrous thickening. The vessels narrow, restricting the flow of blood, and lose their elasticity—hence the popular description as hardening of the arteries; in crude terms it can be likened to the furring up of a hot-water system. It is a condition that commonly precedes strokes and coronary thrombosis.

The intrinsic and growing medical importance of atherosclerosis was sufficient in itself to make it a rewarding subject for the kind of multidisciplinary research which Florey had pioneered, but other reasons can be postulated. Thus the circulation of the blood had been one of his earliest research interests, and was indeed the subject of his first published research paper in 1925. It has been plausibly suggested, too, that growing awareness of his own vascular problems was a factor in the choice. If so, this would make an intersting parallel to the penicillin work. There, it will be recalled, his early interest in mucus was stimulated by his own digestive problems. Mucus contained lysozyme and this in turn aroused his interest in the general phenomenon of anti-biosis; from this penicillin was selected partly because its apparent lytic action seemed to link it with lysozyme. Mucus remained a continuing and absorbing interest and in the postwar years he turned to it with renewed enthusiasm. As a concomitant to the atherosclerosis work he also interested himself again in the role of the lymphocytes in blood.

With many heavy pressures on him the pursuit of these research interests, which meant so much to him, depended very much on the help of his research assistants and D.Phil. students. He was still very much in demand all over the world for important review articles and lectures, the preparation of which was laborious and time-consuming. In the years 1950-60 he gave major lectures not only in Britain but in Spain, Canada, the United States, Australia, India, Belgium, and Switzerland. He had teaching commitments, too, which he took very seriously, and during this time he worked up his pathology lectures into book form.[3] Initially, it was not widely used in Britain (p. 48) but was widely adopted by medical schools in the United States. Eventually it went through four editions, the last appearing shortly after his death.

This change in emphasis in research had to take account of constant improvements in technique and the availability of research workers able to apply them. To the end of his life he was quick to adopt relevant new techniques. The prestige of the laboratory ensured that there was no lack of able people wanting to do research in it, but in making his choices Florey was governed by a keen sense of responsibility towards those who worked with him. The uncertainties of academic life in postwar Britain were such that he could hold out few prospects of long-term appointments. To avoid rousing false hopes he preferred, therefore, to recruit those who came with fellowships or other short-term awards who knew from the outset that they must expect to look elsewhere when these expired. This policy had the important consequence that many laboratories throughout the world subsequently had the benefit of research workers who had been trained under his rigorous tutelage.

The end of the war inevitably saw some dispersal of staff. Duthie went to the Lister Institute, and Regine Schoental to Carshalton, and Berenblum to the Weizmann Institute in Israel. Chain, too, had been invited to go to Israel but in 1948 he left to become Director of the International Research Centre for Chemical Microbiology in the Istituto Superiori di Sanita in Rome, initially on leave of absence from Oxford. To Florey's annoyance he took with him the file of MRC papers relating to the chemistry of penicillin.[4] The parting was undisguisedly a relief to both him and Florey. As we have recorded, they had very different views on such matters as policy in regard to co-operation with industry, the filing of patents, and relations with the press. Chain felt keenly that Florey had been impatient in brushing his arguments aside—though when he approached them he had not been given any encouragement either by powerful men such as Dale and Mellanby—and as we have recorded (p. 128) he was mortally offended at Florey's failure to say a word to him beforehand about the visit to America with Heatley in 1941. For his part, Florey made no secret of the fact that he found Chain's attitudes and manner a great trial. He was not disposed to let bygones be bygones. Years later Lord Bruce, then Chancellor of the Australian National University, put an inquiry to Florey about a young friend who was taking up a position in Chain's laboratory. Florey replied coldly:

Dr Chain certainly worked here for many years, but since he took up the position in Rome I gather from many people who have visited him that little is going on there. I have no personal experience of this, and I should have thought that, as —— has already been accepted there, it is now not much use making any further enquiries about the place.[5]

This does less than justice to Chain, who in fact was doing good research on the ergot alkaloids and had just started a collaboration with the Beecham Group that was to lead to a series of extremely valuable semisynthetic penicillins (p. 306). In 1961 he came back to London as Professor of Biochemistry at Imperial College and carried out research on certain phytotoxins and on the metabolism of glucose.

Apart from the deterioration in his personal relations with Florey, Chain certainly had other legitimate grounds for discontent. Although he had been awarded a Nobel Prize in 1945 the Royal Society did not elect him to its Fellowship—a signal but lesser honour—until 1949, a year after he left England. Nor was he at that time accorded even a minor civil award in Britain, as distinct from both Fleming and Florey, who were knighted in 1944. In 1948 Florey was made a Commander of the Legion of Honour. The balance was not redressed until 1969, when Chain, too, was awarded a well-deserved knighthood. By that time, however, he had been honoured by universities and learned societies in many countries. He, too, became a Commander of the Legion of Honour and held the Order of Merit of the Italian Republic.

The dispassionate observer can only reflect sadly on the incompatibility which drove a wedge between two gifted men who set out together on a project which was to succeed far beyond their expectations. Chain played no part in Florey's life after 1948 so we must digress no further. It is pleasing to record, however, that whatever professional tribulations Chain had to endure he found great happiness during the last thirty years of his life. In 1948 he married Dr. Anne Beloff, an Oxford biochemist who shared his scientific interests; they had a family of three children, including twins, to whom he was devoted.[6]

Despite the immense interest and activity that had been generated in America the international reputation of the Sir William Dunn School of Pathology for research on antibiotics remained paramount. This was fortunate, for it led to Oxford becoming the centre of development for a second important family of antibiotics, the cephalosporins.

This story begins, a little unexpectedly, in the town of Cagliari on the Italian island of Sardinia. It is an ancient city, supposedly founded by the Carthaginians, and has a small university founded in 1626. During the war its Rector was Giuseppi Brotzu, Professor of Hygiene. At the end of the war Brotzu became Superintendent of Public Health in Cagliari and as such was responsible for the local sewage disposal works. As raw sewage has some capacity for self-purification, it occurred to him that this might be some manifestation of antibiosis and accordingly he began to look for micro-organisms that might be responsible. In quite a short space of time he isolated a fungus, which he identified as *Cephalosporium acremonium*, which in culture proved active against a wide range of pathogenic bacteria. As with Fleming's original penicillin, the crude broth showed no apparent toxicity and it proved effective in treating boils and other local infections. Encouraged by this, Brotzu tried to arouse the interest of the Italian pharmaceutical industry, but without success. There the matter might well have ended, had he not persevered and sought the advice of Dr. Blyth Brooke, whom he had met as British Public Health Officer in Sardinia at the end of the war. Brooke was sufficiently interested to consult with the Medical Research Council in London and they suggested that Brotzu should approach Florey in Oxford. Eventually, a culture of *C. acremonium* and a reprint of Brotzu's paper describing it finally reached Oxford in September 1948.

As the inquiries of E. P. Abraham have revealed[7] there is a certain element of comedy behind this, for Brotzu was a man of humour as well as determination. The reprint that accompanied the culture sent to Florey was entitled 'Ricerche su di un Nuovo Antibiotica' and was apparently published in an issue of a journal entitled *Lavori dell' Istituto d'Igiene di Cagliari*, All was not as it seemed, however. It transpired later that, encountering difficulties in finding a journal to publish his work in the troubled circumstances of postwar Italy, Brotzu had simply invented the *Lavori* for his own purpose. The issue in which his paper appeared was the only one that was ever printed!

The culture and Brotzu's information about it was passed to Heatley, who showed that the active principle could be extracted from the culture fluid into organic solvents in much the same way as penicillin. However, at that particular moment he was particularly engaged—with T. L. Su[8], a visiting Chinese research worker for whom he was responsible as supervisor—on a study of micrococcin, an antibiotic also obtained from a sewage organism, which showed promise of activity against the tubercle bacillus. In passing, it may be remarked that after his return to China, Su became swallowed up in the Cultural Revolution but years later contact was re-established through a chance meeting on an ice rink in Peking between one of his students and Heatley's daughter Rose, who was spending a year there (1973-74) as a British Council student. The two were able to meet in Shanghai, where he had become Professor of Epidemiology, and Su was later able to meet his old friends again in Oxford.

In the event, therefore, research on the new antibiotic was undertaken by a group headed by Abraham, working with Kathleen Crawford and H. S. Burton. They collaborated with Brendan Kelly and his colleagues in the Antibiotics Research Station at Clevedon which had good fermentation facilities. It had been set up in 1944 by the Medical Research Council, largely at Florey's instigation, in a former Royal Navy research establishment; he served as a member of the management committee and for a time Heatley was liason officer. Thus began a new research project that was to lead, though not for more than a decade, to an important new generation of antibiotics. It proved to have something in common with one of those Dutch pictures in which mirrors reveal a room within a room within a room. It was also to provide a case history in a new academic attitude towards the patenting of inventions.

The first stage of the research yielded a product named cephalosporin P, because it was active only against the so-called Gram-positive bacteria.[9] Chemically, and in antibacterial activity, it resembled helvolic acid. Clinical trials seemed justified and Glaxo was to have made some for this purpose, but it never materialized. Interestingly, however, a chemically similar antibiotic, fusidic acid, which was isolated in 1962 by Danish research workers, was introduced into clinical practice; as it is well concentrated in bone it is sometimes prescribed for osteomyelitis. From the point of view of clinical potential cephalosporin P was a little more attractive than helvolic acid and a little less so than fusidic acid.

At this point Burton, who was to prove something of a stormy petrel, turned his attention to other problems and Abraham was joined by Guy Newton, who had just graduated at Cambridge, after a distinguished career in the Army, as a DPhil student. They discovered in the culture medium a second antibiotic which, because it was active against Gram-negative bacteria, they named cephalosporin N.[10] This was evidently closely related in some way to penicillin, as it was inactivated by penicillinase, but could not be extracted with organic solvents. They eventually identified it as a new kind of penicillin, penicillin N, which had a side-chain in the molecule different from that in any other variety (p. 172). It proved identical with another antibiotic, synnematin B, obtained in a crude form in Michigan. Clinical trials there had indicated that this might be useful for the treatment of typhoid, being superior in this respect to chloramphenicol, discovered in America in 1947, which can damage bone marrow and lead to the development of blood dyscrasias.

From Brotzu's description it appeared that penicillin N was the main antibiotic present in his culture fluid. Although the Medical Research Council tried to encourage industrial production this came to nothing, probably because it appeared to offer no particular advantage over the increasing number of other known antibiotics, except for the treatment of typhoid, and was particularly difficult to isolate. Abraham and Newton persevered in their investigation, however, because its activity seemed to depend on a molecular configuration not previously reported.

They then detected traces of yet another penicillin-like antibiotic, cephalosporin C, in the culture fluid. A preliminary study showed that although this substance had relatively low antibacterial activity—about 1 per cent of that of benzylpenicillin—this was associated with other interesting properties. In particular, it differed from penicillin in not being inactivated by dilute acid or by penicillinase. Chemically, it contained the beta-lactam ring of penicillin and the same side-chain as penicillin N, but the other ring of atoms present in the molecule was something new.

Although Abraham and Newton were free to pursue further investigation at their own discretion, they were actively encouraged by Florey when they wrote to him in Canberra about this new development. It is likely that it was the resistance to penicillinase that particularly attracted his attention; which had been veering away from antibiotics. Apparently he had only quite recently been persuaded of the medical importance of this. According to Wesley W. Spink—one-time Regent's Professor of Medicine and Comparative Medicine at the University of Minnesota and a President of the American College of Physicians—his conversion took place on the Atlantic City Broadwalk in 1947:

I was with him . . . at the centennial meeting of the American Medical

Association. I was chairman of a general session on antibiotic therapy, to which Florey had been invited as a foreign participant. In his remarks to over 2000 persons in the assembly he stated that he did not think that the appearance of penicillin resistant strains of staphylococcus in clinical medicine constituted much of a problem. This disturbed some members of the panel who thought otherwise. As no one wished to offend an invited guest, nothing further was said at the time. However, as at many other scientific meetings, a quiet conversation on the Atlantic City Broadwalk clarified many issues. During a long walk I presented the evidence of several investigators to him, showing that penicillin-resistant staphylococci did pose a serious threat: he concurred and we parted amicably.[11]

Spink goes on to say that on a visit later, Ethel, too, was fully persuaded of the importance of resistance:

Ethel Florey visited the United States alone in 1956 and included Minneapolis in her journey, staying for several days and seeing at first hand in our laboratories the many strains of penicillin-resistant staphylococci isolated from patients. She needed no convincing on our part that it represented a serious problem in medicine, especially in hospitals. . . . Ethel Florey was a good clinical investigator but she was hampered in her courageous work by physical disability and deafness.

From the point of view of assessing potential clinical use, toxicity and animal-protection experiments were essential. When Florey and Margaret Jennings conducted these they were very favourable. Firstly, they showed that cephalosporin C was even less toxic then benzylpenicillin; in effect, it was not toxic at all. Secondly, it protected mice from otherwise fatal doses of penicillin-resistant staphylococci.

Fortified by Florey's moral and practical support, and the important biological findings, Abraham and Newton tackled cephalosporin C vigorously. The minute concentration of the antibiotic in the culture medium made it very difficult—as in the early days of penicillin—to obtain sufficient material for research purposes. This situation was a good deal relieved in 1957 when the Antibiotic Research Station at Clevedon successfully isolated a much more productive mutant of the mould. The reward of the station was to be closed down by the Medical Research Council some three years later, apparently with Florey's approval,[12] a decision about which Abraham has expressed misgivings.[7] Shortly afterwards Glaxo, who had had a disappointment with cephalosporin P, delivered a useful batch of cephalosporin C. This facilitated the chemical investigation, which nevertheless presented great intrinsic difficulties. Eventually, Abraham concluded that whereas the penicillin molecule contained a five-membered thiazolidine ring cephalosporin C contained a six-membered thiazine ring (containing sulphur and nitrogen). Abraham has recorded[7] that they had some unnerving experiences after they had publicly put their somewhat improbable structure forward in 1961. As he was about to lecture in Australia he received a telegram saying that the structure was probably wrong; in America a Harvard professor shook his head and said that the structure was incompatible with the ultraviolet spectrum. It was a considerable relief when Dorothy Crowfoot Hodgkin and her colleagues at Oxford proved beyond peradventure, by X-ray crystallography, that despite the anomalies the proposed structure was correct.

By this time (1961) the problem of penicillin-resistant staphylococci had become so serious that it was expected that despite its low antibacterial activity—demanding proportionately high doses —cephalosporin C would justify industrial production. How serious the problem was to become is indicated by a comment in a recent (1982) edition of the *British National Formulary* that 'most staphylococci are now resistant to benzylpenicillin'. Just at that time, however, the collaboration of Chain with the Beecham Laboratories began to bear fruit with the advent of methicillin, the first of the semisynthetic penicillins (p. 301) which was effective against bacteria resistant to penicillin. As this is acid-sensitive it can be given only by injection, unlike their introduction Floxapen, which can be taken by mouth.

With this development, the low activity of cephalosporin C made its commercial development unattractive. However, consideration of its chemistry indicated that the side-chain could be removed and replaced by others which might give enhanced activity. These expectations were fulfilled when the phenacetyl derivative was prepared; this increased activity against the test organism some 200 times, giving a product twice as active as benzylpenicillin (penicillin G or II) against some organisms. This opened up great new possibilities for a new series of semisynthetic antibiotics, but the chemical problems proved a great deal more difficult than was expected and it was some years before commercial development was possible. In the event, this stage was not reached until the 1960s, but the intricacies of the chemical research involved are too complex to discuss here; specialist readers should consult the proceedings of a two-day symposium held by the Royal Society in 1979.[13] An extract from the introductory remarks made by John C. Sheehan of Massachusetts Institute of Technology, the first to synthesize penicillin, is worth quoting:

It is remarkable that research in the penicillin area has continued for 50 years and has produced such spectacular benefits to mankind. . . . The penicillin molecule remains unique in intensity of research lavished upon it and in the substantial claim that the penicillins are indeed the queen of the antibiotics and continue after 50 years to occupy a pre-eminent position in medicine.

Florey was naturally not concerned with these chemical developments. There were, however, other developments of a non-scientific nature which were very much his concern and in considering these we must go back to the earliest days of the penicillin project at Oxford and a major source of his disagreement with Chain. The latter, it will be recalled, had urged that their work should be protected by patents, royalties on which should be ploughed back to support further research. He had gone so far as to go to see Mellanby about this but had been brusquely rebuffed (p. 129). In Florey's first discussion with the Rockefeller Foundation when he arrived in New York with Heatley in 1941 the question of patents arose but it was agreed that these should not be sought. After the first visit to Peoria, Thom recorded in a memorandum (p. 131) that the Lancet paper of 1941 had disposed of the possibility of a patent and that in any case Florey and Heatley were not 'patent-minded'.

This succinctly states Florey's technical and personal position at the time. Technically, the consensus of opinion is that the disclosures made in the Lancet in August 1941 were so far-reaching that no effective patent could then have been filed; what happened thereafter is a different matter. Personally, Florey was then averse to the whole idea of seeking to patent—and thus to get financial gain, however altruistically—for a medical discovery. Yet there is evidence that in later years he reversed that position. Wesley Spink records that in 1955, when he was alone with Ethel and Howard in Oxford, the latter 'bemoaned the fact that he had not taken out a patent for penicillin'.[14] He quotes Florey:

I have had great extension of my experiences as a result of penicillin. I have seen much of the world and have many friends. There is only one serious regret that I have about the whole affair. That is, that I did not, on behalf of my colleagues and the laboratory, patent the processes by which penicillin was extracted.

This change of attitude is so fundamental that we must devote some space to the circumstances surrounding it, because the issue became for a time one of considerable political importance and a bone of contention between Britain and the United States.

The first sign of controversy was in the United States, where the immense publicity surrounding penicillin had persuaded many people that it was an American discovery that had been triggered off by Dubos' work on tyrothricin. This aroused the indignation of Florey's former student Epstein (pp. 61, 141) (who by then had changed his name to Falk and was a medical officer in the US Army). Taking up the cudgels on Oxford's behalf in the pages of the *American Journal of Medicine* he insisted that the true starting point was the research on lysozyme and not that of Dubos. While this is substantially true, it is nevertheless a fact that Florey and Chain's original application to the Rockefeller Foundation specifically cited the work of Dubos as evidence that antibiotics 'seem therefore to possess great potentialities for therapeutic application'.

Of much more serious consequence was a statement of Raymond B. Fosdick, President of the Rockefeller Foundation, in the Foundation's Report of its activities in 1943, that it was their funds—including the 1936 grant of $1280 for research on lysozyme (p. 61)—that had made possible the development of penicillin for therapeutic purposes. As is common with such reports it was not published until 1944 and the first public notice of it in Britain appeared in *The Times* of 13 March 1944. This statement was not intended to be controversial, but simply a normal part of the Foundation's account of its stewardship of the funds entrusted to it. Unfortunately, it was seized on in London, in the *Evening News*, as evidence that it was the Americans who had first perceived the significance of penicillin and were thus entitled to claim credit for its development. Questions were asked in the House of Commons and Mellanby—who in 1939 had promised to 'remember' Florey's appeal for £100 and had actually given him £25 (p. 91)—was furious at the implication. He provided the government with evidence to state formally in reply to a question by Mr. John Dugdale, Labour MP for West Bromwich, on 6 April 1944 that Florey had received £6937 of public money since 1939 to support his research, but the circumstances and conditions under which this had been granted were not stated. At the same time as the British Government was being berated for allegedly driving Florey to seek support in the United States, American industry was being attacked because allegedly it had not only appropriated a British discovery but had had the impudence subsequently to make British industry pay royalties on its commercial exploitation.

This controversy caused considerable distress to Florey, who was by no means as hardbitten as many suppose. He wrote a placatory letter to Mellanby, saying that he had had no idea of the consequences that his formal acknowledgment to the Rockefeller Foundation would cause, and saying that the trouble was caused by a last-minute change in the wording which he had failed to notice. Fortunately, in the turmoil of postwar reconstruction it fairly soon subsided, but lasting damage had been done. It was revived in 1952 by E. M. Hugh-Jones, an economics Fellow of Keble College, Oxford. In the summer of that year he raised the matter with J. B. Conant, then President of Harvard, who during the war had been closely connected with the US penicillin project (p. 144) as Chairman of the National Defense Research Committee and Deputy Director of the Office of Scientific Research and Development. He had visited Britain in February 1941 to conclude formal arrangements for an Anglo-British exchange of information in many fields, including penicillin. Conant had lately cited penicillin as an example of Anglo-American co-operation. In a letter[15] dated 4 July 1952 Hugh-Jones made some categorical statements and accusations.

The substance of his complaint was that the British workers had not patented their discovery because in the medical field this was unethical; that when America came into the war in 1941 Britain had freely and without restriction supplied all available information about the production and use of penicillin; and then the whole business had been turned over to commercial interests represented by Merck, Squibb, and Pfizer. The pharmaceutical

companies had then produced penicillin in quantity by deep
culture and had patented this process. When the Ministry of
Supply set up similar plants in Britain during the war they had to
obtain licences from, and pay royalties to, the American companies. When the war was over Britain had to pay a lump sum to
the American interests for the wartime use of the deep culture
process. He claimed that British manufacturers such as Glaxo
and Distillers were still paying royalties to Merck and other
American companies. Hugh-Jones concluded by asserting that all
this was a matter of incontrovertible fact, but it is apparent from
what has already been said that it was an unwarranted oversim-
plification. Nevertheless, it was a view prevalent in Britain, for
in a letter dated 9 August 1952 John Nichols of the Bowman Gray
Medical School at Lake Forest had written to Vannevar Bush—
then President of the Carnegie Institution of Washington—saying that

British doctors allege that America 'stole' penicillin from them during
the war or at least took unfair advantage of them . . . that the Americans
patented the process of growing the mold in deep culture and that today
it is necessary for British manufacturers to pay royalties on all penicillin
grown by this method.[15]

Vannevar Bush was a very powerful man and he was concerned that misrepresentation of the facts might seriously damage
Anglo-American relations, especially in the scientific field. He
therefore invited John T. Connor to make a detailed inquiry into
the allegations that were being made. The choice was a good one.
Connor had been General Counsel of the Office of Scientific
Research and Development working under Bush's direction and
had been particularly concerned with organizing the arrangements for collaboration on penicillin synthesis. In 1952 he was
Counsel for Merck, of which he later became President before
joining the Johnson administration, and thus particularly well
placed to obtain precise and reliable information about commercial arrangements made between private American and British
firms during the war. He made his report to Bush on 28 October
1952. It ran to a dozen pages and it is neither possible nor appropriate to quote it at length here. Nevertheless, as the question of
his judgement over patents was one that caused Florey so much
concern in his later years it is important to record the main conclusions reached, the more so as misconceptions such as those of

Hugh-Jones still persist and have never been authoritatively refuted in generally available publications.

Connor's Report[16] begins with an uncompromising summary of his conclusions:

Only a misunderstanding of scientific research procedures, of patent law, of the facts and understandings surrounding the collaborative development of penicillin from an academic discovery to large-scale commercial production and of the parts played by the Americans and the British in this development could lead people of good will to say that America "stole" penicillin from the British.

The substance of his argument was that so far as British firms made any payment to American counterparts they were in respect not of patents but of 'engineering and other services and costly engineering, scientific and commercial know-how'. This is normal and acceptable practice, without which industry could not operate. It was agreed as such by the Therapeutic Research Corporation, representing British manufacturers. Such exchanges were almost wholly in respect of deep culture processess, the development of which was crucial for large-scale production and was entirely an American initiative. There was, however, no coercion:

Glaxo and Distillers evidently were of the opinion that the time and money they could save by obtaining the benefit of the heavy American investment in developing this "know-how" and these commercially feasible processes were worth the money they agreed to pay for that 'head start'. These opinions apparently were shared by the British government which approved the agreements, but they were not shared by all British manufacturers because several of them went ahead on their own to design, construct and operate penicillin plants in England.

Connor paid particular attention to Hugh-Jones' allegation that the Ministry of Supply had had to pay a lump sum to American interests. He concluded: 'As far as I can find out, no lump sum payments have ever been made by the British Ministry of Supply'.

He cites Glaxo as a specific and important example of the arrangements made. In June 1944 Merck, Squibb, and Pfizer were advised that Glaxo had been asked to run an agency factory for the Ministry of Supply. After some months' negotiations with the Ministry's Mission in America the three companies reached an agreement approved by the British government. In the event, Pfizer dropped out but agreed to the disclosure of technical information to Glaxo and to royalty-free licensing under any British filed patents that might cover the process disclosed to Glaxo. In return for this information Glaxo agreed to pay—for a five-year period expiring 31 June 1951—a small percentage of its net sales of penicillin but this specifically excluded sales to the British government for purposes essential to the prosecution of the war.

Turning from 'know-how' to patents, Connor is equally emphatic:

Up to the present time it appears that no British firm has paid one shilling in royalty to any American firm solely for licenses under any patents covering the deep fermentation methods for the production of penicillin.

The 'present time' to which he refers was October 1952, several months after Hugh-Jones had made his allegations to Conant, and thus his statement amounts to an outright refutation of them. As he was aware, as a chief executive of Merck, of negotiations then going on with British firms which might subsequently have made a minor qualification necessary, he goes on to outline the history of the key patents involved.

These fall into two sets. The first of these were filed by Moyer, with whom Heatley had worked at Peoria. As a government employee Moyer had to assign rights to his inventions to the US Department of Agriculture, but he was entitled to retain foreign rights. He did in fact file in Britain four patents relating to deep culture and at least two of these[17] were finally issued. Similar patents—the so-called Foster-McDaniel patents—were filed by Merck in America in 1941 and 1942, in the names of two of their employees; they were filed in Britain on 14 May 1944. As commonly happens, the validity of these patents was challenged and a working compromise emerged.

Briefly, Commercial Solvents (an American company) who had acquired exclusive commercial licences under the foreign Moyer patents, filed oppositions in several countries to the Foster-McDaniel patents and were joined in Britain by Imperial Chemical Industries and Distillers. To resolve the situation Commercial Solvents, Merck, and Squibb acquired full commercial ownership of Moyer's foreign patent rights and Merck and Squibb obtained non-exclusive licences. The foreign Foster-McDaniel patents were similarly licensed to Commercial Solvents.

In the event, no British firm accepted licences under the Moyer patents acquired by Commercial Solvents. For a short time, however, there was dispute over the Foster-McDaniel patents. Imperial Chemical Industries and Distillers sought from Merck royalty-free, non-exclusive licences under this application and any patents that might result from it. On the ground that these patents would benefit all penicillin manufacturers, and that they had incurred heavy expense in applying for them, Merck resisted this and sought a small royalty. Imperial Chemical Industries and Distillers responded by lodging an objection to the basis of the Merck application on the ground that it did not represent an invention under British law and in any case had been invalidated by prior publication.

The argument grumbled on for some months, and eventually the two British companies agreed to withdraw their opposition on the basis that they would pay a relatively nominal lump sum rather than a royalty. Unfortunately they could not agree what this sum should be, Distillers being less forthcoming than Imperial Chemical Industries. To resolve the dilemma and avoid adopting an inconsistent and seemingly discriminatory licensing policy Merck simply withdrew its application in June 1953.

On 30 June 1953 Connor wrote to Baird Hastings, Florey's American collaborator on the wartime mission to Moscow, and at that time back at Harvard, sending him a copy of his memorandum to Vannevar Bush and informing him of the latest development:

Within recent weeks we have taken steps to abandon the Merck English patent application covering the deep fermentation process, as a result of which we think that the only possible cause of friction has been removed.[18]

Connor concluded his letter to Vannevar Bush by endorsing Conant's view:

I hope that this recital of the complicated facts about the penicillin situation will be useful to you and Dr Conant. From our point of view, the story has been—as Dr Conant has said—"A happy example of Anglo-American collaboration". We know that view is shared by the Glaxo people, and we hope it grows to be the feeling of all British medical people, as all the facts become known.

Connor's memorandum had limited circulation but the list of recipients on the last page includes Sir Harry Jephcott, Chairman of Glaxo. As he and Florey were well acquainted it is most probable that Florey would have seen a copy. If so it must have given him some comfort, for it disposes convincingly of allegations that American companies in some way held Britain to ransom. If there was an error of judgement it was in publishing the original research without first protecting it by patents, but it is very difficult to see how this could have been done in the climate of opinion of the day; it is no use arguing that it can be and is done today. Apart from any ethical considerations there was then in Britain simply no machinery by which academic research workers could patent their results even if they wanted to. Also, as we shall see later (p. 318) there were considerable difficulties about patenting natural products.

By the time the cephalosporin work reached the stage of possible commercial development the situation had been radically changed by the foundation of the National Research Development Corporation (NRDC) in 1948. By 1943 the government was optimistic enough to look ahead to a successful outcome of the war. It was conscious that while British inventive genius was considerable—as exemplified by radar, penicillin, and the jet engine—means for nourishing its fruits in Britain were inadequate; this applied particularly to universities and publicly financed research organizations. In 1943 the Steering Committee on Post-War Employment recommended that public finance should be made available 'for the initial development and testing of new inventions'. No effective action could be taken at that time, but when the Labour Government took office in 1945 Sir Stafford Cripps, as President of the Board of Trade, proposed the creation of a public corporation designed to facilitate the development of inventions from all sources, including industry and private individuals. On 30 June 1948 the appropriate corporation was set up under the Development of Inventions Act, introduced by Harold Wilson. It had powers to assist the development of inventions from the initial research work to the final stages of production by providing both finance and the necessary technical services, such as advice on patenting. Initially, it went carefully and concerned itself largely with inventions arising from public sources; from the mid-1960s, however, it began to provide risk capital for innovation in industry.

Conscious of the allegations that had been made about the unfair exploitation of penicillin, the Medical Research Council suggested to the Oxford workers about 1950 that any commercially promising developments in the cephalosporin field should be patented and the patents assigned to the Council, who would then seek the advice and support of the NRDC. As a logical development, it was soon afterwards agreed that any patents should be assigned direct to the NRDC. Such an arrangement did not require the approval of Oxford University, though they were informed and contented themselves with giving the go-ahead provided they incurred no legal liability. At that time nobody was greatly interested one way or another, as there was no particular reason to suppose that any significant return was likely. Ten years later, however, there had been a complete change of fortune and the cephalosporins had become major money spinners.

Florey, who had encouraged the cephalosporin work from the outset, was a consultant to Imperial Chemical Industries but to his chagrin failed to arouse their interest in the new antibiotic. He was, however, successful with Glaxo—through his acquaintance with Sir Harry Jephcott and his research workers—and the American company Eli Lilly, one of the first to take an active interest in penicillin during the war, also joined in. Other firms, too, became alerted to the possibilities and by the late 1950s NRDC was able to effect some licensing agreements in the United States, Europe, and Japan. There remained, however, a major technical obstacle. The cephalosporin C produced by fermentation had a side-chain that conferred on it very low antibacterial activity. This side-chain could be removed and replaced by others which gave much improved activity but only by chemical procedures too complex and too inefficient to lend themselves to commercial application. The Oxford workers pinned their hopes to discovering an enzyme that would remove the side-chain, just as there is an enzyme that will remove the principal side-chain from benzylpenicillin and give, as it were, the kernel of the molecule to which new side-chains can be attached. A Vice-President and Research Director of Merck who visited Oxford at this time also hoped that progress could be made along these lines. These hopes were not fulfilled, but research workers in Eli Lilly discovered a much more efficient chemical procedure for achieving this end. This led to the preparation of several semisynthetic cephalosporins that underwent successful clinical trials and were marketed commercially. Another development gave futher impetus. The discovery by research workers at Eli Lilly made possible an extensive exploration of side-chain chemistry, a process that led quickly to compounds with increased potency and beta-lactamase stability, and others with oral activity. Together, these achievements account for the many new compounds that have come into clinical use and the huge share they now hold of the antibiotic market.

These developments had startling financial repercussions. Substantial royalties began to accrue to the NRDC about 1965 and it was clear that they would rapidly increase. Nobody could have foreseen the extent of the bonanza, however. By 1978 annual world sales of the cephalosporins exceeded those of semi-synthetic penicillins and amounted to more than £600 million; total sales by Glaxo up to that time exceeded £275 million. Royalties due to NRDC now amount to substantially more than £100 million.[19] It was by far the most successful of the ventures supported by the NRDC and probably the largest royalty earner ever to have emerged from a university laboratory. By expert legal pleading it proved possible to extend the life of the original cephalosporin C patent by six years and of those concerned with modifications of the nucleus by four years, thus ensuring that the basic patents remained operative until at least 1982.

So far as their personal entitlement went, the Oxford workers received substantial and increasing payments and for Florey this meant a welcome accretion of income in the last few years of his life after he had resigned his professorship. His agreed share of the royalties was 0.5 per cent. Sadly, for Newton too—a much younger man— the financial benefit was shortlived for himself, as opposed to his family, for he died suddenly of a coronary thrombosis on New Year's Day 1969, at the age of only 49. He and Abraham had collaborated harmoniously in the Sir William Dunn School of Pathology for twenty years and in the course of a warm tribute to him Abraham wrote:

Guy Newton was an unusually conscientious man of absolute integrity who paid meticulous attention to detail, and he entered a field of research in which these qualities proved highly rewarding. He incorporated unselfishness and a complete lack of pretentiousness in a personality which had a positive and unforgettable flavour.[20]

In the summer of 1965, Abraham and Newton decided that they would use money due to them from the NRDC to found separate charitable trusts to support medical, biological, and chemical research. Abraham supposed that this would present no great difficulty but his lawyers disillusioned him; it appeared that the patents might be regarded as a marketable asset and in divesting themselves of them they might become liable for capital gains tax. Abraham has commented wryly on this unexpected complication:

the consequences of owing a very large amount of tax, when one had given away the money with which to pay it, seemed likely to be rather unpleasant, even in a welfare state, and a matter for some thought.[21]

The matter was referred to the Board of Inland Revenue, who took two years to reach a favourable decision. The first trust was set up in 1967 and two others later. It was only at this stage that formal contact was made with Oxford University; this was necessary because the trust deed stipulated that the money should be used to support medical, biological, and chemical research in the University and its Colleges, with special reference to the Sir William Dunn School of Pathology. A later trust included education as well as research among its objectives. The very considerable income from the trusts has been used over the years to support research, mainly through fellowships and including a visiting professorship in the University of Oxford, and the endowment of a Chair of Chemical Pathology in the Sir William Dunn School. Although Brotzu took no active part in the research, it is a pleasure to record that the University of Oxford conferred an honorary degree on him in 1971.

The great financial success of the cephalosporins revived speculation that similar rewards would have accrued had the same protection been accorded penicillin from the outset. The two basic arguments already stated remain valid; 40 years ago such a procedure would have been regarded as unethical and in any case there was no effective means which academic research workers could have followed to acquire patent protection. In addition, there are, as has lately been authoritatively pointed out, purely technical points about the patenting of natural products which were looked at differently then from what they are now. Briefly, there is the legal dilemma that something must be new if it is to be patentable but how can it be new if it has existed in nature for countless millennia?

Up to 1949—that is, during the most active period of the Oxford work—British and Commonwealth patent law favoured what are called product-by-process claims. Generally speaking, this restricted awards to products made by a clearly defined process. Other countries had, of course, their own legislation. The 1949 Patents Act, which covered the period of the cephalosporin work, was more liberal and allowed what are called product *per se* claims. These cover clearly defined substances, regardless of the means by which they are obtained. In reality, of course, the position is a great deal more complicated than this suggests, but the patent law that gave protection to cephalosporin in the 1950s was substantially different from that operative at the time of the penicillin work in the 1940s. The subject of patenting biological products is, in fact, an exceedingly complex one, as a recent book by R. S. Crespi makes clear.[22] In it, he devotes a considerable amount of space to the penicillins and cephalosporins and makes the following comment:

Much mythology has been generated around these and related questions and unwarranted conclusions have been drawn as to the consequences of the failure of the academic scientists, in Britain at least, to be in the slightest degree patent-minded at that time. No initial appraisal has apparently been proposed of what kind of protection could have been achieved in the circumstances in which the discoveries were made and over the time span from initial observation to isolation of the active substance.

Florey always stressed the great element of luck attending their choice of penicillin for their first serious study of antibiosis. Some years after the war he happened to meet Fletcher in the Hammersmith Hospital and said:

Those days were wonderful days, Fletcher. We none of us can expect to know that kind of excitement again. That sort of thing can only happen once in anybody's lifetime.[23]

For once his judgement was at fault; the cephalosporins were to prove quite as important as penicillin had been. Florey's personal involvement was much less because the circumstances were very different and he was the last to seek undeserved credit. It was, nevertheless, a second major triumph for a laboratory which he had inherited in a state of disarray and had raised to one of the world's most famous centres of medical research.

With only a few exceptions, there was a strong bond between Florey and his research workers. He was meticulous in observing their individual contributions and he was always interested in their subsequent careers. One interesting manifestation of this was his custom of asking each of them for a photograph after they left and this was hung in the upstairs corridor: he said that this idea originated from his Cambridge laboratory. For their part, they had the advantage of training in a school where only the best was good enough. Yet when the time came for him to leave and take up the Provostship of Queen's he characteristically showed no emotion. He was pleased that his successor was a fellow Australian, Henry Harris, a graduate of Sydney University, whom Florey had originally invited to the Sir William Dunn School of Pathology in 1952 with the support of an ANU Travelling Scholarship; subsequently he had remained in the department as Director of Research for the British Empire Cancer Campaign until 1959, when he had gone to the John Innes Institute as Head of the Department of Cell Biology. Florey had always had a high opinion of his experimental work—one of the best brains he had ever had, he once remarked—and he was among those whom he hoped to have persuaded to go with him to Canberra in 1957 in the final throes of the argument about the Directorship of the John Curtin School of Medical Research (p. 290).

10

THE PRESIDENT OF THE ROYAL SOCIETY

In British science, and indeed internationally, the Royal Society occupies a unique position. Founded in 1660, and granted a Royal Charter in 1662, it is the oldest existing scientific society in the world. Its declared general purpose was 'to improve natural knowledge'. It is a private corporation but yet works closely with the government both in an advisory capacity or as agent for the allocation of certain research funds. It is recognized worldwide as the premier national academy of science and as such represents Britain on all international scientific occasions. It is a self-governing body electing its own members, currently some 700 in all. The ordinary Fellowship consists of British or Commonwealth subjects. In addition, there is provision for the election of a member of Foreign Members, now about 80, chosen 'from among persons of the greatest eminence for their scientific discoveries and attainments'. Traditionally, since the time of Charles II, the ruling monarch is Patron of the Society and there is special provision for election of Princes of the Blood Royal. All in all, it is a very august and influential body, and it is fair to say that every British research worker aspires to be elected to it, for to be elected is in itself a public recognition of scientific attainment.[1, 2] Over the matter of penicillin patents, it will be recalled, the prospect of exclusion from the Fellowship had been used by Dale as a powerful threat to induce Chain to desist from his arguments in their favour.

Like all such bodies, the Royal Society has its own hierarchy. It is governed by an elected Council of twenty-one Fellows, who appoint from their number a Treasurer, two Secretaries, and a Foreign Secretary. Of more immediate concern, the Council also elects a President who, *ipso facto*, holds the highest office in British science. It is one of great prestige and influence, and correspondingly coveted. It is to this high office that Florey was elected in 1960, with the expectation that he would serve for five years. For the moment, however, we must go back on our tracks and trace his earlier relationship with the Society.

Election to the Society is understandably no easy matter, and demands in the first place recommendation by at least six existing Fellows. The information on all valid nominations is circulated to every Fellow and a collection of the candidates' publications can be inspected in the library. It is a lengthy process, lasting from July to March. Certificates of recommendation remain valid for seven years in the first instance. As nominations greatly exceed vacancies, it is rare for a candidate to be elected the first year his name is put forward. In Florey's case, his name was put forward in 1937, on the initiative of Mellanby. At that time the number of Fellows elected annually was only 20; today it is 40. In a letter[3] telling Florey about this, Mellanby urges him to forget about it; he had seen many people getting unnecessarily depressed because the years went by and nothing happened. It was advice that Florey himself was to give to candidates in later years. In the event, Florey was elected in 1941. Almost at once (1942-43) he was elected to serve as a member of Council, and he was elected again in 1951-53, during which time he was a Vice-President. The Society honoured him in other ways, recommending him for one of the two Royal Medals in 1951. In 1957 he received the Society's highest award, the Copley Medal; it is a silver medal and an honorarium of £100 accompanies it. In between, he had in 1954 been invited to give the important Croonian Lecture, initiated in 1684 by Dr. W. Croone, an original member of the Society; it was funded by his widow from the rent of the King's Head Tavern in London.

It would be surprising if in the 1950s Florey's thoughts had not turned to the possibility that he himself might in due course be elected President. The honours already accorded him were evidence of the esteem in which the Society held him. Additionally, he had the rare distinction of the Nobel Prize, and, of course, his knighthood. Yet when he came to weigh the odds against him, he must fully have recognized that they were considerable, not only because of the strong competition but also from a particular tradition of the Society.

In its publications and in other ways the Society has for convenience long recognized a division of science into two parts—the mathematical and physical sciences (A) and the biological sciences (B). In the distant past such men as Newton had served long terms as President (in his case 24 years) but for many years it had been the custom for Presidents to serve for five years (although technically re-elected annually) and for Council alternately to elect representatives of the physical and biological sciences. In the nature of things, such a responsible post would go to men of mature age; the average age at election of Florey's immediate predecessors (Sir Cyril Hinshelwood, Lord Adrian, Sir Robert Robinson, Sir Henry Dale) was 61. Hinshelwood was Professor of Physical Chemistry in Oxford and due to end his term of office in 1960. Whoever his successor was, he would be drawn from the ranks of the biological scientists. For Florey, therefore, the 1960 election was critical. He would then be 62 years of age, but if he was not elected then he would by tradition not be eligible again until 1970. By then, had he lived, he would have been 72—not an impossible age, for Sir William Bragg had been elected as recently as 1935 at the age of 73—but his chances would be much diminished.

The office of President naturally demands much more than acknowledged scientific attainment in research. It demands great self-assurance, for the President must not only command respect within the Society but speak authoritatively for it, and for the scientific world generally, on important public occasions. One such, in particular, is the banquet held annually in London on St. Andrew's Day, 30 November. The guests number many hundreds and normally include the Prime Minister of the day and other government ministers, members of the Diplomatic Corps, captains of industry, civic dignitaries, and representatives of the arts and the press. The President's speech made afterwards thus immediately reaches a most influential audience and it is of the first importance that its message should be clear and apposite without causing offence. These occasions, like the annual conversaziones in the summer and other social functions, are ones of great formality. Until very recently white tie and tails, resplendent with orders and decorations, were *de rigueur* when ladies were present; only latterly have dinner jackets become an acceptable alternative. In London, the Society's nearest counterparts in this respect are the Livery Companies. At the end of the war the Society was very far from being an anachronism, but nevertheless to outsiders—and the more perceptive of its Fellows—it had a decidedly old-fashioned and self-satisfied air.

Of Florey's fitness for the Presidency and his ability to discharge all its duties there could by that time be no doubt, but the same could be said of others. Florey's main cause for concern was that in the course of his career he had made enemies, and to the last moment there were great doubts about the outcome.

The processes by which a new President is elected are naturally confidential, but inevitably involve much discreet lobbying on behalf of potential candidates. Nevertheless, anybody can study the strength of the field, and it is indeed not uncommon for interested outsiders to open a book on the outcome when a new election is pending. Those who studied presidential form in 1960 had the following criteria to guide them. First and foremost, the new President would be drawn from the ranks of the biological sciences. He would probably be around 60 years of age and he would have had experience as a member of the Council and probably also as an officer, and been recognized as a medallist or special lecturer; his four immediate predecessors had all complied with these basic qualifications. *En passant*, it may be remarked that only since 1945, with the election of Kathleen Lonsdale and Marjory Stephenson, under Dale's Presidency, had women been eligible for Fellowship. Dale himself looked forward to the prospect of a woman President, but in 1960 this was not in question. At a higher pitch, the accolade of a Nobel Prize was naturally of great significance but whereas Dale and Adrian were laureates when elected, Robinson and Hinshelwood achieved this distinction during the course of their term of office. Additionally, one might look to previous experience as president of one of the other important learned societies; thus both Robinson and Hinshelwood had previously been Presidents of the Chemical Society. In all probability, there would be a strong Oxbridge background. Over and above all this, the new President must be a man of presence demonstrably able to command respect not only within the Society but in the world of public affairs; evidence of this might be seen in some civil award. As a matter of course it would be presumed that the candidate's private life would be above reproach; or at least not the subject of public comment. For Florey, with his long and deep attachment to Margaret Jennings, this was a sensitive point. Although they had both exercised great discretion, their attachment had not passed unnoticed.

Florey was clearly a very strong candidate, but it is interesting to project ourselves backward in time and weigh some of the other considerations that would have influenced students of form in Oxbridge common rooms and elsewhere who were contemplating a mild flutter on the outcome of the 1960 election.

At first sight, one contender seems to stand out above all others. This was A. V. Hill, who had done outstanding research on energy exchanges during nervous and muscular activity. He was a Nobel Laureate in Physiology and Medicine, and had served five times on the Council, including terms as Vice-President, Secretary, and Foreign Secretary. He had been awarded both Royal and Copley Medals, and delivered a Croonian Lecture. He had been President of the British Association for the Advancement of Science and in this capacity had delivered a powerful address on the ethical and scientific problems of overpopulation, which had attracted much favourable notice. His weakness was simply his age: born in 1886, he was 74 years old in 1960, and he had been elected to the Society as long ago as 1918. He must have been a strong contender in 1950, when the choice fell on Adrian, but ten years later his position was weaker, as Florey's would have been in 1970. Sir Edward Salisbury was similarly disadvantaged by having been born in the same year as Hill. After a distinguished career he had lately retired as Director of the Royal Botanic Gardens, Kew; he was a past Vice-President and Biological Secretary and had held office as recently as 1955.

Leaving aside such elder statesmen of science, attention would have been turned to men like Sir Bryan Matthews, Professor of Physiology at Cambridge since 1952. He had been a Fellow for 20 years and had very recently served for three years as Vice-President; he was eight years younger than Florey, having been born in 1906.

There was, however, another name to be pondered closely. This was Sir Lindor Brown, newly elected Professor of Physiology at Oxford after holding a similar appointment in University College, London. His claims were clearly strong. He had been Biological Secretary since 1955 and Vice-President since 1957. He was five years younger than Florey, having been born in 1903.

It was clear, therefore, that the Society was in the position of having a choice of candidates meeting their high standards. This was not necessarily a happy position, however. In such situations, it is not unknown for the votes of the electorate to be so divided that an outsider eventually comes to be elected because he is acceptable to a substantial majority; as we shall see later, it was in such a situation that Florey came to be invited to become Provost of The Queen's College, Oxford. How opinion ebbed and flowed within the Society we do not know, but in the event it was Florey who was their choice and he took up office in November 1960, in succession to his next-door neighbour in Oxford, Sir Cyril Hinshelwood; he was the fiftieth President.

The Royal Society is a very considerable organization, whose various activities are controlled by a complex committee system. It has many separate research funds to administer and widely supports international visits by scientists. It has liaisons, both formal and informal, with national academies of science in many countries and there is thus a regular flow of important visitors. *Ex officio*, the President must represent the Society on many occasions. Although there is a permanent administrative staff, numbering about 70 in 1960, the President's personal burden is heavy even if he confines himself to little more than seeing that the existing machine runs smoothly. In the past, some, like Adrian, had been content to do little more than this and avoid major issues of reform and change, but Florey was not the kind of person to be thus satisfied. He was very conscious that the Society had failed to move with the times and is reported to have said that: 'He hoped to get something done even if he had to carry the Royal Society kicking and screaming into the twentieth century'.[4]

These were brave words, but not ones to which effect could be given without much support, for in themselves they indicate inherent opposition. He was fortunate in finding a powerful ally in Dr. David Martin, head of the administrative staff. He was designated Assistant Secretary to distinguish him from the Honorary Secretaries—Biological, Physical, and Foreign—elected from the Fellowship, but was in effect the chief executive. A chemist by training, he had joined the Royal Society of Arts as Assistant Secretary in 1939. With the outbreak of war he was seconded to the Ministry of Supply and there attracted the particular attention of Robert Robinson, who was then President of the Chemical Society. When the war ended, Martin went to the Chemical Society as General Secretary, instead of returning to the Royal Society of Arts. Under Hinshelwood, Robinson's successor as President, he organized the Chemical Society's centenary celebrations in 1947, and in that same year, at the early age of 32, was appointed Assistant Secretary of the Royal Society. This experience was to prove of great value when, in the last year of Hinshelwood's Presidency, the Society celebrated its tercentenary—an elaborate ten-day event involving 4000 participants, many from overseas.[5]

The Hinshelwood/Martin partnership proved as successful on that great occasion as it had been with the Chemical Society in 1947, but it involved an enormous diversion of the resources of the Royal Society. An elaborate committee system had to be set up to organize the event itself and the Society was also much occupied in fund-raising activities. When Florey took office, these last had proved so successful that an expansion of the Society's activities could be contemplated when the transient dislocation occasioned by the tercentenary was over. It was a favourable moment, therefore, to embark on new projects and Florey did not miss the opportunity. Characteristically, he chose to bring to a head an urgent problem with which, for one reason and another, his predecessors had failed to grapple. This was the question of finding more spacious accommodation for the Society, which had for too long worked under cramped and inconvenient conditions. This was, indeed, a chronic condition which had afflicted the Society throughout its existence. Since 1660, its London home had been successively in Gresham College, Arundel House, Crane Court, and the original Burlington House. Finally, in 1873 it had moved into a new wing of Burlington House built to accommodate it and certain other learned societies. To effect any change Florey had, of course, to persuade his Council—and ultimately the Fellowship at large—of the urgency of the matter.

During his term of office it is customary for the President to give an annual account of his stewardship in the Anniversary Address delivered on St. Andrew's Day.[6] In the first of these (1961) Florey proceeded cautiously. He thanked the Officers and David Martin and his staff for their support; he reported a generous benefaction from the Wellcome Trust to establish a Professorship; he urged the Government to do more for science and technology: he reported important contacts with foreign scientists, including those of China and Russia. Only in two sentences did he refer to a matter that had become uppermost in his mind:

Not the least of our problems is lack of accommodation for [the] responsibilities we seek to discharge. Although I cannot give you any satisfactory assurances on this point now, strenuous efforts are being made to try to overcome this very serious handicap.

For the rest, he contented himself with a review of the history of the blood circulatory system, with particular reference to advances made during the previous ten years as a result of new experimental techniques. He prefaced it by some typically self-deprecating remarks:

In following in the presidential footsteps I have been considerably influenced by the remark made by one of my more candid friends, that I was not so highbrow as my predecessors, and by a comment of another colleague after I had had the honour of delivering a lecture to the Society—he said that it had been a good idea to turn the lights on and off frequently as it kept everyone awake.

Needless to say, his discourse was masterly and incisive. it ended on a note reflecting two of his beliefs:

Science is rarely advanced by what is known in current jargon as a 'breakthrough'. Rather does our increasing knowledge depend on the activity of thousands of our colleagues throughout the world who add small points to what will eventually become a splended picture, much in the way that the Pointillistes built up their extremely beautiful canvases.

In his accounts of the penicillin research he had always stressed that success was the consequence of teamwork and that the study grew out of published work going back for more than half a century.

For those of his listeners attentive enough to remark it, this artistic imagery might have been mildly surprising, for it reflected an interest which meant much to Florey in his later years but which he kept very much to himself. From his early days he had had a keen interest in photography, and later cinematography, and his camera was his constant companion on his travels. By contrast, Margaret Jennings favoured a sketchbook and paints; on one of the many holidays abroad they discreetly contrived to spend together during Long Vacations after the war he asked, on impulse, whether he might try his hand with these. Rather to the surprise of them both he proved surprisingly adept and thereafter oil painting became an absorbing pastime.[7] Visits to art galleries assumed a new interest as he studied the techniques of the masters, and he even kept an easel and paints in his room at the Sir William Dunn School of Pathology. His many paintings are still preserved in his old home at Marston; characteristically, none are signed.

In his Address to the Annual Meeting in the following year he could do no more than indicate that progress had been made in the search for improved accommodation. He reported also progress on another front which he regarded as important—an increase in the total number of Fellows. While this had found general approval, the two principal factions—the physical and the biological scientists—were divided on how it should be effected.

I fancied I detected some signs that the members of most sections thought that they could do with a few more places but that their colleagues in other disciplines were not quite so well placed. And further I believe I saw signs that those on the 'A' side were a little worried that those of us on the 'B' side were not quite up to standard.

To dispel the misgivings of the physical scientists, and with his usual readiness to do battle in the enemy camp, he proceeded to devote the rest of his address to the comprehensive review of the methods used to elucidate the causes of disease. Again he ends by stressing the importance of joint effort.

We hear too much of 'breakthroughs' in these days, for in my opinion such language tends to obscure the fact that all of us depend on the work of our predecessors. This to my mind is nowhere more clearly demonstrable than in the steps that lead to the elucidation of the complicated changes of pathological processes.

By 1963, however, the situation had changed radically and almost the whole of his Anniversary Address was devoted to plans for a move to more spacious accommodation elsewhere in London. Appropriately, and with his usual sense of history, Florey began by reviewing the Society's accommodation problems from the time of its foundation, when rooms had been found for it in Gresham College. He reminded his audience that since 1778, thanks to the personal interest of George III, the Government had always provided accommodation free of rent or any other financial obligation. For present purposes, however, we need consider only the situation in which the Society then found itself and the attitudes towards change expressed by his immediate Presidental predecessors.

To the casual visitor the Royal Society's accommodation in the early 1960s might seem not only adequate but even sumptuous. It occupied a substantial part of Burlington House, an elegant building with its own private forecourt, situated in the heart of London off Piccadilly. Conveniently, it had as neighbours other learned scientific societies—the Geological Society, the Chemical Society, the Linnean Society, and the Royal Astronomical Society. Also in this ivory tower were the Royal Academy of Arts, the Society of Antiquaries, and the British Association. It had a palatial library and a spacious Meeting Room and Council Room. Yet here elegance ended; much of the working accommodation for the staff was a warren of attic and basement rooms, cramped and awkwardly accessible. To drive this point home to his colleagues, he devoted one Council Meeting not to the usual paperwork but to a comprehensive tour of the premises. The other societies grouped round the courtyard were similarly disadvantaged.

It was this situation that Sir Henry Dale inherited when he was elected President in 1940. The military situation was then grave and even the outcome of the war uncertain. By 1944, however, the prospect was much improved and it had been possible to give a good deal of thought to the Society's postwar needs. Dale strongly promoted with the Government the idea of a Science Centre on the south bank of the Thames which would house all the principal scientific societies, including the Royal Society, together with the Research Councils, and possibly also the Patent Office. Apart from meeting the normal needs of all those concerned, it would also serve as a conference centre able to accommodate large international gatherings; this was a facility which London sorely lacked. When Sir Robert Robinson succeeded Dale in 1945 he energetically pursued the same idea. The demands of the Royal Society Empire Scientific Conference and the Newton Tercentenary celebrations in 1946 underlined the urgent need for more and better accommodation, and Robinson devoted a substantial part of his final Presidential address in 1950 to this theme.

This placed Adrian, Robinson's designated successor as President, in a quandary. He, and many of the other Fellows, were by no means happy about the proposal, and he had no wish to be committed to a policy of which he disapproved. The disapproval, it should be said, was not of a science centre but of the Royal Society's participation in it. In a long memorandum to Herbert Morrison, Lord President of the Council, he made a strong plea, saying in effect that the august Royal Society should not be obliged to rub shoulders with the *hoi polloi* of the scientific world:

> It would soon forfeit its reputation if it lost any of its independence and its aloofness from sectional interests, if it did not occupy a position of dignity in a building worthy of its unique status in the scientific world . . . the Society's premises should be self-contained; though they might share services like heating with the rest of the buildings they ought not to share corridors, staircases and entrance halls. . . . In Burlington House the Royal Society has no difficulty in maintaining the almost Olympian dignity and exlusiveness needed for a supreme scientific council. In a Science Centre unless it has a commanding position its prestige is bound to suffer. . . . It ought not to accept anything less than the best the site can offer.[8]

In the event Adrian did not have to make a formal stand on the issue, as the whole scheme gradually petered out, despite efforts by Robinson and a few others to keep it alive. The main reason was that the country's economic difficulties ruled out so ambitious a scheme: a contributory reason was other parties concerned, such as the Patent Office, became involved in studies of alternative sites in Bloomsbury, South Kensington, Holland Park, and the City. It is probable that at this time the majority of Fellows, unaffected by and indifferent to the administrative problems, preferred to stay where they were in Burlington House.

Hinshelwood's Presidency was much occupied with preparations for the Tercentenary celebrations, but the Society's leading role in the organization of the International Geophysical Year (1957-58) was a reminder of the accommodation problem. The scale of that operation is indicated by the fact that the Treasury made a special grant of £550 000 to accommodate the extra staff engaged; extra office accommodation had to be found first in Burlington Gardens and later in Regent's Park.

This was the situation that Florey faced as President, and it is apparent that he had not one problem but two. Firstly, more spacious accommodation had not only to be found, but financed. Secondly, the Fellowship at large had to be persuaded that it was of a quality appropriate to their station in life and demonstrably superior to Burlington House.

An initially promising possibility came to nothing. In 1960 the Civil Service Commission was about to leave Burlington Gardens, immediately to the north of Burlington House. As these premises had been built originally as an examination centre for London University they contained several very spacious rooms and it was thought by the Ministry of Works that they might in some way be useful to all the societies lodged in the Burlington House complex. A joint inspection party, however, decided that the proposal was not feasible.

Concurrently, however, another possibility arose. Only a few days after Florey became President, Martin drew his attention to an article in *The Times* stating that the Government did not intend to pursue its intention to build a new Foreign Office on the site of Carlton House Terrace, and consequently the future of the buildings there was uncertain. The managers, the Crown Estate Commissioners, had rather vaguely suggested that they 'might be suitable as headquarters of cultural bodies'. Acting on this, Florey and his Officers arranged to inspect the property and decided that despite their rundown condition and awkward arrangement they might be made to serve the Society's purposes. They prepared for the Government a document setting out their needs for more accommodation and made a formal application to occupy four houses, nos. 6-9. As is normal in such situations, there was a long delay before anything happened; then, on 25 January 1962, notice was received that the application had been refused.

Meanwhile, however, Florey had not been idle. He was fully conscious that although it was reasonable to expect that the Government, in accordance with policy established over nearly two centuries, would continue to pay the rent of new accommodation, the Society would have to find a very large sum of money to meet the capital cost of essential alterations. What this cost might be was necessarily a matter for speculation until a detailed survey was possible, but a tentative estimate suggested at least £500 000. This was based on a survey arranged by Sir

William (later Lord) Holford, President of the Royal Institution of British Architects, offered as a fraternal gesture. By the standards of the day, and even of the present time, this was a very substantial sum but it was not one to daunt Florey at that stage of his career, and with his considerable experience of large-scale fundraising. In his formal Annual Address to the Society, he reported simply that the Government had turned down the proposal to move to Carlton House Terrace and went on to say:

There the matter might have rested if it had not been for a lunch-time conversation at Oxford, the details of which are perhaps not suitable for an Address such as this.

As the matter had such far-reaching consequences, it is relevant to enlarge a little on the circumstances. Briefly, Florey was having lunch at Halifax House, just across the road from the Sir William Dunn School of Pathology, with Gwyn Macfarlane, who had been a Fellow of the Society since 1956 and a Member of Council during Florey's first year as President. Macfarlane suggested Nuffield as a possible source of funds and Florey asked him to approach Dame Janet Vaughan, Principal of Somerville College, who was a Nuffield Trustee. Macfarlane did so, and found that Dame Janet, like himself, was going to London on the following day; they travelled together and discussed the problem between Oxford and Paddington, so that a properly reasoned case could be put to Nuffield. This was the second time that particular section of the old Great Western Railway was to prove very significant for Florey (p. 43): within a very short space of time he had a firm promise of £250 000. Additionally, he had promises of £50 000 from the Wolfson Trust and £60 000 from the Wellcome Trust, as well as some smaller, but nonetheless helpful, contributions. Armed with this formidable evidence of the Society's capacity for self-help he again approached the Government, this time successfully. On 28 November 1963 it was announced in Parliament that £45 000 p.a. would be made available for the rent of the premises and the upkeep of the exterior. All this Florey was able to announce formally two days later in his Anniversary Address of 1963. He was conscious that there were among his listeners those who did not relish the thought of leaving Burlington House at all; no living Fellow had known any other home.

Fellows will, no doubt, realize that much of the negotiation associated with trying to acquire the new premises has had to be quite confidential, but three successive Councils have been kept fully informed of what was afoot. No dissentient voice has been raised. It is earnestly to be hoped that the Fellows will accept the new arrangements if they can be completed as being a substantial improvement in the Society's resources, although we shall all have regrets at leaving our present splendid library and council room.

He then went on to explain the conditional 'if' included in his statement:

Negotiations are still proceeding with the Crown Estate Commissioners on some architectural arrangements. Until these are completed no agreement can be initialled. We are not unhopeful of a successful outcome. We are all immensely grateful for the extraordinarily generous response to our appeals by the Foundations and individuals I have mentioned but it should not be forgotten that we still have at least £100 000 to collect for the adaptation of the building.

Apart from any reluctance to move at all, Fellows who lacked the eye of faith given to Florey and his supporters might well have been dismayed at the proposed new premises had they had an opportunity to inspect them closely. In the eighteenth century Carlton House was the residence of Frederick, Prince of Wales. Thirty years after his death it was taken over by another Prince of Wales, the future George IV, who totally reconstructed it, adding a grand new screen and portico. Early in the nineteenth century Carlton House stood at the southern end of a fine new road linking Marylebone (now Regent's) Park with St. James's.

By 1825, however, George IV had tired of Carlton House, which he dismissed as no more than 'a house on a street', and moved to a refurbished Buckingham House. He authorized the demolition of Carlton House and the redevelopment of the site as a residential area. The development was entrusted to John Nash and, as might be expected, was on a grand scale. These were no ordinary town houses; they were great mansions occupied in due course by a Duke, an Earl, two Marquises, four Barons, and a handful of exceedingly rich commoners. Nash was responsible only for the exteriors, the original 15 lessees being free to have the interiors designed and built to their own design. In the event, however, eleven of the lessees employed Nash for this purpose too. The outcome was two terraces of splendid houses built to a single grand design. To the south was an unbroken façade of

Corinthian colonnades forming an impressive background to the processional route leading up the Mall to Buckingham Palace. On the other side of the Mall was St. James's Park, perhaps the most elegant in London. The two blocks were separated by the broad expanse of the Duke of York's steps, with a statue of the Duke himself standing on a towering column at the top. The steps led northward into the open space of Waterloo Place. The whole development is regarded as one of the most successful of Nash's many architectural achievements. It was in marked contrast with Buckingham Palace, whose manifold defects led to his fall from grace after the death of George IV in 1830.

Thus in 1963 the Royal Society were on their way to moving into four splendid mansions standing on one of the finest sites in the very heart of London. For many of the Fellows, an additional amenity was that they were no more than a stone's throw from the Athenaeum Club, long the stronghold of the intellectual establishment. One might well ask, therefore, why there should be any opposition to the move and why Florey had to use all his diplomacy to carry the Society as a whole with him.

The reason was, basically, that nos. 6-9 Carlton House Terrace appeared to have many of the disadvantages of Burlington House. Nineteenth-century town houses for aristocrats tend to have fine public apartments concealing warrens of attics and basement rooms for domestic staff, narrow passages and stairways, storerooms without even light. How four adjoining houses of this kind might be turned into satisfactory premises for the meetings and administration of a large learned society was not immediately apparent, especially as a condition of the lease was that the exterior façade should be retained unchanged from Nash's original. Over and above this, the premises were in a poor general state of repair and it was abundantly clear that alterations and improvements would be very costly; on the most optimistic estimate there remained a large gap between donations promised and total cost. There was real danger that the Society might be saddling itself with a crippling financial burden.

Nevertheless, these misgivings about the adaptation proved ill-founded, as is apparent to any visitor to the Society's present house. The spacious entrance hall leads on to a large meeting room capable of seating nearly 300 people; its cost was defrayed by the Wellcome Trust. No amount of ingenuity made it possible to construct this with raked seating, as is usual for lecture halls, but the flat floor means that the room can be used for conversazioni and other assemblies. There is also a smaller meeeting room. On the first floor is the spacious Council Room, with an elliptical table 7½ metres (25 feet) in length; this room was part of the gift from the Goldsmiths' Company. On the same floor is the Library and Reading Room, the gift from the Wolfson Foundation. Others who contributed substantially to the cost of what may be called the public rooms were the Pilgrim Trust, the Drapers' Company, and Mullard Ltd. The Government contributed £125000 towards the building fund. At a more modest level, Florey was able to report in 1964 that Sir Ellerton Becker, a wealthy Australian agriculturalist who had contributed substantially to the Australian Academy of Science (p. 266) had given £5000 'for what might be vulgarly called a bar but which in fact will be a very pleasant meeting place'. At one time he had plans to launch a general appeal in Australia but this came to nothing. Above these are the administrative offices and in the basement a dining room. Florey was very keen on the inclusion of social amenities. The Society was fortunate in completing the conversion in the 1960s, for the standard of materials and workmanship is throughout of a quality which would have been unthinkable—and perhaps regarded as needlessly ostentatious—in the increasing austerity of the 1970s.

But between this final splendour and the original decision to proceed lay years of travail, and a bill which rose from the original estimate of £500 000 to some £850 000. The raising of this huge sum was a grave responsibility for Florey and his officers. Although they were able to make a preliminary survey beforehand, it was August 1965 before Trollope and Colls, the builders, could move on to the site. While such a major conversion inevitably posed great problems, the precise nature of these were not immediately apparent. One proved to be that as private houses the premises had been heated by coal fires and the flues within the walls took quite unexpected courses, sometimes running horizontally for considerable distances. Again, no. 9 had until 1939 been the old German Embassy and many structural alterations had been made, and subsequently made good, of which no record existed. The need largely to avoid the constraints of party walls between the original houses demanded the complicated task of inserting an intricate system of steel girders to take the load.

As always, Florey was generous in acknowledging the help he had received from many quarters. Lindor Brown commented that 'he drove his officers, persuaded the Council and cajoled his office staff until he had a team that was prepared to work as hard as the President'. The work of the officers was spread by the appointment of what he called active Vice-Presidents. Inevitably, however, the main burden fell on himself and on his chief executive, David Martin. In Florey's time the latter's title was changed from Assistant Secretary—which smacked rather of Gentlemen and Players—to the more realistically descriptive one of Executive Secretary. In 1970 he was awarded a well-deserved knighthood and his sudden death in 1976 was a grievous loss not only to the Society but to the whole scientific community. Subsequently they accorded him the honour of a long entry in their annual *Biographical Memoirs*, normally reserved for Fellows.[9]

The Florey/Martin partnership was a powerful one, and each had a profound respect for the ability of the other. Of the move to Carlton House Terrace, Martin wrote:

To be associated with this operation, which Florey masterminded and achieved with a dogged determination, raising the necessary funds and goodwill, was a stimulating experience. . . . I doubt if sufficient recognition of this achievement and Florey's part in it has been properly recorded.

The partnership survived even the unexpected news in 1962 that Florey was to become Provost of Queen's College, Oxford (Chapter XI). Martin was very much opposed to this, fearing that the inevitable disruption in his private life would prejudice his key role in the Society's move to its new home and his other Presidential duties. In the event, Florey not only successfully managed to discharge both obligations perfectly satisfactorily but continued to find time for research. His regard for Martin was once pithily expressed after the latter had been involved in a motor accident in Canada; it was not only David Martin who might have been killed, he said, but the Royal Society itself!

The move from Burlington House to Carlton House Terrace took longer to complete than Florey's term of office as President, and it fell to his successor P. M. S. Blackett (later Lord Blackett) to preside at the formal opening by Queen Elizabeth—accompanied by the Duke of Edinburgh, who came also in his own right as a Royal Fellow since 1951—on 21 November 1967. The occasion was marked by the publication of a history of the Society's various homes,[10] and in the Introduction to this Blackett paid the following tribute:

... I take this opportunity of again recording the Society's appreciation and gratitude to each and everyone concerned. I must, however, single out one name, that of Lord Florey, my predecessor as President, without whose outstanding personal efforts this achievement could not have begun nor have been so successfully accomplished. All of us who are to enjoy these premises are greatly indebted to him.

It was appropriate that on this great occasion Florey should have made the speech of welcome to the Queen.

Politics has been described as the art of the possible, and on this basis Florey showed himself a shrewd politician. The move achieved was an admirable compromise between those who supported the more ambitious scheme of a Science Centre and the diehards who shirked change of any kind and wanted to remain in Burlington House. This view was clearly expressed by Sir Alan Hodgkin, another former President, in his obituary of Adrian:

It is not the purpose of this memoir to argue that Adrian was right and Robinson wrong, or vice versa. . . . The writer's own view is that, although much remains to be done, the arrangements worked out by Lord Florey for the Royal Society at Carlton House Terrace and for the scientific societies housed in its old premises represent a satisfactory compromise between Sir Robert Robinson's grand vision and Lord Adrian's feeling for historical tradition and independence from government.[11]

The success of the operation belies the cautionary note on which Florey ended his last Anniversary Address, in 1965:

The somewhat gloomy thought that possibly through some misjudgement of mine something will now go seriously wrong with the finances of the Society gives emphasis to the fact that I have never ceased to be astonished that the Society should have done me the supreme honour of electing me to this office.

While Florey and his Council had to take careful note of differences within the Fellowship about the move, they had also to consider its repercussions in the outside world. There was some feeling that the Society had become unduly elitist and rarefied, and its removal into sumptuous new accommodation, substantially subsidized by the taxpayer, encouraged such critics. There was also mounting criticism of the scope of the membership, which had certainly failed to take account of the revolutionary changes going on within science. The biological and non-physical sciences were assuming more importance but this was not reflected in the Fellowship. The more serious threat came, however, from applied scientists, who were very poorly represented indeed. As individuals, many Fellows regarded science as an intellectual pursuit of pure knowledge and believed that the application to useful ends of knowledge so gained was an inferior endeavour, best left to others. Such an attitude was doubly inappropriate. Firstly, it was directly contrary to the spirit of the original Royal Charter of 1662, which specifically stipulated that the Society's 'studies are to be applied to further promoting by the authority of experiments the sciences of natural things and of useful arts'. A seventeenth-century Secretary of the Society, Robert Hooke, put its objectives even more directly: 'To improve the knowledge of naturall things and all useful Arts Manufactures Mechanick practises Engynes and Inventions by Experiment.' Two hundred years later this injunction had lost its force. Around the end of the eighteenth century many of the Fellows were dilettantes with no serious interests in science of any kind. That no dire consequences followed was the consequence of a strong reform movement led by scientific members, notably A. B. Granville, who published some highly critical pamphlets. This led to a revision of the Statutes in 1847, which strictly limited the number of Fellows to be elected annually and tightened up the election procedure.

The second objection to the Society's ivory tower dedication to pure science lay not in the obligations put upon it in the distant past but in the pressures of the immediate present. Since the Industrial Revolution the application of science had profoundly affected the structure of western civilization and such recent wartime developments as atomic energy, radar, the jet engine, and penicillin reflected an extension and acceleration of a long continuing change. Increasingly, gifted scientists were making their careers in the applied field—in private industry, in the new national corporations, and in government research establishments. In all of these, they were beginning to have first-rate laboratory accommodation and equipment. They knew their worth, and strongly resented the implication that they were intellectually inferior to those who remained within the shelter of the universities. Individually, their resentment counted for little, but the organizations which employed them were a force to be reckoned with. In a period of growing national economic stringency the Royal Society had more and more to look for outside support, and in the two postwar decades increasingly sought the patronage of industry, particularly very large science-based companies such as ICI, Shell, BP, and Unilever. Such companies became increasingly restive at being asked to support Royal Society activities, however meritorious, when the claims to Fellowship of their own senior scientific staff, of very high calibre, were largely ignored. In the early 1960s this feeling was so strong that serious proposals were made to set up a new body to recognize and support the contributions of the applied scientists. If brought to fruition, such a plan would have been doubly damaging to the Royal Society. Firstly, it would have drawn public attention to its failure to represent the scientific world as a whole; this would not only have been damaging to its reputation but have led to political pressure on the Government to reconsider its level of support. Secondly, such support as industry was currently giving the Society would be largely, if not wholly, diverted to establishing and supporting the new body.

Florey, with the close knowledge of the working of industry he had gained initially through the penicillin project, and subsequently through such direct connections as a senior consultancy with ICI, was more acutely aware of this hazard than many of his colleagues who had led more sheltered lives, though Hinshelwood in 1960 had stressed the importance of finding 'the right balance between the pure and the applied sciences to enable the Royal Society to maintain its full influence in the modern world'. Florey addressed himself energetically to disarming the critics.

In his Anniversary Address in 1964 he characteristically took the bull by the horns:

It has been argued and indeed publicly proposed that this country needs a new Academy, similar to the Royal Society, but devoted to the application of science, particularly in engineering. The feasibility of such a proposal clearly depends in the first instance on whether applied scientists feel the need for a body with the structures of an Academy which would look after their particular interests and which would serve the country during the coming critical years. . . . The last thing I believe we want to see in this country is two possibly antagonistic Academies representing what might come to be thought of as incompatible interests.

He had, however, already announced measures designed to effect the kind of reform that was being urged. Firstly, a modest increase in the size of the Society was to be effected by increasing the number of annual elections from 25 to 32. Within this enlarged compass there was to be greater emphasis on the applied sciences:

. . . it is the technologist who is transforming at least the outward trappings of modern civilization and no hard and fast line can or should be drawn between those who apply science, and in the process make discoveries, and those who pursue what is sometimes called basic science.

He was emphatic, however, that applied science was not to be identified solely with the physical sciences. The role of the biologist—in the widest sense—he believed to be crucial for the future of society. In pursuance of his thought, the Society's membership was to be more open to hitherto peripheral disciplines such as demography, anthropology, psychology, and psychiatry. With a sure instinct that would be more fully appreciated today than it was then, he expressed the view that:

The investigation and understanding of the psychology and even the psychiatry of rapidly expanding populations may well be of paramount importance in the near future.

Such sentiments were not a passing thought prompted by the needs of the occasion. In his later years he was very much preoccupied with the far-reaching social repercussions of science on society. On the same occasion a year later he made a further prescient pronouncement of the same kind very much in tune with current thought.

. . . there is now overwhelming evidence that rapid population growth is bringing with it dire consequences, not only in the great Asiatic countries, but probably even here. Evidence is slowly accumulating that the question is not simply whether food can be supplied for an ever-increasing population, but whether overcrowding *per se* does not lead to obscure and so far ill defined difficulties of mental and social adjustment to a crowded and rapidly changing environment. . . . Perhaps we should be paying more attention to the generally unpleasing form that life is assuming in great cities.

With this initiative, no more was heard of proposals for a new academy of applied science. Cynics scrutinizing the lists of new Fellows in succeeding years might feel that academic scientists still preponderated, and that some of the industrial members had been chosen because of their high standing in the industrial hierarchy rather than for the originality of their researches. Nevertheless, the Society had made a public pronouncement on the importance of applied science in national life, and there were at least hopes that the balance would in the course of time be redressed. Cynics might also have thought there would have been formidable difficulties in creating in Britain a new academy with anything like the prestige of the Royal Society; for the latter to broaden its scope would be a better solution for all concerned.

This move was helpful in restoring unity within the scientific establishment in Britain, but the Society had also to consider its international role. This was, of course, a subject on which Florey could offer sound advice in the light of his personal experience and enthusiasm for good international relations; few scientists of his generation were more widely travelled and connected. He believed that just as in the national context scarce resources of both manpower and equipment could most effectively be utilized by sharing, so more might be achieved by establishing international centres of excellence in particular fields rather than by individual national efforts. Looking at the world generally, he foresaw no great problems with the United States, 'with which scientists of this country have such good relations and with which it is easy to communicate'. Among other things, he had initiated informal meetings with the US National Academy of Sciences—where his opposite number was the physicist Frederick Seitz—which have continued to this day. Looking in the opposite direction the situation was very different:

When we look at the Iron Curtain countries we have to be content with very little. Agreements reached with the Soviet Union and other communist countries spell out in detail exchange arrangements with which we are all pleased, but real international working has scarcely been touched.

Here he spoke with the benefit of the experience of his wartime visit to Moscow. He also led a Royal Society visit to Russia in 1965 and was there again in 1967 on the occasion of the celebration of the 50th anniversary of the Revolution. One interesting link with the Russians was made during the visit to Britain of the Russian cosmonaut Yuri Gagarin, who made the first space flight in 1961. At very short notice Florey organized a lunch for him at Burlington House. His instinct was right but he earned the disapproval of a few of the more conventional Fellows.

It was on Britain's doorstep that he believed the most could be achieved. The European Economic Community had been established in 1957, but Britain's entry still lay many years ahead. Florey, however, had no doubts that Britain was missing an opportunity:

[Co-operation] should not be insuperable in dealing with Western Europe where, although something has been attempted, we are still making far too few conscious efforts to organize co-operative work. At the present time we are even deficient in the amount of scientific discussion we have with our near neighbours. Is it that we are unwilling to become good Europeans? If so we should consider whether this is wise.

In fact, the beginnings of such co-operative ventures were already beginning to be seen. The European research laboratory for research in high-energy physics (CERN), involving twelve countries, was in full operation in Geneva; agreement concerning the European Space Research Organization (ESRO) was reached in 1962; and preliminary moves for setting up a European Molecular Biology Organization (EMBO) had begun. Florey's advocacy of European co-operation was not limited to science. As Provost of The Queen's College, Oxford, he established European Studentships which made it for a time the most cosmopolitan college in the University (p. 359).

A perennial problem facing the Royal Society in general and its President in particular, was that of its relationship with the government of the day. Too close an association threatened its independence; too remote a one threatened its influence. Traditionally, the Society had been the government's chief source of advice on all scientific matters, on the basis that it was in close touch with those directly concerned, but over the years this pre-eminent position had been considerably undermined. Apart from the growing influence of some of the other scientific societies, government had itself sponsored a plethora of other bodies, such as the Department of Scientific and Industrial Research and the Medical and Agricultural Research Councils, whose voices had to be heeded. As he made clear in his 1964 Address, Florey had no illusions on this point:

> . . . the fact must be faced that because of the establishment of these numerous bodies to which the Government turns for advice in the first instance, the direct relation of the Royal Society to government has been diminished during the development of the scientific activity of the twentieth century.

He had no illusions, either, about how time-consuming it could be to serve on these other bodies, but he urged his colleagues not to shirk the task of serving on committees designed to help the organization of science at government level: '. . . I consider it the duty of the Fellows of the Society to do all they possibly can to assist government in the present somewhat critical state of the country's development.' In so doing, they would of course indirectly represent the Society. In Florey's time the changing relationship with government was emphasized by an administrative rearrangement. For a century the Society had dealt directly with the Treasury, the most powerful of government departments, but in April 1964 the Office of Minister of Science was combined with the Ministry of Education to form a new Department of Education and Science; it was with this new body that the Society now had to deal. Concurrently, the Advisory Council on Scientific Policy (ACSP)—which had been set up in 1948 to try to co-ordinate the whole field of non-military science and technology, and on which the Royal Society was represented—was abolished.

Thus the passage of time at least partially resolved a question on which opinion within the Society had long been divided. In 1943—at the instigation of P.M.S. Blackett, who succeeded Florey as President in 1965—the Society had set up a series of committees to consider the needs of postwar research in Britain. This culminated in 1945 in a document *On the needs of research in fundamental science after the war* which was printed by the Society for private circulation; this advocated a powerful role for the Society. Firstly, it argued that grants for really large and expensive items of scientific equipment—telescopes, nuclear machines, and the like—should be made on the recommendation of the Society. Secondly, it recommended the Parlimentary grant-in-aid that it administered for lesser projects should be substantially increased. Blackett's own proposals went even further; he hoped to see the Royal Society as virtually the only national body controlling and administering all government research funds. His dream was never realized, even during Blackett's own period of office (1965-70) which coincided with a Labour government of which he was a strong supporter. The Society's political influence waned rather than waxed. Florey had no illusions about this and he saw no prospect of turning the tide. It is questionable whether he would have wished to do so had it seemed at all feasible. His experience with governments and government agencies —in both Britain and Australia—had not persuaded him that their meddling in scientific research was in any sense an unmixed blessing.

Nevertheless, it is fair to record that not all Fellows agreed with him on this point. In 1980 a later President, Lord Todd (1975-80) was openly critical:

Unfortunately the Society did not take full advantage of the situation [establishment of ACSP]. From 1950 under three successive Presidents [Adrian, Hinshelwood, Florey] the Society gradually lost influence and drifted away from matters of public policy; it became rather introspective and the Presidents were mainly concerned with such problems as accommodation, celebration of the Society's tercentenary and the like. This had unfortunate results in the early 1960s when a number of important—and in my view retrograde—steps were taken which radically altered the relationship between government, science and perhaps more especially the Royal Society.[12]

These allegedly retrograde steps were, of course, taken on the initiative of a government bent on a white-hot technological revolution. In the intense political acitivity of the day it would have been difficult for the Royal Society to have resisted them, even had it been so minded.

While successive governments had been reluctant to delegate responsibility for the administration of substantial research funds it was very willing—apart from its contribution towards new accommodation—to give active support to the Society in other ways. A particular reason for this at that time was the so-called brain drain; able young scientists were crossing the Atlantic in alarming numbers to try their luck in America, much as the young Florey had travelled halfway round the world to seek his scientific fortune in Britian. Since the root of the problem was lack of academic opportunity at home coupled with a reluctance—which the Society had previously done nothing to dispel—to go into industry, it seemed that a palliative would be to found new research professorships for creative workers in relatively neglected fields. This was not an unfamiliar activity, for since 1919 a bequest from Miss Lucy Foulerton had been used to support a research professorship in medicine. In 1961 Florey had persuaded the Wellcome Trust to endow a Henry Dale Research Professorship, to promote research in physiology and pharmacology. At the end of that year he wrote to the Chancellor of the Exchequer seeking support for five new professorships, and he quickly had a favourable response. In 1964 three further Royal Society research professorships were established, and two more in 1967.

To these large new subventions in support of research, and the half million pounds raised for the new premises at Carlton House Terrace, was unexpectedly added a further benefaction, the largest ever received by the Society in its history. This was a sum of £275 000 from the trustees of the estate of Mr. Montagu Napier, to be used in the broad field of cancer research. For the first five years the income was to be used for the benefit of the Institute of Cancer Research at the Royal Marsden Hospital, and thereafter to be used for similar purposes at the Society's discretion. In the event, the benefaction was used to endow a professorship at the Institute. Thus although a substantial further sum had still to be raised to finance the move to new premises the Society was substantially better off materially at the end of Florey's Presidency than at its beginning.

11

THE PROVOST OF QUEEN'S

With the exception of his five years as Professor of Pathology at Sheffield, Florey's working career was closely identified with the Universities of Oxford and Cambridge; even during his brief spell at the London Hospital he held an unofficial fellowship at Caius College, Cambridge, and was there often. From 1935, when he was appointed to the Chair of Pathology, until his death more than thirty years later, Oxford claimed him entirely. He was, therefore, very familiar with the working of these ancient institutions and their unique collegiate systems. With the University he had something of a love-hate relationship, like many of its alumni. As a bushranging Australian, as he sometimes called himself, he was impatient of the atmosphere of privilege, social and intellectual snobbery, and hidebound, unthinking tradition —all more in evidence in prewar years than they are now. At the same time, he recognized the great potential of the University as a seat of learning and never really lost the enthusiasm so apparent in the early letters he wrote to Ethel before their marriage. He was always conscious of how much he owed the University since it had first received him as a Rhodes Scholar. When he was appointed to the Sir William Dunn School of Pathology, Ethel wrote to his sister Valetta that 'The Oxford Chair has been his Mecca for many years . . .' and there is no reason to doubt the truth of this. In his later years he devoted much time and effort to promoting the University's interests, albeit in the direction of changes which he regarded as necessary and beneficial rather than perpetuating the status quo. His somewhat turbulent approach—which sometimes obscured the very point he wished to make— did not, however, endear him to those for whom reform meant unwanted disturbance of a comfortable way of life. There was, therefore, considerable surprise when, in 1962, it was announced that Florey had accepted the Provostship of The Queen's College, for not only was this very much a post closely identified with the entrenched academic establishment, with which he had never expressed much sympathy, but it involved his relinquishing his Chair and the research facilities that went with it. It is necessary, therefore, to consider the circumstances in which he came to be appointed.

To the outsider the constitution of Oxford University is often perplexing. Its details need not concern us here, but it is necessary at least to understand the nature of the colleges and their relationship to the University. The colleges, more than thirty in all, are corporate bodies distinct from the University and governed by their heads—variously known as President, Master, Provost, and so on—and fellows. They control the selection and admission of their own undergraduates who, *ipso facto*, are members of the University and thus come under its statutes. Many of the colleges—but not all—have been richly endowed by past benefactors; Queen's, for example, had acquired much valuable property in the North of England and in Southampton. The University— whose titular head is a non-resident Chancellor, elected for life by Convocation, which effectively comprises all those holding the degree of Master of Arts—is ruled by the Hebdomadal Council chaired by the Vice-Chancellor, which determines central policy and its execution. Under the Council, financial administration is effected by the Curators of the University Chest—whose main source of revenue is through parliamentary grants now allocated by the University Grants Committee—and teaching and all scholarly activity is supervised by the General Board of the Faculties. In practice, students receive their tuition partly through lectures given by members of the University—professors, readers, lecturers, and fellows of colleges—and partly through individual teaching by their college tutors. This elaborate system, parallelled only in Cambridge and to some extent Durham, is not one which anybody would now establish *de novo* but it has evolved over the centuries and is in practice workable. It is, indeed, a good example of commensalism; the University and the Colleges are organisms with lives of their own but yet dependent on each other.

In this system the position of head of a college—or Head of a House as it is commonly called—is very prestigious both academically and socially. It is an acknowledgement of scholarly achievement, though this is by no means the only criterion for appointment. Some colleges habitually appoint from the ranks of their own fellows; latterly others have tended to cast their nets more widely and seek people who have established high reputations in other fields—such as government service—but are ready to return to academic life towards the end of their active careers. For such, there are considerable attractions. The stipend is adequate, if not lavish—approximating to that of a professor who is head of a department—and includes gracious living accommodation in a university city whose elegance is still admired the world over. There is the possibility of a term (at that time two years) as Vice-Chancellor, the highest executive office in the University. The obligatory duties are not too demanding, for the colleges are large enough and rich enough to have adequate administrative staff. Heads of Houses are thus well placed, if they are so minded, to pursue their own interests and activities. On the debit side, is the fact that the Head of a House has no authority except such as he can exercise by persuasion, for he is in effect no more than the chairman of his governing body. This can be a real problem, for Oxford dons notoriously have an innate tendency towards prolonged intellectual disputation over practical matters which need urgent attention. Their professional instinct is to examine all sides of a question. As has been remarked by E. P. Abraham—who himself was a member of the College when he came to Oxford as an undergraduate in 1932—the fellows of Queens had the reputation of being particularly difficult in this respect and Florey was warned by one of them that as Provost 'he was putting his head into a hornet's nest'.[1]

Such a warning was a disincentive in itself, but quite apart from this Florey had over the years not only expressed aversion to any such appointment and had in fact previously turned down at least two similar offers. As we have noted, his professorial appointment carried with it fellowship of Lincoln College; he entered very fully into the life of that college and was a popular member of it. He played an important part in creating a Middle Common Room there—with the help of his friend Mary Lasker —for the benefit of postgraduate students. This was prompted by his often expressed belief that Oxford colleges did little for their graduate students, except take large fees from them in university and college dues; it was the first such Common Room in Oxford. In 1947, when Nuffield indicated that he would like to acknowledge the importance of Florey's penicillin work by a substantial donation, he obtained for the College £50 000 to support three fellowships, initially held by Abraham, Heatley, and Sanders. In 1953 the then Rector, Keith Murray (later Lord Murray), resigned in order to take up an appointment as chairman of the University Grants Committee and Florey was invited to succeed him. He declined the honour and the College appointed Walter Oakeshott, then Headmaster of Winchester College. Doubtless a principal reason was the University requirement (which does not pertain at Cambridge) that on becoming Head of a House he should resign his professorship, with the exceptional opportunities it offered to pursue the medical research which meant so much to him throughout his life. An additional disincentive, no doubt, was that the Rector's stipend was then only £850 p.a. At that time he had many active years still ahead of him; had he decided otherwise, the pattern of his later life would probably have been very different. His chance of being elected President of the Royal Society would not have been enhanced, for it has long been their custom to elect to this office scientists still active in their research fields. All his immediate predecessors— J. J. Thomson, Sherrington, Rutherford, Gowland Hopkins, W. H. Bragg, Dale, Robinson, Adrian, and Hinshelwood—fell into this category. How far this was a consideration that, among others, weighed with him then must be a matter for speculation A few years later Brasenose College had to find a successor to their Principal, Maurice Platnauer, who was to retire in 1960, and it appears that Florey was approached as a possible successor. The suggestion was stillborn, for he made it clear that the headship of a college as such did not appeal to him. He would have been interested only if the College had been able to provide him with adequate research facilities, but there was no means by which this could have been contrived.

The interest of this is not that there was a faction in Brasenose who supported Florey as a potential Principal, but in the fact that as late as 1959 he was still indicating that he was not seeking the headship of any college. Why, then, did he respond favourably to an invitation from Queen's only two years later? This question is not easy to answer satisfactorily, but first it is necessary to consider the circumstances in which he was appointed.

While the Oxford colleges have much in common, each has a distinctive character of its own. The Queen's College* is one of the oldest, founded in 1340 by Robert de Eglesfield, chaplain to Queen Philippa, consort of Edward III. Historically, it ranks sixth in order of foundation. Little is known about Eglesfield, but he came from a landowning family near Cockermouth, a consequence of which is that the college has a traditional connection with the north of England, especially Cumberland and Westmorland (now Cumbria); a number of scholarships and exhibitions were reserved for students from those parts. Like all colleges, it had its ups and downs over the years, especially in the eighteenth century, but at the time with which we are now concerned it was a good middle-of-the-road college in respect of academic achievement, cultural activities (especially music); and athletic prowess.[2] It lacks the social pretensions of Magdalen and the quarrelsome reputation of a few of its Fellows was in contrast with the friendly atmosphere that Florey enjoyed at Lincoln. Overall, nevertheless, it had considerable appeal to anybody minded to become Head of a House, especially when one considers that such opportunities occur only occasionally and sporadically: to miss one may be to lose all.

Ultimately the election of a new Head of a House—like the election of a new chairman of a board of directors or of a learned society—depends on the vote of the governing body. In practice, of course, this entails intensive lobbying before on behalf of candidates favoured by one faction or another. As the process develops, less favoured candidates are dropped and the votes they would have commanded are pledged elsewhere. In most cases the final voting procedure is a mere formality; indeed, in many cases only a single candidate is finally presented.

Queen's was one of those colleges whose Fellows traditionally elected their Provosts from among their own number. The present vacancy was occasioned by the retirement of J. W. Jones. He was one of the large number of Welshmen of modest origins who had established themselves through grammar school (in his case Merthyr County School), and the Universities of Oxford and

---

*In the past, Queensmen were meticulous in referring to their college as The Queen's College, supposedly to distinguish it from Queens' College, Cambridge. Latterly this has come to be regarded as a pedantry of doubtful historical authenticity and I have, where appropriate, used the title Queen's College or simply Queen's.

Cambridge. He was a distinguished lawyer and devoted to the interests of the College: it is said that he knew every member of it by name. He was, however, a man of retiring disposition, very much confined within the limits of the academic world. He had been Provost since 1948, and was cast in much the same academic mould as his predecessor, R. H. Hodgkin (1937-46), though in personality these two men were very different.

Between Hodgkin and Jones, however, the College had followed a slightly different line and in 1945 had appointed Oliver (now Lord) Franks, who had entered the College as an undergraduate in 1923. He had been a Fellow and Praelector in Philosophy, 1927-37, leaving to become Professor of Moral Philosophy in the University of Glasgow. He thus had an impressive and appropriate academic background. At the time of his appointment Franks was only 40 years of age but had already become Permanent Secretary in the Ministry of Supply during his wartime service, and this greatly widened his experience. The governing body had been discerning as far as his ability went but less so in terms of his potential. Franks was a man of quite exceptional talent, which others, too, had noted, and ahead of him lay a career of great distinction. Scarcely had he been appointed than he was asked to be Secretary of the 60-nation conference that was to become the Organization for Economic Co-operation and Development (OECD). There was the possibility of the chairmanship of a nationalized industry. Finally, in 1948, he was appointed-British Ambassador in Washington and resigned the Provostship after only two years in office. In this short time, however, he had managed to established a good committee structure. Later, he was to render signal service to the University as Chairman of the Commission of Inquiry into Oxford University 1964-66. From 1962-76, after retiring from the chairmanship of Lloyds Bank, he was Provost of Worcester College.

It was against this background that the Fellows of Queen's had to consider their choice of a new Provost as Jones approached retirement at the age of seventy. Leaving personalities aside, it was apparent in the 1950s that the star of science and technology was in the ascendant; young people, and their parents, were widely of the opinion that it was qualifications in these fields that would open the doors of opportunity in a brave new world. It seemed logical to seek a successor in this field. This in itself was venturesome for there were few precedents for scientists as Heads of Houses. The only one at that time was Janet Vaughan, basically medically qualified like Florey, who had been Principal of Somerville since 1945. A distinguished earlier example was Sir Henry Tizard, who had been President of Magdalen during and just after the war. On this basis, as well as on personal qualities, one of the existing Fellows emerged as a strong candidate. This was C. W. Carter, a biochemist who had served briefly as Pro-Provost. He was approached after the first meeting at which the succession was discussed, but declined. Thereafter he chaired all subsequent meetings.

With Carter eliminated, a new possibility was George Temple, Sedleian Professor of Natural Philosophy in the University since 1953. For twenty years before that he had been Professor of Mathematics in King's College, London. During the war he had been seconded to the Royal Aircraft Establishment, Farnborough, thus gaining experience in applied science and he had just been appointed Chairman of the Aeronautical Research Council. His academic achievement had been recognized by his election to Fellowship of the Royal Society in 1943. Moreover, he was just sixty years old—an age when useful years still lie ahead but there is little remaining inclination to seek new opportunities elsewhere.

Temple was approached informally and considered the possibility very carefully; eventually, however, he asked that his name should not be put forward. There were two main reasons for this decision.[3] Firstly, although the proposal was flattering and had obvious appeal, it was not one which greatly attracted him personally. Moreover, the appointment carried with it social obligations which his wife's state of health would have made difficult to fulfil. Secondly, and more particularly, he did not wish to stand in the way of another Fellow, Guy Chilver, who was not only a strong alternative candidate but was keen to have the appointment. Chilver was very much a College man. He had been Fellow and Praelector in Ancient History since 1934, and had served both as Dean and, since 1948, Senior Tutor. On the old tradition, he clearly had strong claims, and considerable support.

There was, however, another serious contestant. This was Iain Macdonald, Praelector in French, but for various reasons he could not command an overall majority. Neither could Chilver, though for a time he seemed to be the front runner. With nobody disposed to make a positive move, as opposed to mobilizing opposition to a particular candidate, deadlock ensued; the only solution was to find a new candidate who could command majority support. It was in these circumstances that Florey, a complete outsider, came to be considered. He was, of course, eminently suitable, especially if somebody from the scientific world was sought, though some of the fellows were uneasy about his reputation for abrasive comment in discussion at faculty board meetings and elsewhere. It seemed unlikely that he would accept, however; apart from his known aversion to anything he regarded as an essentially administrative job, he was less than halfway through an exceptionally demanding five-year term of office as President of the Royal Society. The inevitable domestic and professional disturbance would be particularly daunting at that time. Nevertheless, on Florey's own precept that if you don't ask you don't get to know, it was decided to make an approach to him.

Rather unexpectedly, Florey expressed considerable interest in the proposal but made it clear from the outset that if he were to accept it would be only if he commanded strong support within the College. He was not the sort of man who would want to be appointed on a slim majority. He also made it clear that initially the Royal Society would make considerable demands on his time.

As was to be expected, Florey's first reaction was to try to find out more about the proposition. Ironically, he first sought the advice of Temple and was somewhat taken aback to discover that he had already been approached and had turned the proposal down. Temple could not resist enquiring why Florey was seriously interested in Queen's when he had so recently indicated that no such appointment appealed to him. The unexpected reply was that Florey had at his disposal funds sufficient to enable him to build a small laboratory in the grounds of the Sir William Dunn School of Pathology; there he could continue the research which meant so much to him, even if no longer as Professor, as well as being Provost. Privately, Temple doubted whether such a scheme would ever have the University's approval. In the event, no more was heard of it, but Sir Lindor Brown—Professor of Physiology and then Biological Secretary of the Royal Society—later found some accommodation for him in the Department of Physiology,

Following the initially favourable reception, negotiations proceeded satisfactorily, but with one unexpected complication. At the same time, St. John's College was seeking a new President and also conceived the idea that Florey would be an excellent candidate. They, too, sent an emissary, H. W. Thompson, to see him. Florey considered the proposition very carefully but, regretfully, decided that the negotiations with Queen's had by that time reached a stage at which he could not properly withdraw, even had he wished. In fact, although he found both proposals attractive, he remarked privately that he would have preferred St. John's because of its stronger orientation towards the sciences. A further consideration, of course, was that while the offer from Queen's was then firm that from St. John's was necessarily tentative; had he hesitated he might have ended up with neither.

Florey's stipulation that he should command the general support of the Fellowship was observed and he was duly elected Provost on 25 June 1962. He was the first scientist to become Provost—though paradoxically the non-scientific Sir Joseph Williamson, Provost in the latter part of the seventeenth century, had served as President of the Royal Society—and the first never to have had any prior connection with Queen's as undergraduate, research student, or Fellow.

Florey was never the man to wear his heart on his sleeve, and we have no evidence of what his inner feelings were when he first set foot in Queen's as Provost, but certainly a measure of pride and satisfaction can reasonably be inferred. Virtually nothing of the original fourteenth-century foundation building survives and what now strikes the eye is a magnificant building in the classico-baroque style. It is mainly the work of Nicholas Hawksmoor, who assisted Wren—another early President of the Royal Society—in the rebuilding of St. Paul's in London, and Vanbrugh at Castle Howard and Blenheim Palace. The library is one of the finest in Oxford, with wood carvings attributed to Grinling Gibbons, though probably executed by a local craftsman. The College was wealthy enough to maintain an elegant setting for the buildings: well-trimmed formal lawns in the two quadrangles contrasting with the roses and less severe flowerbeds of the Nun's Garden, near some old buildings in a more homely domestic form of architecture, and the Provost's private garden. It was a self-governing community of scholars with some 300 students in residence. If Florey were given to family pride, which he was not, he might have reflected that it was a far cry from the bootmaker's cottage at Bampton, a dozen miles from Oxford, to the splendid Provost's Lodgings in The Queen's College—a transformation effected in only two generations, via the Antipodes.

He was soon to find, however, that general support for his election did not imply support for him in office. He quickly discovered that some Fellows' reputations for quarrelsome disputation were well founded and there ensued a period of considerable frustration. In particular, he found that the committee system set up by Franks was not being used to advantage. Recommendations carefully worked out in committee were questioned when they came before the governing body, who might then proceed to discuss the whole issue afresh. At times, the governing body was split down the middle. He found a fellow-sufferer in Janet Vaughan, Principal of Somerville, who had a great admiration for him. Together they brooded over the mystery of why governing bodies appointed Heads of Houses—presumably because they had a high opinion of their qualities and some personal regard for them—and then proceeded to treat them badly.

The reality of the phenomenon is so well established that passing comment on it is appropriate. The reason seems to lie in the fact that dons are in the nature of things individualistic. They are mischievously given to arguing practical issues at length on intellectual grounds but reluctant to commit themselves finally to a particular course of corporate action. All this can provide endless opportunities for delay and may exasperate a man like Florey who liked to see things happening quickly. He used to complain that the Fellows were 'too clever', meaning that they enjoyed displaying mental agility for its own sake rather than to achieve a useful purpose.

It has been said that Florey's difficulties with his governing body were due to his failure to understand them, but this can be no more than a partial truth. He had, after all, worked with academics all his life and Lincoln College had been almost a second home to him for 25 years. He had had ample opportunity to observe at first hand the devious workings of the academic mind and the technique of college politics. He got off to a bad start by implying at the first meeting at which he presided—he merely sat in on the first two or three—that he had heard the Fellows had a reputation for being a quarrelsome lot, but he hoped he would see none of it. When he complained that he had never experienced such difficulties with the Royal Society or other bodies he had chaired he was not really comparing like with like. As President of the Royal Society he was dealing with fellow-scientists with a common sense of purpose; as he used to put it, 'I can do business with them'. In Queen's, scientists were in a minority and there was much less unity, and there were certianly some members who were deliberately overbearing and obstructive, and occasionally intemperate. Initially, he made the mistake of trying to run the governing body like a University department.

For health reasons, Florey tried as far as possible to avoid being drawn into contentious arguments; as a younger man he might have controlled his unruly team more effectively. As it was, he tended as time went on to—as he said—'sit back and let their ravings sweep over me'. When he did go on the offensive, with something of his old fire, his words were often too abrasive. Even supposing it were true, no governing body would like being told that 'not one of you sitting round this table could run a fish-and-chip shop'.[3]

Florey's lack of confidence in his colleagues led him to seek outside advice, often without prior consultation. This, too, was sometimes a source of trouble, especially as for Florey, himself standing near the pinnacle of affairs, it was natural to turn to authorities far higher than those the College would normally seek or were really appropriate to the task in hand. Thus he turned to Sir George Taylor, Director of Kew Gardens, for advice on the management of the College gardens; gardens were always a delight to him when he could find the time to spend in them. When there was a deficit on catering, which ultimately proved to be due to a dishonest chef, the firm of Lyons was consulted. He complained about bad ventilation—'In my animal house the air is changed every four minutes; I shouldn't think in here it has been changed in four hours'—and called in experts from the Building Research Laboratory. The latter produced a scheme which proved elaborate and unworkable, and eventually the problem had to be taken in hand by the Clerk of Works in the College, as it normally should have been at the outset.

Undoubtedly, the first six months of Florey's Provostship were difficult ones for all concerned. Equally, there is no doubt that once the preliminary skirmishing was over, and the dust had settled, a much more harmonious relationship was established. The most convincing evidence of this is that as he approached the retiring age of 70, the governing body invited him to continue for another three years and were ready to amend the byelaws to enable him to do so. Other evidence is provided by the constructive changes that were introduced during his time. These were mainly of two kinds: the reconstruction of existing accommodation and the building of new, and improvement of the facilities and scope for young graduates. One historically interesting change was that Whildate Farm at Castleford, Yorkshire, was sold to the local borough for housing and recreational development. It was the last territorial link with the eighteenth-century benefaction of Lady Elizabeth Hastings, which up to that time had provided 661 scholarships and 48 Exhibitions for Queensmen.

On the building side there were two urgent needs: to catch up heavy arrears of repairs and maintenance of existing buildings, and overall substantially to increase the college accommodation. In Florey's first year the first part of this programme had an interesting consequence. In order to lay pipes it was necessary to open up the crypt of the chapel, and this revealed seven coffins and chests, one labelled 'Reliquae Fundatoris', presumably the earthly remains of Robert de Eglesfield. In 1964 there was more work of repair, restoration, and maintenance than had ever before been undertaken in a single year. In particular, the cleaning of the stonework was begun, assisted by a grant from the Historic Buildings Fund, launched as a national appeal by the University.

Meanwhile, however, a major programme had been formulated to extend the College's accommodation so that every undergraduate could spend at least two years in residence. This involved three projects. Firstly, College property in the High Street on the other side of Queen's Lane was to be developed to provide accommodation for 52 men; a decision on this had already been taken in principle. Secondly, a large new building was to be put up on a site on the Cherwell in St. Clements, some half a mile away; this was Florey's own concept. It was to accommodate three Fellows and 74 men. Finally, an old student hostel in the Iffley Road was to be converted into flats for married graduates and staff housing. It was an ambitious programme, especially in view of the fact that in the previous few years some £250000 had been spent on internal expansion and improvement. The cost, not counting the purchase of the Cherwell site, was put at £500000. This was quite beyond the College's resources and the bulk of it had to be supported by an appeal directed to old members of the College, to industry, and to charitable foundations. By the end of 1967 £44 000 had been raised and Florey himself had been a successful fundraiser—an activity with which he had long been familiar. In particular, with the help of Isaiah Berlin who went to New York on behalf of Wolfson College, he secured the promise of $220 000 from the Ford Foundation provided the College matched it. To his great disappointment, however, the Nuffield Foundation made no contribution.

Florey did not live to see the completion of this programme; ironically, he died on the very day that work was scheduled to begin on the Cherwell site. Although he paid great attention to the architect's plans, no doubt mindful of his experiences in the building of the John Curtin School in Canberra, the building might well have been a disappointment to him, as it was to many. The design had been entrusted to James Stirling, a internationally famous architect noted for his controversial style. It was, however, not without support in university circles. He was responsible for the Engineering Laboratory at Leicester University, then nearing completion: for this he gained the Reynolds Award in the United States. He was also engaged in the construction of the History Faculty building in Cambridge. His extensive use of glass and red tiles was not to everybody's taste; the new building was unkindly likened to the Palm House at Kew—'more windows than wall'. Nevertheless, Stirling himself viewed it with pride and chose it as one of three examples of his work exhibited at the Museum of Modern Art in New York in 1969 and for years students and young architects came to view it. Whatever his views might have been about its appearance, Florey is permanently identified with the new building; when it was formally opened in 1971 it was named after him and stands as a lasting memorial.

The prior development of the Queen's Lane Annexe was on much more conventional lines, and is regarded as a very successful adaptation of old buildings—preserving the High Street façade unchanged—to modern needs. Florey took a keen interest in it, and worked closely with Norman Wild, Clerk of Works. It stands immediately adjacent to St. Edmund Hall, the last and longest-lived of the ancient academical halls associated with the University. For centuries it had had a close association with Queen's, the governing body of which had the right to appoint the Principal up to 1937. The Principal at the time of the conversion—the Reverend John Kelly—had an alarming experience in the course of the work. An unexploded 18 lb shell dating from the First World War was uncovered close to the wall of his lodgings, and proved to have a timing device in its nose. It was safely removed and taken to Angel Meadow to be exploded, but this was stopped by Magdalen College. It was eventually disposed of on corporation land near Donnington Bridge; how it came to the place in which it was found was never discovered.

Surveying the Oxford scene in the 1960s, and reflecting on his own experiences, Florey concluded that the most pressing need was to attract young graduates from Europe for short-term study and research:

These students will bring an intellectual stimulus and a valuable insight into continental attitudes and ways of thought to members of the College at all levels, and they themselves will acquire some knowledge of English life so that when they return to their own countries they will furnish a reinforcement to the international goodwill and understanding which we all so much desire.[4]

Thus was born the College's European Studentship scheme, modelled on the Rhodes Scholarships which had played so crucial a role in his own career. Concurrently, he pursued a similar line with the Royal Society (p. 42). Briefly, it was designed to provide support for some twenty graduates from eleven western European countries, including Scandinavia. Initially the stipend was £1100 p.a., normally for two years, a very adequate sum in the late 1960s. Sadly, Florey died before he could welcome the first of the students in 1969, but at the time of his death funds for nine studentships had been granted: four from the Ford Foundation, four from the Leverhulme Trust—where he had a friend at court in the person of his old friend at Lincoln, Lord Murray, Chairman of the Trust—and one from Robert Maxwell of Pergamon Press. Shortly afterwards other pledges were made: by the Volkswagen Foundation, the Wellcome Trust, the Royal Bank of Sweden, the Agnelli Foundation of Turin, and the Rothermere Foundation. After Florey's death, J. O. Prestwich energetically took up the appeal where he had left off. The effect on the College was all that Florey could have hoped for. In 1973 the Middle Common Room—in which he took a special interest, as at Lincoln—reported: 'The Florey European Studentships . . . have had a most remarkable impact on the MCR, which must be one of the most cosmopolitan places in Oxford'. Most of the original supporters of the scheme promised support for five years but as the covenants expired it became increasingly difficult, in the depressed economic circumstances pertaining from the mid-1970s, to obtain renewed support; by the end of the decade funds were almost exhausted. Nevertheless, the achievement up to 1980 had been impressive: 76 awards had been made for the study of subjects including the physical and biological sciences, theology, classics, and oriental studies. Between them the Florey students had written about 15 books and published 250 articles in learned journals. Lord Blake, Florey's successor as Provost, rightly praised the scheme as showing 'a characteristic touch of genius'. This is true, but it also showed the other side of his nature: a dogged determination to conjure up support for projects in which he believed.

In the 1960s there was a good deal of concern in Oxford about accommodating within the collegiate system senior graduates engaged in teaching and research in the University who were not Fellows of Colleges. Halifax House in South Parks Road—almost exactly opposite the Sir William Dunn School of Pathology—had been founded in 1947 as a social centre for graduate students, but lacked the intimacy of the Common Rooms of the Colleges, which were urged to stretch their facilities a good deal. Queen's responded to this need in 1964 by electing three additional Official Fellows (one in biochemistry, one in zoology, and one in Russian). In the following year a fourth Official Fellow was appointed, in psychology.

The University of Oxford can fairly be described as a monument to the farsighted liberality of past benefactors and it is easy to lose sight of the fact that the Robert de Eglesfields of the past have their modern counterparts. In the postwar years it was gaining more elbow-room by the foundation of new colleges, mostly for postgraduates. These include Nuffield College, for social studies (founded 1937, but not incorporated until 1958); St. Antony's, for modern subjects (1948); St. Cross (1965) and Wolfson (1966). With the last of these Florey was closely, though only briefly, associated.

Wolfson College owes much to the genius of Sir Isaiah Berlin, a distinguished philosopher, recognized as one of the most powerful intellects of the day and as a man of immense energy and resource. It began life in 1965 as Iffley College, so-called because a vacant site at Iffley was thought to be suitable; today it occupies a magnificent new building, on the site of J. S. Haldane's old home, on the banks of the Cherwell, not far upstream from the Florey Building of Queen's. Like Florey, Berlin was a persuasive fund raiser and succeeded in gaining massive support from the Wolfson and Ford Foundations. These benefactions were formally accepted by the University on 26 July 1966, and Berlin was appointed first President of the new college. Until it received its charter of incorporation, responsibility for administration was vested in the Wolfson College Trust, and Florey was asked to be the first Chairman of the Trustees. Others, besides Berlin, included Dame Janet Vaughan and Sir Isaac Wolfson, Chairman of Great Universal Stores. Florey's responsibility was brief, however. The first meeting was held at Universal House in London on 16 March 1967; just a year later the fifth meeting recorded his death and paid tribute to his work for Wolfson College and the Trust. When the new college was formally opened in 1974 by the Chancellor of the University, Mr. Harold Macmillan, Sir Isaiah Berlin recalled Florey's contribution:

We are fortunate in the Wolfson College Trust. Lord Florey was not only a man of genius, but practical and kind, and he did a great deal for us in every way.

In the early days at Queen's, Florey naturally looked for, and found, support among the scientific Fellows, but there were soon changes. J. L. Harley's achievement as a botanist was recognized by his election to the Fellowship of the Royal Society in 1964. In the following year he was appointed Professor of Botany at Sheffield, though he was soon back in Oxford, as Professor of Forest Science; this, however, was associated with St. John's. Jack Linnett, who had been actively concerned in Florey's appointment, went off to Cambridge in 1965 as Professor of Physical Chemistry. He had a distinguished career there, becoming Master of

Sidney Sussex College in 1970 and serving as Vice-Chancellor 1973-75. Tragically, he died suddenly shortly afterwards, at the height of his powers, at the early age of 62. Linnett had been elected to the Royal Society as early as 1955 and thus for a brief period in 1964-65 no less than four active members of the governing body were Fellows of that august body—Florey himself (President), Temple, Linnett, and Harley. Additionally, Sydney Chapman, Temple's predecessor as Professor of Natural Philosophy, was still associated with the College as Emeritus Fellow; he had been elected Fellow of the Royal Society in 1919. This was a rare distinction for one college, though the non-scientific Fellows seem not to have been greatly impressed. Carter retired in 1965, but Temple did not reach retiring age until 1968. Chilver departed in 1964, to take up an appointment as Professor of Classical Studies in the new University of Kent at Canterbury; like Carter, he retained his contact with the College as Emeritus Fellow. All these vacancies were, of course, filled in due course but new relationships had to be forged.

While his colleagues were gaining honours, so too—in rapid succession—was Florey. In the New Years Honours of 1965 he was created a Life Peer and elected to take the title of Baron Florey of Adelaide and Marston. In April he was formally introduced into the House of Lords, sponsored by Lord Cottesloe, Margaret Jennings' brother, and Lord Adrian, a recent predecessor as President of the Royal Society, whose peerage was one of the last hereditary ones to be granted. While he appreciated the honour, he had no great opinion of the Lords as an institution, regarding it as essentially a talking-shop; if he had points to make, he believed he could make them more usefully nearer to the scene of action. Apart from this, his gradually increasing angina made it necessary for him to apportion his energies carefully. This was perhaps a pity, for speeches in the Lords can carry much weight, and by that time he had the experience and self-assurance to make an effective contribution however intimidating the surroundings. In this he differed sharply from Adrian, who attended frequently and made a dozen speeches. Later in the same year he achieved a much rarer distinction; the Birthday Honours List announced that the Order of Merit had been conferred upon him. The Order—founded in 1902 as a special distinction for emient men and women, and in the personal gift of the Monarch—is strictly limited to 24 at any given time; interestingly, Lord Franks, one of his predecessors as Provost, was similarly honoured in 1977.

Traditionally, the Oxford colleges are religious foundations and college life centred round the chapel, although some of the most recent foundations disdain this amenity. In the case of Queen's, one of the oldest of all, its importance was unquestioned. The chapel is very fine and the ceiling of the apse was decorated by James Thornhill, regarded as the greatest of the English baroque painters. The screen is the work of Grinling Gibbons. As an agnostic, the chapel services meant nothing to Florey but, unlike some contemporary scientists, he was not aggressive in his disbelief. He accepted that as Provost he ought sometimes to appear in chapel and to begin with he was quite happy to read a lesson on the first Sunday of term. He seems to have given this up only when it was gently hinted to him that—judged at least by the high standards of ecclesiastical performance in Oxford—he was not a particularly good reader. He was certainly not indifferent, however, to the beauty of the building and its decoration nor to the music and choristry.

Surprisingly, perhaps, he formed an excellent relationship with the Chaplain, David Jenkins, now Professor of Theology at Leeds University. They were happy to keep to their own sphere of influence and each recognized the efficiency of the other in his own field. Indeed, Florey was so impressed that he persuaded him to take on the job of Domestic Bursar, flattering him outrageously, as Jenkins has acknowledged, by saying that he was the only man on the governing body with 'a scientific approach to things'. It was a brave acceptance, for in Oxford colleges bursars, too, are notoriously favourite victims of governing bodies. Thus they could console each other, as Jenkins recalls:

After one meeting the Provost and I met to gather up the pieces on various items of business and he was somewhat depressed. I told him that although Original Sin rarely took on original forms it was remarkable how diversified and ubiquitous it could be in meetings of the Governing Body.[5]

The Provost's duties included much entertaining both formal and informal, and a major occasion of this kind occurred early in Florey's term of office. By ancient custom, the College petitions each new Queen consort to become its Patroness. On Florey's initiative, Queen Elizabeth the Queen Mother was invited to visit the College on 6 June 1963. It was a day memorable both for the occasion and the glorious weather. Ethel, whose health made it increasingly difficult for her to carry out social functions, was well enough to stand by Howard at the official reception in the Provost's Lodgings. She never failed to do her best, and only a few days before her death in 1966 had welcomed Fellows and their wives to the annual dinner held at the beginning of the Michaelmas Term. For the most part, however, both as President of the Royal Society and Provost of Queen's Florey had to attend, and often conduct, social occasions on his own. Fortunately, by this time in his career he could carry off efficiently and urbanely any occasion, however grand, though never without well concealed inner misgivings until all was over.

After the initial sparring with some of his new colleagues, a mutually satisfactory *modus vivendi* was established and he certainly had no reason to feel that he had made a fatal error. Nevertheless, the reasons why he accepted the Provostship in the first place still remain a matter for speculation. According to his own statement, it was simply because the Provostship would give him an assured income for longer than his professorship would; from the latter he would have had to retire at the age of sixty-seven, which he would have reached in 1965. He was not a man without sentiment but he very much disliked displaying it, and it would be quite in keeping for him to offer such a mundane explanation to conceal higher motives. Nevertheless, it is an explanation that should not be dismissed too lightly. Ethel's health was deteriorating and he had to face the very real prospect that he would have for some considerable time to make provision for an invalid wife. Moreover, although he put a brave face on it to the outside world his own health was a matter of growing concern. While he well knew that the likelihood was that he would succumb suddenly to a major heart attack in the not too distant future, he himself might have to face a period of serious incapacity, with all its financial implications. We may certainly take it, therefore, that the purely financial aspect was an important consideration. Additionally the College must have beckoned as a quiet haven in which he could peacefully, yet usefully, spend his time when his arduous term of office as President of the Royal Society expired in 1965. Yet it is hard to suppose that there was not more to it than this. Florey liked to measure risks rather than to evade them and the prospect of mere comfortable survival would not have been in keeping with his character. To some extent, he must have gone to Queen's because it offered a professional challenge as well as a new way of life. The Sir William Dunn School of Pathology still flourished, but the days of high excitement were past: he had been there for nearly 30 years and the stimulus of doing something quite different must have appealed strongly to him. Certainly, his achievements at Queen's were not those of a man whose main interest was a quiet and comfortable retirement. It is remarkable that throughout his time there he retained his laboratory in the Department of Physiology and steadily pursued his research with the aid of an able young technician.

12

EPILOGUE

The Presidency of the Royal Society is both prestigious and arduous and Florey must have been relieved to hand over the office to Blackett in November 1965. However, the relief was relative rather than absolute; he still lived an energetic life that would have taxed a younger and fitter man. In particular, he still had the Provostship of Queen's and a new, and much happier, relationship with the Australian National University. Although he was no longer responsible for running the Sir William Dunn School of Pathology, he had the use of an electron microscope—a powerful and then still comparatively new research tool—with which to pursue his own particular lines of research. He published half a dozen more research papers on atherosclerosis and the endothelium. He was still in demand as a lecturer and in the period 1966-68 gave the Roy Cameron Lecture to the College of Pathologists; the Frederick Price Lecture to the Royal College of Physicians of Edinburgh; and the Harveian Lecture to the Harveian Society. In 1967 he became a Trustee of the British Museum and was also appointed Chairman of the Trustees of the newly founded Wolfson College in Oxford (p. 361). He maintained an active contact with the Royal Society through a committee set up to review national policy on the support of biological research and a Population Study Group. This last reflected his long interest in demography, quickened by his awareness of the effect of penicillin and other new medical advances on the rate of growth of world population, especially in the developing countries. On the same basis he accepted in 1967 the Presidency of the Family Planning Association; his interest in birth control went back to the papers he had published with H. M. Carleton in 1931. In pursuing these varied interests he had to contend with a steady deterioration in his own health. Additionally, Ethel's health was a matter of growing concern. She, too, had heart trouble and respiratory difficulties. It speaks much for her determination that she kept going at all, visiting America in 1965 to lecture, and then going on to Australia to visit her sister. When Howard was first appointed at Queen's she had joined him in the Provost's Lodging but soon moved out to the quiet of their house in Old Marston.

In the spring of 1966 she made her last journey abroad, this time to the Fulton's house in New Haven, to attend her son's wedding. Charles was then working with the WHO Serum Bank at Yale and he was engaged to Sue Hopkins, an English girl also working in that part of America; in the circumstances it was natural that he should be married from the Fulton's house, for he had come to look on them very much as second parents. Unfortunately, this occasion was a cause for dissention. Howard entreated her not to go in her the very precarious state of health; apart from doing herself serious, perhaps fatal, harm she might well prove a burden to others. In spite of this, she had her way and in the event there were no immediate dire consequences.

Nevertheless, Howard's fears were not unfounded. On 9 October he had invited several important guests for dinner at Queen's, as a preliminary to a discussion of some current scientific business; it was his practice to use the facilities of the Lodgings for his Royal Society work—entertaining people there individually or in small groups. Just before they arrived he was called to the telephone. Briefly, he explained to Jack Harley—who had come down from Sheffield for the meeting and had been staying with him over the weekend—that he had been called urgently to Marston and asked him to act as host in his place. Later in the evening he returned and told Harley privately that Ethel had died. To the others he said nothing, though he was clearly shaken, and proceeded with the discussion for which he had called them together; not until late at night did they learn what had happened. For this, Florey has sometimes been held to have been heartless, but—bearing in mind his extreme reserve about personal matters—the episode is surely not in itself evidence of this. Common experience unhappily provides countless examples of private grief having to be subdued to immediate obligations. It was wholly in keeping with both his strong sense of duty and his lifelong trait of not displaying his emotions—which is very different from not feeling them.

As has been recorded in an earlier chapter, the first phase of Florey's connection with the Australian National University had ended tempestuously with Ennor's visit to Oxford in the spring of 1957, charged with making a final appeal to him to become Director of the John Curtin School. Nevertheless, when the dust settled a different and happier relationship began to be forged. On 27 March 1958 he formally opened the School in the presence of more than a thousand guests, including the then Prime Minister, Mr. R. G. Menzies. Earlier, honorary degrees had been conferred on him and on Sir Norman Gregg, a distinguished Australian ophthalmic surgeon. In his opening address Ennor paid unqualified tribute to Florey, as though no harsh words had ever passed between them. Florey replied gracefully in kind, praising the architects and builders; the contributions that would be made to medicine by clinicians, as represented by Sir Norman Gregg; the support of Prime Ministers of different political persuasions. Nevertheless, moderately but firmly he returned to an old theme; Australia should not be complacent and imagine that scientists would beat a track to her door:

Australia, in the minds of the world in general, is associated with wide open spaces, very large cities, fierce soldiers, horse racing, poor hotels, excellent air services, marvellous tennis players, and at the moment, of course, not quite so marvellous cricketers. But, generally speaking, Australia is not immediately associated with vigorous intellectual activity. . . . But things are changing, and today we are celebrating an event which I am sure will go down as a landmark in the endeavours of Australia to foster experimental science. . . . The School will have to contend for a long time to come with the pull on young men to go for post-graduate training to the great centres which exist and are rapidly multiplying in the United States and which exist in Europe. If it is to attract and hold the best people, it will need not only to be good but it must be superlatively good, just like the building about to be opened.[1]

When so many guests had been invited from a distance it was sad that Gordon Sanders was not included among them. In their addresses both Ennor and Florey went out of their way to praise his contribution to the design of the building, but he always felt the omission keenly.

The Opening Day concluded with a dinner at University House. From many accounts, it is clear that Florey was in particularly good form, relaxed and wholly at his ease among those who might have been his working colleagues. Thus what could have been a somewhat strained occasion passed off splendidly.

No doubt this clear evidence of lack of rancour contributed to a later development. In 1965 Sir John Cockcroft—distinguished atomic physicist and Nobel Laureate—relinquished the Chancellorship, to which he had been appointed in 1961. The Council then invited Florey to become his successor, an invitation which he accepted with real pleasure.

This appointment necessitated a special visit to Canberra so that he could be formally installed as Chancellor. Ethel was invited to accompany him but in view of her health this was not judged sensible. The arrangements were made with Hohnen, the Registrar, and it was agreed that Florey should arrive in Canberra on 4 July, giving him two full days' rest before the ceremony, a point on which he was insistent. He was to leave again in September. While he was there a farewell dinner was organized for Eccles, who was going to the Institute of Biomedical Research in Chicago. Ennor was the host and most of the senior members of the John Curtin School were there. It was a memorable occasion, with no hint of dissent, and Florey was entirely relaxed and happy.

An amusing office memo relating to this visit has somehow got caught up in the Florey archive. Some member of the Chancellery staff had raised the question of insuring him for the homeward journey;

Should we insure him for $14 000 as for members of staff in general? Or for $100 000, as for the Vice-Chancellor? Or as he is not strictly a 'member of staff' should we not insure him at all?

Against this third alternative somebody firmly pencilled 'not at all'. On this occasion Margaret Jennings joined him in Canberra to collaborate in some research he had planned to do in the John Curtin School; they made a leisurely (and safe) return journey via Hong Kong, Japan, and Honolulu.

He was in correspondence with Hohnen again early in 1967, about a further visit as Chancellor in the spring of that year. Advancing years had done nothing to acclimatize him to the Oxford winter, nor eased his financial problems:

I've had a bad month, first nearly three weeks of vomiting and diarrhoea ('gastric flu') and now a filthy cold which caused me to cancel this week's engagements. . . . I should be glad if I could get the travel agency to send the bill to you as I've just been severely depleted by the tax gatherer.

This time he was to arrive in the latter part of March and stay for a month. One sentence in the letter to Hohnen is revealing. He remarks apologetically that he will be arriving on Easter Saturday and hopes this will not be a bother; he can easily get to University House on his own. This was not false modesty; to whatever heights he rose he never expected others to do for him what he could realistically do for himself.

The day after his arrival he wrote home to Margaret Jennings, and his letter shows how serious was the illness he still so stoically concealed from the world:

I am afraid my optimism received a terrible blow on arriving at Sydney, for I had a most frightful attack almost as soon as I set foot on the ground . . . I staggered through customs—very easy and no long distance to walk. I felt so bad on arriving at the hotel that I asked for a wheel-chair and was eventually carried up to my room where I was firm enough to say that in no case did I want a doctor. After sitting still for half an hour things began to get better and I got into bed and with the aid of much dope had an unconscious night.[2]

This severe attack was not enough to delay him and he went on to Canberra to fulfil his full programme as Chancellor. Half a dozen other letters home to Margaret Jennings contain many interesting comments about developments in Canberra and about their personal relationship.

On this occasion he met Ennor on a footing different from that of the past. He had just relinquished his position as Dean of the John Curtin School—supposedly because after having served for three years as Deputy Vice-Chancellor he was not appointed Vice-Chancellor in succession to Sir Leonard Huxley—and been appointed Secretary to the Commonwealth Department of Education and Science. He dined with Ennor, his Minister, and several senior civil servants and they discussed scientific organization. The Minister he dismissed as 'very opinionated—perhaps you have to be to be a Minister'. The Vice-Chancellor designate was Sir John Crawford, Director and Professor of Economics in the Research School of Pacific Studies. Florey spent the best part of a day with him discussing University business at the end of his visit. Clearly he had no regrets about having finally turned down the Directorship of the John Curtin School, an appointment which was about to be discussed amid what he called 'a tremendous hoo-ha': 'I don't believe people here realise it is not a job that would hold much attraction for a good scientist'.[3]

But the real interest of these letters is the warmth and plans for the future that pervades them, and the reason for this is that at last there is the possibility of marriage and permanent companionship. Howard confesses unashamedly to boredom at the general Canberra scene, but sees how different it will be when they can survey it together. Sadly, this was not to be. On 12 February in the following year he wrote his last letter to Canberra, again addressed to Hohnen:

I suppose the time is coming when I shall have to make some arrangements for coming out to Australia. . . . I have just received an invitation to attend the Tenth Quinquennial Congress of the Association of Commonwealth Universities in Sydney. I do not know whether the University would like me to go to that or not, but perhaps I could go down to Sydney to represent them on one or two days. . . . I have also been rung up by Lord Todd who tells me that Birch has asked him to open the Chemistry Laboratory and has suggested that it would be a good thing for the Chancellor to be present. . . . I wonder if you would be kind enough to let me know what the programme is likely to be for the end of July, August and the beginning of September. I hope this will be convenient to you and I hope to be accompanied by my wife.

A stark pencilled note at the bottom of this letter in the Canberra files records 'died 22 Feb. 1968' (a date which is in fact incorrect by one day, doubtless due to the time difference between Britain and Australia). Thus ended a close relationship with the University that had endured for nearly quarter of a century. It had certainly had its ups and downs, and there is no doubt that Florey had gone through long periods of frustration and disenchantment in which he nearly severed the connection altogether. That he did not do so is a measure of his basic devotion—both sentimentally as a loyal Australian and practically as an academic anxious to make a success of a unique opportunity—to the concept of the Australian National University. It must be acknowledged, too, that over the years the University had to exercise much patience in its dealings with a younger and more impatient Florey.

Among the Florey papers is a single photostated page from a book, with the section headline 'The Smiling Chancellor'. It is in fact from Martin Gilbert's official life of Winston Churchill and

it quotes Lord Winterton's reflections on a speech by Churchill
as Chancellor of the Exchequer when presenting his Budget in the
1920s:

The remarkable thing about him is the way in which he has suddenly
acquired, quite late in his Parliamentary life, an immense fund of tact,
patience, good humour and banter on almost all occasions; no one used
to 'suffer fools ungladly' more fully than Winston, now he is friendly
and accessible to everyone. . . .'

The provenance of this slip of paper is uncertain, but the parallel
is apt. In spite of all that had gone before, it is as a smiling Chancellor that Florey is remembered in Canberra.

In the 1960s he was very conscious of living literally on bor-
rowed time. The severe attack he suffered in Sydney was only
one of many before and after. A fortnight after Ethel's death he
made a new will, and to this he pinned a brief note to be given in
due time to Margaret Jennings: 'I have made the will to which
this is attached in the supposition that I shall die quite soon . . . I
am sorry you will have so much to do'. Their relationship over
the years had left neither in any doubt that ultimate happiness
was to be found in marriage, when all could be shared, and the
strains of living independent lives put behind them. It was only
Howard's strong sense of duty that now caused him any misgivings; marriage when death might strike literally at any moment
was not lightly to be entered into. However, a period of remission
persuaded him that the step was thinkable and when he left for
Canberra in the following March it was privately understood between them that they would be married soon after his return.
Oliphant, expected in England in June, might be their first
visitor at the Provost's Lodging, he wrote. It may well be,
however, that he was strongly tempted to quit all his responsibilities and spend what time was left to him in the peace and
quiet of his charming house and garden at Old Marston. One of
his earliest letters from Australia included the significant sentence 'Perhaps I really am a fool to have Queen's round my
neck'. This is probably not so much indicative of disenchantment with Queen's—with whom his relations were by then much
happier—as of a readiness to surrender himself entirely to the
domestic bliss that had so long eluded him.

The wedding took place on 6 June 1967 at the Old Register

Office in St. Giles; they were both anxious to avoid any sort of press publicity, and for this reason, the arrangements were made quietly by Florey's solicitor, Mr. F. R. Williamson. The wedding was as quiet as the law permits—the only other people present were Jim Kent and Cecilia Little, Margaret's housekeeper, who had been asked to be witnesses. Afterwards they all went back to Queen's for a quiet celebration with a few of their closest colleagues from the laboratory in the garden of the Lodgings.

During this period of growing ill-health he lost nothing of his zest for research, remarking that 'there are so many things one could do!' Only two or three weeks before his death he carried out some delicate operations on mice to dissect the carotids. Kent recalls that he had still lost none of his old skill and steadiness of hand. It is pleasant to record that Kent's long years of technical assistance, which so admirably complemented Florey's own experimental skill, were acknowledged by the University of Oxford by the award of an honorary degree of Master of Arts in 1978.

All too briefly life at the Provost's Lodgings was transformed. Florey now had a loving companion and confidante always by his side. By instinct a cheerful and forthcoming host, he now had a congenial hostess to entertain with him. Even the dark hours, when he had attacks of severe pain, were lightened; if they occured in the daytime his perceptive wife could steer the conversation away from him while he waited for relief. But on one Wednesday in February 1968 relief did not come. On 21 February he suffered so severe an attack that for the first time he stayed in bed and during the afternoon Margaret was sent for urgently. Quietly they decided between themselves that he should not go to hospital but be nursed at home; their desire above all was not to be separated by strangers. He was, however, beyond recovery and died that same day. The funeral service was in the church of St. Nicholas just across the road from his house in Old Marston, but many more than were able to attend this wanted to pay their tribute to his memory. Their opportunity was provided later by a Memorial Service at Westminster Abbey, attended by hundreds.

A memorial tablet to Sir Christopher Wren, architect of St. Paul's Cathedral and third President of the Royal Society, reads *Si monumentum requiris, circumspice* ('If you would see his monument, look around'). In a wider sense, these words would be an appropriate epitaph for Florey, for by the time of his death there was virtually no part of the world in which the use of penicillin had not become a normal feature of medical practice. In his later years the social consequence of this development preoccupied him greatly. For a physician the saving of life is of paramount importance, but yet it had to be acknowledged that life saving on the scale that penicillin made possible was not an unmixed blessing; in many parts of the world it was already leading, along with other medical advances, to an explosive growth of population greater than local resources could sustain. This posed a moral dilemma which had been succinctly stated by A. V. Hill in his Presidential Address to the British Association for the Advancement of Science in 1952:

The conquest of disease has led to a vast increase in the world's population. The result may be starvation, unrest and even the end of civilization. If ethical principals deny our right to do evil that good may happen, are we justified in doing good when the foreseeable consequence is evil? . . . The forces of good and evil depend not on the scientist but on the moral judgment of the whole community.

The introduction of penicillin into medical practice throughout the world is Florey's true and indestructible memorial, but there are others more tangible. In 1980—on 18 October, the day of St. Luke the Evangelist, patron saint of physicians and surgeons and also, appropriately, of artists—a memorial tablet was unveiled in the porch of the church of St. Nicholas in Marston. It was a moving service, with the address given by David Jenkins, the Chaplain of Queen's in whom Florey had found such a strong supporter (he was by then Professor of Theology in the University of Leeds). The beautiful parish church was filled with the music of Bach, which he loved, and the organist and choir were from the College.

Surprisingly, Florey had until then no national memorial but through an unexpected sequence of events this omission was made good in the following year. Among the Australian medical men who had made their name in London was Sir Neil Hamilton Fairley, a specialist on tropical diseases and a friend of Florey from Adelaide; he was elected Fellow of the Royal Society in 1942, a year after Florey. He died in 1966, after a long period of ill-health, but his two sons were both trained in medicine at

Oxford and one, Gordon, became a leading cancer specialist. Tragically, he was murdered in 1975 by the IRA in a bomb attack presumably directed at someone else and subsequently a memorial to him was placed in the crypt of St. Paul's Cathedral. By chance, this was located immediately above one to Fleming, whose ashes are buried there, and when she was visiting the crypt in 1980 Lady Hamilton Fairley suddenly realized that there was no comparable memorial to Florey in London. She sought the advice of an Australian friend there, Dr. C. J. Hackett, also an Adelaide graduate, who in turn consulted with Margaret Florey, Henry Harris, Edward Abraham, and Gwyn Macfarlane. With their backing the Dean of Westminster was approached and he gained the warm support of the Royal Society, the Australian National University, and the Australian Academy of Science. The proposal thus began to acquire a decidedly Australian flavour, and this was enhanced when the Dean's Verger suggested that the stone should be of marble from South Australia. At this stage chance took a hand, which Florey would no doubt have appreciated. Hackett went to see the Agent General for South Australia, who quite by chance happened to be opening that evening an exhibition of the work of Paul Trappe, a South Australian sculptor; as a result, Trappe was ultimately commissioned to engrave the stone according to a design by John Peters (Plate 18). Only a few days later the Premier of South Australia arrived in London and when he heard of the proposal at once undertook on behalf of his Government to provide the stone. The support of the South Australian Government would have been natural in any circumstances, but was doubtless enhanced by the fact that near the close of his life Florey had been offered the Governorship of the State. The Australian Government arranged carriage. All this naturally took time and as the unveiling ceremony was to take place on 2 November 1981 there was some anxiety among the organizers at delay in the arrival of the stone. However, it reached London safely on 26 October, conveyed by the Royal Australian Air Force.

The service in the Abbey was a great contrast to that in the little parish church at Marston, but none the less warm. Frank Fenner, formerly Director of the John Curtin School in Canberra and yet another Adelaide graduate, gave the Address[4] and the lessons were read by the Australian High Commissioner, R. V. Garland, and the President of the Royal Society, Sir Andrew Huxley. By a fortunate chance, Florey's old friend Pansy Wright, Chancellor of Melbourne University and now Sir R. Douglas Wright, was able to be in London at the time.

It was an occasion happily representative of Florey's life and interests. The simple memorial stone, 60 × 90 cm in size, was unveiled by Margaret Florey and a floral tribute was laid by his son Charles and grandson Daniel McMichael. It is placed close to those commemorating the astronomers John and William Herschel and the naturalist Charles Darwin, symbolic of the way in which Florey's research bridged the gap between the physical and the biological sciences. The wording is simple, but precisely defines his achievement: 'His vision, leadership and research made penicillin available to mankind'.

When made a life peer Florey took the title Baron Florey of Adelaide and Marston, the alpha and the omega of his life. The plaque at Marston is matched by a bronze head by John Davie near Prince Henry Gardens, Adelaide; there is also a portrait by Allan Gwynne-Jones in the University there. A portrait by the Adelaide artist William Dargie is proudly displayed in his old school, St. Peter's Collegiate.

With that of other Presidents, Florey's portrait—by Henry Carr—hangs in the rooms of the Royal Society. Finally, there is a portrait by Frederick Deane which was subscribed to by his past and present students and colleagues and hangs in the Sir William Dunn School of Pathology. He wrote a letter of thanks in characteristic vein:

I would like you all to know how much I valued your very kind and generous thought in having my portrait painted. I am told that it is very good and I can only hope that now it is hung in the Department its fierce expression doesn't intimidate my successors. . . . I am surprised in going round the world to find what a good reputation the laboratory has for doing real experimental pathology and for teaching the young people to have a dynamic outlook on the problems of medicine. This is not due to the efforts of any one person but is a reflection of how extremely fortunate I have been in having such good colleagues and helpers.

Other memorials perpetuate his name. In 1969 the Royal Society and the Australian National University raised by subscription a fund sufficient to endow Florey Fellowships to assist promising young postdoctoral scientists to do medical research, on a two-year basis, in Britain or Australia. This active encouragement of two-way academic traffic between Britain and Australia would certainly have been very warmiy approved by Florey. Howard Florey Lectures were established in 1981, to allow eminent scientists to give lectures, in alternative years, at universities in Australia and Britain. The first Lecturer was Sir Andrew Huxley, President of the Royal Society, who visited Australia in 1982; Frank Fenner was the second, coming to England in 1983. In Canberra, a Howard Florey Professorship was established in the John Curtin School, to be held by the Director; the first holder was Colin Courtice. The British drug industry endowed a Fellowship at Lady Margaret Hall; its first holder was Margaret Jennings. Buildings, too, have been named after him; the Florey Building of Queen's College, Oxford; the Howard Florey Institute in Melbourne; his former house in Sheffield, now a students' hall of residence. Sheffield gave him an honorary degree in 1960, and the Registrar had to make enquiries about a suitable robe. In passing it is interesting to note that Florey wrote back very precisely: 'I am 5′ 8¼″ tall and my hat size is 6¾'. There are Florey rooms in Lincoln College Library and in Wolfson College.

This association of his name with academic and learned bodies vindicates the opinion Mellanby had expressed in 1944, that scientific men throughout the world would correctly evaluate Florey's role in the development of penicillin and rightly rate it 'on a much higher level than that of Fleming'. It has done little, however, to establish his reputation in the eyes of the general public, who know little and care less about the inner workings of such august bodies as Oxford University and the Royal Society, and their sister bodies in the Antipodes. The issue of a banknote bearing his portrait in Australia (Plate 19) might have done something to redress the balance there, but unfortunately it is on a 50-dollar bill—a higher denomination than most Australians use even in these days of inflation; a straw poll carried out by the writer in 1981 showed that many had never even seen one. It is a sad fact that, for reasons already discussed, Florey's name is not identified in the public mind with the successful use of penicillin. No doubt he would have wished it otherwise but he was not the kind of man to repine over what might have been. Such a comment poses a final question—what kind of a man was Florey?

If we look at his life at a purely professional level it is clear that his strength lay in an unusually powerful combination of qualities. His intellectual ability was formidable, sufficient to enable him to do more than hold his own in any academic circles. But he himself had no illusions that this amounted to brilliance. All his life he moved in circles where clever men abounded, and he was quite ready to admit the superiority of others in the realm of abstract thought. But cleverness for its own sake did not attract him, and the intellectual virtuosity that tends to pervade conversation and debates in Oxbridge common rooms made no appeal to him; this was one of his problems at Queen's. For him knowledge was a means to an end, whether it be to advance scientific understanding still further or to achieve some practical objective. He once rounded savagely on a Fellow of Lincoln who was much given to decrying others, asking him bluntly what he had ever achieved that entitled him to be so disparaging. Yet he was a past master at displaying his own knowledge if the occasion arose, whether it was giving a lecture to a learned audience or presenting his case for the support of his research. A particularly important example was his initial exposé of the penicillin situation lasting nearly an hour, to Alan Gregg at the Rockefeller Foundation in New York in 1941. Of this Heatley has given the following account:

I remember him best of all for that performance—and he was so tired after that long journey. He was very lucid in the presentation of his facts, and fully explanatory. It was unemotional, but still very telling, and in a startling sort of way it revealed the wide grasp of his scientific mind. . . . I realized suddenly how great a man he was. None of us in the penicillin team could have matched him, and he was so clearly the leader. I count that hour in Gregg's office as one of the greatest experiences of my life.[5]

This was certainly Florey displaying his professional repertoire at its most impressive. In referring to him as the leader, Heatley touches on another important aspect of his character. He had great powers of leadership, but exercised them not by self-assertion but because he was positive and practical, the kind of man whom others instinctively turn to and follow. Implicit, too, in Heatley's comment is another important attribute, physical and mental stamina. He had an extraordinary capacity for steady application to the task in hand, whether it was prolonged delicate operations in the laboratory, as in the extirpation of lymph nodes; the preparation of detailed reports and research papers; or embarking on important discussions or a programme of experiments at the end of long and tiring journeys. A particular source of strength lay in his ability to keep several different activities going at the same time. He drove himself hard but he got the best and the most out of others by example rather than compulsion, and his keen and direct interest in the experimental work of his department. Among those who were fortunate enough to work with him the first-rate was regarded as the norm. As it was known, too, that he set a strong pace those to whom this was a disincentive rarely found a place with him. The essence of his research strategy was to build up a team whose diverse talents made it possible to attack a problem from various directions. Of necessity, this involved skills of which he himself had little or no knowledge, but once he was satisfied that a colleague knew what he was about, and was devoting himself to the task in hand, he interfered as little as possible. When he did venture a comment, it might sound diffident but was always very much to the point. He was punctilious in acknowledging contributions made by others, whether immediate colleagues or earlier workers in the same fields as his own. In his own personal research he not only had much manual skill in delicate work, but a remarkable knack of planning his programme so that the maximum information could be extracted from a particular experiment. He was very incisive, too, in getting under way; when visiting a strange laboratory he was ready to start work the day he arrived and fretted at delay.

Such an assessment of the sources of his professional success is not too difficult to make, for it is based—like scientific experiments—on observation and experience; most people would probably reach roughly the same conclusions. But the situation is very different when one attempts to evaluate his character at a more personal level, for two particular difficulties are at once encountered. The first is that, perhaps rather more so than with most people, his personality clearly changed considerably over the years; there is a world of difference between the young Florey

—impetuous and abrasive, fresh from Adelaide—making his way in the prewar years, and the urbane dignified figure who later emerged as President of the Royal Society, Provost of Queen's, and Chancellor of the Australian National University. To some extent, as has been argued earlier, this reflects deliberate restraint for the sake of his health; he knew that too much excitement was bad for his heart. No doubt it partly represents also the normal mellowing effect of age; in most people the zest for dispute commonly wanes with advancing years. Even so, the contrast between the young and the old Florey is very striking and the parallel with Winterton's recognition of a sea-change in Winston Churchill at about the same age is interesting.

The second difficulty lies in Florey's lifelong instinct to bottle up his emotions and conceal them from the world. This, again, is not unusual to some degree in many people but Florey carried it to such an extent that one is always doubtful about taking at face value the explanations he gives for some of his own major decisions. He was a master of the understatement; his instinct always was to offer some mundane reason even though in truth it was largely an emotional one. A particular instance was his acceptance, to everybody's surprise, of the Provostship of Queen's. He told his friends that it was because he could remain in salaried employment there longer than he could as a professor, but there was surely more to it than just that. It is hard to believe that it did not involve some agreeable sense of achievement, for in Oxford, where half his life was spent, to be Head of a House is no mean thing. He was not a man driven by ambition, and certainly not by ambition for material goods, but like any normal man he prized the successive distinctions that punctuated his passage through life, even though he did not go out of his way to seek them. He received them always with characteristic modesty. To one letter of congratulation on his receipt of the Order of Merit in 1965 he wrote in typical phraseology: 'I assure you one of the pleasures of the occasion is to know that one's friends are not engaged in low mutterings . . .'.

As is not uncommon, the fierce front and forbidding demeanour were in reality a protective shield to conceal a sensitive nature. Like all scientists, his professional interest was with things rather than people but throughout his life he derived great enjoyment from art in its various manifestations. He enjoyed ballet and opera and found in them a valuable source of relaxation. In his recollections of his wartime visit to Moscow visits to both loom large. At home, good recordings of classical music were a constant evening recreation throughout his life. Mozart was perhaps his greatest favourite and, largely missing the romantic period, stirring composers such as Berlioz and Prokofiev particularly appealed to him. Throughout his life his camera—both still and cine—was his constant companion and he used it skilfully. He always enjoyed good paintings but it was only comparatively late in life that he became a practitioner of the visual arts; as his interest in painting developed his interest in galleries turned increasingly to study the techniques of the masters, very much as he had built up his scientific techniques by losing no chance of working with those in the vanguard of progress. It would be wrong to exaggerate his knowledge and understanding of the arts but they were more than dilettante and —judged, of course, by amateur standards—his painting showed real talent.

Such pleasures were, of course, of an essentially personal nature, not necessarily shared with others. But it is wrong to suppose, as some have done, that Florey was not a man who—given a suitable opportunity—could relax and enjoy himself thoroughly in the company of other people. He was a popular member of the Lincoln College Common Room; that he was not equally so at Queen's can quite simply be attributed to the fact that there he had responsibilities as Provost, whereas at Lincoln he had none. In North Africa his military hosts clearly found him a particularly agreeable and forthcoming member of the mess. In Australia, Oliphant and others still remember relaxed and comfortable parties on the beach. At the Royal Society the Executive Secretary, Sir David Martin, often remarked on the exceptional easiness of their necessarily close business relationship. At the Australian National University—after the heat of battle had subsided and his obligations were largely formal—he became the smiling Chancellor. The explanation of the paradox—of which he was himself aware—is perhaps that he was a man who became absorbed in what he was doing; he worked hard and he played hard and found it difficult to achieve an intermediate stance.

Although the Nobel Prizes make their recipients famous overnight, Alfred Nobel himself was of a very retiring nature. On the subject of biographies he once wrote to his brother: 'Who has time to read biographical accounts? And who can be so simple or so good-natured as to be interested in them.' Grateful though he no doubt was for the generous benefaction of Nobel—with whom he had something in common in living an immensely energetic life despite the handicap of ill-health—it was doubtful whether Florey, despite his own modest view of his achievements, would have subscribed to this view. All through his life he had a keen interest in history which, like photography, added spice to his travels. He would have been more likely to have inclined to Carlyle's belief that history is the essence of innumerable biographies, and his modesty did not blind him to the fact that the introduction of penicillin into general medical practice had not only profoundly affected his own career but the course of history. Equally, he would have welcomed the fact that any account of his own life would of necessity have to record also the contributions of his colleagues, a matter always very much in his mind.

REFERENCES

In the preparation of this work many sources have been consulted and where appropriate cited in the main text and listed in the following pages. For the benefit of readers not familiar with standard abbreviations for scientific journals, conference proceedings, and so on—as given, for example, in the *World List of Scientific Periodicals*—most of these have been written out in full. Certain key sources, however, are frequently cited and to avoid lengthy repetition the titles of these have been shortened and only the page or file number quoted for precise identification. These shortened titles are as follows.

98HF. Florey archives lodged by Lady Florey with the Royal Society in London. They have been carefully and expertly catalogued and for the most part separated into folders in some 300 box files. The reference indicates first the number of the box file; second, the number of the folder within the box; and third the number of the individual item.

ANUHF. Florey archives lodged by Lady Florey with the Australian National University, Canberra. They relate almost entirely to his relationship with the ANU in general and the John Curtin School of Medical Research in particular. When consulted in 1981 they had not been catalogued but remained in parcels in their original files as dispatched from Oxford. The first reference number refers to the parcel; the second to the file within it.

CSA/EBC. Chain archives lodged by Lady Chain with the Contemporary Science Archives, Oxford. This material is mainly stored in folders in box files. The first number refers to the box file; the second to the folder within it.

MRC. Florey letters and papers in the archives of the Medical Research Council, London. The number is the file number.

Antibiotics. *Antibiotics*, by H. W. Florey, E. Chain, N. G. Heatley, M. A. Jennings, A. G. Sanders, E. P. Abraham, and M. E. Florey. Two volumes. Oxford University Press, London (1949). Continued as M. E. Florey *The clinical application of antibiotics*. Four volumes (1952-60).

Biographical Memoir. E. P. Abraham 'Howard Walter Florey' in *Biographical memoirs of Fellows of the Royal Society*, vol. 17, pp 255-302. Royal Society, London (1971).

Macfarlane. Gwyn Macfarlane, *Howard Florey, the making of a great scientist*. Oxford University Press, Oxford. (1979).

Bickel. Lennard Bickel, *Rise up to life: a biography of Howard Florey who made penicillin and gave it to the world.* Angus and Robertson, London (1972).

Symposium. John Parascandola (ed.) *The history of antibiotics: a symposium.* Held at Honolulu, 5 April 1979. American Institute of the History of Pharmacy, Madison, Wisconsin (1980).

Penicillin Production. Albert E. Elder (ed.) *The history of penicillin production. Chemical Engineering Progress Series,* no. 100, vol. 66, 1970. American Institute of Chemical Engineers, New York (1970).

Hare. Ronald Hare, *The birth of penicillin and the disarming of microbes.* George Allen and Unwin, London (1970).

Penicillin Chronology. Dean H. Mayberry (compiler), *Penicillin Chronology, Northern Regional Research Centre.* Science and Eduction Administration, US Department of Agriculture (1980).

KB. Letters and papers in archives of Kemball, Bishop Ltd, now with Pfizer Ltd, Sandwich, Kent.

Chapter 1

1. *Biographical Memoir.*
2. *Bickel.*
3. P. M. S. Blackett and H. C. Coombs. *Memorial to the Rt. Hon. Lord Florey O.M., F.R.S.* Australian National University/Royal Society (1969).
4. John C. Eccles and William G. Gibson, *Sherrington,* Springer International (1979).
5. Frank Fenner 'Howard Walter Florey' in *Dictionary of scientific biography* (ed. C. C. Gillispie) vol. V, p. 41. Scribner, New York (1972).
6. *98HF,* letters to H. W. Florey from Mary Ethel Hayter Reed 1925-26.
7. *98HF,* letters to Mary Ethel Hayter Reed from H. W. Florey 1922-26.
8. *Macfarlane.*
9. R. G. Macfarlane in *The dictionary of national biography 1961-70.* Oxford University Press, Oxford (1981).
10. F. G. Mann. *Lord Rutherford on the golf course.* F. G. Mann, Cambridge (1976).
11. David Wilson. *Penicillin in perspective.* Faber and Faber, London (1976).

Chapter 2

1. S. R. Douglas. 'George Dreyer.' *Obituary Notices of Fellows of the Royal Society,* **4**, Dec. (1935).
2. *British Journal of Experimental Pathology,* **4**, 146 (1923).

3. Lord Todd and J. W. Cornforth. 'Robert Robinson.' *Biographical memoirs of Fellows of the Royal Society*, Vol. 221 (1976).
4. *CSA/EBC*, B67.
5. *CSA/EBC*, B67.
6. *CSA/EBC*, B67.
7. *The Times*, 12 September 1980.
8. *New York Times*, 20 March 1983, p. 20 E.
9. L. Colebrook, 'Alexander Fleming.' *Biographical memoirs of Fellows of the Royal Society*, Vol. 2 (1956).
10. L. Colebrook, 'Almroth Edward Wright.' *Obituary notices of Fellows of the Royal Society*, **17**. Nov. (1948).
11. *British Journal of Experimental Pathology*, **11**, 192 (1930).
12. *Annals of Botany*, **13**, 549 (1899).
13. *British Journal of Experimental Pathology*, **11**, 251 (1930).
14. *Journal of Obstetrics and Gynaecology*, **38**, 550, 558 (1931).
15. Dunham Lecture (1965).
16. *Hare*, pp. 67-87.
17. Ronald Hare, 'New light on the history of penicillin.' *Medical History*, **26**, 1 (1982).
18. André Maurois, *Life of Sir Alexander Fleming, discoverer of penicillin* p. 131. Jonathan Cape, London (1959).
19. Ronald Hare, *Medical History*, **26**, 1 (1982).
20. *British Journal of Experimental Pathology*, **10**, 226 (1929).
21. *Hare*, pp. 93-101.
22. *Hare*, p. 109.
23. Ronald Hare, *Medical History*, **26**, 1 (1982).
24. Macfarlane, pp. 347-57.
25. P. W. Clutterbuck, R. Lovell and H. Raistrick. 'The formation from glucose by members of the *Penicillium chrysogenum* series of pigment, an alkali soluble protein, and penicillin, the antibacterial substance of Fleming.' *Biochemical Journal*, **26**, 1907 (1932).
26. *Hare*, p. 102.
27. *Hare*, pp. 102-3.
28. *Hare*, p. 106.
29. *Hare*, p. 108.
30. *Hare*, p. 116.
31. *Journal of Bacteriology*, **29**, 215 (1935).
32. L. Colebrook, 'Gerhard Domagk.' *Biographical memoirs of Fellows of the Royal Society*, vol. 10 (1964).
33. G. Domagk. 'Eine Neue Klasse von Desinfektions mitteln.' *Deutsche Medizinische Wochenschrift*, **61**, 829 (1935).
34. *Hare*, pp. 155-61.
35. *Lancet*, *1*, 1279 (1936).

36. 'The antisulphanilamide activity (*in vitro*) of *p*-aminobenzoic acid and related compounds.' *Chemistry and Industry*, **18**, 133 (1940).
37. Ann Parry. *The Admirals Fremantle 1788-1920*. Chatto and Windus, London (1971).
38. G. Papacostas and J. Gaté, *Les associations microbiennes: leurs applications thérapeutiques*. Gaston Doin et Cie, Paris (1928).
39. E. B. Chain. 'Thirty years of penicillin therapy.' *Proceedings of the Royal Society of London*, B, **179**, 293 (1971).
40. *CSA/EBC*, B107.

Chapter 3

1. *Korrespondenzblatt fur Schweizer Ärtate*, **17**, 385 (1887).
2. *Antibiotics*, pp. 1-73.
3. A. Lode, *Zentralblatt für Bakteriologie, Parasitenkunde und Infektionskrankheiten und Hygiene (Originale)* **33**, 196 (1903).
4. *Antibiotics*, pp. 19-26.
5. *Antibiotics*, p. 22.
6. R. Dubos, *Journal of Experimental Medicine*, **70**, 1 (1939).
7. W. H. Helfand, H. B. Woodruff, K. M. H. Coleman, and D. L. Cowen in *Symposium*, p. 32.
8. *Antibiotics*, p. 25.
9. E. B. Chain, 'Thirty years of penicillin therapy.' *Proceedings of the Royal Society, London, B*. **179**, 293 (1971).
10. Chain, 'Thirty years of penicillin therapy.'
11. *CSA/EBC*, B61.
12. *CSA/EBC*, B61.
13. *CSA/EBC*, B67.
14. *98HF*, **36**, 6, 3-4.
15. N. G. Heatley, personal communication.
16. E. B. Chain. Symposium, p. 20.
17. *CSA/EBC*, B65.
18. *CSA/EBC*, B67.
19. *MRC* 3001/3. 'The treatment of wound shock.', *MRC Memorandum no. 1 (1940)*.
20. E. B. Chain, History of penicillin discovery, in *Symposium*, p. 15.
21. K. P. Dimick, G. Alderton, J. C. Lewis, H. D. Lightbody, and H. L. Fevold, *Archives of Biochemistry*, **15**, 1 (1947).
22. E. B. Chain and H. W. Florey, 'Penicillin.' *Endeavour*, **3**, 3 (1944).
23. Trevor I. Williams and Herbert Weil, 'The phases of chromatography.' *Arkiv för Kemi*, **5**, 283 (1953).
24. M. S. Tswett, *Bericht der Deutschen botanischen Gesellschaft*, **24**, 384 (1906).

25. S. B. Binkley, D. W. MacCorquodale, S. A. Thayer, and E. A. Doisy, *Journal of Biological Chemistry*, **130**, 219 (1939).
26. I. Berenblum and R. Schoental, *British Journal of Experimental Pathology*, **24**, 232 (1943).
27. *CSA/EBC*, B104.
28. *CSA/EBC*, B104.
29. *CSA/EBC*, B67.
30. *CSA/EBC*, B67.
31. N. G. Heatley, personal communication.
32. H. W. Florey and R. H. Ebert, *British Journal of Experimental Pathology*, **20**, 342 (1939); H. W. Florey, R. H. Ebert, and B. D. Pullinger, *Journal of Pathology and Bacteriology*, **48**, 79 (1939).
33. B. D. Pullinger (1976), quoted in *Macfarlane*, p. 263.
34. *Macfarlane*, p. 310.
35. J. H. D. Kent, personal recollection.
36. E. Chain, H. W. Florey, A. D. Gardner, N. G. Heatley, M. A. Jennings, J. Orr-Ewing and A. G. Sanders, 'Penicillin as a chemotherapeutic agent.' *Lancet*, Aug. 24 (1940), p. 226.
37. *CSA/EBC*, B67.

Chapter 4

1. E. P. Abraham, E. Chain, C. M. Fletcher, H. W. Florey, A. D. Gardner, N. G. Heatley and M. A. Jennings, 'Further observations on penicillin.' *Lancet*, 16 August (1941), p. 177.
2. *CSA/EBC*, B104.
3. Samuel Mines, *Pfizer . . . an informal history*, Pfizer, New York (1978).
4. *CSA/EBC*, B104.
5. *Antibiotics*, p. 642.
6. *MRC* 1752 (1941).
7. E. P. Abraham, E. Chain, C. M. Fletcher, H. W. Florey, A. D. Gardner, N. G. Heatley and M. A. Jennings, 'Further observations on penicillin', *Lancet*, 16 August (1941), p. 177.
8. *MRC* 1752 (1941).
9. *CSA/EBC*, B104.
10. N. G. Heatley, personal information.
11. Letter from Sir Joseph Banks to Richard Chevenix 23 March 1805, *re* Wollaston's failure to disclose his process for making malleable platinum.
12. *Penicillin chronology*, p. 2.
13. *Penicillin chronology*, p. 3.
14. *Antibiotics*, p. 649.
15. R. Coghill, *Penicillin production*, p. 17.

16. *Hare*, p. 172
17. W. R. Marshall, *Penicillin production*, p.v.
18. Harry L. Yale, *The early history of the development of penicillin G at Squibb* (n.d).
19. *Bickel*, pp. 124-129.
20. *Bickel*, p. 128
21. H. L. Yale, (n.d).
22. 'Penicillin data exchange exempted from antitrust laws.' *Oil, Paint and Drug Reporter*, 20 December (1943).
23. W. H. Helfand *et al.*, *Symposium*, p. 39.
24. H. L. Yale (n.d).
25. W. H. Helfand *et al.*, *Symposium*, p. 46.
26. W. H. Helfand *et al.*, *Symposium*, p. 50.
27. *Penicillin chronology*, p. 6.
28. W. H. Helfand *et al.*, *Symposium*, p. 41.
29. Robert D. Coghill, *Penicillin production*, p. 17.
30. Albert L. Elder, *Penicillin chronology*, p. 9.
31. Robert D. Coghill, *Penicillin production*, p. 16.
32. W. H. Helfand *et al.*, *Symposium*, p. 51.
33. Samuel Mines, *Pfizer . . . an informal history*, p. 74 (1978).
34. Albert L. Elder, *Penicillin production*, p. 11.
35. Robert D. Coghill, *Penicillin production*, p. 19.
36. Allan J. Greene and Andrew J. Schmitz, Jr. *Penicillin production*, p. 86.
37. Robert D. Coghill, *Penicillin production*, p. 21.
38. Albert L. Elder, *Penicillin production*, p. 8.
39. Albert L. Elder, *Scientific Monthly*, June (1944), pp. 405-9.
40. Albert L. Elder, *Penicillin production*, p. 4.
41. A. N. Richards, 'Production of penicillin in the United States.' *Nature, London*, **201**, 441 (1964).
42. J. C. Sheehan, *The enchanted ring: the untold story of penicillin.* MIT, London (1982).

Chapter 5

1. *98HF*, 46.1.4.
2. *CSA/EBC*, B104.
3. *MRC*, 3188/I.
4. *KB*, File 1.
5. *98HF*, 19.4.82.
6. *KB*, File 1.
7. *KB*, File 1.
8. *KB*, File 4.
9. *KB*, File 3.
10. ICI Board Minute 11049.

11. *KB*, File 4.
12. M. E. Florey and H. W. Florey, *Lancet*, **1**, 387 (1943).
13. *98HF*, 288.3.2.
14. M. E. Florey, *The clinical application of antibiotics*. Oxford University Press (1952-60). [A sequel to *Antibiotics*].
15. *MRC*, 3188 11.
16. *MRC*, 3160/3/I 11.
17. *MRC*, 3188/25.
18. S. A. Waksman, 'Antagonistic relations of micro-organisms.' *Bacteriological Reviews*, **5**, 231 (1941).
19. W. H. Wilkins and G. C. M. Harris 'Investigation into the production of bacteriostatic substances by fungi.I. Preliminary examination of 100 fungal species.' *British Journal of Experimental Pathology*, **23**, 166 (1942).
20. Interview recorded for National Library, Canberra (5 April 1967).
21. E. Chain, H. W. Florey, M. A. Jennings and T. I. Williams, 'Helvolic acid, an antibiotic produced by *Aspergillus fumigatus mut. helvola* Yuill.' *British Journal of Experimental Pathology*, **24**, 108 (1943).
22. D. M. Crowfoot and B. W. Low. 'A note on the crystallography of helvolic acid and the methyl ester of helvolic acid.' *British Journal of Experimental Pathology*, **24**, 120 (1943).
23. S. A. Waksman, E. S. Horning and E. L. Spencer, *Science*, 96, 202 (1942); *Journal of Bacteriology*, **45**, 233 (1943).
24. H. W. Florey, M. A. Jennings, and Flora J. Philpot, *Nature, London*, **153**, 139 (1944).
25. W. E. Gye, *Lancet*, **2**, 630 (1943).
26. *Antibiotics*, p. 282.
27. Robert D. Coghill, *Penicillin production*, p. 19.
28. E. P. Abraham. Personal communication.
29. *Antibiotics*, p. 785.
30. H. T. Clarke, J. R. Johnson, and R. Robinson, *The chemistry of penicillin*. Princeton University Press (1949).
31. Lord Todd and J. W. Cornforth 'Robert Robinson (1886-1975).' *Biographical Memoirs of Fellows of the Royal Society*, **22**, 415-527 (1976).
32. See J. C. Sheehan, *The enchanted ring*.
33. *MRC*, 1752/1.

Chapter 6

1. *Royal British Legion Journal, August* (1977).
2. *98HF*, 34.18-7.
3. 'Investigation of war wounds: Penicillin', carried out under the

direction of Professor H. W. Florey and Brigadier Hugh Cairns. A.M.D. 7/90D/43. War Office, October (1943).

4. 'Penicillin in warfare.' Special issue of *British Journal of Surgery*, **32**, 110-224 (1944).

5. *98HF*, 34.18.

6. 'Penicillin in warfare', *British Journal of Surgery*, **32**, 211 (1944).

7. *98HF*, 34.23.

8. W. S. Churchill, *The second world war*, *V*, 373. Cassell, London (1952).

9. For Hastings' and Shimkin's account of the mission see 'Medical research mission to the Soviet Union.' *Science*, **103**, 605, 637 (1946). See also Michael Shimkin 'Roads to Oz. I. A personal account of some US-USSR medical exchanges and contacts 1942-1962.' *Perspectives in Biology and Medicine*, **22**, 565 (1979).

10. G. F. Gause, 'Gramicidin S and Early Antibiotic Research in the Soviet Union.' *Symposium*, p. 91.

11. *98HF*, 48. A. G. Sanders' diary of visit to USSR 1943-44.

12. N. Borodin, F. J. Philpot, and H. W. Florey 'An antibiotic from *Penicillin tardum*.' *British Journal of Experimental Pathology*, **28**, 31 (1947).

13. *Bickel*, p. 223.

14. *Bickel*, p. 233.

15. *Bickel*, p. 231.

16. Winston S. Churchill. *The second world war*, *VI*, p. 478. (1954).

17. M. Kiese, *Klinische Wochenschrift*, **7** August (1943).

18. Yukimasa Yagisawa, 'Early history of antibiotics in Japan.' *Symposium*, pp.69-90.

Chapter 7

1. *CSA/EBC*, B25.

2. *HF98*, 34.18.

3. *HF98*, 34.18.52.

4. *CSA/EBC*, B28.

5. *Biographical memoir*, pp. 293-302.

6. *Lectures on General Pathology*. Lloyd-Luke, London (1954).

7. *98HF*, 288.3.11.

8. C. G. Bernhard, E. Crawford, and P. Sörbom. *Science, technology and society* in the time of Alfred Nobel (see especially pp. 307-403). Published for the Nobel Foundation by Pergamon Press, Oxford (1982).

9. See *Les prix Nobel en 1945*. Stockholm (1947).

10. *Les prix Nobel en 1945*, p. 263.

11. *Les prix Nobel en 1946*, p. 221. Stockholm (1948).

12. *CSA/EBC*, B67.
13. *MRC*, 1752/1.
14. W. Howard Hughes, *Alexander Fleming and penicillin*, p. 73. Priory Press, London (1974).
15. *MRC*, 1752/1.
16. Correspondence quoted in J. C. Sheehan, 'The enchanted ring.
17. *HF98*, 34.18.
18. Mary Lasker, personal communication.
19. For an account of the memorial fund and its changing fortunes see Patricia Spain Ward, 'Antibiotics and international relations at the close of world war II.' *Symposium*, p. 101.
20. *Symposium*, p. 101.
21. *CSA/EBC*, B46.
22. *98HF*, 297.2.7.
23. Broadcast, 13 April 1950. Private communication from Professor Florencio Bustinza.

Chapter 8

1. *ANUHF*, 17.1.
2. *Sydney Morning Herald*, 23 September (1944) p. 3.
3. P. H. Partridge in *The defence of excellence in Australian universities*, p. 13.
4. *Proceedings 10th International Congress History of Science*, (Ithaca 1964) *Vol. 1*, pp. 179-196.
5. T. H. Laby, 'A university for the Commonwealth.' *Australian Quarterly*, **1**, 32 (1929).
6. *Alfred Conlon: a memorial by some of his friends*, privately printed (1963).
7. Letter from Blamey to Curtin 24 October 1944. P.M.'s Department files. Commonwealth Archives.
8. *98HF*, 288.39.
9. Letter from Minister of Health to Prime Minister 4 January 1944 P.M.'s Department Files. Commonwealth Archives.
10. Letter from F. M. Burnet to A. C. D. Rivett 16 February 1945.
11. Australian National Institute for Medical Research (1945).
12. *ANUHF*, 11.18.
13. *ANUHF*, 11.18.
14. *ANUHF*, 10.13.
15. *ANUHF*, 11.19.
16. *ANUHF*, 11.19.
17. Minister for Post War Reconstruction (John J. Didman) to Prime Minister 25 February 1948.
18. *ANUHF*, 11.17.

19. *ANUHF*, 10.1.
20. *ANUHF*, 11.25.
21. *ANUHF*, 11.25.
22. Report of Meeting at Vice-Chancellor's House 6 October 1949.
23. *ANUHF*, 12.6.
24. *ANUHF*, 12.18.
25. *ANUHF*, 13.12.
26. *ANUHF*, 13.12.
27. *ANUHF*, 13.12.
28. *ANUHF*, 13.12.
29. *ANUHF*, 13.12.
30. *ANUHF*, 12.16.
31. *ANUHF*, 13.5.
32. *98HF*, 297.23.
33. *ANUHF*, 13.5.
34. *98HF*, 289 3.
35. *ANUHF*, 13.5.
36. *ANUHF*, 13.5.
37. *Alfred Conlon* (1963).
38. *98HF*, 297.33.
39. *98HF*, 297.35.
40. *ANUHF*, 13.5.
41. *ANUHF*, 13.5.
42. *ANUHF*, 14.11.
43. *ANUHF*, 15.3.
44. *ANUHF*, 14.1.
45. *ANUHF*, 14.3.
46. *ANUHF*, 14.3.
47. *ANUHF*, 15.3.
48. *ANUHF*, 15.3.
49. *ANUHF*, 15.3.
50. *ANUHF*, 15.3.
51. *ANUHF*, 14.1.
52. *ANUHF*, 15.1
53. *ANUHF*, 14.11.
54. *ANUHF*, 14.11.
55. *ANUHF*, 14.8.
56. *ANUHF*, 15.1.
57. *ANUHF*, 15.1.
58. *ANUHF*, 15.1.
59. *ANUHF*, 13.17.
60. *ANUHF*, 15.1.
61. *ANUHF*, 15.1.
62. *ANUHF*, 15.1.

Chapter 9

1. Hubert A. Lechevalier. *Symposium*, p. 113.
2. A. Schatz, E. Bugie, and S. A. Waksman, *Proceedings of the Society for Experimental Biology and Medicine, N.Y.*, **55**, 66 (1944).
3. H. W. Florey, *Lectures on General Pathology*, Lloyd-Luke, London (1954). (Revised editions 1958, 1962, 1970).
4. *MRC*, 3088/a/I.
5. *ANUHF*, 1513 (1954).
6. See E. P. Abraham in *A biographical dictionary of scientists* (ed. Trevor I. Williams) 3rd edition A. & C. Black, London (1982).
7. E. P. Abraham, 'A glimpse of the early history of the cephalosporins.' *Reviews of Infectious Diseases*, **1**, 99 (1979).
8. *British Journal of Experimental Pathology*, **29**, 473 (1948).
9. H. S. Burton and E. P. Abraham, *Biochemical Journal*, **50**, 168 (1951).
10. E. P. Abraham, G. F. Newton, and C. W. Hale, *Biochemical Journal*, **58**, 94, 103 (1954).
11. Wesley W. Spink, *Infectious diseases*, p. 101. Dawson (1978).
12. *MRC*, PF 100A.
13. 'Penicillin fifty years after Fleming'. A Royal Society Discussion organized by James Baddily and E. P. Abraham, Royal Society, London (1980).
14. Spink, p. 101.
15. Quoted in letter from J. T. Connor to Vannevar Bush 28 October 1952.
16. Legal file, Merck Sharp and Dohme, 1952.
17. British Patents 618415, 618416.
18. J. T. Connor to Baird Hastings, 30 June 1953.
19. NRDC. *Evidence offered to the committee to review the functioning of financial institutions (The Wilson Committee) 1978.*
20. *E. P. Abraham, Chemistry in Britain*, **5**, 368 (1969). See also *Nature, London*, **221**, 885 (1969).
21. E. P. Abraham, *Review of Infectious Diseases*, **1**, 105 (1979).
22. R. S. Crespi, *Patenting in the Biological Science*, Wiley, Chichester (1982).
23. *Bickel*, p. 222.

Chapter 10

1. E. N. da C. Andrade, *A brief history of the Royal Society*. The Royal Society, London (1960).
2. *The record of the Royal Society of London. 4th edition.* The Royal Society, London (1940).
3. *98HF*, 291.8.18.

4. Alan Hodgkin, 'Edgar Douglas Adrian.' *Biographical Memoirs of Fellows of the Royal Society*, Vol. 25, p. 53, 1979 (quoting Philip Bowden, FRS).
5. Sir Harold Hartley, *The tercentenary celebration of the Royal Society of London, 1960*. The Royal Society, London (1961).
6. The Anniversary Addresses are published in full in the Philosophical Transactions of the Royal Society.
7. Lady Florey, personal communication.
8. Royal Society paper A/4(50), 18 September 1950.
9. Sir Harrie Massey, 'David Christie Martin'. *Biographical Memoirs of Fellows of the Royal Society*, Vol. 24, (1978).
10. *The Royal Society at Carlton House Terrace*. The Royal Society, London (1967).
11. Sir Alan Hodgkin, 'Edgar Douglas Adrian'. *Biographical Memoirs of Fellows of the Royal Society*, Vol. 25 (1979).
12. Lord Todd, R.S. Anniversary Address (1980).

Chapter 11

1. *Biographical memoir*, p. 278.
2. See R. H. Hodgkin, *Six centuries of an Oxford college*. Basil Blackwell, Oxford (1949).
3. George Temple, personal communication.
4. Queen's College *Record* (1968).
5. David Jenkins, Memorial Address, 18 October 1980.

An exhaustive conspectus of the organization of the University of Oxford in the 1960s will be found in *University of Oxford: report of the commission of inquiry* (*The Franks Report*). Clarendon Press, Oxford (1966).

Chapter 12

1. *Australian National University News*, **33**, August (1958).
2. *98HF*, 297.94.
3. *98HF*, 297.99.
4. John Curtin School of Medical Research: *Report for 1981*.
5. *Bickel*, p. 141.

INDEX